COLUMNS 2

2012 — 2013

Murphy Givens

COLUMNS 2

2012 — 2013

Murphy Givens

www.nuecespress.com

Corpus Christi, Texas

Library of Congress Control Number 2015902764

Givens, Murphy

COLUMNS 2   2012 — 2013

Includes index.

1. South Texas — History.
2. Nueces County — History.
3. Corpus Christi — History.

ISBN   978-0-9832565-7-1

Published by Nueces Press, Corpus Christi, Texas.

Cover design by Jeff Chilcoat
Cover photograph by Doc McGregor

www.nuecespress.com

PUBLISHER'S NOTE

Murphy Givens has written columns on South Texas history for the Corpus Christi Caller-Times since 1998. In addition, his talks on public radio are widely heard. Some readers have told me that the first thing they do each Wednesday is open the Caller Times to read Murphy's column.

As a student of local history and collector of Corpus Christi area ephemera, I am continually amazed at the information contined in Murphy's columns and the photography which accompanies them. It seems to me that Givens must have read every book, newspaper and document containing information on South Texas history.

Jim Moloney
Nueces Press
www. nuecespress.com

INTRODUCTION

Gustave Flaubert said his favorite historical periods were those which were ending since that meant something new was being born. I realize that many columns in this compilation are about the beginning or end of some historical period — when Henry Kinney set up his trading post on Corpus Christi Bay, when Richard King bought his first 15,000 acres to begin a ranch on Santa Gertrudis Creek, when the Civil War began and ended and trail drives started to Kansas. But then, history is about change. This collection of columns is about the process of change and the people who made it happen. It's a cliché to emphasize how much things have changed, but that's why we find history so fascinating.

All the columns in this collection first appeared on the Viewpoints Page of the Caller-Times. When I retired from the newspaper in 2009, it was agreed that I would continue to write a weekly column on Corpus Christi and South Texas history. These columns are part of the result. The columns appeared in the newspaper almost exactly as written. Since then, they have been edited for this book. They appear here in the order they were published; there was no attempt at any chronological progression based on subject matter.

I realized when I first began writing about history that people are more interested in historical events than in what I think about them. So I keep myself out of the writing as much as I can. It is a useful discipline, one I had to break to write this introduction. A woman called me once to ask my advice. She said she was writing a book about her life, but didn't know what to say. Think of it. What a formidable task she faced, sitting down to a blank page with nothing to say. Sometimes I feel the same way, the fingers fairly itching to get started, but from the head nothing; the words refuse to come. Writer's block, they call it. But this book was made easy because all the columns were already written, the episodes of staring at a blank screen all past, leaving only the editing, the assembling, the putting together, for which I owe an enormous debt of gratitude to my publisher Jim Moloney. As always, any errors are my own.

Murphy Givens

TABLE OF CONTENTS

GROWING UP

One hundred years ago the year 1912 marked the beginning of great change for Corpus Christi. A lot of things were going on that laid the foundation for what the city would become. It didn't all happen in 1912 but much of it started then. That's when progressive sparks began to fly.

You hate to start with a list but . . . the City of Corpus Christi began building a new Municipal Wharf. A new City Hall had just been built the year before. The city was about to begin paving downtown streets and putting up the bluff balustrade to separate downtown from uptown. Nueces County was about to start to work on building a new courthouse (the 1914 Courthouse, still with us) and an elegant new causeway to Portland.

Who knows whether public investments spurred private growth or whether it was the other way around? Certainly, private investment came in very close conjunction with public investment. The Nueces Hotel was going up on the site of the old Anderson homestead on Water Street and the Beach Hotel, later called the Breakers, was under construction on North Beach.

In its 40th year, Market Hall was torn down to make way for a new City Hall, built at a cost of $55,000. The new three-story brick City Hall on Market Square was built during the Clark Pease administration. The new building had two large halls on the third floor, city offices, two rooms for the police department, jail quarters, and one room leased to Western Union. It later had a charity hospital on the third floor. The building served as City Hall for 40 years before a new one was built on Shoreline.

Besides building a new City Hall, the city was taking steps in 1912 to improve its downtown streets to accommodate the automobile. Paving began on Chaparral, Mesquite and Water, with the city paying one-fourth the cost and property-owners paying three-fourths. In all, the plan called for paving 150 blocks of city streets.

13

Some of the street bond money was set aside to build a concrete balustrade on the side of the bluff, an ugly, muddy and slippery slope when it rained. Alexander Potter, a New York engineer hired to design a water supply system for the city, drew up plans to terrace the bluff and build the balustrade. Conrad Blucher used Potter's design to make detailed plans for the bluff improvement project.

Giant walls, with reinforced concrete base anchors, were built. The bluff was terraced to prevent erosion and in places the height was cut down and in others built up. A tunnel connecting uptown to downtown was added later. The bluff improvement project was finished during the administration of Mayor Roy Miller.

Though planning was begun in 1912, the Municipal Wharf was not completed until 1914. It was built on a landfill off Cooper's Alley where the old Mann wharf once stood. It served as the town's primary shipping wharf.

In 1912, the county began planning to replace the 1875 Courthouse, designed by Rudolph Hollub, a former Union Army engineer, and generally called the Hollub Courthouse. In 1913, voters approved a $250,000 bond issue to build a new courthouse. The six-story 1914 Courthouse became a showpiece. The newspaper was effusive: "Modern architecture is seen to abound in the new courthouse . . . the building is unique . . . a massive structure of splendor . . . a credit to the hand of man . . . one is dazzled as he looks at the tall columns over the doorway . . . "

Besides taking steps to build a new courthouse, the county also began planning to build a causeway to Portland. Since the 1840s, travelers crossed the bay by using the underwater Reef Road, a raised natural reef of oyster shells that divided Corpus Christi Bay from Nueces Bay. The first work ordered by the Nueces County Commissioners Court on Jan. 11, 1847 was to stake the Reef Road so travelers on horseback or in buggies wouldn't stray from off the reef and into deeper water.

After the turn of the century, people still crossed the Reef Road in horse-drawn wagons and buggies, which looked from a distance as if they were traveling on water. You could say that Nueces County had the wettest road in the world.

Starting in 1912, the county began work on building an arched causeway across the old Reef Road. The new causeway cost the county $166,000 to build. It didn't last long. It was damaged in the 1916 hurricane then destroyed in the 1919 storm.

COTTON ON MUNICIPAL WHARF,
CORPUS CHRISTI, TEXAS.

Corpus Christi's Municipal Wharf was built on a landfill off Cooper's Alley. It replaced the old Central Wharf as the town's main shipping pier.

The pride of Corpus Christi, when it opened in 1913, was the 278-room Nueces Hotel, the tallest building south of San Antonio. It was built by several investors who were later bought out by cattle rancher W. W. Jones. This aristocrat of hotels was famous for its Tropical Garden and Sun Parlor.

Other big news in 1912 was the opening of the Corpus Beach Hotel, built by John Dickensen on North Beach. It was surrounded by oleanders and palms. A streetcar stopped at the front door and the grounds ran down to the water. People lounged under shingled sheds on the beach while waiters fetched drinks and snacks. The Beach Hotel was later remodeled and renamed The Breakers.

Corpus Christi made great strides toward becoming a modern city during the administrations of Clark Pease (1909 to 1913) and Roy Miller (1913 to 1919), but if we need a starting point (and we do for this column) then we can look to 1912. At the time, it was still a small village of 8,000 souls, but 1912 set the style for what Corpus Christi would become.

— Jan. 4, 2012

When Nueces County completed the causeway across Nueces Bay in 1915, automobiles could cross to Portland and the north for the first time. To the right is the SAAP trestle which was completed in 1886.

The Nueces County Courthouse, designed by Harvey L. Page, served the county from 1914 until 1977.

Alexander Potter designed the bluff balustrade. The first section was completed in 1915 and it was extended north in 1916.

The new City Hall was built on the site of the old Market Hall, between Peoples and Schatzel Streets. After it was replaced in the 1950s, the building became La Retama Library. Today the site is Retama Park.

The Nueces Hotel stood at the edge of Corpus Christi Bay until the seawall was built. While it was a place of refuge in the 1916 and 1919 hurricanes, it was damaged by Hurricane Celia and torn down.

The Beach Hotel was built by John Dickensen in 1912 and renamed the Breakers. It was heavily damaged in the 1919 hurricane. The hotel was the only structure on North Beach to be reopened and used after that storm. Damage from Hurricane Celia caused it to be torn down in 1970.

LOOKING BACKWARD

I read recently about an experiment in Europe which found that subatomic particles called neutrinos traveled 60-billionths of a second faster than light — which, said the article, means Einstein was wrong and you can travel backwards in time.

They will be a long time on the job creating the technology for that, but, say we could move back in time, what would we find in Corpus Christi in the 19th Century? We can get a glimpse of what life was like in, say, the 1870s from reminiscences of early residents, little vignettes of the past.

"When the cows come home" was more than a colorful cliche. Milking was a regular chore and butter was churned at home. William Rankin, born in Corpus Christi in 1856, recalled how people in town kept cows. "As a rule," Rankin said, "we had several cows of our own; some families had from one to three cows." Anna Moore Schwien, born a slave, said her mother's calves would stray over to Büsse's place in Blucherville (behind where the Central Library is today) and she would be sent to bring them home.

Schwien also recalled the clothes women wore. "The women in those days dressed so well. The materials were of the finest, and the dresses fit well. Not a day passed that the women didn't dress in the afternoon after their naps. Dressing was carefully done and was followed by sewing or other pleasant pastimes. I have in my trunk the chemise that Sarah Belden made for her trousseau — it is of pure linen and entirely made by hand with the finest of stitches."

Eli Merriman, longtime newspaper editor, remembered quilting parties at Banquete when he was a boy. "In the early days, quilting parties were common with the ladies. Some ladies dipped snuff, a custom among the best at that time. I remember being sent down to the creek after hackberry roots to make snuff brushes for the quilters. There were so many ladies around the frame that I had to crawl under the quilt to distribute brushes."

19

E. H. Caldwell came to Corpus Christi in 1872 and later owned a hardware store. He recalled that courting often involved moonlight drives in a convoy of rented buggies. "We always had a chaperon to lead our party in her own buggy, setting the pace at the terrific speed of four or five miles an hour. We would go about seven miles out of town, then return to arrive before 11 p.m., the time limit set by the livery stable. To stay out beyond this time, well, it just wasn't done." They attached lanterns to the carriages to see their way back.

Men riding into town, said Caldwell, wore six-shooters and slung rifles from their saddle horns. Exuberant ranch hands leaving the Ruby or Favorite Saloon late at night would shoot their guns on the way out of town, a practice called "waking up the sheriff."

Caldwell got into trouble for using his pistol when a yellow dog rushed out barking and snapping at his horse's hooves. "I resented this indignity and foolishly took out my pistol and shot the dog dead. Within half an hour, the neighbor filed complaint and the sheriff came by the house and asked me to accompany him to court. The judge read the complaint, that I was carrying a concealed weapon, and asked if I were guilty. I had to say I was. He gave me a fine of $50. I thanked the jury and added that half of them at that moment were carrying concealed weapons, which was almost certainly the case in those times."

Merriman recalled that it was customary then to visit newly married couples on their wedding night. They would make a loud commotion and get the happy couple "to come out and receive congratulations and set up the treat to the boys outside."

After Lelia Nias married John B. Dunn, and they moved into a small cottage, she put up wallpaper in her new home. "She used a flour paste and that night an army of rats invaded the home. They ate the paper to get the paste behind it, as high as they could jump, and these rats were high jumpers."

Andy Anderson, son of a ship captain and bay pilot, recalled boyhood pranks. "The boys called Judge Russell the Old Duck Shooter because he liked hunting so well. He used to wear a beaver hat. Some boys stretched a wire across the street and it just happened that the Old Duck Shooter was the first one to come along and it knocked his hat off. He was provoked, but he didn't know who did it."

In another prank, they "ran a long string from the clapper of the Methodist Church bell, down the building, and all the way up to the

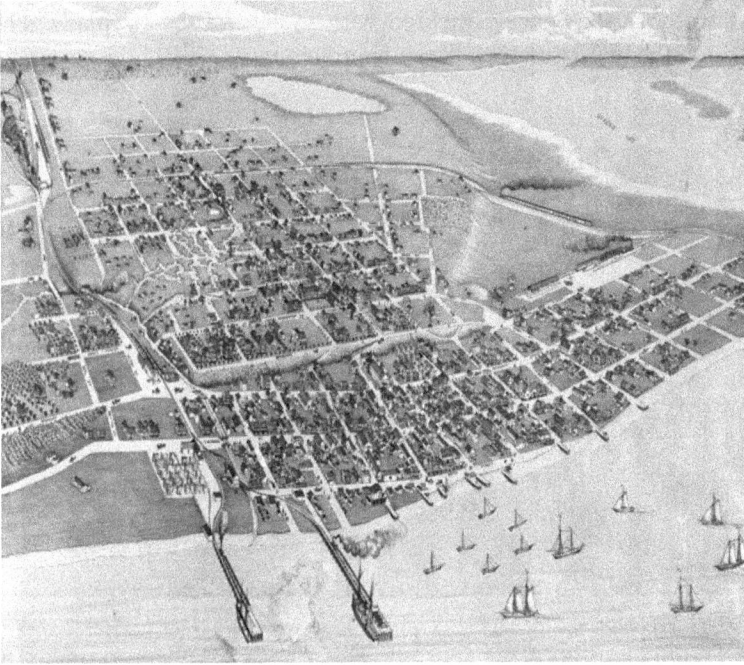

In 1887 Augustus Koch drew this bird's-eye view of Corpus Christi. You can't see it here, but the streets in the drawing correspond to the streets laid out on the 1879 map of the city.

bluff, using a whole ball of twine. They would pull the string and ring the bell. At first no one could find out how it was done, but someone finally discovered the string and cut it off at the bell."

Anderson's neighbor, a Mr. Gold, "would take me with him to the reef when he went after oysters. We would drive out in a cart and horse. He would bring a great load of oysters back to his home, where he would open them; there was a big pile of shells in the yard."

A medicine show, when they sold Hamlin's Wizard Oil from a wagon, was a big attraction. "Four fellows would sing beautifully," Anderson said, "and the whole street would be full of people listening to the singing. Finally, someone arranged for them to give an entertainment at Market Hall. You paid 25 cents to hear them sing and they had a full house every night. They sold lots of Wizard Oil."

Anderson said on one New Year's Eve they saw the old year out by playing a card game called Smut. The loser of each hand would

21

get his nose (and face) smeared with soot from the fireplace. They greeted the new year with black-smudged faces.

— Jan. 11, 2012

Eli Merriman

E. H. Caldwell

Captain Andy Anderson

Anna Moore Schwein

TWO BRUTAL MURDERS

George C. Hatch, a county clerk in Dyersburg, Tenn., came to fight in the Texas Revolution and rode with Sam Houston's scout "Deaf" Smith. Hatch's nephew Jim Bowie was killed at the Alamo and Hatch was at the battle of San Jacinto.

In 1841, Hatch brought his family and slaves to Texas in covered wagons and settled in Colorado County near Columbus. On Sept. 12, 1842, Hatch was in San Antonio when Mexican Gen. Adrian Woll raided the town and took prisoners, including Hatch, to Mexico.

Woll's captives were locked in the dungeon in Perote Castle. Hatch and a man named David Morgan, who were chained together, managed to escape. They had a long trek to freedom, suffering hunger and hardship before they reached Point Isabel and took passage on a boat to New Orleans.

The Niles Weekly Register on May 20, 1843 reported: "David Morgan and George C. Hatch, two of the San Antonio prisoners who escaped from the castle of Perote, arrived at New Orleans."

In 1854, Hatch moved his family to Live Oak Peninsula and bought 3,800 acres. He built a two-story house on the bluff overlooking Ingleside Bay. The house was built of Florida pine brought by lumber schooner. Hatch raised cattle and hogs.

When the Civil War broke out, Hatch was too old to fight (he was born in 1799) but four sons enlisted in the Confederate Army. After the war, Hatch took his slaves to Corpus Christi and released them. He refused to take a loyalty oath to the Union.

He decided to leave the country. A first cousin, Christopher Hatch, of Morehouse Parish, La., was trying to encourage former Confederates to move to British Honduras to the Hatch Colony, later called the Toledo Settlement. After the war, many former Confederates moved to British Honduras (known today as Belize).

George C. Hatch and a widowed daughter, Annie Hatch Byrne, became exiles in British Honduras. (His wife died in Goliad during the war.) The Southern planters had a rough time adjusting to the soil and damp climate. They tried to grow cotton, but found it unreliable, then discovered that sugarcane was the best crop. In late April or early May 1869, after three years in exile, George C. Hatch and his daughter returned to Texas.

Three years later, on Sept. 5, 1872, Hatch was on his way from Ingleside to Corpus Christi. As he approached the north end of the Reef Road, on the Portland side, he was shot to death in his buggy. This was at what we call Indian Point today. Eli Merriman, a young reporter, saw the body and shot-up buggy. The old man was slumped over in his buggy, his pockets cut out and his horses stolen.

A posse rode into Mexico and came up to the man riding Hatch's horse. They killed him, but lost the trail of the other two. John B. Dunn, riding with the posse, indicated that the murderers were dealt with in time. "Outside of five or six persons," he wrote, "no one knows whether they were caught or not." Dunn said that the names of the killers were made known to them and written down and put in their hats. "It is sometimes amusing to hear people say that the murderers were never caught. Well, ignorance is bliss."

After Hatch was killed, his son John returned from California a wealthy man. He made a fortune selling beef to the gold miners. He bought out his brothers and sisters and moved into the family home. He planted a 75-acre vineyard and introduced wine-making to the Ingleside area.

By a grim coincidence of fate, two of the more sensational murders in the Coastal Bend involved members of the Hatch family, three decades apart. Eunice Hatch, 18, wife of James Marion Hatch Jr., grandson of George C. Hatch, was cruelly murdered in 1902.

She was found in her home on a farm a few miles west of Corpus Christi on April 21, 1902. Her head had been split open by a hatchet. The body was found by John Priour, an uncle of the husband, James Marion Hatch Jr. Her parents, Mr. and Mrs. W. H. Lindley, lived at Ingleside. Hatch and his young wife had an infant daughter, Myrtle, who was crying in her crib when her mother's body was found.

Suspicion focused on Andres Olivares, who worked on the nearby McCampbell place. He had been a guest in the house, but Eunice told her husband not to bring him back. "I don't want Andres over here any more," she told him. "I don't like the way he looks at me."

Blood was found on Olivares' clothes and his shoes matched prints at the murder scene. Some men urged Sheriff John Bluntzer

Eunice Hatch and her husband James Marion Hatch Jr. A farmhand, Andres Olivares, killed her in a brutal hatchet attack in 1902.

to let them have Olivares and turn his back. But Jim Hatch stopped that. He walked up to the prisoner and talked softly to him for a time. People tried to overhear the conversation, but could not. Olivares hung his head and listened.

Though he pleaded guilty at the arraignment, Judge Stanley Welch ordered a not-guilty plea to be entered. The trial lasted one morning. That afternoon, the jury found him guilty. The judge ordered Olivares to be hanged on June 3, 1902. After the sentence, the newspaper printed Olivares' confession: "I did it but I do not know what was in me at that moment. I killed that woman, Jim Hatch's wife."

On the day of the hanging, Olivares was taken to a scaffold built at the 1854 Courthouse and the jailer fixed the noose around his neck. Olivares said, "Adios, amigos!" before Sheriff Bluntzer sprang the trap. Those who witnessed the hanging were Hatch, the husband, and the victim's father, W.H. Lindley.

Like the murder of George C. Hatch on the Reef Road in 1872, the 1902 hatchet slaying of Eunice Hatch, followed by the hanging of Andres Olivares, was the talk of Corpus Christi for a long time.

25

Andres Davila, convicted of murdering Eunice Hatch, was decorated with a rope in the reproduction in the Corpus Christi Crony on June 7, 1902. He was hung at the Nueces County Courthouse on June 3, 1902.

— Jan. 18, 2012

PIONEER FIREMEN

William Long "Billy" Rogers as a young man survived a massacre at the start of the Mexican War and it was whispered that he tracked down and slit the throats of the killers, one by one. On the border, a slit throat was called Billy's Cut.

Rogers, a former sheriff, built a new home in 1871. In the early hours of Aug. 1, 1871, people woke to shouts and gunshots, a fire alarm. At the corner of Chaparral and Cooper's Alley, Rogers' new house was burning. The heat of the fire was so intense that a bucket brigade could not get close. The house was destroyed.

Rogers started building another home exactly like the one that burned and he began organizing a volunteer fire company. The town was receptive. That October, Chicago's great fire alerted people to the danger of fire in a town of old wooden buildings. The citizens of Corpus Christi raised $681 to buy a fire engine and contributors held a meeting on Nov. 28, 1871 to choose officers for the Pioneer Fire Company No. 1. William Rogers was elected president. Volunteers for the town's first fire organization included many prominent citizens.

Andy Anderson asked to be excused from jury duty, explaining to Judge Russell that he was in the fire company. "That's no excuse," the judge said. "If there's a fire, we'll all go to it."

On Nov. 28, 1871, the fire engine arrived from New Orleans, a hand-pumper with a walnut body, which could shoot a stream of water 60 feet and had a suction pipe to siphon water from the cisterns. The city began digging fire wells and it approved building an engine house on Market Square.

Rogers and Richard Jordan were building a structure on Market Square to provide space for city government at no cost to the taxpayers. The builders leased lower stalls to vendors and let the city use the upper floor. The first tenant of Market Hall was Pioneer Fire Company No. 1.

After a fire destroyed his home in 1871, William Rogers founded a volunteer fire department, the Pioneer Fire Company No. 1. Rogers was elected president.

The first fire fought by the Pioneers was at the Colored Baptist Church on the bluff, which burned on Jan. 13, 1873. From this came the need for a hook and ladder brigade for the few two- and three-story buildings in town. Corpus Christi soon had two organizations of firemen — the Pioneer Fire Company No. 1 and the Lone Star Hook & Ladder Company. They combined forces in 1874 into a single Corpus Christi Fire Department, a volunteer organization.

A 787-pound fire bell was installed in a bell tower on Market Hall. After a hurricane sent the bell crashing to the ground, it was mounted on a concrete base and kept at ground level behind Market Hall.

The annual Firemen's Parade and Ball was observed on the last Tuesday of November. This citywide celebration was the social event of the year. There was a parade during the day, with fire engines and hose carts covered with flowers, and competitive events were held between the fire units, followed by a supper and dance at Market Hall.

The fire department grew with the addition of the Protection Hose Company No. 2, Security Hose Company No. 3, and Shamrock

Hose Company No. 4. Their hoses were stored in the Beach section (downtown), Irishtown (north of the Courthouse) and the bluff.

The department was funded by citizens and merchants through donations. The volunteer firemen paid dues and furnished their own uniforms. When a fire broke out, firemen and horses pulled hose carts and fire engines to the scene. The original hand-powered fire engine was replaced in 1877 with a Silsby steam engine.

Sam Shoemaker, trained as a steamboat engineer on Mississippi River steamboats, became engineer of the steam fire engine. His two sons were also volunteer firemen. Names most closely linked to the early fire department are those of William Rogers, Felix Noessel, and Sam Shoemaker.

To fight fires, firemen used cisterns and fire wells at the end of blocks, but lack of water was a nagging problem. The solution was to use water from the bay, at least within reach of the hoses. Fire piers were built 30 feet into the bay. During a fire in the downtown area, fire engines sat on these piers and water was pumped from the bay.

Near midnight on July 14, 1892, fire broke out in the Lay home in the 200 block of Chaparral. As the fire spread to the J. B. Mitchell Warehouse, firemen rushed to the scene. But the fire spread to the Biggio, Molander and Daimwood houses and jumped to Royal Givens' grocery store. While they were fighting the fire in the front of the store, a wooden annex at the rear caught fire, then jumped to Louis de Planque's photo studio on William. Finally, the firemen brought the fire under control.

Next morning showed the 200 block of North Chaparral littered with charred timbers and ruined furnishings. Tin goods from Givens' grocery were stacked in the street with armed guards standing by. Furniture and possessions rescued from burned buildings lined the street. It was the worst fire in city history, Corpus Christi's great fire.

Following this disaster, Corpus Christi got serious about establishing a municipal water system. Less than a year later, the city celebrated its new waterworks with water piped in from the Nueces River. The newspaper reported that, "Hydrants are opened and water rushes out with tremendous force. The city is safe against fire."

When Market Hall was torn down in 1911-1912 and a new brick City Hall built in its place, the city organized a full-time, paid fire department. The equipment used by the volunteers was junked, though many volunteers were hired as firemen in the new department. This was about 1913. Since the file on the early fire department is missing from the library, I couldn't find out when the annual Firemen's Ball was discontinued, but it came about when the volunteers were replaced by the city-run fire department between 1912 and 1914.

The full-time professional firefighters were admired and respected, but I doubt whether they have ever been as loved by the community as the Pioneers, Lone Stars and Shamrocks were when the Firemen's Parade and Ball was like Thanksgiving and the Fourth of July rolled into one big city celebration.

— *Jan. 25, 2012*

Corpus Christi volunteer firemen in front of Market Hall. The date of the Louis de Planque photo is unknown but it was not long after the Pioneer Fire Company No. 1 was founded, in 1871.

The annual Firemen's Parade and Ball was observed on the last Tuesday of November. This citywide celebration was the social event of the year. There was a parade during the day, with fire engines and hose carts covered with flowers.

Members of Shamrock Hose Company No. 4. Their hoses were stored in the Beach section (downtown), Irishtown (north of the Courthouse) and on the bluff.

RANKIN'S GROCERY

William S. Rankin's parents came to Corpus Christi from Glasgow, Scotland in 1853, part of a wave of immigrants attracted to South Texas by Henry Kinney's land promotions.

James Rankin and wife Agnes (Brown) brought four daughters and one son from Scotland. Three more boys were born in Texas, including William, born on Sept. 27, 1856 in a house at Lawrence and Mesquite. His father James operated a livery stable on Mesquite.

During the bombardment of Corpus Christi in the Civil War, the Rankin family camped out in the country on the John Gallagher sheep ranch west of town.

"We stayed there a few days," Rankin once said. "We could hear the cannon fire. One day, another boy and I went to FitzSimmons' store and got groceries and went back. The Gallaghers had plenty of meat and cornbread." But he remembered the war years as a time when food was scarce, when they traveled to Cuero or Victoria to get cornmeal, and used parched corn kernels to make coffee.

After the war, when he was 10 years old, one of Bill's chores on Saturday was to go out in the country, southwest of town, to fetch butter. He would take his younger brother along. "We would take our time and play along the way. We got three pounds of butter for $1, nice country butter. She would give us each a great big slice of home-made bread and a big glass of buttermilk before we started back."

"Some of our fun as boys," Rankin recalled, "came from teasing old Dickie Power. It was his custom to go from his home on the bluff (he lived where the Cathedral is today) downtown every evening about dusk, passing our home on the way. Some boys planned a joke on Mr. Power. The FitzSimmons' boys across the street and I made an imitation snake, coloring it in bands of red, green, yellow and black, and to the tail we fastened a large and noisy rattlesnake rattle and to the other end a long string.

"We hid the snake in our garden inside the fence and laid the string under the fence and across the street, where we awaited the coming of old Mr. Power. Soon as we saw him, and just before he reached the spot where the snake was hidden, we jerked the string, the snake darted across the sidewalk with a terrific rattle, and Mr. Power jumped and screamed, 'Snake! Snake!' When he discovered us boys across the street, and realized we had played a trick on him, he was very angry and threatened to whip us."

In the yellow fever epidemic of 1867, several members of the Rankin family became sick. Rankin's father James and his sister Agnes both died. Rankin, 11, and his younger brother came down with the fever but were among the lucky ones who recovered.

In 1872, when Bill Rankin was 16, he became a house painter. During the Nuecestown Raid (also called the Noakes Raid) in 1875, when Mexican bandits raided the town and burned Thomas Noakes' store, Rankin was at work painting the upstairs of the McCampbell Building in Corpus Christi.

"Charles Vandervoort, Chris Yung, McKenzie and I were painting together, when John McClane (the sheriff) rode by shouting, 'Mexican raid! Mexican raid!' We locked up the house and ran out. I had never carried a gun up to that time in my life, but that night I was assigned, with others, to guard the outskirts of the city and was part of the armed patrol."

Rankin formed his own company, went to New Orleans and brought back a stock of supplies, and went into the retail grocery business. His first grocery store was on the corner of Chaparral and Peoples, but he later moved into the McCampbell Building, which he had painted during the Noakes Raid a few years before.

"Judge John McCampbell's family lived upstairs; the judge had his office there; downstairs there was a store. It seemed that everyone who went into business in that building failed. When I asked for a lease for a couple of years, Judge McCampbell said, 'You think you'll stay for two years?' I made a success of it, though, staying four years and making good money there. I always worked hard and always had a good time and never knew what my competitors were doing because I was too busy."

Rankin once said he could buy "the finest smoke-cured bacon and hams for 15 cents a pound, the best Wisconsin cheese for 20 cents, and so much fresh country butter I had to tell the farmers to take it back home and eat it themselves. You could go to the market with

William Rankin's grocery store in the 1880s occupied the ground floor of the McCampbell Building at Mesquite and Peoples, across the street from Market Hall.

25 cents and get enough meat for six people, with a soup bone thrown in for the dog and a chunk of cat meat besides. Now you can't get even the soup bone for 25 cents."

On April 16, 1885, William Rankin married Louise Weiderman of New Orleans, whom he had met when she visited Corpus Christi. They were married in New Orleans and returned aboard the Morgan Line steamer "Aransas." The couple's first home was a cottage on Mesquite, where the Amusu Theater later went up. In 1893, Rankin built a large house on South Broadway, copied from a home he admired in New Orleans. The two-story house, with nine rooms, cost Rankin $9,000 to build.

Rankin built the original Corpus Christi National Bank building (he made the first deposit in the bank) and he became one of the stockholders in the Miramar Hotel on North Beach, which burned soon after it was built. He was a charter member of the first Country Club, which was on North Beach then, and he was a longtime deacon of the First Presbyterian Church.

Bill Rankin's wife Louise died in 1942 and he died in 1948 when he was 92. Rankin was a boy during the bombardment of the city in the Civil War, survived the yellow fever epidemic of 1867, stood guard during the Noakes Raid, and was a purveyor of groceries in

William Rankin, pioneer grocer

the days when kids came in to buy Blackjack Chewing Gum and people called canned peaches air-tights.

— *Feb. 1, 2012*

THE GRINGO BUILDER

Uriah Lott, a native New Yorker, started a wool-buying business in Corpus Christi in the late 1860s. But his ambition was to build railroads and within three decades, from 1875 until 1905, he became, as J. L. Allhands called him, "The Gringo Builder" in a book by that name.

Lott was born on Jan. 30, 1842 in Albany, N.Y. After the Civil War, he traveled to Corpus Christi, where he learned to grade wool and hides and opened his own commission house in 1869. He turned his attention to his dream of building a railroad from Corpus Christi to Laredo, which gained the backing of ranchers Mifflin Kenedy and Richard King.

Many opposed Lott's project because some feared it would ruin the ox-cart trade, the town's principal commerce. One newspaper said, "What, do away with our wagon trade! Never!" Huge Chihuahua carts pulled by teams of oxen, horses and mules brought wool and hides from Chihuahua, Mexico, some 500 miles away. After 1871, carts hauled copper, lead and silver ore from mines in Mexico that was shipped from Corpus Christi to smelters in Hamburg, Germany.

The long trains of ox-carts were almost a daily sight in Corpus Christi. Chaparral Street would be crowded with ox-carts unloading and loading. On the return trip, the carts carried merchandise back to Mexico. In 1871, Corpus Christi's major wool dealers handled three million pounds of wool. The majo dealers were Doddridge, Lott & Company, Bryne & Buckley, Norwick Gussett, Headen & Son, John Woessner, J. B. Mitchell & George Evans, and Edey & Kirsten, which was bought out by Uriah Lott.

An election in 1874 on a $200,000 county bond issue to finance the railroad was called off after opposition became so strong. Within a year, though, Corpus Christi began to realize that the wool trade was going to San Antonio and Brownsville as the amount of wool handled in Corpus Christi in 1874 dropped to about one-third of what it had been in 1871. Lott's projected railroad to Laredo was revived.

With $6,500 that he borrowed from Richard King, Lott bought a steam locomotive from the Baldwin Locomotive Works, which arrived in September 1875 on the steamship "Mary." The locomotive bore a brass legend that read "Corpus Christi." On Thanksgiving Day 1875, people gathered at Cooper's Alley and Mesquite Street to watch Lott drive the first "golden" spike of the Corpus Christi, San Diego and Rio Grande Narrow Gauge Railroad. The spike, gilded to look like gold, was stolen that night.

A new arrival in town named J. P. Nelson asked Lott if he could get the grading contract. Lott said he had a man already doing the grading. Nelson went to look at the work and told Lott that no railroad could be built on such a poor grade. He said he would grade a piece to show the difference. When Lott came by to inspect the work, he found Nelson fixing his silver watch with the sharp end of his grading hoe and Lott said, "A man who can fix his watch with a grubbing hoe can have the grading contract of this railroad."

A month after the golden spike was driven and stolen, Lott sold excursion tickets, at 50 cents a ticket, to ride to the end of the track. Passengers sat on wooden benches as they rode 18 miles to Martha Rabb's pasture (at today's Robstown). By Jan. 1, 1876, 25 miles of track had been laid and the line had one wood-burning locomotive and 14 cars.

Lott and a man from Pennsylvania, J. J. Dull, who made the iron rails, traveled to San Diego to meet with local citizens. Next morning, on their way out of town, the two men ran into bandits from Mexico who had a dozen captives tied to trees. They stripped Lott and Dull of their valuables and clothes and tied them to a bush. One of the captives worked his way free and ran to San Diego and raised the alarm. Some 40 men rode to the scene as the robbers fled.

Lott ran out of money and was forced to sell the line to the Palmer-Sullivan Syndicate and the Texas Mexican Railway acquired the project and finished the line. When the tracks reached Laredo in 1881, the new company allowed the former owners to celebrate the inaugural run. Richard King, Mifflin Kenedy and Uriah Lott invited friends to ride to Laredo in a private car. On the way, they drank lemonade that had been spiked with King's favorite whiskey, Rose Bud, and were in high spirits when they reached Laredo.

Uriah Lott was the driving force behind building railroads in South Texas.

The name was changed to the Texas Mexican Railway. In 1902, on the night of July 17, every employee of the railroad and another 450 hired hands were put to work converting the line from narrow-gauge to standard-gauge. The 162-miles of track had been prepared and the operation was done overnight.

The Tex-Mex gained a reputation as the friendliest and perhaps most unusual railroad in the world. If an engineer spotted a buck grazing by the tracks, he would stop the train and let passengers take a few shots. He would stop for a cowboy who needed a ride and ranch wives would give conductors shopping lists to be filled. In the early years, passengers would toss up mesquite and ebony cordwood to the tender to speed things along. The train often had to stop when cattle wandered onto the tracks, which made for a leisurely schedule.

Even though he went broke on his first venture, Lott didn't give up on building railroads. He helped build the San Antonio and Aransas Pass Railroad, the SAAP, which reached Corpus Christi in 1886, and he was the driving force behind the St. Louis, Browns-

No. 101, a coal-burner, was brought to Corpus Christi from Oklahoma in 1902. It ran out of Robstown hauling workers and supplies for the construction of Uriah Lott's St. Louis, Brownsville & Mexico Railroad.

ville and Mexico Line, the Brownie, which made its inaugural run from Corpus Christi to Brownsville to July 4th, 1904. Today's towns between Corpus Christi and Brownsville owe their founding to the Brownie. The first town to spring up was at the junction of the Brownie and the Tex-Mex on ranchland owned by Robert Driscoll, hence the new town was called "Rob's Town."

Because of the part that Uriah Lott played in building railroads, he was one of the most influential men in the development of South Texas, but he didn't feel that Corpus Christi appreciated what he had accomplished and said at some point that he would live to see grass growing in the streets of Corpus Christi. His railroads changed the landscape of South Texas, but brought him no wealth. The old Gringo Builder died virtually penniless in the Casa Ricardo Hotel in Kingsville in 1915.

— *Feb. 8, 2012*

WARSHIPS ATTACK CITY

Soon after the Civil War began, on April 12, 1861, an acting volunteer lieutenant, 45 years old, reported to the New York Navy Yard. Lt. John W. Kittredge — a native New Yorker with a sallow complexion — was given command of the bark Arthur, a three-masted warship assigned blockade duty in the Gulf of Mexico.

In December 1861, Kittredge sailed the Arthur to its blockade station off Port Aransas. Before his arrival, Texas ports on the western end of the Gulf had been lightly blockaded and blockade runners were able to operate at will out of Indianola, Corpus Christi and other seaports. This was about to change.

For the next few months, Lt. Kittredge caused havoc along the coast, capturing blockade runners and sending raiding parties ashore to pillage and burn, creating panic as barrier island residents moved inland.

On the morning of Jan. 25, 1862, the schooner J. J. McNeil, a blockade-runner, stood in for Pass Cavallo and Indianola, loaded with coffee and tobacco from Veracruz. After unloading, it was supposed to take on a cargo of cotton for Mexico, but the McNeil ran into the Arthur and was captured. The captured ship and its cargo would be sold, with the captain and crew sharing in the prize money.

In February, Kittredge captured a sloop, the Bellefont, and landed marines on Mustang Island, where they burned the homes of the bar pilots who guided ships through the pass. They crossed over to St. Joseph's and burned the wharf at the village of Aransas.

In April 1862, Kittredge took launches for an expedition on Aransas Bay. The bays were too shallow for the Arthur. Kittredge's men attacked three ships off Shellbank Island in Aransas Bay and captured two, which they were forced to leave behind when Confederate reinforcements arrived from Fort Esperanza on Matagorda Island.

41

Kittredge and men in their launches confused Blind Bayou on St. Joseph's for an opening to the Gulf. When they came to the end of the bayou, they scrambled out of their launches, ran across the island to the Gulf side, and signaled to the waiting Arthur, which sent in a cutter to rescue them just before the Confederates arrived.

After this close call, Kittredge laid low and stuck to the boring routine of blockade duty. He resumed the offensive in the summer. A coastal survey ship, the Sachem, was converted into a gunboat and added to his fleet, along with the Corypheus, a captured yacht.

On July 9, Kittredge captured the schooner Reindeer, loaded with cotton, and next day captured the sloop Belle Italia, giving him the light-draft ships he needed to sail into Corpus Christi Bay and attack Corpus Christi.

Corpus Christi knew that Kittredge was coming and the city's provost marshal, Charles Lovenskiold, ordered concrete rubble loaded on three old ships, which were then sunk in Corpus Christi Bayou to block Kittredge's entry into the bay.

The Confederate officer sent to prepare a defense of Corpus Christi was Maj. Alfred Marmaduke Hobby. His family had settled at St. Mary's in 1857 and opened a general store. When the war broke out, Alfred M. Hobby organized the 8th Texas Infantry Regiment, with himself as colonel and his brother Edwin as captain.

Kittredge's flotilla arrived on Tuesday morning Aug. 12, 1862. The sunken sloops filled with concrete hardly slowed them down. The gunboat Sachem easily towed them out of the way. Kittredge sailed into the bay with the Corypheus, Reindeer, Belle Italia, and Sachem. That night, the lights of his ships were seen clearly from the town.

Next morning, Kittredge landed under a flag of truce and met Maj. Hobby on Ohler's Wharf. Kittredge said he intended to inspect U.S. facilities in the town. Hobby told him the U.S. government had no facilities in the town and that he was there to prevent Kittredge from coming ashore. After an exchange of threats, Kittredge gave Hobby 48 hours to evacuate the inhabitants.

People evacuated, going up the river to Nuecestown (where Calallen is today) or to the Gallagher sheep ranch three miles west of town. That night, they slept on blankets on the ground or under wagon beds. Next day, some evacuees put up quilts on poles to escape the broiling sun. When the truce was over, three guns — an 18-pounder and two 12-pounders — were placed behind old

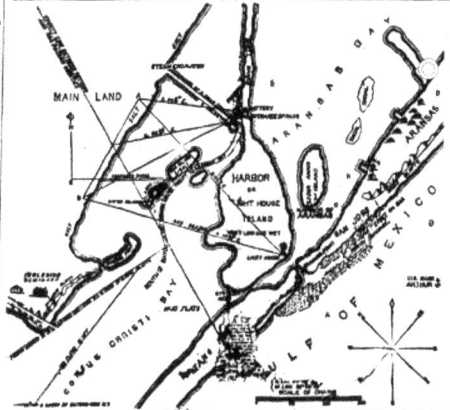

The New York Herald on Aug. 27, 1862 featured a map and article detailing Lt. John Kittredge's naval operations in Aransas and Corpus Christi bays.

fortifications made by Zachary Taylor's soldiers in 1845. At dawn on Friday, Aug. 15, 1862, Felix von Blucher, a Confederate major, aimed the 18-pounder at the Corypheus, fired, and the shell hit near the ship. The ships returned fire, with the shells landing on the fortifications, throwing up sand. The exchange of shots continued on Saturday, then guns fell silent on Sunday.

On Monday morning, the Belle Italia moved in close to shore and put 30 men in launches and a 12-pounder howitzer and landed them on North Beach. The plan was to take the Confederate battery from the rear. The men were carrying rat-tail files to use to spike the guns.

Maj. Hobby ordered a charge on the landing party and they were forced back to their launches, dropping rat-tail files in the sand. One Confederate was killed, shot during the charge.

Thomas J. Noakes' sketch of the battle of Corpus Christi in August 1862. Union forces from John Kittredge's fleet of warships landed a shore party on North Beach and bombarded Corpus Christi.

After the shore party was rescued, Kittredge turned his guns on the town, firing 500 to 600 solid shot and explosive shells at random targets, then the ships sailed away. The weary evacuees returned to find many damaged houses. Spent cannonballs were collected — they called them "Kittredges" and used them for door-stops.

Confederates learned what Kittredge's next move might be. The Union blockade commander had gone ashore before around Flour Bluff to supplement his shipboard fare with fresh eggs and buttermilk. This time, a trap was laid by Capt. John Ireland and Kittredge was captured, with his seven-man gig's crew, without a shot being fired. He was taken to the town he had so recently bombarded and crowds of people came out to see "that pirate Kittredge," though he was treated with courtesy. He gave his parole and was sent North. Kittredge was later court-martialed and discharged for striking an ordinary seaman.

Many of the town's residents fled after the bombardment, leaving behind a virtual ghost town for the last two years of the war.

— Feb. 15, 2012

PERRY DODDRIDGE

I recently wrote about Uriah Lott, who built railroads that transformed South Texas. The man who infected Lott with the railroad fever was his business partner, Perry Doddridge. If ever there was a classic example of someone who worked his way from the bottom to the top, from dire poverty to great wealth, it was Perry Doddridge.

He was born at Lower Peach Tree, Ala., on June 1, 1832. Both parents — Noah Doddridge and Nancy Latham — died at Galveston in 1839 when Perry was seven years old. When he was 14, Perry Doddridge worked as a clerk in Brownsville for the riverboat line operated by Richard King and Mifflin Kenedy. He was promoted to shipping agent and stationed at Mier, Mexico, and then he was appointed deputy director of customs at Roma. He left to begin his own business of buying and selling wool and hides, in partnership with a man named Jonas Jacobs.

The Rio Grande is a shallow and slow-moving stream today, but in Doddridge's time riverboats owned by King and Kenedy that were built to "float in a light sweat" traveled up the river to Rio Grande City, Camargo and Roma when the river was high, about seven months of the year, from June to November. During a drought when the river level was low, other routes were used. That's how Doddridge came to Corpus Christi.

Corpus Christi's newspaper, the Nueces Valley, reported on July 3, 1858 that, "Mr. Perry Doddridge passed through our city from his business home at Roma last week with a large amount of specie, hard silver dollars, en route for New Orleans, using this port in preference to the river route of the Rio Grande and Point Isabel."

Doddridge moved to Corpus Christi and on June 12, 1862 he married Rachel Fullerton, the 16-year-old daughter of Capt. Samuel Fullerton. At the end of the Civil War, Doddridge opened a business in Corpus Christi and later he and Allen M. Davis bought out the wool-buying firm of Edey & Kirsten. Doddridge remained closely associated with ranchers Richard King and Mifflin Kenedy and their financial interests. After Richard King's death, Doddridge was named one of the three executors of the estate, with Henrietta King and Mifflin Kenedy.

In the yellow fever epidemic that swept Corpus Christi in 1867, Perry and Rachel Doddridge lost their four-year-old son in September, near the end of the epidemic.

In 1871, Doddridge opened the first bank in Corpus Christi, at the corner of Chaparral and Lawrence, and signed on two partners, Davis and his brother-in-law, Uriah Lott, another wool dealer. The firm was known as Doddridge, Lott & Davis. They were bankers and buyers of wool and hides and had four large warehouses used for the Mexican trade.

Early on, Doddridge promoted building railroads and was known as the granddaddy of the plan to build a line to the border. He was among prominent citizens who organized the Corpus Christi & Rio Grande Railroad, planning a narrow-gauge railroad to Eagle Pass, but the plans fell through. After he was elected mayor of Corpus Christi in 1873, he revived the idea of a narrow-gauge railroad to the border with Uriah Lott, his business partner, who soon left the firm to build the railroad.

During those years, the Doddridge home on the bluff (the old Fullerton mansion) was one of the town's main social centers. Except in the summer when the Doddridges traveled, every Thursday evening was open house at the Doddridge place where "old and young amuse themselves brilliantly and feast on the best fare," wrote Maria von Blucher. E. H. Caldwell wrote in his memoirs that the Doddridge home "was a frequent gathering place for many of us young people. No extremes of formality or expensive show was expected. We attended dances, played games, conversed, and generally passed happy times."

Perry Doddridge's bank went under in 1893 during the "money panic" and collapse of the Ropes' boom. Not only did the bank fail, but Doddridge spent his personal fortune amassed from the wool trade in paying depositors 60 cents on the dollar, which left him bankrupt. Mary Sutherland in "The Story of Corpus Christi" said the entire city sympathized with Doddridge, "a good, honest man, self-made, and whose greatest sin was his trust in his fellow man. He never recovered from the shock of the destruction of his life work."

Perry Doddridge, an orphan from Lower Peach Tree, Ala., became a prosperous wool merchant and mayor. He built Corpus Christi's first bank.

After the bank failed and Doddridge lost his fortune, he held various jobs until he was appointed a county commissioner. He attended a commissioners' court meeting two days before he died, on June 11, 1902. An obituary in the Corpus Christi Crony noted that, "For 30 years every move for the advancement of the region and the improvement of its people has been fathered or fostered by Perry Doddridge. Both of the railroads now terminating in Corpus Christi owe much of their inception to him." He was also behind dredging the Morris & Cummings ship channel across the bay and he was instrumental, as president of the school board, in building the first public schools in Corpus Christi. Rachel Doddridge died the following year and left the Doddridge property on South Broadway to the First Presbyterian Church, which stands on that site today.

One of the city's principal streets was later named for Perry Doddridge, but other than that the Doddridge name is mostly forgotten. He was one of those influential men whose deeds become superseded by time and his story unknown to all but a few. Which is

In the early 1890s, girls rode their bicycles in front of the Doddridge & Davis Bank on Chaparral, across from the St. James Hotel.

one more reason why city officials should be wary of changing historic street names, an issue that surfaces every so often. The old names serve as a valuable link or window to the city's past. Now, when you drive down Doddridge Street, you will know something about the man behind the name.

— Feb. 22, 2012

SOME TREASURE TALES ARE TRUE

Probably every place on the Gulf of Mexico from the Florida Keys to the Yucatan Peninsula has its lost treasure legend. Certainly the Texas coast has its own legends, including some that are true and some that are romantic fantasy.

One true story started on April 9, 1554 when a fleet of Spanish galleons set sail from Veracruz for Spain loaded with the plunder of the conquistadors. It was said to be the richest treasure fleet that ever sailed.

When a storm scattered the fleet, several galleons went down, three reached Spain, and one limped back to Veracruz. Three ships — the Santa Maria de Yciar, San Esteban, and Espíritu Santo — wrecked on Padre Island. Three hundred survivors, including soldiers, sailors, priests, women and children, were attacked and killed by Karankawa Indians as they fled down the island. Only two men survived, a Spanish friar and another man who hid at the wrecked ships.

In 1904, Alex Meuly of Corpus Christi claimed he found the remains of one of the Spanish galleons 420 feet from shore, 35 miles down the island. He claimed it held a vast fortune in gold. He built a special trailer to transport the treasure, but for some reason he could never find the ship again.

But ancient and encrusted Spanish doubloons were found so often in one sand dune on the island that it was called Money Hill. Some of the coins were dated 1525. One story told of a man going egg-hunting on the island and returned with his pockets filled with Spanish coins. Another man, an Englishman known as "Buttermilk" Bill, found $4,000 in gold coins near Devil's Elbow.

Many of the treasure tales along our section of the coast are connected to the pirate Jean Lafitte, who was driven from Galvez's Island in 1820 and established two bases in this area, at Cedar Bayou and at the south end of St. Joseph's Island, across the pass from today's Port Aransas. The wife of one of his pirates, a woman known later as "Grandma" Frank, told the story that Lafitte's treasure — more than $500,000 he took away from Galveston — was buried in a mott of live oak trees at False Live Oak Point. After the last of the treasure was buried, and Lafitte came back alone, he supposedly told Mrs. Frank, "There is enough treasure in those woods to ransom a nation."

Other tales say that Lafitte buried his treasure on the Oso, or at the mouth of the Nueces, or at a place later called the Treasure Dunes at Packery Channel. These were all legends passed down through history, with not a shred of factual evidence to support their veracity, though not all the Lafitte stories are so fanciful. After a hurricane hit on June 24, 1880, a Galveston paper reported that a farmer while plowing struck on an old iron pot which held $15,000 in Spanish coins, believed buried by Lafitte or his men.

Another treasure tale from Padre Island has the ring of truth to it, and may be one where the treasure is still there, waiting to be found.

John Singer and his wife and children were shipwrecked on Padre Island in 1847. They made the most of it and settled down on Padre Balli's old ranch. Singer was the brother of Merritt Singer, who invented the Singer sewing machine. At the beginning of the Civil War, John Singer, knowing they would be suspect as Union sympathizers, planned to vacate the island. He buried anywhere from $60,000 to $80,000 (accounts vary) in gold, silver and jewelry in stone jars between two stunted live oaks. After the war was over, he returned to find that a storm had erased his landmarks. He searched for a long time, but never found his treasure buried in the sands of Padre Island.

Jacob Zeigler, who ran a hotel in Corpus Christi in the 1860s and 1870s, distrusted banks, people said, so he buried $50,000 in gold coins on North Beach and died without revealing the location. For years, people dug around a dense mott of salt cedars on the other side of the bayou on North Beach, looking for Zeigler's gold.

Another tale involves the Mexican revolutionary leader Pancho Villa. In 1955, an aging woman, who had been Villa's nurse, said he ordered saddlebags filled with gold to be buried at Roma, San Antonio, Robstown and Corpus Christi. She gave details about their location, but a former Pancho Villa lieutenant scoffed — "It is infantile to suppose that his money would be buried in the United States. Isn't there enough Mexican soil in which to bury fortunes?"

Silver coins were recovered from the 1554 ship wreck off the coast of Padre Island in 1967. They are part of the artifacts on display at the Corpus Christi Museum of Science and History.

Let's go back to where we started, with the Spanish treasure fleet of 1554. When news of the disaster reached Mexico, a salvage expedition was mounted, one of the great treasure hunts of all time. Native divers from Yucatan brought up silver and gold from the San Esteban, which was easily found since its masts were above water, and they found the Santa Maria de Yciar and Espíritu Santo by dragging a chain between two ships. The recovered treasure was catalogued and duly sent on to Seville.

Four centuries later, a hurricane uncovered the resting place of one of the ships near the Mansfield cut. In 1967, a salvage firm recovered items from the galleon, including silver and gold coins, a small gold crucifix, cannonballs, astrolabes, even fossilized cockroaches. The state sued the salvage firm and the treasure was obtained by the state. The Texas Antiquities Committee confirmed that three sites 2.8 miles north of the Mansfield cut were the remains of three Spanish galleons of the great treasure fleet wrecked in 1554. What was left of the Santa María de Yciar was destroyed when the Mansfield channel was dredged. The collection from the San Esteban is part of the Shipwreck Exhibit at the Corpus Christi Museum of Science and History.

We know that hundreds of years ago Spanish galleons wrecked on the island and, from time to time, gold doubloons have been dug out of the sand dunes of Padre Island. And who knows, maybe the Grandma Frank tale is true and the old pirate Jean Lafitte's treasure was buried somewhere among the trees at False Live Oak Point.

— Feb. 29, 2012

NAMES AND SLOGANS

The map of South Texas would look a lot different if some early names had stuck. Ingleside, for example, was called Hatch's Settlement in 1858, then Palomas — Spanish for doves — until the name was changed to Ingleside. For years we heard that "Ingleside" was taken from a poem by Robert Burns, "The Cotter's Saturday Night." I read that old Scottish poem several times, but never found "Ingleside" in it. The closest is the line — "They, round the ingle (fireside), form a circle wide." Maybe another poem by Robert Burns has Ingleside in it.

Port Aransas was called Turtle Cove, Star, Ropesville, Tarpon, then Port Aransas. Rockport was Rocky Point before it was Rockport. It changed its name to Aransas Pass, then back to Rockport. Aransas Harbor changed its name to Aransas Pass after Rockport gave up the name. Bayside was known as Black Point and Indianola was first called Powderhorn.

A railroad stop called Corpus Christi Junction was renamed Gregory. Mesquital, named for a mott of mesquite trees, changed its name to Taft, in honor of rancher Charles Taft, half-brother of President Taft. Sinton was named for a Taft Ranch director, David Sinton, who wanted to call the place Berlin.

Refugio for a time was called Wexford, after County Wexford in Ireland, but they reverted to the original name for Nuestra Señora del Refugio Mission. San Patricio was originally called Villa de San Patricio de Hibernia.

Beeville was called Maryville, after Mary Hefferman, the survivor of an Indian massacre in 1836. The name Beeville came from Gen. Bernard E. Bee, who was secretary of war during the Republic of Texas; it was not named for his son, Hamilton Bee, a Confederate general known for his ability to retreat.

Bishop was first called Julia and Alice, named for Alice King Kleberg, was first called Bandana. Three Rivers was called

Hamiltonberg, after landowner Annie Hamilton and Freer was known as Government Wells. San Diego was first called Perezville and Lagarto was called Roughtown, for its rowdy saloons, then that was changed to Lagarto for the alligators in Lagarto Creek.

Corpus Christi for its first two years was called Kinney's Rancho, but by 1841 Kinney was calling it Corpus Christi after the bay. But years before, in 1836, Peter Grayson laid out a city called Grayson on the present site of Corpus Christi. Grayson, the attorney general of the Republic of Texas in 1837, had the place surveyed for a town site in 1838, just before he killed himself during a painful illness. Grayson was a town on paper only.

OLD COMMUNITIES

For much of its early history, Corpus Christi was confined by its downtown and uptown areas. On its northern end, near the Courthouse, was Irishtown. On the west side of the bluff, a block west of today's Central Library, was Blucherville, where the Bluchers built their homes. Past Blucherville was an area called Little Mexico.

Across the bayou to the north was the Rincon (meaning corner or secluded place), which was later called Brooklyn, then North Beach, and finally Corpus Christi Beach. In the 1870s, a small wooden bridge over the bayou connected Corpus Christi to Brooklyn. So we had our own Brooklyn Bridge 10 years before the "Eighth Wonder of the World" opened in New York in 1883.

To the northwest was the community of Juan Saenz, which had a post office in 1906 and about 150 people. A few miles away was Nuecestown, 12 miles from Corpus Christi, which was often called Twelve-Mile Motts in its early years. Calallen, near Nuecestown, was founded in 1908 by rancher Calvin J. Allen. There was also Annaville, which began in 1940 when Leo Steward and his wife Anna built a store and put out a sign that said "Annaville." North Pole was between Calallen and Annaville. Each Christmas, people would drive there to get their letters stamped "North Pole, Texas." The name was said to have come from railroad surveyors, who called it North Pole because it was the highest elevation along the line. Another version said the place was called Sykes until one cold winter when they began to call it North Pole.

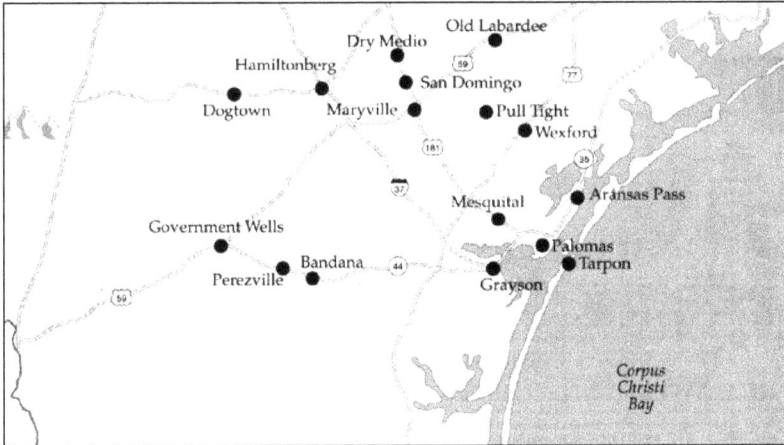

How the map of South Texas would appear if some of the old town names had stuck. Instead of Corpus Christi there would be Grayson, Tarpon instead of Port Aransas, and Perezville instead of San Diego. Art by Alberto Martinez, Caller-Times.

To the south was Flour Bluff, the name dating back to a smuggling incident in 1838 when a cargo of flour was dumped on the peninsula. But the community dates to about 1890. On the way to Flour Bluff was Aberdeen, where the Seaside Cemetery is today, Brighton, on the shore of Laguna Madre and named for Brighton, Tenn., and Encinal.

To the west was Kostoryz, founded in 1904 by Czech farmers and named for Stanley Kostoryz. Farther out was Clarkwood, platted and founded in 1909 by Z. H. Clark. The name came from combining Clark's name with an earlier name of Woodland Park.

As Corpus Christi grew, it swallowed up Brooklyn, Aberdeen, Clarkwood, Flour Bluff, Brighton, Sunshine, Juan Saenz, Riverside, Calallen and Annaville, as urban uniformity pressed on. Some names have survived, more in memory than actual usage, while others have disappeared, like the communities themselves.

SLOGANS

South Texas towns adopted some colorful nicknames and slogans, which are interesting in what they reveal about a town's aspirations or self-image.

Portland once called itself the "Gem City of the Gulf." Ingleside called itself "The Atlantic City of Texas," then dropped that in favor

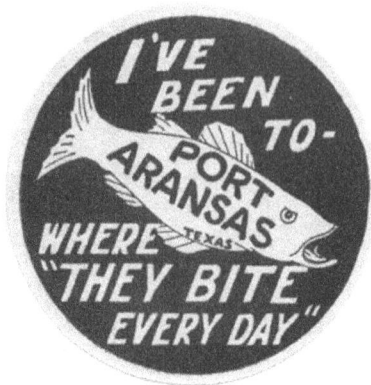

of "The Playground of the South." Aransas Pass had a long slogan — "The City of Certainty, Where the Sails Meet the Rails." My favorite was Taft's slogan, which could have been taken as a direct challenge to its citizens, as if they were idle and unprofitable — "Where Permanent Prosperity Rewards Honest Effort."

Robstown's slogan, without a civic blush, was — "God's Most Livable Land and Most Lovable People." Alice called itself "The Windmill Town" then "Hub City." Because of its truck farms, Odem billed itself as "Evergreen Acres." The slogan for Mathis was, "As Good As the Best and Better Than the Rest," and Port Aransas cast the line, "Where They Bite Every Day."

Corpus Christi once called itself the Naples on the Gulf, then Bluff City, followed by Texas Riviera, and finally Sparkling City by the Sea. Now, when that is used, it is usually in a rather testy and ironic sense, for Corpus Christi is known as a town where its citizens are always up in arms about something. Corpus Christi could easily adopt Port Aransas' old slogan — Where They Bite Every Day.

— March 7, 2012

A BOOM TOWN BEFORE THE WAR

In 1939, Corpus Christi learned that a naval air station would be built in Flour Bluff and the following year Congress allocated money to begin construction. Sand dunes and fishing shacks at Flour Bluff were leveled and by June 1940 some 9,000 construction workers were at work. Many thousands came to Corpus Christi hopeful of getting a job.

The city was humming with activity. Hotels were packed and added beds were put in lounges; the Nueces Hotel even put beds in its famous Sun Room. People rented out extra rooms to the influx of workers. A Depression-era migrant camp on North Beach filled with workers and families who came to find work building the Navy base.

Corpus Christi was one huge construction site. The downtown area was a maze of detours and traffic jams. New sewer lines were being laid, ditches dug, streets paved or dug up for water and sewer lines. Dredge soil from the bay was piled in small mountains along the bayfront for use in raising the grade below South Bluff. The south end was raised several feet to conform to the grade of the seawall. As the bayfront was being transformed, the city's largest building, the 20-story Robert Driscoll Hotel, was rising on the bluff.

The greatest activity was at a site of scrub brush and sand in Flour Bluff where the Naval Air Station was being built at a frenzied pace. The base was built in seven months, a project that in normal times would have taken years to complete. The naval air station was dedicated on March 12, 1941. Auxiliary fields around the city were quickly built and commissioned.

Corpus Christi's population in 1940 had doubled from the last census 10 years earlier, to 57,301. Within a year, it was estimated it had gained 30 percent, to 75,000. People grumbled about an increase in prices that came with the growth; at Shoop's Grill, a roast duck dinner cost a 80 cents and haircuts went from 50 cents to 65 cents.

The first stock of the new miracle hose — Nylon — went on sale at Perkins Brothers at $1.95 a pair.

In 1941, as Britain battled to survive and the German army pushed deep into Russia, Americans were divided between isolationists, who opposed any U.S. involvement, and the internationalists, who felt the U.S. must help Britain defeat Hitler's Germany. That debate, and with it the time of sleepwalking, was about to end.

Sunday, Dec. 7, 1941, began in Corpus Christi as a cool placid day. Two new subdivisions — Hilltop Terrace and Dahlia Terrace — opened that day. The D. N. Leathers housing center was celebrating its first anniversary. A movie playing that day was "I Wake Up Screaming" with Betty Grable at the Ritz. People were humming a popular song by the Andrews Sisters, with the lyrics: "Buckle down, Winsocki, buckle down; you can win, Winsocki, if you'll only knuckle down."

It was a lovely December day, shortly after noon, when people heard on radio that Japanese planes had attacked the U.S. bases at Pearl Harbor. At the new Naval Air Station, leaves were cancelled. At the Caller-Times, phones were ringing off the wall with people wanting news. Printers in Sunday clothes began work on a special edition. In the midst of the chaos, reporters laughed when a man called wanting to know the time. Telephone operator Virginia Adams said when the news was announced on radio, the switchboard lit up. "The lights were all over the board. You couldn't take care of them, there were so many."

That Monday at the cavernous Assembly & Repairs hangar at the Naval Air Station, sailors and civilian workers listened to President Roosevelt's "a date which will live in of infamy" speech. After the president finished, there was a moment of silence in which people looked at each other, every face reflecting unasked questions.

After Pearl Harbor, men crowded the recruiting offices on Starr Street trying to enlist, raring to fight. The city learned about its first casualty of the war, "Billy Jack" Brownlee, in the Army, was killed in the Japanese bombing of Hickam Field. Only later did the city learn that Warren Joseph Sherrill, a Navy yeoman, was killed on the USS Arizona.

The war brought new rules to ration supplies of critical material and everyday conversation was sprinkled with talk of red tokens and blue tokens and airplane stamps, shoe stamps, sugar stamps. Civilians were allowed two pairs of shoes a year. Men wore pants

A man in front of the S&Q Clothiers at the Nueces Hotel read a Caller Extra reporting the Japanese attack on Pearl Harbor on Dec. 7, 1941.

without cuffs and housewives saved cooking fats to boost the supply of grease. Ordinary citizens received a black "A" sticker for their car windshield entitling them to three gallons of gasoline a week.

Beginning in 1942, the Navy operated a radar training school on Ward Island. People in town had no idea what the big secret about Ward Island was until after the war. Security measures were imposed around Corpus Christi and cars were searched for cameras, some beaches were off-limits, and people were not allowed to take a boat out in the bay without a photo ID.

The first blackout drill was held on Jan. 19, 1942. The next blackout, 10 days later, was the real thing, prompted by a U-boat sighting. During 1942 and 1943, U-boats roamed the Gulf, sinking American and Allied ships, mostly tankers carrying oil and gasoline, the lifeblood of war. In late January 1942, a U-boat was sighted near the Aransas Pass channel. To prevent ships from being silhouetted against the background of city lights, a dusk to dawn blackout was enforced. Air-raid wardens patrolled, looking for specks of light.

On April 21, 1943, President Roosevelt and Mexico's President Avila Camacho visited the Naval Air Station to discuss the war. It

Parked on the beach at the Corpus Christi Naval Training Center, Presidents Franklin D. Roosevelt (left) and Manuel Avila Camacho of Mexico watch an aerial display by a formation of Catalina Patrol boats and a squadron of dive bombers.

was FDR's second visit; he came to the Port Aransas area to go tarpon fishing six years earlier. At the time of Roosevelt's visit, 20,000 civilians were employed at the Naval Air Station, many of them young women. During the war, young women from all over the country worked in the Assembly & Repairs Department repairing Navy planes. Throughout the war, young women wearing regulation coveralls were a common sight on the streets of Corpus Christi.

— March 14, 2012

A MAJOR COG IN WAR MACHINE

Corpus Christi, with the world's largest naval air training center, was an important part of the war machine. Some 35,000 aviators trained at the Naval Air Station and auxiliary fields played a major role in winning the war in the Pacific.

Only weeks before the attack on Pearl Harbor, the first class of cadets received their wings. In that group was Gerald F. Child. Less than a year later, Child and his PBY crew were the first to locate the Japanese fleet steaming toward Midway. Before his plane was shot down, Child kept visual contact with the Japanese carriers, which helped give the U.S. Navy a great victory, considered the turning point of the war in the Pacific.

Future President George Bush, the father, astronaut and Senator John Glenn, and Hollywood stars Tyrone Power and Robert Taylor were among those stationed at the Naval Air Station during the war.

In 1944, two German POWs escaped from a POW camp at Mexia, 360 miles away, and fled to Corpus Christi, hoping to reach Mexico. This set off the biggest manhunt in the city's history. People began to see Nazis everywhere. A merchant seaman with an accent was jailed and two Russians, here to study refinery operations, were arrested after they were heard talking in a strange language. A boy told police he had seen the escaped POWs hiding by his school, which turned out to be three men in a crap game.

The POWs were staying at a tourist court on North Beach. When someone reported them and the deputies showed up, the prisoners thought they were there to collect a bill. Eugene Kurz and Heinz Grimm, Luftwaffe pilots, refused to answer questions and demanded interrogators call them "sir." They were sent back to Mexia.

At the end of the war, German POWs were housed at the Naval Air Station in a compound enclosed by barbed wire near the South Gate. The POWs worked at manual labor jobs for which they were paid 80 cents a day; people found them to be cheerful, good workers. In the evenings they were shown movies. They liked Walt Disney films.

On April 12, 1945, on the eve of victory in Europe, an Associated Press bulletin reported the most shocking news since Pearl Harbor, the death of President Roosevelt at Warm Springs, Ga. At George Evans Elementary, students gathered at the flag pole to sing two of the president's favorite songs, "Abide With Me" and "Home on the Range." The country went into mourning.

After atomic bombs were dropped on Hiroshima and Nagasaki, Corpus Christi learned later that James Burney, a native of the city, a geophysicist, was among the scientists who unlocked the secrets of atomic fission. When the war in the Pacific ended on Aug. 15, 1945, a wild victory bash was held in Corpus Christi. Pedestrians jammed the streets, overflowing the pavement, and cars streamed down Chaparral, tooting their horns and making a good deal of noise. Artesian Park was roped off as merrymakers were dancing, shouting, singing, drinking, until the early morning hours. It was a day of kindness between strangers.

Juliet Knight (Wenger), a reporter, was at City Hall when it was announced the war was over. "The building emptied into the streets, as did others around us. Everyone was shouting and singing, hugging each other. The joy of long-awaited peace exploded. For a moment in time, everybody in the city, regardless of class or race, loved one another."

With the war over, people no longer had to worry about events in some distant part of the world. They were suddenly free to be very much occupied with their own lives. In December 1945, for the first time since 1941, Corpus Christi streets were decorated for Christmas, at peace with the world.

The war was over, but wartime shortages were not. The huge bureaucracy that controlled rationing was still operating and food, liquor and cigarette shortages continued. Butchers and restaurant owners in Corpus Christi appealed to the Office of Price Administration at Dallas for relief from the "meat famine." Some restaurants and butcher shops closed. There were bread lines in April 1946 after stores received a fraction of their usual supply. An Andrews Sisters' song during the war said, "You get no bread with one meatball." For a time in Corpus Christi, there was no bread and no meatball. When wartime rationing ended in 1947, food prices soared.

Gerald F. Child was one of the first to graduate from flight training at the Naval Air Station in 1941. A year later, at the battle of Midway, Child and his PBY crew were among the first to locate the Japanese fleet. They kept visual contact for three hours before their plane was shot down by a Japanese fighter. They stayed in the water overnight before being rescued. Child won the Navy Air Medal three times before the war was over.

Privately owned yachts that had been confiscated by the Coast Guard and used to patrol the Gulf looking for U-boats were returned to their owners in early 1946. That April, the city's beloved former mayor Roy Miller died. He was a progressive mayor and one of the most ardent leaders behind building the port of Corpus Christi. In a postwar boom, as building supplies became available and government permits were no longer needed, new subdivisions sprouted up like mushrooms after a rain.

When voters approved switching to a city manager form of government, Mayor Roy Self and the City Council hired an unqualified man, the only applicant, as city manager after a short interview. The apparent lack of serious intent prompted the recall of Mayor Self and Council members Raymond Rambo, Neal Marriott, Nels Beck and B. G. Moffett. Rather than face a recall election, Self and the four council members resigned and a special election was called for March 2, 1946 to fill the vacancies in city government.

On June 18, 1946, people lined Chaparral in front of Lichtenstein's for a victory parade for Admiral Chester W. Nimitz, a native of Fredericksburg who commanded U.S. forces in the Pacific. The Nimitz Day Parade was considered the city's largest since the Port Opening Day parade in 1926.

The German POW camp at the Naval Air Station was closed on March 16, 1946 as the prisoners were repatriated to Germany.

Much of the town turned out June 18, 1946 for a parade honoring Texas-born Fleet Admiral Chester W. Nimitz. A crowd estimated at 10,000 lined Chaparral for the Nimitz Day Parade. Special guests were 30 Gold Star mothers. The five-star chief of naval operations vowed that "Corpus Christi will always be an important byword in naval aviation." Still, the Naval Air Station became a shadow of its wartime self and its auxiliary fields were closed. The constant drone of planes overhead was gone and Corpus Christi was no longer filled with the buzz and excitement of thousands of Navy servicemen.

— March 21, 2012

1950s: NEW PLAYGROUND

Corpus Christi gained a new playground when the Padre Island Causeway opened in 1950. The island had always been remote, hard to get to, but with the causeway and bridge it would never be the same.

It was a brilliant day when the causeway opened on June 17, 1950. People waited for hours for the noon opening. After the opening dedication, cars streamed across to this new playground, the next Miami Beach, it was said.

The $1.2 million cost would be repaid through a toll. The charge was $1 for a car, $2 for a car with trailer, 10 cents for A bicycle. The causeway opened the lonely island to thousands of visitors. There were predictions that easy access to Padre Island would pull visitors away from the amusement park on North Beach, but any harmful effects were not readily apparent. A year after the Padre Island Causeway opened, the old wooden bridge across the Nueces Bay was replaced with a concrete causeway.

In the last weekend of June, a crisis erupted half a world away when North Korea struck across the 38th Parallel and invaded South Korea. On Friday, June 30, President Truman decided to send U.S. troops into Korea. Later that summer, reserve Company B of the 15th Marine Infantry, composed of 80 young men from the Corpus Christi area, departed from the Missouri Pacific Depot for the Korean War. Some men in Company B ended up with the 7th Marines in the desperate fighting around the Chosin Reservoir. During the Korean buildup, troopships departed from the Port of Corpus Christi and traveled through the Panama Canal to Korea.

At the end of January 1951, an ice storm crippled and isolated Corpus Christi. Buses and taxis were parked, there were no flights in or out, and telephone circuits were knocked out. Frozen rain and low temperatures caused accidents, closed schools, and ruptured water pipes, but they didn't break the records. The city's all-time low (since records were kept) was a frigid 11 degrees set on Feb. 12, 1899. The lowest in the freeze of '51 was 18 degrees. But the slippery streets kept people home. Those venturing out, the newspaper reported, often wound up "where the law of gravity demanded."

In the early 1950s, a campaign by Dr. Hector Perez Garcia, founder of the American GI Forum, led to the cleanup of almost 3,000 open pit privies in the city.

A new red-brick City Hall opened on Shoreline in 1952. Exposition Hall held its first show in 1952 and Memorial Coliseum opened in 1954. Before the end of the decade voters passed bonds, after two attempts failed, to air-condition the Coliseum. Also in 1954, La Retama Library moved from the W. W. Jones mansion into the old City Hall on Mesquite.

The year the new City Hall opened on Shoreline was a year of scandal for the city. Mayor Leslie Wasserman was indicted on charges he accepted bribes in return for oil and gas leases on city-owned land. Others were indicted with him. The cases never reached court and a recall movement failed. The following year, the group behind the recall movement succeeded in electing Albert Lichtenstein mayor.

A severe drought punished South Texas in 1953. The city's reservoir near Mathis ran low and water rationing was instituted. The reservoir, built in 1936 after the La Fruta dam collapse in 1930, was about one tenth the size of the reservoir after the Wesley Seal dam was completed in 1958.

It was a big event when Corpus Christi's first TV station went on the air on June 20, 1954. KVDO — nicknamed K-Video — broadcast on ultra high frequency (UHF) channel 22. Most sets were made for very high frequency (VHF) and needed a converter to pick up KVDO. The station had no cable link to any of the three national networks. KVDO's programs originated in its studios on Staples Street or were canned shows that aired weeks late. TV viewers in the city would have to wait for Ernie Kovacs and "Queen for a Day."

One KVDO program was "Video Kitchen" with Pat Kline. One afternoon, she came in to prepare for her cooking show and discovered they had switched her gas range to an electric range, due to a change in sponsors. As the show began, she put a Pyrex pan of water on to boil. No one had removed the paper packing from the burners and they caught fire. The show host grabbed a pan of water

66

The beach was packed with visitors on July 4, 1950, the first holiday after the opening of the new Padre Island Causeway two weeks before. The previously remote island quickly became Corpus Christi's newest playground.

and poured it onto the cooking element, shorting out electric circuits and knocking KVDO off the air until the next day.

KVDO's monopoly of the local TV market didn't last long. Two VHF stations — KRIS (Channel 6) and KSIX (Channel 10) went on the air two years later. KSIX-TV began broadcasting from a studio near Robstown called "the farm." The only thing in the room was an orange crate and a microphone when Gene Looper began to read: "This is KSIX-TV signing on the air on Channel 10."

That year, 1955, Lichtenstein's bought out Perkins Brothers on the bluff and renamed it Lichtenstein's Uptown. It was a time when the downtown and uptown areas began a slow decline. With the growth of suburbs after World War II, new shopping centers thrived and some downtown merchants, to survive, opened branch stores in the shopping centers. In 1957, Lichtenstein's opened a store in Parkdale Plaza, the city's largest shopping center.

Drive-in restaurants go back to the 1920s when the Pig Stands were opened in Dallas and spread across the country. I read some-

Pick's on Ayers, founded in 1938 by J. B. Pickens and later owned by "Pop" Salvo, was one of Corpus Christi's most popular drive-ins. Doc McGregor photo was taken on April 7, 1941.

where that the Pig Stands invented the chicken-fried steak sandwich, fried onion rings, and Texas toast and that they originated drive-through service. Besides the Pig Stands, drive-ins had spread by the 1940s and then reached their heyday in the 1950s.

Popular drive-ins in Corpus Christi were Zackie's No. 1 and No. 2, the Purple Cow, Pick's on Ayers, known for its fine enchiladas, the High Hat at Staples and Marguerite, not far from where City Hall is today. There was the Toot & Tellum on Staples, the Jitter-Bug Drive-In on Antelope, and several Pig Stands; the busiest was near the Bascule Bridge.

—March 28, 2012

BRIDGE — TUNNEL FIGHT

One of the major crime stories of the 1950s occurred in October 1955 when a man named Don Worden was killed and buried in the sand on Padre Island. His wife said she killed him in fear for her own life. She was not indicted. That decade recorded a dramatic rescue in February 1959. After their boat sank in a storm, Leslie Schmidt, his wife, and three children spent three cold, hungry days clinging to a buoy in Corpus Christi Bay.

Corpus Christi's big quarrel in the 1950s was over how to replace the bascule bridge, built in 1925 over what had been Hall's Bayou. When the port opened in 1926, the major attraction was the bascule bridge. It never had a formal name; "bascule" is a French word for see-saw which describes the counter-balanced bridge. The bridge was 121 feet long, 52 feet wide, weighed 1,500 tons, and cost $403,000. It was painted black and coated with grease to protect it from salt air.

The Corps of Engineers opposed building this bridge, arguing that the opening was not wide enough for the increasingly larger ships entering the port. But the city opted for the cheapest bridge possible. As the Corps warned, the 97-foot opening was a tight fit for cargo ships, which often scraped the sides of the bridge, sometimes putting it out of commission. The master of a Dutch cargo ship said the tight squeeze "scared the hell out of me." Sailors called it threading the needle.

The bascule bridge was also a nuisance for motorists. When an approaching ship's siren sounded, the bridge was raised, stopping traffic. Drivers fumed because ships were far out in the bay. But ships had to signal the bridge when they were a mile away and the tender had to raise the bridge. It would stay raised about 20 minutes, but the wait seemed endless to motorists.

The problem intensified as the volume of traffic grew, the frequency of the bridge being raised increased, and the size of the ships became larger. But how to replace it? In the early 1950s, the town debated whether to dig a tunnel under the port entrance or build a high bridge over it.

High bridge today sounds like an oxymoron, with the Harbor Bridge arching high over the entrance to the port, but in the 1950s the bascule bridge was low, squat, and ugly, high only when one end was raised. Those backing a tunnel argued that a high bridge would tower over the city like a big ugly birdcage — envisioning an even larger bascule bridge.

The issue was decided when the State Highway Commission offered $9 million to build a high bridge, but not a dime for a tunnel, with the rationale that the state did not want a toll tunnel on a toll-free state highway. On March 24, 1954, the City Council voted to build a high bridge and Mayor Albert Lichtenstein, leader of the tunnel faction, resigned in protest.

Construction of the high bridge began in June 1956. It took three years and four months to build. The sides of the cantilever truss bridge were joined on March 13, 1959. The new Harbor Bridge opened to traffic on Oct. 23, 1959. It was a big day for the city. The old bascule bridge was sold for scrap. A few hated to see it go. Before it became a bottleneck, it was a symbol of the city's growth and prosperity.

Harbor Bridge loomed over North Beach. Two major events had profound consequences for North Beach, which was called the "Playground of the South." The first was the construction of the causeway to Padre Island in 1950 which gave Corpus Christi a new playground of surf and sun to compete with North Beach's aging carnival attractions and eroding bayside beach. The second was the construction of the Harbor Bridge.

Even before the bridge was built, North Beach was in decline. The long waits to cross the bascule bridge hurt, but traffic was still funneled through North Beach. Harbor Bridge rushed traffic away, bypassing and isolating North Beach. North Beach merchants could look at the traffic exiting Harbor Bridge and remember how it used to be when all the cars streamed past their front doors.

In its heyday in the 1930s and 1940s, North Beach was the place to be, with a carnival every day, the smell of salt air, the lapping waves and feel of warm sand. Tourists crowded the city's playground. On an average weekend, the North Beach Amusement Park, the carnival midway, the Ferris wheel, merry-go-round and other rides would attract as many as 4,000 visitors. On a holiday weekend, the number could climb to 20,000 or more. The city's boom years in the 1940s were prosperous times for North Beach.

Over time, the numbers began to drop after the Padre Island Causeway opened in 1950. In 1957 the amusement park and boardwalk were closed and torn down. Business owners convinced the City Council to change the name from North Beach to Corpus Christi Beach, to emphasize that it was a part of the city, but the name change didn't help. Whatever it was called, the strip of land would never again be "The Playground of the South."

Just before Christmas 1958, the Navy announced it would close the Overhaul & Repair Department at the Naval Air Station, which had been in operation since World War II. The Navy employed some 3,000 civilian workers to repair Navy aircraft engines. The closure was a severe blow to Corpus Christi; the Navy's O&R was the largest employer in the area. Despite protests from civic leaders, the decision stood and in 1959, the O&R was shut down. Later, the city would gain when the new Army Maintenance Center (now the Army Depot) moved into the old O&R facility.

The decades of the 1940s and 1950s represented phenomenal years for Corpus Christi, when major civic improvements included building the Seawall, the JFK Causeway, the Nueces Bay Causeway, the Wesley Seale dam, and Harbor Bridge. It was an era of expansive optimism, an era of big change.

— April 4, 2012

A steamship approaches the bascule bridge opening in 1935. The bridge served the city as the main span over the port entrance for 33 years, from 1926 until Harbor Bridge replaced it in October 1959. The bascule was dismantled and sold for junk in 1961.

Harbor Bridge, under construction in 1958, dwarfed the old bascule bridge.

THE MERCER LOGS

A new book — "The Mercer Logs: Pioneer Times on Mustang Island, Texas" — is worth reading but I can't help being a little disappointed. I wish there was more of it. To read the Mercer Logs is to step into another world, strange and fascinating.

The Mercers settled on Mustang Island in the 1850s. They became a family of bar pilots who kept diaries written in the third-person style of a ship's log, telling of ships that passed by, of weather conditions, of the depth of water on the bar, of deaths, marriages and events in people's lives on the island.

The book notes that the logs — which run from March 1, 1866, to Aug. 31, 1877 — were written mainly by Robert Mercer, the father, and two sons, Ned and John. Sisters Agnes and Jane were also contributors. No matter who wrote a particular entry, the logs reveal an amused tolerance, a live and let live attitude that was prevalent on the islands.

Robert Mercer, a lawyer in Lancashire, England, moved to this country in 1830 and started a wheat farm in Indiana. He would take his crop by flatboat to New Orleans and after one trip, he visited Mobile, Ala., and moved the family there in 1852. Three years later, he moved to St. Joseph's Island on the Texas coast. Within a year, Mercer built a cabin on Mustang Island and moved across the pass. The Mercers settled on the north end of Mustang Island, which was the beginning of what would become Port Aransas.

In the Civil War, the Union blockading squadron landed federal troops on Mustang Island and burned the Mercer cabin and slaughtered sheep and cattle on their ranch. The family moved to Indian Point, near today's Portland, to sit out the war. Robert's wife Agnes died in 1863 at Indian Point.

After the war, the Mercers returned to Mustang Island and rebuilt their home. Edward, called Ned, and John got pilot's licenses to follow their father's trade. The pilots charged a fee ($3 per draft foot) to guide ships over the bar and through the pass, which they called the dugout.

Arriving ships would hoist a flag to signal that they wanted a pilot. The Mercers had a lookout perch on the roof of their cabin to watch for arriving ships. Sometimes a captain would risk crossing the bar and navigating the channel without a pilot so he could pocket the fee. The logs would note — "The captain took no pilot."

The Mercers were also salvage operators, beachcombers, they grew vegetables, kept chickens and pigs, and ran a small cattle ranch called El Mar. The father died in 1876 and was buried in the sands of the island. Later, his coffin was dug up and reburied in Holy Cross Cemetery in Corpus Christi.

A bar pilot's duties being irregular, and living on the island allowing for a relaxed standard of conduct, the Mercer pilots were hard-drinking, tobacco-spitting men and Mustang Island was a hard-drinking place. The logs make note of drinking bouts: "John got drunk as hell and damnation and had company in the shape of Capt. Clubb and Parry Humphrey." . . . "Dick Allen came to the house with a bottle of whisky with him and stopped all day. He is worse than the seven devils. His tongue never stopped for a minute and he was here all day."

To cherry pick a few selections from the log entries in the book:

— *April 26, 1866: Killed a rattlesnake in the yard. He had a young chicken in his mouth.*

— *August 10, 1866: The mosquitoes were powerful bad last night. We had to make a smoke for the horses and ourselves too.*

— *August, 1870: John took a turn amongst the water tanks; found out they want clearing away in front. But too powerful warm; will wait till sunset. A fellow would not be worth a damn if he worked all day. It makes a fellow want to write the log.*

— *January, 1872: Cold as hell and plenty ice all around the house. The setters at the house paying particular attention to setting close to a big fire. Cold as damnation with an indication of snow. The wind blows powerful hard; it keeps tally with the cold.*

— *April 28, 1872: Ned and Frank hunting eggs. Walked and waded all over the country. Got a few eggs and got*

The Mercer home on Mustang Island had a lookout perch on top of the house to watch for ships hoisting a signal flag requesting the services of a bar pilot.

darn well played out. All hands back safe. Took it easy (for the) balance of the day . . . Don't like hunting eggs.

— *Jan. 1, 1874: Ned and Emma bought two pigs. One got out of the pen. Ned, Tom and Bett gave him a hell of a chase but the pig outrun them. They run him to the Point but it got dark and he evaporated.*

— Feb. 25, 1875: Had a fight between Alex Goodbread's dog and our dog Jack. Jack cleaned him out. He thought he could lick Jack but he was the most damned fool dog living. Jack always run from him before, but he stood his ground this time and fought for his rights and got them.

— April 21, 1875: Alex Goodbread (the schoolteacher), the contemptible damn lanky picket cuss, shot and killed our dog Jack. Hope the damn hound may never have any luck or raise grub enough to feed him and that he may lose everything he has, is the prayer of his friend and admirer, John Mercer.

— "Thursday, Nov. 30, 1876. Steamer Mary in trying to cross the bar at dead low water failed. She pounded her bottom out. Set the colors of distress. John, Ned, Tom Brundrett, Tom Lacey, Parry Humphrey started for her in the Doaga (pilot boat). The sea was very heavy. Made several trips to get alongside her. The cargo between decks was leaving in big piles. The Mary struck at 7 a.m. and her fires were put out in 30 minutes. She settled very fast. No lives were lost."

The book, edited by John Guthrie Ford, was published by the Port Aransas Preservation and Historical Association. It is full of interesting material, thoughtfully arranged, and one can recognize the hard work it took to transcribe and organize. Ford explained that the entries were selected to keep the book within a manageable length. While I understand what they were up against, with 4,000 entries, I look forward to a book on the Mercer diaries that will include most of the entries, fully indexed. I value this effort, but a more comprehensive book would be an important record of a lost way of life, one strange and fascinating to us, but at one time as natural as the tides themselves.

— April 11, 2012

NOAKES TRIES TEACHING

Thomas Noakes left England when he was a teenager, crossed the Atlantic as a cabin boy and reached Texas sometime between 1845 and 1848. In the 1850s, he settled at Nuecestown — Twelve-Mile Motts — 12 miles up the river from Corpus Christi.

Noakes married a neighbor's daughter and started to farm. Noakes was well-schooled; he could paint and he kept a diary. In the fall of 1865, after the Civil War, rancher George Reynolds asked him to teach school at Nuecestown.

Noakes didn't want to teach, but times were hard and he needed to provide for his family. He went to Corpus Christi to see William Carroll, called "Little" Carroll, a teacher at Hidalgo Seminary. Carroll explained how he organized the lessons and next day Noakes audited Carroll's class.

Most exercises were written on the blackboard, Noakes wrote. "The writing lesson is copied on the board, from the grammar or the arithmetic, by the teacher and recopied by pupils. After which, every pupil recites what he has written to the teacher, who examines the writing at the same time, thus the pupils learn to write, cipher or speak grammar at the same exercise." This was followed by spelling, geography, and arithmetic, in which pupils went over multiplication tables and Carroll copied sums on the blackboard.

"Commencing with the top of the class," Noakes wrote, "each boy does his part, the teacher doing the figuring on the board, as the pupils direct him, each pupil holding his slate and copying the sum when it goes on. When the sums are completed, the pupils take their slates to the teacher, who inspects the manner in which they are written. In the reading lessons, each pupil reads a short passage, while the pupil next to him stops him (as they term it) that is, at a comma, he exclaims, 'comma one' and so on."

Noakes went to see Horace Taylor, the former teacher, to borrow a blackboard. Now he was ready to conduct school.

Noakes began teaching on Oct. 1. He started school at nine, went to lunch at 12, and quit at 4 p.m. "I experienced much less difficulty from my students than I expected and found them anxious to learn. I experienced the greatest difficulty for want of books, slates, everything required to carry on a school. I found the schoolhouse deficient as much as the pupils, the windows being gone, sashes and all."

After school, Noakes had farm chores to do until dark, such as rounding up cows, butchering meat, digging a well, tanning a hide. Noakes settled in to his new pursuit and noted that teaching required more patience than education. He made a deal with a parent named Stevens to teach his children without fee in return for him providing Noakes with lunch each day. The Stevens' place was near the schoolhouse.

On Nov. 13, a freezing norther blew in and "the windows of the schoolhouse being out, the wind and rain made it very disagreeable. After dinner, I made a fire, but it was very cold and most of the children being thinly clad, I dismissed school at 3 p.m." On Saturday, he fixed the windows of the schoolhouse.

That Sunday, there was an explosion at the Hinnant home. A bottle filled with gunpowder was being used as a candle holder. When the candle burned down, the gunpowder exploded. "My best pupil, a young lady of 16 (Mary Hinnant) was hit in the face and arm by fragments of glass and badly cut, besides being much burned." Noakes visited her and was distressed to see "what was once a pretty face all burned, cut and swollen. I now have four pupils sick with fever and one wounded from a gunpowder explosion."

On Dec. 5, Noakes kept a fire burning at the schoolhouse. "Some days, school-teaching goes very much against me, and this was one of the days. I sometimes feel as though I must get on my horse and ride off somewhere to get away and leave everything and then again there are moments when I feel more satisfied."

When his friend John Williams died, Noakes wanted to be executor of the estate, which would entitle him to a percentage of the sale. But George Reynolds and James Bryden, influential stock raisers, sought that for themselves. Noakes was furious, writing that Reynolds and Bryden "hate to see me make a cent and if they can keep me poor, I will be dependent on them. By allowing me to keep a small school, they intend to keep me from starving while they get their children educated."

A self-portrait of Thomas J. Noakes. He tried his hand at teaching at the school in Nuecestown in the fall of 1865.

Noakes tried to prevent Reynolds and Bryden from "their contemplated self-appropriation of John Williams' estate" but had no success. On Dec. 22 he told his pupils he was giving up the post of schoolteacher and bid them farewell.

"I did intend to say more, but so many sorrowful looking faces being turned on me at the same time quite unmanned me. I had to thank them for their attention during the short time we had been together."

He rode into Corpus Christi to buy groceries for Christmas, paying 60 cents a pound for coffee, 50 cents a pound for sugar, and $1 for a small tin of preserved peaches, "those things being considered the height of luxury." Noakes, amid mental turmoil, was depressed on Christmas Day, feeling that "everything was crooked and everybody corrupt." Two days after Christmas he rode into Corpus Christi and withdrew his application to become administrator of the Williams' estate. He saw that Bryden and Reynolds were in town and at home vented his spleen in his diary: "In these people we see the old adage verified, that if a beggar gets on horseback he will ride to the devil."

A Mr. Doak, a short-tempered young man from Louisiana, took Noakes' place as schoolmaster. On Dec. 31, Noakes summed up his brief tenure as a teacher. His income for the year did not exceed $4 and he noted that, "The only gain I made has been confined to experience and that may be good pay for future purposes, but it's a very poor article to live on."

— April 25, 2012

LONE STAR FAIR — 1

One hundred and sixty years ago, Corpus Christi was a crowded and exciting place. Hundreds of people were in town for Henry Kinney's Lone Star Fair, the first state fair held in Texas. The fair had been planned for months, perhaps inspired by the success of the Great Exhibition in London, the first world's fair that attracted some six million visitors.

The always optimistic Kinney, founder of Corpus Christi, expected some 20,000 to 30,000 people would come to his Lone Star Fair. This was really ambitious when you consider that Corpus Christi was a small, remote and provincial place. Kinney had no state or local funding to put on the fair, so he financed it himself, on money borrowed from friends. John P. Schatzel, former U.S. consul at Matamoros who moved to Corpus Christi, put up $45,000 and Forbes Britton borrowed $1,000 in gold to invest in Kinney's scheme. Many other rash investors put up money.

Months before the fair was set to open, Kinney advertised the sale of livestock and land that would be held at Corpus Christi beginning on May 1, 1852. The Texas State Gazette at Austin reported that Kinney expected up to 30,000 people would come to the fair, though the editor thought this was an extravagant statement. Kinney, with infinite attention to detail, was doing everything he could to make the fair a success. Corpus Christi's newspaper, the Nueces Valley, reported he was "untiring in his exertions to make the fair worthy of himself and the masses who will be in Corpus."

Kinney distributed thousands of handbills promising lavish entertainments and luxurious accommodations for visitors. He sent John Holbein to London to promote the fair and encourage emigration. He wrote letters to state leaders and got prominent citizens to serve on the fair committee. He enlisted Gov. Peter Hansborough Bell to open the fair and convinced one of the state's leading citizens, Ashbel Smith of Galveston, to preside.

Corpus Christi was buzzing with excitement. New buildings were going up and old buildings were refurbished. A race course was built. The Nueces Valley reported that, "Constant additions are being made to the already extended catalogue of amusements for the occasion, so that it is impossible that this feature of the fair can be a failure."

Kinney sent "Legs" Lewis, with $3,000 in his pockets, to New Orleans to buy silver cups and goblets to award as prizes. The New Orleans Delta reported that the 70 silver exhibit prizes — on display at the store of Hyde & Goodrich on Chartres Street — were of the "most highly wrought and elaborately finished specimens that we have ever seen." The New Orleans Delta also wrote that, "Extensive sales of land are to take place at the Corpus Christi Fair, and to capitalists this affords a fine opportunity for the profitable investment of money. Every species of amusement will abound, money will be plentiful, land cheap, speculation rife, and all the beauty and chivalry of Texas will be there."

As the day for the fair approached, the Texas Republican reported that every movement in and around Corpus Christi seemed to have some connection with the great fair. At the port of Indianola, ships departing for Corpus Christi included the sloops Belle, California, Mary Ann, Wandering Willie and Major Harris, a light-draft steamboat. The Major Harris was Kinney's own steam-powered packet boat, built at Cincinnati expressly for the shallow waters of Corpus Christi Bay. It began operating just in time to convey passengers to Corpus Christi from the New Orleans steamboats arriving at Indianola.

One of the early arrivals in town was Thomas S. Lubbock (for whom Lubbock was later named) with a letter of introduction to Kinney. Lubbock was seeking work as auctioneer at the livestock sales, and Kinney hired him. Many others were coming in. Henry Maltby's Circus arrived from San Antonio with its featured star, Ella Nunn. Ranger Capt. Rip Ford, veteran of the Mexican War, came to town. So did steamboat captain Richard King, riding up from Brownsville, and Sally Skull, known as a woman who carried a gun and was not reluctant to use it. She shot a man during the fair; Rip Ford said the man pulled a gun on her.

The Indianola Bulletin reported that a large number of people had already assembled in the town, as well as a great variety of livestock, and "everything wore a promising appearance, and the

A silver cup, later owned by Mifflin Kenedy, was given at the Lone Star Fair in Corpus Christi in 1852.

A prize pitcher awarded at Henry Kinney's Lone Star Fair in Corpus Christi in 1852.

committee of managers were engaged in arranging the plan of exhibition and distribution of premiums."

In Corpus Christi, streets were crowded with people with an out-of-town look, walking around, looking at the points of interest, visiting the warehouse where exhibits were displayed. They could stop for refreshments at stands with ice and lemonade throughout the town. The beach side of Water Street became a camping ground for families from the country. Many visitors stayed at the Union House on Chaparral, the old Union Theater built in 1845 when Zachary Taylor's army was concentrated at Corpus Christi. It had been converted into a hotel.

Maria von Blucher in a letter to her parents ("Maria von Blucher's Corpus Christi") wrote that, "Corpus Christi is filling with people and animals of all kinds: jaguars, bobcats, bears, panthers, bullfighters and bulls, cocks — cartloads full, their purpose being fighting, the chief pleasure of the Americans — circus riders, fast runners, German girls and barrel organs. It vexes me that the women of our nation (Germany) sink so low here. For the prizes, Col. Kinney has bought magnificent and most valuable silver things, worth many dollars, all the objects very tasteful . . . Kinney has also bought a steamboat, which transports the new arrivals promptly off the big schooners." Of all the excitement of the fair, Maria von Blucher was looking forward to the bullfight featuring Don Camerena, a celebrated matador from Mexico City. She wrote her parents that her husband Felix would take her to the bullfight "and I am indeed anxious to see it."

— *May 2, 2012*

LONE STAR FAIR — 2

Corpus Christi was a lively and crowded place 160 years ago, for a small town of 600 people, because it was hosting Henry Kinney's Lone Star Fair, the first state fair held in Texas.

The main purpose of the fair was to enable Kinney to sell land to get out of debt. His idea was to attract people to the fair, hoping some would buy thousands of acres he had to sell. A secondary purpose was to drum up support for Mexican revolutionary leader Gen. José M. J. Carbajal.

When the fair opened on May 1, 1852, Corpus Christi was crowded with visitors, but nothing approaching the 20,000 that Kinney expected. Somewhere between 1,000 and 2,000 people came. They came from New Orleans, Galveston, San Antonio, Brownsville and many from the Rio Grande border.

A New Orleans correspondent wrote that the arena was crowded each night with "elegantly dressed American and Mexican ladies, flirting their fans with the same coquetry that they would at an opera, officers of the army, frontiersmen of Texas, with their fine shooters in their belts and the handle of a Bowie knife peeping from their bosoms, friendly Comanche and Lipan Indians, and Mexican rancheros." A band from New Orleans played each evening in front of Kinney's home on the bluff as leading citizens gathered for libations and music, puffing cigars and savoring the liquor.

Exhibits displayed in a warehouse included Mexican blankets, saddles, bridles, spurs, wool, cow hides. William Dinn showed off his agricultural products from his farm outside Corpus Christi. Auctions were held in the mornings with longhorn cattle bringing $5 a head, mustang ponies $20 and mules about $30 a head. At land sales, town lots sold for $100 and rural lands went for $1 to $3 per acre. Horse races were held in the day and circus acts in the evening, along with cockfights, riding contests, even lectures on philosophy and literature.

One featured performance was Mexico City's famed bullfighter Don Camerena. A young red bull named Colorado nearly gored the famous bullfighter; the match was declared a draw.

Don Camerena was not the only person from Mexico disappointed at the fair. Gen. Carbajal was a featured speaker at the fair. Carbajal, a longtime friend of Kinney, was trying to separate the northern states of Mexico from the central government. Gen. Carbajal, who went to college in Virginia, set forth his cause and that of the people of Tamaulipas against the wrongs inflicted by the tyranny of the Mexican government, words that resonated with Texans who could remember their own revolution in 1836. But Carbajal attracted little support. His revolution just dwindled into insignificance.

Near the end of the fair, on May 12, the prizes were awarded, later reported in the Nueces Valley on May 20, 1852. Richly embossed silver cups, chalices, urns, gravy bowls, brought back from New Orleans by Legs Lewis, were handed out for the best flock of sheep, the best herd of brood mares, the best herd of mustangs, and so on.

Gail Borden Jr. (of evaporated milk fame) won a prize for his canned meat biscuits. Thomas Flintoff, an itinerant painter from England won a prize for his paintings of Corpus Christi. John Dix won for the best flock of sheep. R. Clements won for the best herd of mustangs. Mrs. Manning was given a prize for two quilts. Henry Maltby was given an award for his "highly artistic feats of the ring and circus." Henry Kinney won three prizes, for a stallion, Mexican bridle, and milk cow. His wife Mary took a prize for the cotton grown on their Oso Ranch. Each prize bore the inscription: "From H. L. Kinney and General Committee of the Lone Star Fair, Corpus Christi, May, 1852."

On the last day, Ashbel Smith, chairman of the fair, spoke at the Maltby circus pavilion, praising Kinney's enterprising character and noting the great expense he incurred in putting on the fair. He presented Kinney with two pieces of plate brought from New Orleans — a silver urn and a fruit basket — for his hospitality. Kinney spoke of past endeavors and chances taken in establishing a trading post at Corpus Christi, the dangers from Indian and Mexican raids, but he resolved, he said, pointing toward the bay, "to live or die on the spot."

After two weeks, the Lone Star Fair ended. Word spread from returning fair-goers that it was a flop. The sloop Wandering Willie arrived at Indianola with passengers returning from Corpus Christi.

Henry L. Kinney was photographed by Mathew B. Brady in Washington, undated but probably not long after Kinney's Lone Star Fair was held in 1852. The photo was reprinted in Frank Leslie's Illustrated Newspaper on Dec. 22, 1855.

The Indianola Bulletin reported that the arrivals said the fair fell "infinitely short of what was expected, and in the main, is rather a failure. We can but suppose that the amusements and exhibitions were of a limited character."

A similar report was carried in the Texas State Gazette in Austin. "We learn from a gentleman just from Corpus Christi that the fair was considered rather in the light of a failure. There were present about 500 Mexicans, about 200 filibusters, including the renowned Carbajal, about 200 citizens from different parts of the country — being in all about one thousand persons. The sales of cattle, horses, and land, for which undoubtedly the fair had been gotten up, were meager to what was expected."

The failure of the fair wasn't bad management on Kinney's part, just bad logic. Corpus Christi was a long way from anywhere, far from population centers and travel was too difficult. So the expected 20,000 people did not show up to rescue Kinney from bankruptcy. His creditors closed in, demanding payment, and Kinney was forced to give up his Mustang Island ranch and mortgage other holdings. Kinney later said he spent $50,000 on the fair, which attracted thousands of people, and that, "No such pageant had ever been known in this section of the country before." Of course, Kinney had a natural gift for self-promotion.

After the fair, the streets must have looked deserted. The circus performers, bullfighters, Mexican revolutionaries, soldiers, Indians, politicians and sightseers all left town. It was the first and last state fair in Corpus Christi and it would be long remembered.

— May 9, 2012

THE MEXICAN TRADE

Corpus Christi was called the Old Indian Trading Grounds, not that Indians traded there, but it was an old Karankawa haunt where Texas traders landed goods to smuggle into Mexico. Of course they would have taken exception to being called smugglers, but so they were.

Much of South Texas along the coast was linked to this trade. Victoria merchant John Linn landed tobacco at the Old Indian Trading Grounds in 1829, planning to meet a man with pack mules to take it to Camargo, Mexico. Henry Gilpin arrived that year in a schooner full of merchandise for Mexico. Four years later, he returned with goods worth $80,000 for Zacatecas.

It was a lucrative trade. Because of disunity and prevailing political turmoil, Mexico never developed strong commercial ties with its disaffected northern states. Trade caravans from Mexico City to the north were rare. American traders moved in, bringing leaf tobacco, cotton domestics, and cheap goods that American manufacturers produced in abundance, shipped from New Orleans. For merchants, the markup was three or four times what the goods cost. In return, they bought wool, hides and other products from Mexico, also at fat profit margins.

Early on, this trade moved through Matamoros where American firms were well-established. In Mexico, customs duties and tariffs were collected on goods shipped in by sea, but were not collected on goods freighted overland. And for a time, the Matamoros port was closed to all foreign trade. This encouraged merchants in Matamoros to land goods on remote Texas beaches and transport them overland, bypassing tariff charges and customs duties. That's why John Linn, Henry Gilpin and other smugglers — ah, traders — landed merchandise at the Old Indian Trading Grounds.

Henry Kinney, seeing that it was a good spot to land goods for Mexico, set up his trading post in 1839. The place was called

Kinney's Rancho, then Corpus Christi. Kinney was joined by Frederick Belden and Henry Gilpin, moving up from Matamoros. In 1841, only 70 to 100 people lived at Kinney's Rancho, but it was a thriving place with wealthy merchants engaged in the Mexican trade. Traders included J. P. Kelsey, William Mann, Henry Redmond, William Cazneau, and of course Kinney. Caravans carrying $100,000 or more in goods required protection, so Kinney hired gun hands. Several of his hired guns became prominent men on the border, such as H. Clay Davis and J. R. Everitt.

Henry Clay Davis, from Kentucky, is an interesting story. On a trip to Camargo, he met the beautiful daughter of Mexican rancher Don Francisco de la Garza. He asked for her hand in marriage. The rancher refused, saying that if he gave his consent the American would take Hilaria away and he would never see her again. When Davis promised to build a home across the Rio Grande, the rancher gave his consent. Davis married Hilaria and they established Davis Ranch (or Davis' Landing), which became a transit point for goods shipped from Corpus Christi into Mexico. Davis Ranch became Rio Grande City.

J. P. Kelsey, from New York, also following the Mexican trade, set up a tent at Kinney's Rancho in 1842. He claimed to be the first to call Corpus Christi "Corpus Christi." He married the town's first schoolteacher, Amanda Brooks, a young woman from Ohio, and they moved to Davis Ranch. They became founding settlers of Rio Grande City.

Former Ranger J. R. Everitt, another Kinney gun hand, built an adobe house opposite Mier, Mexico, and called it Buena Vista. Henry W. Berry, also hired to protect Kinney's trading post, stayed in Corpus Christi and became the first sheriff of Nueces County. Most of Corpus Christi's settlers were traders or people hired in connection with the Mexican trade.

The Mexican War disrupted trade, but after the war ended in 1848 trade returned. Kinney and William Cazneau organized the Chihuahua Train, a caravan of 100 wagons to carry goods to Chihuahua, 500 miles away. Kinney hoped to establish a trade route to compete with St. Louis traders who freighted their goods down the Santa Fe Trail into northern Mexico, a market larger than, say, France.

In the early years, traders conveyed goods to Mexico and sold them, but as trade ties built up Mexican traders arrived at Corpus

Ox carts in Mexico. Similar carts were used to haul wool and hides to Corpus Christi, which was founded as a transit point for trade with the Chihuahua region of Mexico.

Christi to buy and sell and American merchants were content to sit and wait for the trade to come to them. Goods were transported both ways, with leaf tobacco, cotton prints and Colt six-shooters going to Mexico and hides, wool and silver dollars and bullion coming to Texas.

As a port of trade, Corpus Christi was bypassed in the 1850s as Indianola, on Matagorda Bay, grew. Much of the Mexican trade was siphoned off by Indianola merchants and sent up the Old Cart Road to San Antonio and to Mexico. Trade was curtailed again during the Civil War, but after the war Corpus Christi began to reclaim a share of the Mexican trade because it was hundreds of miles closer than other Gulf ports. After the 1875 hurricane nearly wiped out Indianola, more of the Mexican trade returned to Corpus Christi.

Not only did Corpus Christi become one of the world's leading wool markets, it was also handling raw ore from mines in Mexico, from as far away as Zacatecas. Caravans — "trains" — of Chihuahua wagons, pulled by up to 22 mules per wagon, hauled cargoes of copper, lead and silver ore, which were shipped from Corpus Christi to Hamburg, Germany.

Robert Adams, an early settler, said it was not unusual to see trains of 50 wagons with 20 mules pulling each wagon. Another said it was thrilling to see trains of wagons, sometimes a mile long, snaking into town. On a given day, trains of Chihuahua wagons — heavy and creaking with wool and hides or bullion and lead — arrived from Mexico.

Shipment of Mexican ore was initiated by wool merchants Edey & Kirsten. The firm was bought out by Uriah Lott, who became the driving force behind building railroads in South Texas, progress that put an end to the Mexican trade. But for four decades, from 1839 to the early 1880s, it was the dominant part of the local economy. In the early years, the Mexican trade was almost the sole source of wealth for the town. It was the reason Corpus Christi was founded.

— May 23, 2012

HE LEFT SOME LOOSE ENDS

In 1829, Henry Addington Gilpin landed on the site of today's Corpus Christi, 10 years before Henry Kinney built his trading post. Why Gilpin, from a prominent Nova Scotia family, came to South Texas is a mystery, which was not unusual for the time and place. It was not unusual because Texas attracted people who could lose themselves and escape whatever drove them west.

Gilpin came from a well-regarded English family. His grandfather, the Rev. William Gilpin, was a celebrated author in England. A collection of his works is at the Dalhousie University Libraries in Nova Scotia. A son, John Bernard Gilpin, was appointed deputy consul and later consul for His Majesty's government at Newport, Rhode Island.

John Bernard Gilpin had 13 children by two wives. He first married a woman in Pennsylvania and they had seven children. After she died, he married Mary Elizabeth Miller in Newport, R. I., and they had six children, including Henry A. Gilpin, who was born on May 13, 1808. He was six years old when his mother died in 1814 after complications from the birth of a sixth child.

In 1833, the father, John Bernard, retired and moved to Kings County, Nova Scotia, where he lived until he died. Several sons by his first and his second wife became prominent doctors and ministers in Canada. One son, a midshipman on a British warship, was killed in action off the Spanish coast in 1811. Another, Henry, disappeared. He went to Texas.

Before he came to Texas, Henry Gilpin, one account says, worked in a bank in New Jersey and "left suddenly." In 1829, he bought trade goods for Mexico and arrived on a schooner from New Orleans. After he landed at the site of today's Corpus Christi, he went to Matamoros where he fell in with other traders. In Mexico, Gilpin learned to speak Spanish. He met Frederick Belden from New York and they became business partners. Gilpin led trade caravans to Chihuahua. On a trip in 1833 he carried $80,000 worth of goods to Zacatecas.

Gilpin and Belden moved to Corpus Christi in the 1840s, transporting trade goods into Mexico to evade customs' duties. With profits that could reach four times the cost of the goods, great wealth was made from the Mexican trade.

When Zachary Taylor's army concentrated at Corpus Christi in 1845, Gilpin was offered a job on Taylor's staff as an interpreter, but he stayed in business. During the war, he operated out of Camargo as an agent for Belden and partners and returned to Corpus Christi after the war.

In 1852, the year after his father died in Nova Scotia, Gilpin was elected chief justice of Nueces County, equivalent to today's county judge. When Thomas Parker was sheriff and Gilpin chief justice, Gilpin benefited from the relationship. At a sheriff's sale, Parker sold Gilpin 1,476 acres of land for $50, or 2.9 cents an acre. This tract became the foundation for Gilpin's ranch at Penitas.

Gilpin was chief justice in 1862 when the Union blockade commander, Lt. J. W. Kittredge, landed with a flag of truce at Ohler's Wharf on Aug. 12, 1862. Kittredge was met by Gilpin and Col. Alfred Hobby, in charge of Confederate forces. Kittredge warned them to evacuate civilians before he bombarded the town.

Gilpin and Belden were partners in a ranch called Carmel near Lagarto. When Belden died in 1868, Gilpin was named administrator of the estate, which he managed for Belden's widow. In 1873, Gilpin was elected to the Texas House for a district that covered 22 counties and ran from Corpus Christi to Brownsville, Laredo to El Paso.

In the Nuecestown Raid in 1875, Gilpin was in his buggy heading to Corpus Christi when he was captured by bandits, along with other travelers on the road. The bandits took the captives' horses and made them walk or run as they headed for Nuecestown. A bandit who knew Gilpin shouted, "Andale! Don Enriquez! Andale!"

Gilpin, like his father and grandfather, was a well-read and scholarly man. After he retired and moved to Penitas, he devoted his time to the study of weather and astronomical observations. Ruth Dodson, whose family lived nearby, wrote an article about Gilpin for the Southwest Review in 1933. Dodson wrote that Gilpin's ranch house was surrounded by a fence and a gravel walk led to the front steps. The house had a wide gallery where the judge liked to sit. He

Bas relief of Henry Addington Gilpin, who landed trade goods bound for Mexico in 1829 at the site that would later become Corpus Christi.

was an exotic neighbor, with an English accent, and he would invite friends to tea.

Several single women, Dodson wrote, "set their cap" for Judge Gilpin, without success. "Then, to the surprise of everyone, a daughter came to visit him. I don't know when this was, but the daughter, her Episcopal husband, and her three children came to visit him within my memory — it must have been in the early 1880s. We lent them horses to ride while they were here. I think they came from New York."

Based on a slim trail, Gilpin apparently married and fathered two children, a son named Charles Pope Gilpin and a daughter named Caroline Mathilde Gilpin, before he decamped for Texas.

Gilpin did not live alone at the Penitas ranch. He "kept bach" with a man named Graham. "I can't remember when Mr. Graham's home was not with Judge Gilpin," Dodson wrote. "They were well suited to be company to each other, although Mr. Graham was very much younger."

Gilpin sold the livestock on his ranch for $30,000, but the money evaporated and he was living in dire poverty when he died on Nov. 11, 1895. According to Dodson, George Reynolds was appointed executor of the estate, which included 800 acres of land, mortgaged for $1,200, and the home and possessions. "Mr. Reynolds, being executor, could not bid on the land," Dodson wrote, "so he had his son John do it. It went for the $1,200 debt." Quite a bargain, though not as good as Gilpin's original price of 2.9 cents an acre.

Besides the land and the house, Henry Addington Gilpin left some loose ends about his family ties and the cause of estrangement that sent him off to Matamoros and Corpus Christi. Whatever secrets he brought to Texas were buried with him.

— May 30, 2012

BATTLE OF SALADO CREEK

In the last of several probing attacks in 1842, Mexican Gen. Adrian Woll with a large army captured San Antonio on Sept. 11. Though it was a Sunday, district court had been called and judge, lawyers and witnesses in town were taken captive.

Texans rushed to repel the invaders. Gen. Matthew "Old Paint" Caldwell mustered volunteers in Gonzales and sent Z. N. "Wildcat" Morrell and 12 men on fast horses to find Ranger Capt. Jack Hays, who was away on a scouting trip.

Before they left, Morrell ground up parched corn and mixed it with sugar, which he called cold flour. Although they saw plenty of game, they were under orders not to shoot for fear of alerting Woll's men. When they found Hays, they had eaten nothing but a few bites of Morrell's cold flour and were close to mutiny.

Hays told Morrell to talk to them. "I remembered an old saying," Morrell said, "never try to influence a man against his inclination when he is hungry, but I determined to try." Morrell told them that when they left Caldwell's camp he felt like he was 40 years old and after he fasted a day, he felt he was 35 and when the cold flour and the coffee ran out, he felt he was 21 and ready to fight.

"Old Paint" Caldwell arrived and took command as the senior officer, with Hays commanding the scouts. They decided that Hays, who knew the terrain, would choose a place for a battle and try to lure Woll there. Hays chose Salado Creek, seven miles northeast of San Antonio, where an embankment would serve as a breastwork. Caldwell would lie in wait and Hays would bring Woll to him, using an old Comanche trick.

On Sunday morning, Sept. 18, Hays, Morrell and a few men rode to a half mile of the Alamo. Hays, in view of Mexican soldiers, cut capers, waving his hat and shouting insults about the Mexicans' manhood. It worked. As the Mexican cavalry gave chase, Hays and men raced away toward Salado Creek, throwing away blankets and coats to lighten the load on their winded horses. They reached camp with every man alive.

That afternoon, Woll arrived with infantry, cavalry and artillery. He had 1,200 men to Caldwell's 225. At Salado Creek, Mexican soldiers formed in line of battle opposite Caldwell's Texans, who were behind the embankment under a canopy of pecan trees. Woll's artillery tried to drive the Texans from behind their cover. When grapeshot hit the pecan trees, they said it sounded like tearing calico. Woll, seeing that artillery was not doing the job, ordered a charge.

The Mexicans advanced, Morrell wrote, under a splendid puff of music, with pikes and swords flashing in the sun. Woll's infantry approached and were within 30 feet of the Texas lines when the rifles of the Texans fired a tremendous volley, leaving hardly a man standing. Those not hit ran to the rear. Woll lost 60 men killed and many wounded while the Texans lost one killed and several wounded. Hays' selection of a battlefield worked to perfection.

When Woll's men captured San Antonio, they plundered Hays' Ranger headquarters and took a new pair of pants belonging to Bigfoot Wallace, called "Foot" for short. Before the battle at Salado Creek, Wallace vowed to find and shoot any oversized Mexican wearing pants big enough to fit him. During the battle, he found the man, shot him, and secured the pants. He said he figured the Mexicans owed him a pair.

After the battle, the Texans were puzzled when they heard gunfire from behind Woll's position. They soon realized Woll was firing on reinforcements rushing to join them. By chance, Woll's troops came upon Capt. Nicholas Dawson bringing 53 men from LaGrange to join Caldwell. Dawson's men, caught in the open, raised a white flag to surrender, but they were cut to pieces by Woll's artillery. Only 15 men survived.

For Morrell, it was an anxious night, knowing his son Allen was with Dawson. When the sun rose, he rode to the scene of the slaughter, a mott of mesquite bushes on the prairie. From a distance he could see scattered bundles of clothing. On closer view, they were bodies. He began turning them over, looking at faces, looking for his son. He recognized nearly every one. Some were neighbors, their wives now widows, some the sons of neighbors.

Morrell couldn't find his son. "A number of bodies were turned over before I could recognize them. One or two were so badly mangled I could not recognize them. Supposing that one of these

Ranger Capt. Jack Hays chose Salado Creek as a good place for a battle with the superior forces of Mexican Gen. Adrian Woll.

might be my son, I examined their feet for a scar he carried from childhood. By this time I was satisfied he had escaped or was among the prisoners. I wrote down the names of the dead so that I might make a correct report to the bereaved."

Woll retreated, shadowed by Hays, with Caldwell following. They crossed the Medina River (near today's Castroville) and reached the Hondo River. The pursuit was disconnected, desultory. Caldwell was not eager to tangle with Woll after he had seen what Woll's guns did to Dawson's men.

Hays came upon Woll's rear guard, a battery with infantry support, on the Hondo River. When Caldwell arrived, Hays urged an attack. Caldwell demurred. Hays asked for volunteers to join his Rangers to take the battery. As they charged uphill, the Mexican artillery overshot them. Every soldier manning the cannons was killed as Hays' men silenced the guns.

After Hays captured the cannon, the plan called for Caldwell to attack. Hays held the battery, but no support arrived. Caldwell later explained that due to boggy ground and tired horses, he declined to support Hays' charge and thought it prudent to avoid a pitched battle. Woll's forces retreated unmolested and crossed the Rio Grande, taking their hostages with them.

Morrell and many other Texans were appalled that they didn't try to prevent their Texas compatriots from being carried off into captivity in Mexico. "Old Paint" Caldwell never lived down his timid failure to attack the retreating Woll.

—June 6, 2012

BLOODBATH IN MIER

After the battle of Salado Creek, Republic of Texas President Sam Houston authorized an expeditionary force to punish Mexico after Mexican Gen. Adrian Woll captured San Antonio and carried off Texas hostages.

Houston authorized Gen. Alex Somervell to launch reprisals by carrying the war across the Rio Grande into Mexico. In Somervell's collection of unpaid volunteers — called the Southwestern Army of Texas — were several Texas leaders, including Thomas Jefferson Green and William S. Fisher. Jack Hays, the Ranger captain, was part of that force, and he was put in command of a battalion of scouts. With him were Rangers Ben McCulloch, Sam Walker and Bigfoot Wallace, who was still wearing the britches he took from a dead Mexican soldier after the battle of Salado Creek.

Hays led the way for Somervell's expeditionary forces, which numbered about 750 men. Houston called them light troops, meaning irregulars, but many were adventurers not amenable to military discipline. Since Houston was short of money, arms, men, everything needed to make war, Somervell's men would have to live off the land; their pay would come from whatever they could carry off. Houston could not afford a war; this was a pay-back raid.

Somervell's forces arrived at Laredo on Dec. 8, 1842 and camped downstream from town. Mexican soldiers at Laredo evacuated across the Rio Grande. Next day, some of the Somevell's men plundered Laredo, which they considered a Mexican town, ignoring Houston's orders to conduct civilized warfare. As the stragglers made it back to camp, Somervell ordered them arrested and their plunder returned to Laredo.

Somervell said the men who wished to go home could do so and about 200 left for home. Somervell took the others across the river and captured the town of Guerrero, where they demanded 100 horses and when these were not available demanded $5,000 in lieu of the

Gen. Pedro Ampudia (from "Mier Expedition Diary"
by Joseph D. McCutchan).

horses. The alcalde (or mayor) brought $700 and said that was all
that could be raised. When Somervell ordered the men to cross into
Texas and return home, some refused to obey. Five captains, with
their men, decided to proceed downriver to obtain horses and
provisions to see them home. Some 200 men left with Somervell
while 310 remained behind.

Jack Hays made the same offer to his Rangers that Somervell
made to his men, that they were free to go on, but Hays warned the
Rangers that the descent into Mexico could hold an unpleasant
surprise. Though he was not one to back off from a fight, he had
information from his network of border spies that a large Mexican
force was being rushed to deal with the Texans. Don't go, he said,
but Bigfoot Wallace and Sam Walker, among others, did not heed
the warning.

As Somervell led the remnant of his command to the junction of the Frio and Nueces for mustering out, back on the Rio Grande those men and their leaders who wanted to press on elected to proceed under the command of an old border fighter, William S. Fisher. As it turned out, this was a mistake. If the Texans thought they could march into Mexico, take their revenge and portable plunder, especially horses, and march out again, the reality was otherwise, as events would show.

On Dec. 21, 1842, Fisher's men crossed over to Mier, the largest town next to Matamoros on the lower Rio Grande. They rode into town and demanded food for themselves and forage for their horses. The alcalde promised the food and forage would be delivered to the Texans' camp next day. They waited until Christmas Day for the demands to be met. They captured a Mexican who told them that Gen. Pedro Ampudia had arrived with 1,000 soldiers.

The Texans rode into town at sunset. They were expected. A bullet whizzed past the ear of Bigfoot Wallace, killing the man behind him. Mexican soldiers rushed out of the houses lining the streets. The Texans, fighting at close quarters, used bowie knives and rifle butts against the Mexican soldiers. They made sallies against Ampudia's cavalry and artillery. The fighting was ferocious, more like a street brawl than a military engagement.

After it was over, the streets of Mier were littered with bodies of those who had been shot or stabbed or their heads bashed in by rifle butts. Some 600 Mexican soldiers were killed and 100 Texans, enough to fill a graveyard.

Under a flag of truce that was sent over from the Mexican side, the Texans sued for peace, at the bidding of William S. Fisher, who was sick, and against the strong advice of Thomas Jefferson Green, who wanted to keep fighting. Fight first, said Green, negotiate later. He was so upset he broke his sword rather than give it up.

At the time they surrendered, they had the fight virtually won, they learned later. General Ampudia and other Mexican leaders had their horses saddled and waiting and were ready to flee if the Texans did not accept the truce. "We fought Ampudia, and had him whipped, and they sent a flag of truce and Colonel Fisher very foolishly listened to him," said George Washington Trahern. "We fought him two days and two nights, and he was ready to retreat, they were all ready to retreat. And Fisher let this flag of truce come in, instead of shooting at it."

Bigfoot Wallace survived. He thought that as many as 800 Mexicans were killed and said the battle was harder-fought than the battle at San Jacinto. From where the surrender took place, he saw row upon row of dead Mexican soldiers, with a priest moving among them making the sign of the cross. The bodies of 100 Texans killed in the fight were dragged through the streets, followed by a cheering crowd of children and adults.

It was a bloodbath. The battle at Mier left more casualties than any engagement between Texas and Mexico since San Jacinto. For Texans, Mier would leave such a bad taste they could hardly keep from spitting at the mention of the name.

— June 13, 2012

'THAT DITCH IS FOR US'

After the surrender at Mier, 200 Texas prisoners were marched under heavy guard down the river toward Matamoros. It was the last day of 1842 and very cold. The captives built fires at night and when the fires burned down they slept in the warm ashes.

The towns they passed through along the river — Camargo, Reynosa, Guadalupe — became scenes of noisy and triumphant fanfare for their Mexican escorts. Their approach was announced with bugles, trumpets, and the excited pealing of church bells, as if it were a day for one of the saints. The captives were herded through the main plazas of the towns, surrounded by prancing horses of the cavalry guards and taunted by jeering mobs. The Texans knew enough Spanish to yell insults at their hosts.

The main body of the captives reached Matamoros on Jan. 9, 1843. One evening, they were penned up in a cattle corral and the Texans, as if they were in a play, some comic interlude, pawed the ground and snorted like mad bulls. When they were later put in a sheep pen, they bleated like lost lambs.

After a week, they left for Monterrey, guarded by a troop of cavalry, 600 infantry and one piece of artillery. They were fed very little and the stitching came out of their boots, then the boots fell apart, and they passed through the towns barefoot, ragged and starving.

Their putative leaders — William Fisher and Thomas Jefferson Green — were sent ahead by horseback and were treated much better, though Green wrote letters of complaint when they were not allowed bedding at one of their nightly stops. But Green praised his host at Monterrey. "Our table was supplied from the best French restaurant in the city; and our kind host, old Colonel Bermudez, was all the time apologizing for not having things good enough for us."

As the main body marched from Monterrey to Saltillo, beginning on Feb. 2, plans were made to escape, under the leadership of Ewen

Cameron, the big Scotsman. They reached their prison quarters at the Hacienda Salado, 100 miles west of Saltillo, on Feb. 10. Fisher and Green had arrived the day before.

At Hacienda Salado, they found six Texans already there, three captives from the Santa Fe Expedition in 1841 and three captives taken in San Antonio during Woll's raid. The plan to escape was refined.

Next morning at daybreak, Capt. Cameron gave the signal by raising his hat and the Texans attacked their guards, overpowering them in fierce fighting and taking their weapons. The whole compound was in motion. Some guards fired hastily, dropped their guns and fled. There was a cheer as the Texans realized the courtyard was theirs and the Mexican guards surrendered. An inventory of their casualties showed five Texans dead and as many seriously wounded in the melee.

They borrowed a couple of hundred horses, mostly from their cavalry escort, and Bigfoot Wallace captured a large pacing mule that belonged to a Mexican captain named Arroyo.

Fisher and Green were not with them; they had been taken some distance away from Hacienda Salado before the breakout. Ewen Cameron was in charge. The escapees left by the main road to Saltillo, heading toward the Rio Grande. All 193 Texans were mounted. They rode 60 miles, fed their horses, slept two hours, then left the main road to ride around Saltillo. They decided to leave the road and strike out over the mountains, but soon learned they had made a terrible mistake. It was barren, arid, desolate country, without water or food, and they became lost. They spent six weary days trying to get through.

Men were dying of thirst and starvation. Horses were killed and eaten. Bigfoot killed the big pacing mule and devoured mule steaks. He said they drank the red blood with gusto "as if they were drinking to one another's health in the saloons of San Antonio."

They were lost in the mountains, suffering from thirst, and losing stragglers. They were too weak to carry their guns. The horses were eaten or abandoned. Some of the men, delirious, wandered off to die alone; their bodies would never be found. It was as if the land of Mexico was closing in around them, trapping them, preventing their escape.

Bigfoot dried some of the mule meat, which he carried in a haversack, and he would chew on bits from time to time until his

Sketch of Bigfoot Wallace from A. J. Sowell's "Texas Indian Fighters."

tongue became too dry and swollen to swallow. Bigfoot, with Ewen Cameron and two others, broke away from the main body. They thought by the looks of the land that water was near and, by a supreme effort of survival, used the last of their strength to reach it. They had a vision of splashing in a lake. They were captured by Mexican cavalry 150 yards from a pool of water.

When they were given water, Bigfoot grabbed the gourd and refused to give it up. He said it was the best he ever tasted. He drank all the water in the gourd, despite the guard's warning that it would kill him, then fell on the ground and promptly went to sleep. He hadn't slept for five or six days. When morning came, he opened his haversack and found the last of the mule meat. A guard asked what he was eating. "Mule meat," he said. "Whose mule was it?" the guard asked. "My mule," said Wallace. "It was not," said the Mexican. "He belonged to Captain Arroyo."

Almost all the escapees were recaptured, except for five who died, four who made their way back to Texas, and four who simply disappeared, dead somewhere in the mountains. After a few days spent rounding up stragglers, the prisoners were marched back to Hacienda Salado where Bigfoot Wallace and Henry Whaling noticed that the Mexicans were digging a big ditch. Whaling said, "That ditch is for us."

— June 20, 2012

THE BEAN POT

After wandering the hills without water, after eating their horses and drinking their own urine, after nearly dying from exhaustion, the escaped Mier prisoners looked like walking corpses. They were marched back to Hacienda Salado, the place they had escaped from, where they learned that Gen. Antonio López de Santa Anna had ordered them to be shot as punishment for the escape. A big ditch was being dug for them.

While Santa Anna had been treated with every courtesy when he was a captive of the Texans, after San Jacinto, he would still rather shoot Texans than eat breakfast. Despite his preference, Santa Anna was prevailed upon to modify the order and rather than kill all the prisoners kill only one of 10, a decimation, as close to mercy as Santa Anna was capable of.

The men to be executed would be chosen by lot. Since 176 prisoners were at Hacienda Salado when the order was given, 176 beans — 17 black and 159 white — were put in a clay jar. The prisoners were chained and guarded, allowing no chance to rush and overpower the guards. Each man had to draw a bean.

Bigfoot Wallace noticed that white beans were placed in the jar and the black beans put on top, not mixed up. He thought they were trying to ensure that Ewen Cameron, who led the escape, got a black bean, since he had to draw first. Someone whispered "dig deep, Captain" and Cameron pulled out a white bean. William F. Wilson, chained to Cameron, drew a white bean. William Eastland, cousin of Nicholas Dawson, massacred at Salado Creek, was the first to draw a black bean.

Waiting to draw a bean to see who would live and who would die was worse than charging a blazing cannon, said Bigfoot Wallace. The black beans, Wallace noticed, were larger. His big hand shook and he could barely get it in the jar. He felt around until he had two beans; he dropped one and held up a white bean. One story told later said he offered to swap his white bean with a young man with a black one. Not true, he said; he meant to stay alive as long as he could. "When I put my hand in and found two beans, one big and one small, I pulled out the small one because I thought the black beans looked bigger. I had only one life to give for William Wallace."

A gambler from Austin drew a black bean and muttered, "Just my luck." The guards taunted the condemned men, telling them better luck next time. Henry Whaling got a black bean, then demanded food. "I do not want to starve and be shot too." They gave him rations.

The condemned men were led away. An infantry company called the Red Caps would be their executioners. The prisoners, blindfolded, asked to be shot from the front, but each man had a soldier standing behind him and each was shot in the back at point-blank range. Henry Whaling was shot several times before he died.

One corpse being piled up was not a corpse. J. L. Shepard was shot in the shoulder; he only feigned death. When the soldiers left, he escaped into the mountains. He was captured after 10 days, brought back, and executed.

The survivors — hollow-eyed and hollow-bellied — were put on the road to Mexico City. Some died on the way. "Foot" Wallace was still wearing the Mexican pants he acquired in the battle at Salado Creek, though little more than the waistband was left and he wore a long shirt that reached his ankles. His shackles were too tight and his arms turned black. In one town, a woman told a guard to take off his shackles; the guard refused, saying only the governor could make such an order; she said she was the governor's wife. The shackles were removed.

A few miles from Mexico City, orders came down from Santa Anna, with callous cruelty, that Ewen Cameron was to be executed even though he had drawn a white bean. As the prisoners were marched away, they heard gunfire and knew Cameron was dead.

The prisoners arrived at Mexico City on May 1, 1843 and were kept there until October. They were put to work building roads, carrying sand in sacks. The prisoners cut small holes in the sacks to let the sand dribble out as they walked to lighten the load.

In October, they were moved to the dungeon at Perote Castle, 300 miles from Mexico City, between Puebla and Veracruz, an ancient stone fortress. Some prisoners from the Santa Fe Expedition and

The Drawing of the Black Bean by Frederick Remington

from Woll's San Antonio raid were already there. Earlier that year, 16 Texans escaped from Perote through a hole dug under the walls; eight were recaptured.

In the damp dungeon at Perote Castle, Bigfoot said the men were so hungry they supplemented their diet by catching and eating rats. The men were hitched to carts like oxen and made to haul rocks down from the mountains. Some prisoners died and some were released through the good offices of British and American ambassadors. Bigfoot Wallace and three other men were freed on Aug. 5, 1844.

The following month, on Sept. 16, 1844, those who remained in the prison were freed. It was said Santa Anna had promised his wife on her deathbed that he would free them, and for once in his life, said Bigfoot, he kept his promise.

Four years later, during the Mexican War, Bigfoot Wallace surprised himself when he failed to blow the head off a Mexican soldier bearing a white flag. Bigfoot called it the single greatest act of restraint in his life.

"I didn't see the flag," Bigfoot said. "I just saw his face. He was the man who held up the clay jar of beans at Hacienda Salado."

At the end of the Mexican War, the remains of the Texans executed in the black-bean drawing at Hacienda Salado were

A partial view of the castle of San Carlos de Perote, in the state of Veracruz, between Veracruz and Mexico City.

exhumed and returned to Texas and reburied, with the remains of Capt. Dawson and his men, on a steep bluff overlooking LaGrange, known today as Monument Hill.

— June 27, 2012

THE BLACK LAND SPECIAL

An excursion train called the Black Land Special pulled out of Corpus Christi on Nov. 9, 1924. On board were 110 prominent farmers, businessmen and civic leaders — all wearing pearl-gray Stetsons — on their way to cities across Central and North Texas to promote the fertile black-land farming region of South Texas.

The man credited with organizing the Black Land Special was Maston Nixon, a young cotton farmer near Robstown, a man of talent and energy.

Nixon was born in 1896 in Luling. His father, a banker, was involved in politics and Maston named his ponies after politicians. When his father died, he was sent to boarding school in San Antonio, the West Texas Military Academy. His first job was to harness a mule to the ice wagon, for which he was paid the grand sum of $5 a week. He saved the money and invested in an oil company, the Dixie Oil and Refining. He eventually owned 10 percent of the company.

Nixon enlisted in the army in 1917 and, as a second lieutenant, was drilling recruits when two men came to see him about his stock in the oil company. They offered him $46,500 in cash or the same value in stock in a new company. He took the cash and regretted it for the rest of his life. "It was the worst business decision I ever made," Nixon said. The new company became Humble Oil.

Nixon served as an artillery captain in France at the end of World War I and was stationed with occupation forces in Germany. After he was discharged in 1919, he moved to a cotton farm at Petronila, which he owned with his stepfather. He married Hallie Fincham of San Antonio and started an experimantsal cotton seed farm at Robstown.

The inspiration for the Black Land Special started with Nixon after he helped establish the Robstown Chamber of Commerce and served as its first president. During that time, he had a survey run on black

Members of the Black Land Special, each man wearing a pearl-gray Stetson, prepared to leave by train on a 1,500 mile trip across Central and North Texas to promote black land farming of South Texas.

land farm acreage that was unfarmed but available for sale in Nueces, Jim Wells, Kleberg, and San Patricio counties. He learned that while there were several thousand farms in the four-county area, hundreds of thousands of acres were available for farming.

Thus began his idea of encouraging farmers to settle in the black-dirt farm region of South Texas. The best way to promote the region, to tell its story, was discussed. Someone suggested they hold a county fair and send out invitations to farmers throughout Texas. Then someone thought of hiring a train and, rather than bring people here, take farmers and farm products to show them what could be grown here.

Nixon, as chief organizer, enlisted the help of Missouri Pacific, Southern Pacific and Tex-Mex Railroads, which helped cover expenses for the 12-car excursion train. He got Texas A&M University to help prepare the exhibits. He got one of the best Army bands in Texas — the 20th Infantry Band at Fort Sam Houston — to make the trip to entertain the crowds.

The Black Land Special departed the San Antonio & Aransas Pass depot in Corpus Christi on Saturday, Nov. 9, 1924. Farmers, businessmen and civic leaders from the four-county area were ready to carry the message of prosperity to Central and North Texas. Among the 110 men wearing pearl-gray Stetsons were Gilbert McGloin, A. M. French, Joseph Hirsch, Edwin Flato and Nixon's stepfather, E. O. Stubbs.

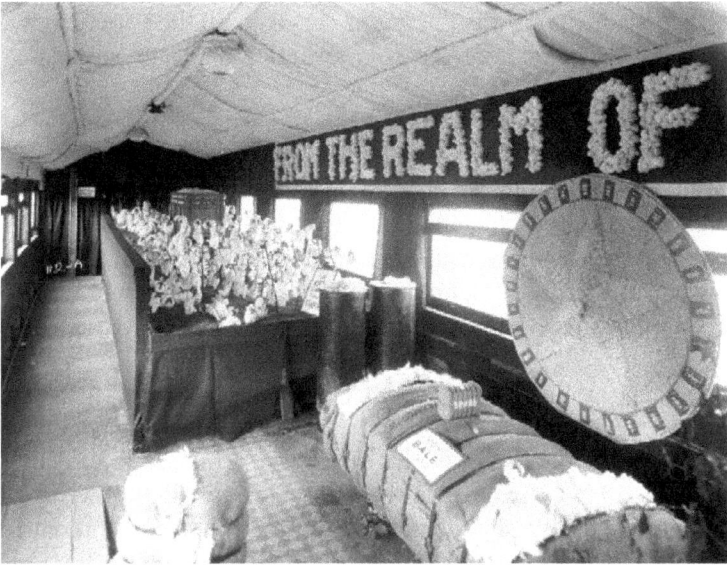

The Black Land Special included four railroad cars with exhibits of farm products from the Corpus Christi area. A banner in the cotton car read — "From the Realm of King Cotton."

An editorial in the Corpus Christi Caller said the train was a revelation. Even people who had spent their lives in this section were surprised, the paper said, by the variety of products in the exhibit cars. They knew the products were grown here, yet the massing and grouping of them in four cars "could not fail to make one feel proud that he was a part, no matter how small, of all this wealth."

At the first stop on Monday morning at Lockhart, 800 people visited the Black Land Special. At Taylor on Tuesday, 1,500 people saw the film "Land of Plenty" and visited the exhibits. At each stop, the 20th Army Band, followed by the delegation in their pearl-gray Stetsons, paraded through the downtown to the theater. There people would see the film about the farming techniques and products of the Coastal Bend, then they would visit the exhibit cars.

The first was the cotton car. A reporter at Bartlett called the exhibit "a veritable cotton paradise." One end of the car was a miniature cotton field, with real stalks and a miniature cotton wagon. The other end featured manufactured products and over all was a banner of fluffy cotton that read, "From the Realm of King Cotton."

The second exhibit was the grains car, with all the varieties of corn and grain and a map of the four counties made of various grain seeds.

The third railroad car included pecans, date palms, among other trees, and an exhibit entitled "How We Make Money." This depicted a golden horn of plenty in which went cotton, grain and other products and out of which poured silver dollars.

The fourth car showed all the varieties of fruits and vegetables grown in the region, including flapper cabbage, Bermuda onions, "carrots that made your hair curl and beets that put roses in your cheeks."

The men in the pearl-gray Stetsons returned after two weeks. Everywhere they went — Sherman, Paris, Ennis, Mexia, Corsicana, Waco — they were greeted by large and enthusiastic crowds. An estimated 55,000 Texans saw the movie and 65,000 visited the exhibits. The trip was judged to be a wonderful demonstration of the farming fertility of the black land soil of the Corpus Christi area.

Maston Nixon — who went on to build the Nixon building on the bluff and found the Southern Minerals Company — later said, "We were not selling land but trying to sell the goodwill of our area and show the people what good farm land we had." Within five years after the trip, 100,000 new acres were brought into production in the Coastal Bend, in large part a direct result of the seeds planted by the Black Land Special, called the greatest promotion ever devised for any section of the state.

— July 4, 2012

TAYLOR STREET

Like other cross streets that run from the bluff to the bay, Taylor Street is short, only four blocks now, but for a short street it has a long and colorful history. The street was named for Gen. Zachary Taylor, the commanding general who brought half the U. S. Army to Corpus Christi in 1845 in preparation for the Mexican War.

When Taylor and the army were here, Corpus Christi was hardly a village. It was a trading post set up to sell goods to Mexican smugglers. Taylor's soldiers considered it part of Mexico, although claimed by Texas. "We are over the line in Mexico and ready for anything," Lt. John James Peck wrote his wife. Another lieutenant, U.S. Grant, described it as "a small Mexican hamlet with an American trading post at which goods are sold to Mexican smugglers."

There was no Taylor Street as such at the time, but from the top of where the street is today the view from the bluff would have shown hundreds of tents stretching along the shore. The famous Daniel P. Whiting lithograph depicts the scene in 1845, though the perspective is from North Beach.

Taylor's soldiers dug a deep well at the site of Artesian Park, just north of Taylor Street, but the water smelled like rotten eggs and was undrinkable. For drinking and cooking, army teamsters hauled water from the Nueces River 12 miles away.

Taylor Street was named and laid out in the grid of streets by Henry Kinney in 1852, the year Corpus Christi was incorporated. The street in the 1850s included the John Dix home at Taylor and the bay, built of shellcrete, and the Russell home, where Dix's married daughter lived. During the Civil War, Confederates suspected that Dix, a Union backer, had an understanding with the federal blockading ships that he would hang a light from his home to save it from being shelled during bombardment. The home of his daughter, Helen Dix Russell, a block west, became known as the

A postcard from 1907 shows the Seaside Hotel at the end of Taylor Street, facing south, with its arbor of salt cedars by the bay.

Ironclad Oath house. It was where federal occupation authorities required former Confederates to take the oath of allegiance to the restored Union.

After the war, a private school for girls was operated in the John Dix home by Mary Eliza Hayes Dix. She taught black girls sewing and white girls standard academic subjects.

The most famous structure on Taylor went up in 1878. After a long struggle to raise money, the town's Episcopalians built the Church of the Good Shepherd on the corner of Taylor at Chaparral, next to where Taylor's soldiers dug the artesian well. The church's 60-foot-high steeple could be seen far out in the bay.

I looked up the Sanborn Fire Insurance Map for 1885 on microfilm. It shows half a dozen houses, a carpenter's shop and a blacksmith shop on Taylor Street then. After the turn of the century, in about 1904, the old Dix home was converted into the Seaside Hotel, owned by Jack Ennis, a Beaumont oilman.

The Seaside Hotel was famous for its grove of salt cedars. Guests could sit in the shade under a roof of cedar limbs and watch sailboats on the bay. It was a popular place. In 1908, William Jennings Bryan stayed there after he lost the presidential election to William Howard Taft, who came to visit Corpus Christi the following year.

A story told about Jack Ennis said he was sweeping the cement floor under the salt cedars when a woman guest took him for a hired hand. She asked how much he earned. "Oh," he said, "about enough

Taylor Street (top photo) looking toward the bay about 1910-1912. The First Baptist Church was on the left then the Church of the Good Shepherd with its tall steeple. At top right was the Central Christian Tabernacle. Barely visible on a pier at the end of the street was the Seaside Pavilion. The bottom photo showed the same street looking toward the bluff from the Seaside Pavilion. The salt cedar grove is visible at the edge of the bay.

to pay for my tobacco." She gave him two dollars and told him to buy something for himself. When she checked out, she was told her bill had been cancelled and she was given a note from Ennis — "No woman as kind-hearted as you shall pay a cent at my hotel."

After the success of the Seaside Hotel, Ennis built the Seaside Pavilion on a pier off Taylor Street. The Seaside Pavilion was a combination hotel, dance hall, and carnival. Rooms cost 75 cents a day. A Sanborn map shows a bar and bath houses on the first floor, a ballroom on the second, and hotel rooms on the third.

About 1908, the Seaside Electric Theater was built across the street from the Seaside Hotel. Motion pictures had been shown in town for four years, but they were shown in converted storefront buildings. The Seaside Electric was the first in town built exclusively as a theater. It featured a four-piece lady orchestra.

Two photos, taken about 1910 or 1912, show Taylor Street a century ago. Looking east from the bluff, on the left or north side of the street, is the new First Baptist Church. The church had been held in an old blacksmith shop before the new church was built. A block down is the Church of the Good Shepherd and at Taylor and Water is the Seaside Hotel, then the Seaside Pavilion on the pier in the bay.

On the right side of the street, looking east from the bluff, is the Central Christian Tabernacle, followed by the residence of W. S. Gregory. He bought the place from Edward Cooper, who founded Cooper's Clean Bakery. Down the street is a photographer's studio, a confectionary and real estate office. At the eastern end is the Seaside Electric. Historically, the street was three blocks long until the seawall was built, starting in 1939, and dredged fill expanded the bayfront by a block.

There was once a blacksmith shop at Taylor and Mesquite. Today, that area is dominated on the bluff end by the Caller-Times. At the bay end is the towering One Shoreline Plaza, which is just east of where the Seaside Hotel and its grove of salt cedars once stood. One Shoreline Plaza is another landmark that can be seen far out in the bay, as the steeple of the Church of the Good Shepherd was in the 19th Century.

— July 11, 2012

TRAIL DRIVERS

Abel Head "Shanghai" Pierce was a regimental butcher in the Confederate Army. He compared the position to that of brigadier general — "always in the rear on an advance, always in the lead on a retreat."

Like Shanghai Pierce, the cattlemen and cowboys who made the trail drives right after the Civil War were mostly former Confederate soldiers and officers. After four years of fighting, men back from the war had endured hardship — sleeping on the ground, spending long hours in the saddle or on the march, coping with all kind of weather.

These former Confederates were among the first to go up the trail after the war. Of course, not all were ex-soldiers. Some were younger brothers, who were too young to fight, and others were former slaves who, out of necessity, had learned to handle cattle when the other men were away fighting.

When the war ended, returning soldiers were broke. Their Confederate pay was worthless. Though Texas did not suffer as much physical destruction as Southern states where the fighting was heaviest, there was little industry. There were few jobs or even the prospect of jobs, and there was very little hard money. Commercial ties were mostly severed. An economy had to be rebuilt and the men in tattered gray had to start over. They had to make something seemingly from nothing.

But on the ranges of Texas — especially South Texas — there was an abundance of half-wild longhorn cattle. In Texas, the price of cattle had dropped to $1 a head, about the value of the hide. But in the great packing-house cities of Kansas City, St. Louis and Chicago, the value ran from $20 to $40 a head. Cities in the East were hungry for beef. Texas cattlemen began exploring ways to get their half-wild longhorns to that market.

Some herds went north in 1866 for Baxter Springs in southeast Kansas or Sedalia, Mo. They ran into trouble from bands of armed men called Jayhawkers and Redlegs. As the men driving the herds were mostly former Confederates, the Jayhawkers and Redlegs were men who had fought on the Union side. They used the fear of tick fever as a pretext to ambush men with herds and steal their cattle. The herds that got through, however, sold for high prices.

Texas cattlemen learned that the Union Pacific Railroad had reached Abilene, a small town of log-hut buildings, but a railhead nevertheless, in western Kansas, far away from the trouble in eastern Kansas and western Missouri. Herds could be sold in Abilene and shipped by rail to the stockyards of Kansas City, St. Louis and Chicago.

Drovers turned their herds toward Abilene. They followed the most famous of all cattle trails, the Chisholm Trail. Perhaps 75,000 head reached Abilene in 1867. Every year thereafter the herds grew larger as trail-driving became a science and progressively easier, though there would always be flooded rivers to cross and stampedes on stormy night.

Stories of the men who went up the trail can be found in "Trail Drivers of Texas," stories like that of W. F. Cude, a Confederate soldier who was captured and released on parole. "Four of us left Jackson, Miss.," Cude wrote, "and walked to Beaumont in 16 days. My shoes had worn out. When I got to Houston, I went to a store and got a new pair of shoes. I told the clerk to charge them to Jeff Davis." Back in Texas, Cude signed on as a trail hand to take a herd to Kansas.

R. G. Head enlisted when he was 16. He spent four years in the Confederate Army. After the war he got work as a trail hand with pioneer drover John J. Meyers, who led the first herds to Abilene. T. M. Turner, nicknamed "Louisiana," was a Confederate scout who wanted to be a cowboy. After the war he went to Goliad and started with a herd for Abilene.

D. C. Rachal (his name was Darius Cyriaque, but he simplified it), an ambulance driver in Hood's Brigade, was in battles from the Wilderness to Gettysburg. After the war, he came home and started a ranch at White Point across Nueces Bay from Corpus Christi. He began to drive herds to Kansas. In Rachal's case, "drive" is the right word. He was known for driving a trail herd at a fast pace, then letting the cattle graze and fill out when they got to Kansas. The technique took his name. A trail boss hurrying his herd along would say, "Rachal 'em, boys, Rachal 'em."

South Texas was the start of the cattle trails, which could diverge by up to 50 miles depending on grass conditions, drought, and flooded rivers. The great cattle drives to railhead towns in Kansas ended with the spread of barbed wire fences and the coming of railroads to Texas.

As I thumbed through "Trail Drivers," I found there are no typical stories — each being different in its own way — yet they are all typical. Like this one. A cattleman named Randolph Paine bought cattle at $12 a head and drove 3,000 steers to Abilene. He sold them for $30 a head and brought the money back to Denton County in a wagon. In this way, cattle went north in a flood and gold came back to a destitute land. Except for what the cowboys spent in the cow towns of Kansas — raising hell and waking up the sheriff — the money came home to become the economic mainstay of Texas during the lean times of Reconstruction.

The men in gray returned to Texas after the war and, almost by accident, devised a great industry, one of the greatest of the 19th Century. It was far more important to Texas than the romantic image suggests. The trail-drive era lasted two decades, from 1866 until the late 1880s, when fencing and railroads brought it to a close. Before it was over, though, an estimated 10 million cattle were driven north and sold for $250 million. This money was used to sustain and develop Texas. I don't know how to measure it. I don't know what to compare it with. But, taken all together, it was a tremendous enterprise.

In the first five years after the war — from 1865 to 1870 — the cattlemen, trail bosses and trail hands were trailblazers in every sense of the word. Many if not most of them were former Confederate soldiers. Like the longhorns they walked to market, they were a tough and special breed. We shall not look upon their like again.

— July 18, 2012

GOODBYE BOOZE

The fight over Prohibition in 1916 was one of the most potent divisive political issues in Corpus Christi history. A campaign was mounted in Nueces County to ban liquor four years before national Prohibition became the law of the land.

The campaign aimed at an election to close 43 saloons in Nueces County, 37 of them in Corpus Christi. The Prohibition campaign was assisted by a traveling evangelist, Rev. Mordecai Ham, who conducted a revival and preached about the evils of demon rum. Corpus Christi, he said, was as liquor-sodden and sinful as Sodom and Gomorrah.

While the "drys" had Mordecai Ham to push their cause, the "wets" had Mayor Roy Miller and County Judge Walter Timon, two of the best stump speakers in South Texas. Passions reached a fever pitch, with Corpus Christi divided evenly between wets and drys.

Children wore ribbons to show which side their parents supported — white ribbons for Prohibition and red for Anti-Prohibition. Merchants who supported one side or the other were boycotted. It was all but impossible to sit on the fence.

A big Temperance parade was held the weekend before the election. Boys were sent ahead of the parade to search for roofing tacks that reportedly had been spread to puncture tires of the parade cars. The parade stopped in front of the saloons while the women serenaded bar customers with "Goodbye Booze" and "Nueces County Going Dry."

On election day on Tuesday, March 10, 1916, women milled around every polling place. They couldn't vote, but they could hector the male voters. Some threatened to divorce their husbands if they discovered that they had voted wet. There was a huge turnout, with 92 percent of eligible voters — 3,377 men — voting.

The drys won by 218 votes. The town's bars closed at 9:30 p.m. on April 21, Saturday night. The city's saloons were re-opened as other businesses. The famous Ben Grande became a grocery store. The Market Saloon became a chili parlor. The nearest place to buy beer was Rockport, 30 miles away.

Four years later, national Prohibition took effect after passage of the 18th amendment. The Volstead Act banned the manufacture, sale and transportation of intoxicating liquors. This ushered in the bootlegging era, which lasted until the end of Prohibition in 1933.

During Prohibition, welding shops in Corpus Christi turned out small copper stills and moonshiners set up portable stills in their backyards. Disposing of the mash, which had a strong odor, was a problem. Law-enforcement officers drove around sniffing the air for the stench of sour mash.

In one incident, a large diesel-powered boat from Mexico with a load of bananas docked at the Municipal Wharf. The bananas were deck cargo. The real cargo was tequila, which was openly sold during daylight hours and delivered at night by rowboats.

Bootleggers would burn sugar to add to clear liquor to give it an amber color, like bourbon. They stored moonshine in oak barrels with charcoal to speed up the aging process. For those with more refined tastes, cases of tequila, mescal and whisky were smuggled from Mexico. Mexican distilleries produced an ersatz bourbon called "Waterfill," an ersatz Scotch called "Frazier," and they sold brands called "Straight American," "William Penn," and "Old Taylor."

Mexican whisky smugglers — "tequileros" — used pack mules to haul cases of liquor across remote South Texas ranches. It was a profitable business. A bottle of tequila that sold for 60 cents in Mexico would bring $15 in Corpus Christi. Pack trains of smugglers were protected by well-armed guards, forerunners of today's violent drug smugglers.

There were deadly encounters between the tequileros on one side and Texas Rangers and U.S. Customs agents on the other. In one incident, the Hebbronville Enterprise reported on Nov. 23, 1923 that, "U.S. Mounted Customs Officers . . . trailed a bunch of horseback liquor smugglers from Jenning's Ranch in Zapata County to Bruni's Pasture in Webb County, where they overtook them. There was a running gunfight in which one smuggler was killed. The officers seized 450 quarts of liquor, four horses, four riding saddles, three pack saddles, two Winchesters and 200 rounds of ammunition."

State and federal agents in Texas had their hands full. The state's long coastline and proximity to Mexico made it ideal for smugglers.

A panel truck loaded with 300 gallons of smuggled liquor was seized by the U. S. Customs Service near Sinton and taken to the Federal Courthouse on Starr Street. A Doc McGregor photo.

Some liquor shipments reached Texas from Canada, via British Honduras, with ships transferring the cargo to smaller vessels outside U.S. jurisdictional waters.

Padre Island was a favorite landing place for rum-runners. Louis Rawalt, a professional beachcomber who lived with his wife in a wooden shack on Padre Island, once wrote about an incident in 1925. Rawalt said a British smuggling ship named "I'm Alone" was shelled and sunk by the U.S. Coast Guard near the southern end of Padre Island. The ship had been chased by a Coast Guard cutter across the Gulf. The captain refused to surrender and threw his cargo overboard before the Coast Guard cutter shot the ship full of holes.

Rawalt heard through the island grapevine to be on the lookout for liquor so he drove down the beach in his pickup, searching for bottles, and saw nothing but an old gunnysack in the sand. He was looking for bottles or cases but kept seeing gunnysacks. He stopped to investigate; the sack he opened had a dozen sealed tin cans labeled insect spray. He pried open the lid and inside was a bottle of Bourbon whisky, "Old Hospitality."

Rawalt hid 110 sacks behind the dunes, filled a duffle bag with 72 bottles and headed for Port Isabel, where he could sell the whisky.

Louis Rawalt rolls along a barrel of tar salvaged on the beach while his three-year-old son Charlie follows behind.

The ferry captain was suspicious, so Rawalt told him what he had found and gave him a few bottles. Rawalt sold the whisky at Port Isabel and was on his way home when he saw the ferry captain coming back down the island in a pickup truck. Rawalt realized the ferry captain had followed his tracks into the dunes and found the hidden whisky. When Rawalt went to check, it was all gone.

Since the "I'm Alone" was carrying a thousand cases, burlap bags washed ashore with sealed tins of whisky for a long time. They were scattered up and down the island and Rawalt said people tramped through the sand for weeks looking for their share of "Old Hospitality."

— July 25, 2012

SAN JOSE OR ST. JOSEPH'S?

Changing the name of Corpus Christi Beach back to North Beach corrects a mistake made in 1959. Most people never accepted the change; they always called it North Beach. There is another name change in the region that should be reconsidered. In 1973, St. Joseph's Island was changed to San Jose.

This story started with Sid Richardson, the Fort Worth wildcatter who amassed an immense fortune and bought himself an island. Richardson's great wealth came from the discovery in the 1930s of the Keystone Field in West Texas followed by the discovery of the Eola field in Louisiana. He died in 1959 on the island he owned — St. Joseph's. When he died, Richardson was the second richest man in Texas, behind H. L. Hunt and a bit ahead of his friend Clint W. Murchison.

Richardson and Murchison grew up in Athens, Texas, became friends and later in life business partners. It was said that hardly a day passed that the two didn't talk to each other on the phone, to gossip and make deals. In one deal, they purchased 800,000 shares of the New York Central Railroad. When a reporter asked Richardson about buying the railroad stock, he said, "I do not like publicity. I bought it for an investment. A man is getting in a hell of a shape if he can't buy something without people wanting to know what he's doing."

Richardson, a Democrat, was a friend of Franklin D. Roosevelt. Once on a train, Richardson met Dwight D. Eisenhower and they became fast friends. Richardson tried to persuade Eisenhower to run for president as a Democrat, but when Eisenhower decided to run as a Republican, Richardson broke his lifelong Democratic ties to support him.

But we're drifting away from the island. There is a story, perhaps apocryphal, about Richardson's decision to buy St. Joseph's Island. His friend Murchison bought most of Matagorda Island. (It was

Clint Murchison's son who once owned the Dallas Cowboys.) Richardson was visiting Murchison on Matagorda when Murchison teased him — "Sid, why don't you quit sponging off me and buy your own island."

In 1936, Richardson bought the 17-mile-long, five-mile wide St. Joseph's Island between Mustang and Matagorda islands. Long operated as a cattle ranch, the island had been owned by the Richard H. Wood family. The Woods sold it in 1922 and it went through several owners before Richardson bought it.

After buying the island, Richardson needed to build a house on it. He asked Murchison how much he spent on his Matagorda home. Murchison said, "About $35,000." He was pulling his friend's leg; he probably spent that much on the glass alone. But Richardson was determined to build his own island home for $35,000. He hired his nephew, Perry Bass, a young geologist, to build him a resort home. He finally went back to Murchison and said, "How much did you say you spent on this house?"

"Oh, $35,000 or so," Murchison lied.

"Well," said Richardson, "Mine will cost a little more. I may have to spent about $75,000."

When it was finished, Murchison visited his friend's new place and looking over the impressive lodge home, with its wrought-iron staircase, he knew Richardson had spent at least $200,000 on it.

"Sid, how much did you say this house cost you?"

"I'm not going to tell you," Richardson said. "You got me into this, you SOB."

Richardson ran 2,000 head of cattle on the island, kept a hunting reserve, and built a landing strip for important visitors. President Franklin D. Roosevelt paid him a visit when he was in the area fishing for tarpon in 1937. Dwight Eisenhower came to go duck-hunting in 1951 just before he ran for president.

Sid Richardson died on St. Joseph's on Sept. 30, 1959. He was 68 and had suffered an apparent heart attack. Richardson, a bachelor all his life, left $2.8 million to each of Perry Bass's four sons. The rest of his $105 million estate went to the Sid W. Richardson Foundation. Perry Bass inherited the island.

After Richardson's death, Perry Bass began the effort to change the name from St. Joseph's to San Jose. Bass thought San Jose sounded more beautiful than St. Joseph's, which was sometimes shortened to St. Joe, and there was some historical

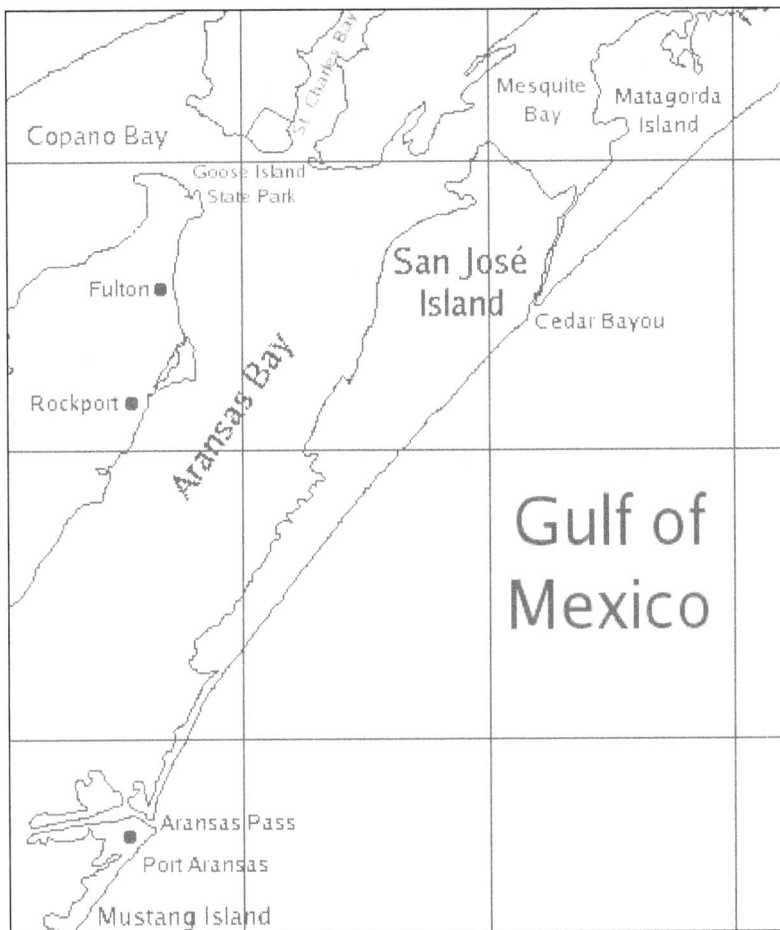

St. Joseph's Island is identified on this modern map as San Jose Island.

validity to changing the name. Bass could point to an old Mexican land grant of 1834 and some ancient Spanish maps that identified it as Isla de San Jose.

On the other hand, for more than a century the name had been Anglicized by English-speaking residents, who settled on the island before the Texas Revolution. They called it St. Joseph's. When Zachary Taylor's troops landed there in 1845 and planted the first American flag to fly over Texas soil, they called it St. Joseph's.

The island's decline began with the Civil War. The community at the south end, across the pass from today's Port Aransas, was called "Aransas." It was a settlement of bar pilots, lightermen and island ranchers. The demise of Aransas began when the Union blockade created havoc with coastal commerce. Even worse were attacks by shore parties from the blockading ships. In one attack in February 1862, federal troops burned much of the town, including homes, warehouses and wharves. After the war, attempts to revive the settlement failed and St. Joseph's lost its population.

The name was officially changed on Jan. 10, 1973. Judge John H. Miller of the 36th District Court signed an order designating the island as San Jose. A statute passed by the Legislature authorized the change. While some people adapted to the change and began to call it San Jose, others, especially descendants of the early settlers on the island, continued to call it St. Joseph's. It goes by both names today.

Changing longtime historical names like St. Joseph's, I believe, disrespects the past and the people who came before us. For more than 140 years — from the early 1830s until 1973 — it was called St. Joseph's by the people who lived there and by the coastal residents nearby. Balanced against that weight of usage were a few old maps that identify it as Isla de San Jose and the political clout of the late Perry Bass, who died in 2006. I don't know what the process would be. I don't know how it could be done. But San Jose should be changed back to St. Joseph's Island.

— Aug. 1, 2012

GHOST TOWNS OF THE COAST

Texas in 1836, during the revolution, had 50,000 people, roughly the population of today's Victoria. The coast was deserted, with the few settlements like Victoria and San Felipe de Austin far inland. Five years after the revolution, the population jumped to 250,000, the equivalent of today's Corpus Christi. This influx resulted in the creation of new towns on the coast, all founded within a decade after the revolution.

Aransas City (near today's Rockport) was established in 1837, Lamar in 1838, Corpus Christi in 1839, St. Mary's in 1842, Indianola in 1844, Saluria in 1845, and Aransas village on St. Joseph's Island in 1845. Only Linnville was there before the Revolution. Of these, only Corpus Christi survived.

Aransas City, on Live Oak Peninsula, was founded by James Power, the Irish empresario who built his home and store there. The town site was near the south end of today's Copano Bay Causeway. Aransas City was the first port of entry for the Republic of Texas. A village sprang up on the other side of Copano Bay called Point Lookout. The founder, James Byrne, renamed it Lamar, after Texas President Mirabeau Lamar, and suggested the customhouse at Aransas City be moved to Lamar. The president, his vanity stroked, obliged the request. From that point, Lamar's fortunes improved and Aransas City's declined. In 10 years, Aransas City was dead. Henry Kinney, a merchant at Aransas City, built a trading post on a high bluff on Corpus Christi Bay. This was the beginning of Corpus Christi.

Lamar, after it gained the customhouse, prospered, as a growing port town with an industrial salt works. In the 1850s, Sam and James Colt, the revolver makers, bought a quarter interest in 14,000 acres on the Lamar Peninsula. Whatever the Colts had in mind — whether they were investing in Texas land or planned a Colt manufacturing operation near Lamar — it died with the Civil War. The town of

133

Lamar was half destroyed in a Union attack and never regained its importance. Like Aransas City, its rival, Lamar withered away.

The village of Aransas, on the south end of St. Joseph's Island, was laid out in 1845. It was the home of sailors, ranchers, and lightermen who unloaded big ships that couldn't come through the Aransas Pass. One prominent citizen was James Babbitt Wells, who had commanded the Texas Navy yards at Galveston. Robert Mercer, bar pilot, lived at Aransas before he moved across the pass to found the Mercer settlement, later called Port Aransas.

Like Lamar, the demise of Aransas began with the Union blockade. In 1862, a Union shore party destroyed many of the buildings at Aransas. After the war, the people moved across the pass to the Mercer settlement on Mustang Island.

St. Mary's was built at Black Point on Copano Bay. Beginning in the 1840s, much of the lumber shipped to Texas was unloaded at St. Mary's wharf. A road connected Corpus Christi to the port at St. Mary's. The decline began after a railroad from San Antonio bypassed St. Mary's and ended at Rockport. In 1887, the third hurricane in a decade wrecked the town and St. Mary's wasted away. Today's Bayside includes part of old St. Mary's.

In 1831 or 1832, John Linn, a merchant engaged in the Mexican trade, built warehouse facilities at a spot on Matagorda Bay. Linn's Landing became Linnville. On August 8, 1840, a large Comanche war party, 500 warriors or more, attacked Linnville. Many of the residents escaped to a ship in the bay. The Indians plundered the warehouses and burned the town. After Linnville was destroyed, its residents moved three miles south and established Lavaca, later called Port Lavaca.

Prince Karl of Solms-Braunfels, head of the German Immigration Society, landed German families at Indian Point, a sandy shore along Lavaca and Matagorda bays, 12 miles below Port Lavaca. The German settlers called the place Karlshafen, which became Indianola, Queen of the West.

Indianola grew explosively, passing Galveston to become Texas' busiest port. It was nearly destroyed by a hurricane on Sept. 16, 1875. Another storm struck on Aug. 20, 1886, followed by a fire that consumed what the storm left standing. The last disaster sealed the fate of Indianola.

Not far from Indianola, on the northeastern corner of Matagorda Island, the town of Saluria was projected in 1845. The founders

A drawing of Indianola in September 1860, taken from the royal yard of the barque Texana by Helmuth Holtz. From the Library of Congress.

included James Power and Alexander Somervell, who led the Texas raid into Mexico in 1842 that resulted in the battle of Mier. Power deeded most of the town site to Somervell and two other men.

Mary Maverick, who lived for a time at Decrows Point across the pass from Saluria, provides a glimpse of Prince Karl of Solms-Braunfels and Gen. Alex Somervell. "His Highness, son of the Grand Duke of Braunfels, was on his way to the Colony of New Braunfels of which he was the founder. The prince and suite spent a day and night with us and the Somervilles (Somervells). General Somerville was a noted laugher — he saw the Prince's two attendants dress His Highness, that is, lift him into his pants, and General Somerville was so overcome by the sight that he broke into one of his famous fits of laughter, and was heard all over the Point."

Somervell was killed in 1854 in mysterious circumstances. He left Lavaca on a boat for Saluria carrying a large amount of money. His body was found lashed to the boat and the money gone. His killer was never found.

The 1850 census showed 200 people on Matagorda Island, most of them residents of Saluria. In 1862, during the Union blockade, Saluria's residents fled to the mainland. Confederate soldiers at nearby Fort Esperanza were ordered to destroy bridges and ferries linking Saluria to Indianola. Saluria was burned by Confederate troops, an act more destructive than any committed by Union

135

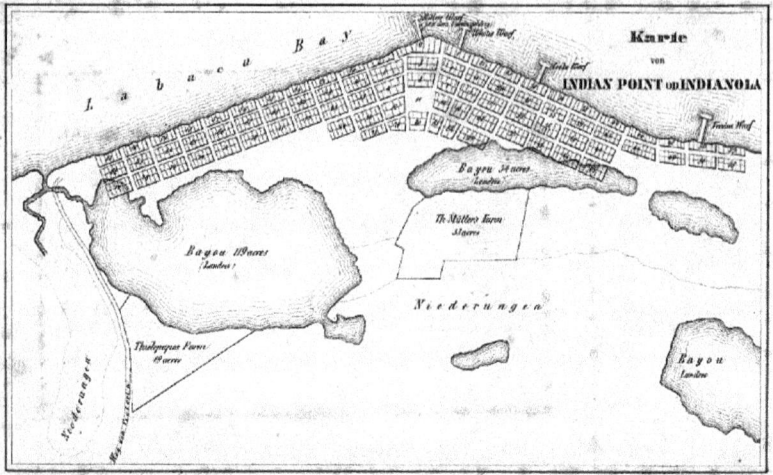

This map shows Indianola stretched out along Lavaca Bay with lakes hemming it in on the southern side.

soldiers during the war. Some believed that John Bankhead Magruder, the Confederate commander of the Department of Texas, was doing a favor for Galveston by destroying a competing port.

Efforts to rebuild Saluria were dashed by the hurricane of 1875, the same that all but destroyed Indianola. Besides the widespread destruction, the storm flooded the town's cisterns with saltwater and destroyed the town's water supply. Saluria never recovered.

Many of the early shipping towns on the Texas coast flourished, declined and died. Saluria, Linnville, St. Mary's, Lamar, Aransas City and Aransas village are long gone. Only traces remain, like old shellcrete cisterns. Indianola today is a small fishing village with a large graveyard. Last time I was there, a restless feeling was in the air, as if the spirits of the dead still hovered about old Indianola. It is a melancholy place.

— *Aug. 8, 2012*

THE 1960s — 1

Every decade has its own identity. As I looked through newspaper clips from the 1960s, it brought back many memories, not all good. It was a decade many of us endured, rather than enjoyed. It was a decade of the Vietnam War, the assassination of President Kennedy in Dallas, his brother killed in Los Angeles, and Martin Luther King Jr. shot to death on a motel balcony in Memphis. It was a time of riots, protests, and the sexual revolution. It was a decade of the Beatles, miniskirts and beehive hairstyles. The uplifting event came near the end, in 1969, when man walked among the craters on the moon.

In Corpus Christi, the big event of 1960 was the opening of the Corpus Christi International Airport. Dignitaries were flown from Cliff Maus Field to the new airport at Clarkwood. Sand flats on North Beach had served as a landing site until 1928 when the first airport was built off Old Brownsville Road. After the first airport manager, Cliff Maus, was killed in a plane crash, the airport name was changed to Cliff Maus Municipal Airport. It was laater shortened to Cliff Maus Field and served until the new airport opened on Aug. 7, 1960.

That fall, Hollywood starlet Kathy Grant (Kathryn Grandstaff) campaigned for her father, Delbert Grandstaff, in his unsuccessful bid for the U.S. Senate. She was remembered locally as Miss Buccaneer-Navy of 1949. She married Bing Crosby in 1957.

It was a severe jolt when the Navy closed the Overhaul & Repair facility at the Naval Air Station in 1959. The O&R was the largest employer in town. In 1961, when John F. Kennedy took office, Corpus Christi exulted with the news that the O&R would be re-opened as ARADMAC, the Army Aeronautical Depot Maintenance Center with an awkward acronym. The number of employees rose steadily, to nearly 5,000, as the depot repaired helicopters for the Vietnam War.

When Mayor Ellroy King chose not to seek re-election, three slates fought over the prize: Odell Ingle's Corpus Christi Party, JoeSalem's Alert Party, and Ben McDonald's Progress Party. On April 4, voters elected McDonald mayor with three members of his slate elected to the council.

In April 1961, Corpus Christi lost out to Houston in competition for a NASA laboratory center, but gained a consolation prize with a NASA tracking station. It was built at Rodd Field, the old World War II auxiliary base. NASA scientists determined that orbiting capsules would pass over Corpus Christi more often than any other location in the United States and more frequently than any location in the world except for two sites in Australia.

Alan Shepard, America's first man in space, and Virgil Grissom, the second man in space, visited the tracking station in June. Both had been stationed at the Naval Air Station years before. Tracking Station No. 16 monitored the orbits of early space flights, including John Glenn's first orbital flight on Feb. 20, 1962.

The Corpus Christi tracking station was one of the few equipped to help astronauts get back to Earth in the event of an emergency. The Rodd Field station was one of NASA's main tracking stations throughout the Mercury, Gemini and Apollo projects that resulted in the moon landing in 1969. The station on Corpus Christi's far Southside was an important link between American astronauts in space and the ground controllers in Florida and Maryland, and then the Manned Spacecraft Center at Houston.

In June 1961, Vice President Lyndon Johnson led a Washington delegation to Padre Island as Congress was debating legislation to establish a national seashore. They were treated to a fish fry on the island, followed by a reception for Johnson and Lady Bird at Exposition Hall. The following year, President Kennedy signed a bill creating the island park.

On Aug. 5, 1961, Corpus Christi voted to annex Flour Bluff while Flour Bluff voted to incorporate as a separate city. The Corpus Christi City Council passed an annexation ordinance and city police began patrolling in Flour Bluff. Suits filed by Flour Bluff residents to block annexation were appealed to the U.S. Supreme Court, which ruled that it did not have jurisdiction in the matter.

Annexation was still a hot issue the following year. Voters by a narrow margin approved doubling the size of the city by annexing 49 square miles of land that included the Naval Air Station, Clark-

On June 21, 1961, Vice President Lyndon B. Johnson and Lady Bird arrived at Exposition Hall on Shoreline Boulevard for a reception following a visit to Padre Island. Corpus Christi Mayor Ben McDonald was in the back seat

wood, Annaville and Calallen. Those opposed to annexation, led by former mayor Farrell Smith, argued that extending city services to the annexed areas would cost more than $800,000. The vote was 8,030 for with 7,252 against to add more streets, more houses, more suburbs. With the annexed areas, Corpus Christi's population climbed to 184,163.

During the Berlin crisis of 1961, a Corpus Christi man, Col. Glover S. Johns, Jr., was sent to Berlin as commander of the Army Battle Group dispatched when the East German Communists began building the Berlin Wall.

The Weather Bureau warned on Friday, Sept. 8, 1961 that Hurricane Carla was aimed at Corpus Christi. On Sunday, Corpus Christi boarded up. Mayor Ben McDonald returned from a whitewing hunting trip to the Valley and set up a cot in City Hall.

The downtown was evacuated after reports warned that Carla's storm surge could top the seawall. North Beach and the islands were also evacuated. Some 15,000 people in Corpus Christi sheltered at

Hurricane Carla on Sept. 11, 1961 took a large bite out of Ocean Drive near Montclair when waves generated by the storm washed out the ground underneath

the Courthouse and the schools. The National Guard was called out before the storm hit.

On Monday morning, Carla made a sharp right turn and slammed into Port Lavaca. Around Corpus Christi there was damage but much less than expected. Winds knocked down power lines, uprooted trees, and broke windows. Bridges were washed out on Ocean Drive. Old island passes were reopened and the Padre Island Causeway was damaged. The state's new Port Aransas Causeway, from Aransas Pass to Harbor Island, was wrecked.

It was a near miss for Corpus Christi. After the storm, experts said if Carla had not veered and if it had struck Port Aransas as expected, with the pass funneling the storm directly at Corpus Christi, it would have swamped North Beach and downtown Corpus Christi, even with the seawall, just like the deadly hurricane of 1919.

— Aug. 15, 2012

THE 1960s — 2

On the larger stage, the 1960s was a decade of the Bay of Pigs, the Cuban Missile Crisis, the Vietnam War, student protests, the assassinations of President Kennedy, his brother Robert, Martin Luther King Jr., and urban riots that followed the King assassination. It was a time of violent upheavals, but it was also a time of great progress. Miniskirts were short and hopes were high. As I looked back through newspaper clips of the 1960s, the speed of change seemed remarkable.

In Corpus Christi, one symbol of change was the dismantling of the greasy old bascule bridge — the work was finished on June 3, 1961 — and the port entrance widened under the new Harbor Bridge. One of the first of the larger ships to use the wider entrance was the USNS Card, a small aircraft carrier. Three years later, the Card was sunk by a mine in Saigon harbor. As the Port observed its 40th anniversary in 1966, it completed a project that deepened the ship channel to 40 feet and extended it to the Viola Turning Basin.

Work started in 1961 on I-37 in downtown Corpus Christi and by 1969, construction reached Live Oak County 48 miles away; it was completed in the 1980s. The second span of the Nueces Bay Causeway was finished in 1963. By December 1965, the first segment of the Crosstown Expressway, Morgan to Port, opened to traffic. Everything was in flux with construction of I-37, the Crosstown Expressway and the re-construction of South Padre Island Drive.

As the city's transportation infrastructure was being improved, the end of an era came on June 20, 1962. The Missouri Pacific ran its last passenger coach out of Corpus Christi, ending passenger service for the city. For eight decades, Corpus Christi had passenger train service, beginning in 1880 when the Tex-Mex began operating to Laredo. In the heyday of railroads, Corpus Christi had three railroad depots with daily service to Laredo, Brownsville and San Antonio.

The end of the passenger train era was recorded on June 20, 1962 when the Missouri Pacific ran its last passenger coach out of Corpus Christi.

On Jan. 10, 1962, a freeze killed the palm trees on Shoreline. That summer, after the fifth case of polio struck in Corpus Christi, thousands took the Sabin oral polio vaccine on sugar cubes. Some 500,000 doses were administered in Nueces County.

In January 1963, a courtroom was packed when Mrs. Loraine Lambert Graning was sentenced to life in prison for murdering her husband. Testimony revealed that she and her 16-year-old son from a previous marriage killed her husband, Melvin B. Graning, 61, supervisor of Western Electric, which built the NASA tracking station at Rodd Field. Graning, 61, had been struck in the head, then hauled in the trunk of a car to the Nueces River near Calallen. He was dazed but still alive when his head was held under water until he drowned.

In August 1963, some 400 Corpus Christi residents, black and white, marched on City Hall to demand the city appoint a Civil Rights Commission. Later that year, the council created the commission and appointed former mayor Ben McDonald as chairman and Frances "Sissy" Farenthold as one of the members.

In May 1964, TV viewers in Corpus Christi finally got access to all the national network programming when Channel 3, KIII, went on the air, joining KRIS and KZTV.

In a decade of senseless violence, one of the worst crimes in the Corpus Christi area was committed on April 12, 1965 when three Corpus Christi fishermen were shot to death by two California runaways.

142

Lady Bird Johnson, the First Lady, spoke at the dedication of Padre Island National Seashore on April 9, 1968. The podium was built of island driftwood.

Paul Eric Krueger and John Phillip Angles were headed for Mexico. They stopped at Corpus Christi, rented a small boat and traveled down the Laguna Madre. They had an AR-15 rifle and M-1 carbine. Paul Krueger opened fire on three men fishing from a pier, shooting them as they fell into the laguna. The dead men were Noel Douglass Little, Van Dave Carson, and John David Fox. After they were caught, Angles, 16, was sent to the State School for Boys at Gatesville. He was released in 1968. Krueger was sentenced to life in prison. He was released after 12 years.

In 1965, employees at the Army Depot went on a heavy schedule, working 60-hour weeks, to keep up with repairing helicopters needed for the Vietnam War. An old Navy aircraft carrier was converted into a floating aircraft repair shop called USNS Corpus Christi Bay. It operated off the coast of Vietnam, but its home port was Corpus Christi and its personnel were trained at the Army Depot.

On Jan. 9, 1967, an inch of snow fell on Corpus Christi while some inland points recorded up to nine inches. The Kennedy Memorial Causeway to Padre Island became toll-free in 1967.

After Carla, the second major storm of the decade was Hurricane Beulah. Corpus Christi was on the edge of the storm, which produced record rains and flooding after it made landfall near Brownsville on Sept. 20, 1967. One unusual effect from Beulah was that commodes all over Corpus Christi backed up from increased pressure in the sewer system.

On April 8, 1968, Lady Bird Johnson, the first lady, dedicated the Padre Island National Seashore. Thousands attended the celebration.

For Corpus Christi in the 1960s, the city was doubled in size through annexation. It was also the greatest decade for highway construction. Harbor Bridge, opened in 1959, was the prelude to the construction of I-37, the second span of the Nueces Bay Causeway, raising the South Padre Island Drive to expressway standards, and building Crosstown Expressway. We are still living with those big projects of that earlier time, but we don't have the equivalent new ones to pass on to the future.

One of the hit songs of the 1960s, though it was not connected to Corpus Christi, was Jimi Hendrix's "Crosstown Traffic," with the line, "I'm just trying to get to the other side of town." Another song from that era was "Let It Bleed" by the Rolling Stones and when you consider the assassinations, riots and Vietnam War, could a better title be found for the 1960s? It's a good thing the arrow of time moves in only one direction, so we won't have to go through the 1960s again.

— Aug. 22, 2012

SELF-RISING POLITICS

Noah Smithwick, who came to Texas in 1827, stayed at Green DeWitt's colony near the eventual town of Gonzales. Smithwick wrote about the simple fare he encountered in those times, which usually consisted of venison, cornbread, and honey. He wrote that Texas children had forgotten or had never known what wheat bread was like.

"Old Martin Varner used to tell a story of his little son's first experience with a biscuit," Smithwick wrote in "Evolution of a State."

"The old man managed to get together money or pelts enough to buy a barrel of flour. Mrs. Varner made a batch of biscuits which, considering the resources of the country, were doubtless heavy as lead and hard as wood. When they were done, Mrs. Varner set them on the table. The boy looked at them curiously, helped himself to one and made for the door with it. In a few minutes he came back for another.

"Doubting the child's ability to eat it so quickly, the old man followed him to see what disposition he made of the second. The ingenious youngster had conceived a novel and altogether illogical idea of their utility. He had punched holes through the center, inserted an axle and triumphantly displayed a miniature Mexican cart."

Smithwick, a blacksmith, opened a shop in San Felipe de Austin next to that of another blacksmith, Gail Borden Jr., who would eventually gain fame as the inventor of condensed milk.

Borden was interested in food preservation. He developed what he called a "meat biscuit." He would boil eight pounds of beef to reduce it to one pound of extract. To this he mixed in flour and seasonings and baked it. The result was his meat biscuit.

Borden won a gold medal at the Great Exhibition in London in 1851 and he won a prize at Henry Kinney's Lone Star Fair in Corpus

Christi in 1852 for his "Patent Meat Biscuit." If Gail Borden's gold-medal meat biscuits were so good, I wonder why we're not eating them today.

You can't write about the role of biscuits in Texas history without mentioning W. Lee "Pass-the-Biscuits-Pappy" O'Daniel. He was a popular radio personality, with his Light Crust Doughboys, and later started his own Hillbilly Flour Company. When his radio program came on at 12:30 each day, it was said the entire state stopped to listen.

Like his biscuits, Pappy O'Daniel could rise to the occasion. When he ran for governor in 1938, he entertained crowds with his band, the Hillbilly Boys, while his staff passed out hot biscuits. How can you not vote for a candidate who gives you hot biscuits? O'Daniel was a colorful demagogue, with his country homilies, like Huey Long in Louisiana, long before the Coen brothers displaced his character and put him in Mississippi in their movie, "O Brother, Where Art Thou?"

I vaguely recall a story about O'Daniel. A political opponent accused Pappy of keeping a large supply of cheap whisky hidden in a back room at his house and he answered the charge with, "That's a lie! I keep it in a China cabinet" (next to the sherry and cut-glass goblets and fine bone china). But I forget. Maybe that was Pa Ferguson, also known as "Two Governors For the Price of One" Ferguson. I tried to look up the quote, but couldn't find it, so maybe I imagined it.

The novelty of the O'Daniel campaign, with country music and hot biscuits and honeyed oratory, attracted huge crowds across the state. It was said of O'Daniel that you never had to worry about him using big words in his stump speeches because he didn't know any big words. He would rail against Communists and labor union goons and rhapsodize on "beautiful, beautiful Texas" with his best radio voice.

It was also said of O'Daniel that when he was elected governor and took office in 1939 that he knew absolutely nothing about how state government worked. But is that unusual? How many governors have we had who actually knew what they were doing? In my opinion, Texans long ago reached an understanding with their governors; they don't expect much of them and the governors, for their part, don't do much. Then both are free to ignore each other until the next campaign cycle. One of the unsolved mysteries of

"Pappy" O'Daniel gave a two-fingered salute during a campaign speech in Corpus Christi. The sign read: "The BURNING issue in Texas State Government is Graft-Corruption-Bribes-Scandals."

the universe is why we even need a governor . . . but I'm off on a different rabbit trail.

Last time I mentioned Pappy O'Daniel, a few years ago, I received a note from Bobby Lewis of Alvin in which he recalled when the O'Daniel campaign stopped in his hometown. "O'Daniel was campaigning with his Light Crust Doughboys," Lewis wrote. "They came to Alvin and attracted a crowd of 150 or so, including myself and several buddies. While O'Daniel was speaking, the Doughboys were baking biscuits on the bus. A fire alarm sounded and everybody took off to see where the fire was, except us boys. We were waiting for those biscuits. O'Daniel continued to talk, as though he were speaking to thousands. When he finished, the cook brought out a large sheet pan of hot biscuits, emptied them into a sack, and gave them to us boys. We lit out to the old railroad trestle on Mustang Bayou, sat with our feet dangling, and ate biscuits until the last cow in Brazoria County came home."

I don't know whether the huge crowds turned out for the country music, O'Daniel's oratory — "beautiful, beautiful Texas" — or the hot biscuits. I tried to find a recipe for Pappy's biscuits, without luck. Anyway, I have my own biscuit recipe, an old family recipe, which I wrote about a few years ago.

As for Pappy, there's something else to chew on. While governors of Texas of the last half century included a glaring lineup of lawyers, bankers, farmers, ranchers, oilmen, a movie theater owner, a drilling contractor, a baseball team owner, even a one-time elevator operator, Pappy O'Daniel was the first, and probably the last, self-rising flour salesman to occupy the governor's office

The best biscuit recipe I've found came from my grandmother. It is probably as old as the country itself. I translated the instructions for ingredients into modern terms. The original called for lumps of sweet lard "the size of hen's eggs" and "two cents worth of flour."

You need 2 1/2 cups of all-purpose flour; 4 teaspoons baking powder; 1 teaspoon salt; 1/2 teaspoon cream of tartar; two tablespoons brown sugar; 4 nor 5 tablespoons butter (preferred) or margarine or Crisco; two tablespoons of Crisco for the pan; and 3/4 cup or so of milk. Blend the dry ingredients, cut the shortening in until it resembles coarse meal, add milk, turn the dough onto a floured board. Knead a few times and roll it out or pat it out to 1/2-inch thickness; cut the biscuits out and bake on a well-greased cookie sheet in a hot oven (450 degrees) for 12 to 15 minutes. With care, this recipe will produce flaky and sumptuous biscuits.

—Aug. 29, 2012

GATHERING MOSS

Several things I found interesting of late in my reading of Texas history during our interminable hot summer . . . A high ranking Mexican official in the government who made an inspection tour of Texas in 1828, Manuel de Mier y Terán, noticed that the forests around Nacogdoches were being destroyed not for firewood or lumber but for Spanish moss, as recorded in the book "Texas by Terán."

Settlers collected Spanish moss "which they consume in great quantities because they use it in mattresses and in mixing the mud with which they plaster the walls of buildings. They fell trees in which that moss hangs. In order to bring in 150 wagons of moss, how many trees will it be necessary to chop down?"

Apparently, Spanish moss was prized as mattress-filler because it repelled bugs. I recall an entry from the Mercer Diaries that mentioned using moss to stuff a mattress.

In Stephen F. Austin's colony, settlers used ring-barking to kill trees without having to spend a lot of labor chopping them down. Mier y Terán saw this when he visited the cotton plantation of Jared Groce.

"The fields are largely cleared; around the land one sees hundreds of tree trunks that — having been cinched — no longer grow. All over this country they use the word *cincho* for a big stretch of thick trunks which they have stripped the bark until they leave the bare wood, wherein the tree dies and rots." It was a spectral and melancholy landscape, Mier y Terán thought, because of the skeletons of trees.

Mary Austin Holley, Stephen F. Austin's widowed cousin, also took note of ring-barking on a visit to Bolivar, 40 miles from the mouth of the Brazos, in 1835 (from "Mary Austin Holley: The Texas Diary, 1835-1838.") "Walked about the place in search of the great live oaks so much talked of," she wrote. "Did not find but one

— a bee tree — that had been girdled and (stripped) of its leaves to my sorrow — what wanton barbarism."

* * *

The great Sam Houston — always first in line for a drink — was a man who gave and received healthy insults. He was both loved and hated, admired and despised. How did he ignite such contradictory emotions? One clue can be found in John Holland Jenkins' memoirs. Jenkins, a 14-year-old recruit in the Texas Army, was at Gonzales after the fall of the Alamo when Houston spoke to the soldiers at DeWitt's Tavern about the crisis Texas faced. "I yet consider him about the finest looking man I ever saw as he stood over six feet tall, in the very prime of mature manhood," Jenkins wrote in "Recollections of Early Texas." A week later, as the army began its retreat, Jenkins saw another side of his hero.

"I suppose he must have noticed how young I was and how tired I seemed, for having a Negro riding along behind him, he ordered him to dismount and told me I could ride awhile, at the same time bidding me to ride immediately in advance of the army and not get too far ahead. I mounted the horse and felt I would be willing to die for Houston . . . The horse was very spirited and I, becoming absorbed in the scenery, allowed him to go a little too fast, and was rudely aroused and checked by the voice of my hero saying, 'God damn your soul! Didn't I order you to ride right here?' "

Jenkins was shattered. "Of course he had cause to rebuke me . . . but with these few harsh words General Houston completely changed the current of my feelings toward him, and my profound admiration and respect was turned into a dislike I could never conquer. In the subsequent history of our state, when he was a candidate . . . my vote was never cast in his favor, for memory was ever faithful in bringing back that loud curse and my feelings as I listened."

* * *

When Comanches rode into San Antonio for a peace parley on March 19, 1840, it erupted in violence and 35 Comanches were slain in what came to be known as the Council House fight. Mary Maverick in the book "Memoirs of Mary A. Maverick" recorded the scene outside her house on the Main Plaza where a wounded Indian was dying.

"A large man . . . came up and aimed a pistol at the Indian's head. I called out, 'Oh, don't, he's dying,' and the big American laughed and said, 'To please you, I won't, but it would put him out of his misery.' Then I saw two others lying dead near by." As she was visiting a neighbor across the street, Dr. Weideman came up and placed a severed Indian head on the window sill. "The good doctor bowed courteously, saying, 'With your permission, Madam,' and disappeared. He returned with another bloody head. He explained that he had viewed all the dead Indians and selected two heads, male and female, for the skulls, and also selected two entire bodies, male and female, to preserve as specimen skeletons."

Dr. Weideman took the Indian heads and bodies to his home, Mary Maverick wrote, and put them into a large soap boiler. He later emptied the boiler, containing water and flesh from the bones, into a ditch which furnished drinking water for the town. "It dawned on the dwellers upon the banks of the ditch that the doctor had defiled their drinking water. There arose a great hue and cry and all the people crowded into the mayor's office. Dr. Weideman was arrested and brought to trial; he was overwhelmed with abuse . . . He took it quite calmly, paid his fine and went off laughing." In the context of the times, there was no question which was the greater offense. The outrage was over contaminating the town's water supply, not the taking of Comanche heads.

Mary Maverick said the doctor, who was good with the sick and would take no pay for his services, set up his Indian skeletons in his garden and dared anyone to steal from his premises. He drowned a year or two after the head-hunting incident while trying to cross Peach Creek near Gonzales.

— Sept. 5, 2012

152

CACTUS JACK

John Nance Garner's political career carried him from a Texas county judgeship to Congress to Speaker of the House to Vice President in the Roosevelt Administration. He was a leading candidate for president until Franklin Roosevelt chose to run for a third term.

Garner read law with a lawyer in Clarksville and was admitted to the bar when he was 22. He was elected county judge of Uvalde County, then the Legislature in 1898. He wanted to be elected to Congress and, in congressional redistricting, helped configure the sprawling new 15th District, which included Corpus Christi, to boost his chances.

In the 1902 primary, Jim Wells, the powerful political boss in Brownsville, sent word to Corpus Christi Democrats that, "Garner's our man." Garner won the primary and defeated a Corpus Christi Republican in the general election. In January 1903, Garner visited Corpus Christi and asked supporters, "What is the one thing dearest to your heart?" A man said, "We want a channel dredged through Turtle Cove (mudflats that blocked navigation) to give Corpus Christi deepwater access to the Gulf."

In Washington, Garner and his wife Ettie lived in a boarding house. They took the streetcar to work. She performed his secretarial duties and cooked their lunch on a gas range in his office. They spent Sundays at the zoo where Garner liked to watch the seal catch fish. He made $5,000 a year; she made $1,200 as his secretary.

Garner doubled his income playing poker. One session of Congress, he won $15,000; most sessions, his poker winnings exceeded his salary. He described his attraction to the game. "A poker table is one of the greatest places to test a man's courage, to tell whether he is a bluffer, whether he is weak or strong. People demean playing poker, but that's the way to find out a lot about human nature."

John Nance Garner in 1903 after he won election in the newly created 15th congressional district in South Texas. (Photo from the Library of Congress.)

Garner worked for his district. In 1908, he succeeded in getting an act passed authorizing construction of a new federal building and established a federal court in Corpus Christi. He struggled to fulfill Corpus Christi's request for deepwater access. Government policy dictated that Texas needed only one major port — Galveston. Garner got funds appropriated to dredge a channel through Turtle Cove, though it was a shallow channel. A board of engineers found that the Turtle Cove mud bank made dredging too expensive and concluded that Harbor Island, 20 miles closer to the Gulf, was a better location for a deepwater port.

After the 1919 storm wiped out dock facilities on Harbor Island, Corpus Christi supporters, including Garner, argued that Corpus

Vice President John Nance (Cactus Jack) Garner at his desk in 1938.

Christi would be a safer location for a port. On May 22, 1922, President Warren Harding signed a bill to begin dredging a channel to Corpus Christi. Port Opening day came on Sept. 14, 1926. Though Garner no longer represented Corpus Christi in Congress, due to redistricting, the port was built in large measure because of his early support. It is simplistic to look back at the building of the port and think it was inevitable. Just for the record, a long chain of decisions in Washington made over the years with Garner's guidance led to that point. He kept the promise he made in 1903. As a result, what had been a small town when Garner was elected to Congress became a large city and gateway to international trade.

When Garner was elected Speaker of the House in 1931, friends told him, "You've got to dress up and look respectable." Garner thought it a good idea. "Mrs. Garner went downtown with me and had me measured for formal clothes, striped pants, evening clothes, the whole outfit. I bought $485 worth of clothes. I never had so many clothes in my life. John McDuffie of Alabama used to kid me about them."

After he was chosen as Franklin D. Roosevelt's vice presidential running mate in 1932, Garner soon regretted it. "Worst damn-fool mistake I ever made was letting myself be elected vice president. I

155

should have stuck with my chores as Speaker of the House. I gave up the second most important job in government for one that didn't amount to a hill of beans."

Garner was more conservative than Roosevelt and did not fully support New Deal legislation he helped pass. "They (Roosevelt's advisers) didn't have as much consideration for the taxpayers as I did, I might say. The value of the dollar, or where they got it, never occurred to them." But any disagreements he had with FDR he kept to himself. "It didn't make any difference how much we disagreed. I wasn't going out and shout it to the public. I was the vice president, part of the administration."

Garner broke with Roosevelt over the court-packing plan. "The most popular president we ever had was advocating control of the Supreme Court. He was the boss of the executive department, as he should be; he had more influence in Congress than any president I ever served under. And he wanted to influence the Supreme Court in determining constitutional questions. I think that was an unreasonable ambition."

Roosevelt asked him: "How do you find the court situation, Jack?"

Garner said, "Do you want it with the bark on or off, Captain?"

"The rough way," Roosevelt replied.

"All right, you are beat. You haven't got the votes."

Garner was the Democratic frontrunner in 1940 until Roosevelt chose to run for a third term. Garner retired, said he was "crossing the Potomac for the last time," and went home to Uvalde. After Ettie died in 1948, he moved out of the main ranch house into a small frame building. "People come by to see me," he said. "They want to see what a former vice president looks like. They expect to see some big imposing man, and it's me, just a little old Democrat." He died on Nov. 7, 1967. He was 98 years old.

Years before, Corpus Christi presented Garner with a gold watch for his efforts to build the port, the Intracoastal Canal and the federal courthouse. He carried the gold watch all his life. Ideally, the new U.S. District Courthouse should have been named for Garner, but it was never considered. No member of Congress did more for Corpus Christi than "Cactus Jack" Garner, yet he has been neglected by a city that owes him so much.

— Sept. 12, 2012

WAR AT PASS CAVALLO — 1

In April 1861, at the beginning of the Civil War, Texas authorities and the U.S. commander in Texas, Gen. David Twiggs, agreed to a peaceful withdrawal of U.S. troops from Texas. Those on the Rio Grande would depart from Brazos Santiago. Those at San Antonio and inland points would take ship from Indianola.

The first contingent left Indianola on the Daniel Webster while another contingent camped at Green Lake behind Indianola, waiting to board the Star of the West outside the bar at Pass Cavallo off Matagorda Island. On April 17, U.S. troops at Indianola slept on the wharf to be ready to leave first thing in the morning. Two steamers would take them to the Star of the West out in the Gulf. Next day, when they arrived off Pass Cavallo, there was no Star of the West.

The peaceful exodus of U.S. troops from Texas was no longer possible. The bombardment and surrender of Fort Sumter meant war had commenced. Confederate Col. Earl Van Dorn, a veteran of the Mexican War, was in command of Confederate troops in Texas. He was on board the Confederate steamer General Rusk which anchored within hailing distance of the troopship. A voice shouted from the Star of the West: "Ship ahoy! Avast there! You'll run into us! What vessel is that?" The answer came back over the water: "The General Rusk. I have some troops for you. Stand by to catch our line."

Confederate soldiers, concealing their weapons, boarded and captured the ship. The captain of the Star of the West was indignant, swearing that a dirty trick had been played on him. A nearby Union gunboat, Mohawk, was unaware of what was happening. The General Rusk escorted the troopship, a prize of war, to Galveston, where it received a joyous welcome as a symbol of one of the first victories of Confederate arms. The Star of the West was already famous. In January, it had tried to land supplies to the besieged Fort Sumter in Charleston harbor and was fired on by Confederate batteries, the first shots fired in the Civil War.

During the Civil War, Union and Confederate forces clashed over control of the barrier islands and the major passes, including Pass Cavallo and Aransas Pass.

On Matagorda Bay, four steamers from Galveston arrived with 1,000 men to reinforce Van Dorn. U.S. forces at Indianola were blocked from escape and forced to surrender. They gave their parole, promising not to take up arms against the Confederacy, and were allowed to sail to New York aboard three small schooners. Major C. C. Sibley of the Third Infantry said they had a miserable journey with the troops crowded on deck on the open transports.

That was the first action of the war along the western stretch of the Texas coast. That summer, blockading ships of the U.S. Navy tacked back and forth off Aransas Pass between Mustang and St. Joseph's islands and Pass Cavallo, the entry into Matagorda Bay. Confederates manned gun batteries on Mustang and Matagorda islands to prevent Union ships from entering the passes and disrupting the increasingly important traffic in the inner bays.

An old earthworks redoubt called Fort Washington, built in 1842 when the Republic of Texas feared an invasion by Mexico, was located by the Matagorda Island Lighthouse. Three artillery companies under the command of Maj. Daniel Shea, with four 24-pounder guns, were stationed there to guard Pass Cavallo.

On Dec. 7, a Union warship fired on the battery and Shea's 24-pounders returned fire, forcing the ship back to the Gulf. The action made it clear that the gun battery was vulnerable to the long-range guns of U.S. ships.

In January 1862, the U.S. frigate Santee and gunboat Midnight opened fire on the battery. They wanted the Confederates to waste their ammunition and they wanted to test the range of their guns, but Shea's four guns remained silent. The captain of the Midnight reported that he saw the battery of four heavy guns near the base of the lighthouse. When he opened fire with shell, sand and sandbags went flying and the gunners retired a little from the batteries. After a lot of noise and little damage, the Midnight ceased firing, without ever provoking return fire.

Shea's three companies were ordered to build a new fort two miles away, out of range of the Union warships but still in position to guard Pass Cavallo. Some 500 slaves were conscripted to help build the fort. Earthen walls 12 feet high, 15 feet thick and 200 yards long were reinforced with logs strengthened with shell concrete. The new fort, called Fort Esperanza, meaning hope, mounted eight 24-pounders and one behemoth, a 128-pounder Columbiad. They all fired solid shot.

On Jan. 25, the schooner J. J. McNeil, a blockade runner laden with coffee and tobacco from Veracruz, was captured by the U.S. bark Arthur, a three-masted sailing ship commanded by Lt. John Kittredge. On board the McNeil was Captain Hopper and his ailing wife. Kittredge sent the McNeil off under a prize crew and, under a flag of truce, landed Captain and Mrs. Hopper on Matagorda Island.

Maj. Shea met Kittredge. In his report, Shea said two Union warships, the gunboat Midnight and the bark Arthur, anchored off Pass Cavallo and two launches approached flying a white flag. On shore, Kittredge said he wanted to release Captain Hopper and his wife, who was too ill to be sent on to New York. He told Shea he knew the caliber of his guns and could reduce his battery but that he

The Star of the West was captured off Pass Cavallo by Confederate forces days after war commenced with the fall of Fort Sumter. Reproduced from "Indianola" by Brownson Malsch.

had no orders to fire on the coast unless he was fired on. Shea said they talked for 30 minutes. They agreed to respect a white flag and that its absence would mean a fight.

Since Captain Hopper had given his parole he was honor-bound not to reveal specific military information. However, since no parole had been requested of Mrs. Hopper she was free to divulge anything she could remember. Mrs. Hopper told Shea the gunboat Midnight had six 32-pounder guns and a swivel-mounted Parrott rifle and the bark Arthur had a crew of 74 men and drew 14 feet. Since she knew the size and names of the guns, Shea assumed that her husband, despite his parole, had whispered the information in her ear.

—Sept. 19, 2012

160

WAR AT PASS CAVALLO — 2

Along the Texas coast, the first year of the Civil War saw skirmishes between blockading ships of the U.S. fleet and Confederate bastions guarding Aransas Pass and Pass Cavallo. One of the first actions in the war was the capture of the Star of the West troopship off Pass Cavallo and the surrender of U.S. forces waiting to embark at Indianola.

In February 1862, Major C. G. Forshey, a Confederate engineer inspecting defenses on Matagorda Island, reported that "the enemy has discovered the valuable and daily increasing trade passing by our inland navigation route. A constant run of small craft is visible, and it would be easily cut off at this point but for the batteries here." Salt that supplied most of Texas and Louisiana came from the Laguna Madre and lakes below Corpus Christi. Lead and military supplies from Mexico came up on blockade runners operating in the inner bays. Cotton and sugar went out in return, part of the valuable commerce sustaining the Confederacy.

On Oct. 25, 1862, the USS Westfield sailed past Fort Esperanza into Matagorda Bay. Defenders of the fort retreated to Indianola before they could be cut off. On the Westfield, a U.S. Marine, Henry Gusley, wrote in his diary that the ship ran aground in the shallow waters of the bay and had to be towed off. "In the meantime, some of our officers visited the adjacent shore, for the purpose of obtaining some fresh provisions, and found the feelings of the inhabitants so thoroughly Secesh they refused to sell a morsel of anything to a Union man. Immensely patriotic, no doubt, these Lone Stars thought this action was very foolish it would have proven if we had used the force at our hands and taken what we wanted gratis."

The Union sailors were not shy about taking what they wanted, sending in foraging parties to supplement to their ship fare. On Thanksgiving Day 1862, 10 Union sailors from the mortar schooner Henry Janes landed on Matagorda Island to kill a beef. They were captured and sent to Houston as prisoners of war. A week later, in early December, with Union forces becoming more threatening, most of the residents on Matagorda moved to the mainland and Confederate troops at Fort Esperanza burned the town of Saluria on Matagorda Island and drove most of the cattle to the mainland.

The Union gunboat Kittatinny and the hard-luck mortar schooner Henry Janes (which lost 10 of its men on the beef-hunting trip) tried to enter Matagorda Bay. The Kittatinny struck bottom, hard, but did not run aground. In the next two days, they captured two blockade runners, the Matilda, sailing under English colors but loaded with contraband cargo, and the Diana. Both were sent on as prizes.

In November 1863, Union invasion forces under the command of Gen Nathaniel P. Banks captured Brownsville and began to move up the coast. They captured the Confederate Fort Semmes, commanding Aransas Pass, and the 13th and 15th Maine and 20th Iowa moved on toward Fort Esperanza guarding Pass Cavallo.

A cold norther blew in on Nov. 19 as Union troops crossed Aransas Pass and marched up St. Joseph's Island. They reached Cedar Bayou, separating St. Joseph's from Matagorda Island, on Nov. 23. Confederate Maj. Charles Hill, waving a white flag, appeared on the opposite side of the bayou. He wanted to find out what happened to the Confederate men at Fort Semmes. A sergeant from the 15th Maine, James Saunders, swam across the channel to talk. After an angry exchange, the Confederate shot Sgt. Saunders and Union troops on the opposite bank fired on and hit Maj. Hill. His body was found in the dunes. The Union troops crossed Cedar Bayou on flatboats and marched up the island.

On Nov. 27, they reached Fort Esperanza and fired on Confederate pickets, driving them inside the walls. The Union soldiers prepared for a siege. They dug rifle pits linked with trenches and batteries were placed. Cannon fire was exchanged on Nov. 29. A Union soldier saw a cannonball rolling in the sand and foolishly stuck out his foot to stop it. It caused such damage his foot was amputated.

The 500 to 700 Confederate troops inside the fort were in dire straits, with gunboats lobbing shells into the fort and a strong land force attacking their western side. They spiked the guns, set powder magazines on fire, and evacuated the massive fort.

The fort's defenders escaped by the previously constructed rope bridges and ferries across Saluria Bayou to the mainland behind Green Lake.

Thomas Nast drawing depicted Union troops in Indianola in December 1863 after Gen. Nathaniel Banks' invasion forces captured Fort Esperanza. Reproduced from "Indianola" by Brownson Malsch.

Confederate soldiers camped on the Caney, 40 miles away, heard rumors. A soldier, Rudolf Coreth, wrote his family in New Braunfels that "Saluria has been taken without our having been able to fire a shot, because the fort was not protected at all on the landward side and the batteries were all directed toward the water."

It was bitterly cold that November. Union soldiers camped outside Fort Esperanza had no tents and were short of rations. They butchered the wild cattle on the island and used the hides of the slaughtered cattle to cover their rifle pits, where they huddled for warmth with two men to each pit.

In January, the 13th Maine was sent on a reconnaissance expedition on Matagorda Peninsula to feel out the Confederate position at the mouth of Caney Bayou. Two captured riverboats, the Planter and the Matamoros, ran aground. The boats warped free with kedge anchors. On the trip up the long narrow peninsula, a sailor on the gunboat Sciota, escorting the 13th Maine, took aim at a cow and shot a captain in the head (Charles March), killing him.

That winter, frequent raids were launched from Matagorda Island to Indianola, Port Lavaca and Matagorda Peninsula. Union troops occupied Indianola in December. Confederate forces moved back to the Caney River, 50 miles away. In February, Union forces were ordered back to New Orleans, leaving only small garrisons at Pass Cavallo and Aransas Pass, then these were pulled out two months later. One of the last actions of the war occurred at Pass Cavallo on Feb. 19, 1865 when the USS Pinola captured an armed Confederate schooner, the Anna Dale.

The massive turf-covered walls of the abandoned Fort Esperanza, built by slave labor in 1862, survived until they were destroyed by hurricanes in 1868 and 1878. Until recent times, the rifle pits dug by Union soldiers and the traces of the gun emplacements at the old fort could be found in the sands of Matagorda Island.

— Sept. 26, 2012

THE CROW'S NEST

You gather raw material, background information, relevant facts, then wait until the material no longer lies quiet on the mind. It might be weeks or months before the time comes and the piece begins to take shape.

That's how I write. It was not how Bob McCracken wrote because the demands of meeting a deadline required him to find something to write about every day for his column The Crow's Nest. That's not easy. For McCracken, writing a daily column became a constant struggle. Writing was like sweating blood.

Robert Burrow McCracken was born in Marfa in 1910. He attended schools in Floresville and Corpus Christi and studied journalism at the University of Missouri. He returned to Corpus Christi during the Depression and lived in a tent on the beach until a reporting job opened up.

When McCracken began work on the paper in 1933, The Crow's Nest was written by different reporters on the staff, the task rotating each day. McCracken began to write the column more often until he became the sole author. He moved up in the newsroom, becoming assistant to the editor in 1939, managing editor in 1941, then managing editor of the Caller and the Times in 1945. Whatever his duties, he still wrote The Crow's Nest.

The late Juliet Wenger wrote about McCracken in her book "News to Me." She said he was shy by nature, which made the public demands on him painful. "As a teenager," Wenger wrote, "I read his column and occasionally stood in front of the window of the newspaper office, on Mesquite Street at that time, and watched him at work. He was everything I admired. When I went to work on the Caller, he was my boss. I found in him common sense, objectivity, and the kindest humor."

McCracken had a Clark Gable appeal, she said, that women could not resist and they pursued him, though he was married with two children. "One of the assignments I grew into," Wenger wrote, "was to be his shield. When a woman asked him to drive her home from some event, he could not be so impolite as to refuse. Instead, he gave me a signal, and I rudely shouldered my way into his car and sat between him and the woman in the front seat."

When he quit smoking on doctor's orders, Wenger said he wrote himself into a corner about how much guts it took to quit. "Then he started smoking again. When no one was looking, he would light a cigarette and hand it to me. When he passed by my desk, he would take a drag. Often, there were two cigarettes going at once in my ashtray." Did he drink? Only every chance he got, but that was a failing common to the newspapermen of his time.

In February 1944, two German POWs escaped from a camp at Mexia. They were recaptured on North Beach and taken to the County Jail, where one of them was interviewed by McCracken.

"The Lookout got a face-to-face look at what this war is about. So far as he knows, the hour spent in the company of 21-year-old Lt. Heinz Joachim Grimm afforded his first contact with a member of Hitler's master race. It was a depressing experience. Here was a young man of fine appearance, cultured, polished, intelligent. Change his heavy German sweater for a lightweight pullover model, his ersatz trousers for a pair of slacks, his army shoes for white bucks, and he could have passed for an American college student. But when he spoke, the illusion faded. Then his professional arrogance, his ingrained contempt for everyone not of his race or class, his sarcastic politeness, stamped him for what he was, a misguided zealot and an utter fool."

In 1945, McCracken wrote about a landlord-tenant dispute. When *Jackson v. Mayes,* involving a lease of the Elks Club building, came to trial, Judge Joe Browning told the jury to find in favor of Bush Jackson. The jurors twice returned verdicts in favor of Joe Mayes. The jurors were locked up on Saturday night and on Sunday morning the judge told them to bring back a directed verdict for Jackson or he would lock them up for another night. In criticizing the judge, McCracken wrote that "people don't like the idea of such goings on, especially when a man in the service of his country (Mayes) seems to be getting a raw deal."

Judge Browning cited McCracken, the reporter and publisher for contempt and ordered them arrested. McCracken took his portable typewriter to write The Crow's Nest from jail. They were released

Logo for McCracken's column.

after five hours. On May 28, 1947, in *Craig v. Harney,* the U.S. Supreme Court reversed the findings of Judge Browning, noting that what happens in a courtroom is public property and a judge cannot use the power of his office to protect himself from criticism. It remains a landmark decision.

McCracken thought it was cruel punishment for men in South Texas to wear ties in the hot summer and he led the charge for men to shuck coats and ties. The last Saturday in April became Bob McCracken Day when men's clothing stores held sales for sport shirts. He also led a campaign, with less success, for restaurants to quit serving crackers wrapped in cellophane.

McCracken's thoughts in a dry season, written on March 29, 1956, held that a sure way to end a drought was for the city to institute water rationing. "It has been the experience, if the Lookout's memory serves him correctly, that each time a water shortage exists and rationing is undertaken, the rains come, but not until everyone is on the verge of pulling out each other's hair, midnight lawn sprinkling has started and recall has been threatened."

Bob McCracken died on Oct. 29, 1958. He was only 47 but suffered from emphysema. An editorial noted: "From his precarious perch atop The Crow's Nest, The Lookout surveyed the South Texas scene — and the world beyond — for more than two decades. The column was unique, just as its author, Robert B. McCracken was

167

Bob McCracken in his office at the Caller-Times, date unknown, but probably in the early 1950s.

unique." There was an unsuccessful campaign to have the new high bridge named the Lookout Bridge, in honor of McCracken.

Over the course of its history, dating back to 1883, the Caller-Times had two editors so closely identified with the paper that they became the institution's public personality. The first was Eli Merriman, one of the founders of the paper, and the second was Bob McCracken, the Lookout who kept watch from The Crow's Nest.

— Oct. 3, 2012

LITERARY COWBOYS

It would be hard to find three more different writers, in style and substance, than Mayne Reid, O. Henry and J. Frank Dobie, yet all three had strong connections to South Texas that made them distinct voices in the literature of the Southwest.

One of the most colorful writers in the 19th century was Mayne Reid, an Irishman, son of a Presbyterian minister, who came to the United States in 1839. He enlisted in the Army during the Mexican War and landed with Winfield Scott's army at Veracruz. He was wounded during the storming of Chapultepec Castle and, some accounts say, was the first man to scale the walls and raise the American flag. By his own account, he gained a battlefield promotion to captain for heroism, a rank he used for the rest of his life.

After the war, Capt. Reid was stationed at Fort Inge, near today's Uvalde, for a time. Reid absorbed the stories of the Texas frontier and turned these into very successful novels that were read around the world. The great Russian writer Vladimir Nabokov ("Lolita," "Speak, Memory") was a fan of Mayne Reid and read his novels as a youngster in Russia.

Reid's most popular novels were ''The Rifle Rangers,'' ''The Scalp Hunters'' and ''The White Chief.'' You won't find them in the bookstores today; they have long been out of print. Perhaps Reid's most famous novel was ''The Headless Horseman,'' based on an old South Texas folk tale set on the Nueces River. In this tale, two friends swap clothes, hats, horses and the wrong man gets killed.

* * *

Capt. Mayne Reid (left) set many of his stories, including the "Headless Horseman," in South Texas. William Sydney Porter (O. Henry) (right) was convicted of embezzling funds from an Austin bank before he became a world-famous author.

As a young man of 19, William Sydney Porter (he later adopted the pen name of O. Henry) left his uncle's drugstore in North Carolina to become a ranch hand in the brush country of South Texas. He worked on the Hall Ranch in LaSalle County near Cotulla.

"In those days," wrote O. Henry in "The Call Loan," "cattlemen were the anointed. They were the grandees of grass, kings of the kine, lords of the lea, barons of beef and bone." O. Henry not only wrote about cattle barons, but the cowboys who rode the range and rounded up the cattle. He wrote of the Cisco Kid, "whose habitat was anywhere between the Frio and the Rio Grande. He killed for the love of it — because he was quick-tempered — to avoid arrest — for his own amusement — and any reason that came to his mind."

O. Henry (or, rather, Porter) had his own brush with the law. After working on several ranches in South Texas, he went to work for a bank in Austin, from 1891 until 1894, and was accused of some misappropriation of funds. To make a long story short, he was convicted of embezzling $784.08 from the bank and sentenced to three years in prison in Columbus, Ohio. While in prison he began to write the stories that would bring him fame.

In the "Double-Dyed Deceiver," O. Henry wrote about the Llano Kid who killed a man during a card game and in making his escape he stole a horse to make his way from Laredo to Corpus Christi. "On the Rio Grande border," O. Henry wrote, "if you take a man's life you sometimes take trash; but if you take his horse, you take a thing the loss of which renders him poor, indeed, and which enriches you not — if you are caught."

In "The Caballero's Way," O. Henry described the brush country of South Texas. "More weird and lonesome than the journey of an Amazonian explorer is the ride of one through a Texas pear flat. With dismal monotony and startling variety, the uncanny and multiform shapes of the cacti lift their twisted trunks and fat, bristly hands to encumber the way. The demon plant, appearing to live without soil or rain, seems to taunt the parched traveler with its lush grey greenness."

* * *

Another writer who caught the essence and flavor of the land was J. Frank Dobie, born and bred on his father's ranch in Live Oak County. His early life on the ranch became the foundation for his works. Dobie's books include "A Vaquero of the Brush Country," "Coronado's Children," "On the Open Range," "Tongues of the Monte," "Apache Gold and Yaqui Silver," "The Longhorns," "The Mustangs," "The Voice of the Coyote," "Up the Trail from Texas," and many others.

Dobie wrote about his boyhood on the Dobie ranch in an article for the Corpus Christi Caller in 1959. "No play world could have been more interesting than the one I, my older sister and brothers made for ourselves and lived in on the ranch. With pegs, twine and sticks we built big pastures and stocked them with spools, from which my mother's sewing machine had used the thread, for horses; with tips of cattle horns, sawed off in the branding chute in the ranch corrals, for cattle; and with oak galls for sheep and dried small shells for goats. The goats could not be branded, but we branded the other stock with pieces of baling wire heated red-hot."

He recalled that the Dobie house was in a mott of live oaks overlooking the valley of Long Hollow; how the house had a paling fence around it, with flowers, and a dirt yard kept bare to show snake trails; how the wild buffalo clover reached the stirrups of his saddle; how the horses would stamp on the caliche at their stables to knock off red ants crawling above their hooves; how the stillness of

J. Frank Dobie in 1955. He grew up on his father's ranch in Live Oak County which provided the foundation for much of his work.

the day was broken by windmill lifting rods; how coyotes serenaded at night in stereo; how fresh and green the mesquite looked in early spring; how his horse Buck would point his ears when he walked into the pen to rope a mount — "seeming to ask if I were going to ride him or Brownie."

In "Coronado's Children," Dobie wrote: "All I regret now is that the stones of Fort Ramírez have been carried away. I should like to stand on them once more in April, and gaze across the winding Ramireña upon the oak-fringed hills beyond. Yet the hills could hardly be so lush with buffalo clover — as we used to call the bluebonnet — and red bunch grass, so soft and lovely, as they are in the eyes of memory."

— Oct. 10, 2012

172

BEES AND CIVILIZATION

Mary Austin Holley, a cousin of Stephen F. Austin, visited her brother and famous cousin on trips to South Texas in 1831 and 1835. Her resulting book gives a glimpse of Texas in the 1830s.

On one of her trips she found a bee tree that had been ring-barked to kill it. She called it "wanton barbarism." Mary Austin Holley was fascinated by bees. I found an odd remark in her book.

"It is a very curious fact in the natural history of the bee," she wrote, "that it is never found in a wild country, but always precedes civilization, forming a kind of advance guard between the white man and the savage. The Indians are perfectly convinced of the truth of this fact, for it is a common remark among them, when they observe these happy and industrious insects, 'there come the white man.' "

As the devil's advocate, how would she know what was a common remark among Indians? Still, she was voicing a widespread belief of that time. But was it true? Did the honeybee signal what Mary Austin Holley described as "the advance of civilization"?

I don't know, but another visitor was skeptical of that claim. Dr. Ferdinand Roemer, a German scientist who traveled to Texas from 1845 to 1847, explored Texas from Galveston to New Braunfels to Waco. His book "Texas" was published in 1849. In 1847 in the San Saba Valley, Roemer wrote, "We had scarcely gone a short distance when the cry, 'A bee tree! A bee tree!' brought us to a halt. Mr. (Robert S.) Neighbors, who possessed the keen sight of the pioneer, observed the flight of bees to an old live oak tree.

"Our entire company halted. No real backwoodsman will pass up a bee tree without robbing it, no matter how much he is in a hurry. Axe blows followed in quick succession and the chips flew. Suddenly a burst of joy broke forth, for some of the golden honey began dripping upon one of the men wielding the axe. After a few more strokes, honeycombs filled with honey became visible. Everyone ate as much of the sweet honey as he desired . . . Several combs were left in the hive to serve as food for the bees in winter, a custom followed by the humane settlers."

The opinion was prevalent in Texas, Roemer wrote, that "bees are not original inhabitants of the wilderness, but advance with the white man as the buffalo retreats before him. I had occasion to verify the latter statement relative to the buffalo in Texas, but I could not convince myself of the truth of the former . . . We found bees in the middle of the wilderness many days' journey from the settlements. As a matter of fact, it is hard to understand that the extension of their territory should be dependent upon the presence of the white man."

I know nothing about bees, except to stay away from them, but surely Dr. Roemer was right and Mary Austin Holley was wrong.

* * *

William Bollaert was another observant visitor in the 1840s. The Englishman spent two years traveling through Texas, from 1842 into 1844. On a visit to San Antonio on Sept. 20, 1843, Bollaert sketched the Alamo and met one of its ardent champions.

"On going to the Alamo to make sketches an old Mexican woman brought me out a chair and table. She had lived near the Alamo from a child and had known nearly all those who had fallen in the wars. 'Yes, sir,' said she, 'I knew them all. Poor Travis! What a tiger Santa Anna must have been. I shed many a tear during that siege.' . . . Whilst she was recounting the horrors of the siege, I was sketching and sympathizing with her, when she looked over my shoulder. 'Ah, Señor, had you but seen the Alamo on a Feast Day, not like it is now, in ruins, you would have been delighted' . . .

"She flattered my drawing and resumed her observations. 'Ah! Señor, the front of the church was so beautiful. On one side of the doorway stood San Antonio, on the other San Fernando with other saints. The bells rung a merry peal; they were broken up and thrown into the river, some say 50 quintals weight (5,000 pounds), the enemy not being able to melt them into bullets. I never look into the ruins of the church without shedding a tear; not half the walls are now to be seen and those grown over with weeds . . . but I have seen the Texas flag float over the poor old walls. It was then all walled in. There were large barracks for the troops and gardens with fruit trees, vegetables and flowers . . .'

William Bollaert, an Englishman traveling through Texas, sketched the Alamo.

"The old lady, looking at the sketch, said, 'I am glad you love the Alamo. Here, I'll give you a crucifix made from the stone. Tis but ill-done but will serve as a remembrance of the Alamo.' "

The year before he sketched the Alamo, on March 23, 1842, Bollaert visited Corpus Christi. He arrived with Capt. Wade and others on the vessel Washington. He wrote: "Arrived at 3:30 p.m. It is high bluff land, with muskit (mesquite) timber. Messrs. Kenney (Henry Kinney) and Aubry (William Aubrey) are the principal traders here. Their log house is fortified and they have a piece of artillery. We learnt that Carnes and his party had been for some time past doing military duty here, but had left for San Patricio where they were surprised and murdered by the Mexicans. This spot at present may be looked upon as a good point for trading with Mexico. When the question is settled between the two countries, then Corpus Christi will become a place of some importance."

* * *

Galveston was the immigrant portal to Texas. It was our Ellis Island. A young German woman, Emma Murck, landed in Galveston in 1854, just before her 21st birthday. She later married Hermann

175

Altgelt, the founder of Comfort, Texas. She described the ship's arrival at Galveston in her memoirs, translated from German as "Descriptions from Texas Life."

"As soon as we landed, a crowd of people, mostly Germans, rushed aboard ship to welcome the newcomers, to hear news from the fatherland and, what became apparent to me, to find out if there were any girls aboard, at that time a rare article . . . I remember the following incident. A middle-aged man, a baker by trade, looks over the passengers. He spies a pretty blond peasant girl. At first he tries to hire her as a cook, offers her, 8, 10, then 12 dollars a month salary, which to us seemed very high, according to our notions. In vain. The young German girl declared she was going inland to her brother who sent her traveling expenses. 'I want to marry you right now!' the baker replied. Whereupon, to my secret satisfaction, he got this answer, 'To be married is exactly what I do not want.' "

— Oct. 17, 2012

THE NOLAN BROTHERS

Matthew and Thomas Nolan, young Irish orphans, enlisted as bugle boys in the U.S. Army, the 2nd Dragoons, in 1844. Mat was 12 and Tom was 10. Their older sister Mary became a nurse. They landed in Corpus Christi with Zachary Taylor's army in 1845 and went on to serve throughout the Mexican War.

At war's end in 1848, the Nolan boys returned to Corpus Christi and joined the Texas Rangers. Mat, 16, enlisted with "Rip" Ford's company of Rangers while Tom signed up with John Grumbles. When the Rangers were disbanded, with the U.S. Army taking over frontier protection, Mat and Tom Nolan returned to Corpus Christi. In 1858, Mat, 24, was elected sheriff of Nueces County, defeating Samuel Miller, who owned a ferry on the Nueces River. Mat hired his brother Tom as his deputy.

Two years later, on Aug. 4, 1860, a man named John Warren started a fight at the La Retama Saloon, a new establishment on Chaparral Street owned by James Barnard. John Warren, 30, originally came from Florida; he owned a butcher shop on Market Square. (There was another John Warren in Corpus Christi at the time; John G. Warren, 38, from Tennessee, owned a variety store.)

John Warren the butcher was known as a troublesome drunk who would provoke a fight. On Aug. 4, 1860, he got drunk in the La Retama Saloon and threatened to kill two men, including the saloon owner James Barnard, for wrongs real or imagined. After the ruckus at the La Retama, Sheriff Nolan took Warren to his room at Ziegler's Hall and put him to bed, telling him to sleep it off. The county had no jail or place to lock up prisoners at the time.

Instead of sleeping it off, Warren returned to the La Retama and tried to enter the saloon. Barnard told him to get out. Warren persisted and was ejected. Warren pulled a Bowie knife and stabbed Barnard several times, leaving him near death, then Warren went to Ziegler's Hall where he had a pistol in his room.

The news spread. A rider hurried after Sheriff Nolan, who was on his way out of town. The sheriff and his brother Tom went after Warren and found him in Richardson's store, next to Ziegler's Hall. Warren raised his pistol and shouted, "Stand back or I'll shoot you!" Tom tried to take the weapon and during the scuffle he was shot in the forehead at pointblank range. Warren turned the gun on the sheriff and fired. Though he was only a few feet away, he missed. Sheriff Nolan winged Warren as he ran away.

Other men heard the shots and chased Warren into Zeigler's Hall, where he was shot to death, his body riddled with bullets. An inquest was held, but no blame was attached to the Nolan brothers for their handling of the situation. Thomas Nolan died 11 days later, on Aug. 15, 1860. He was 24, the first law enforcement officer killed in Corpus Christi, and Nueces County, in the line of duty. The obituary in the Ranchero on Aug. 18, 1860 spelled out the deputy's career.

He was born Oct. 8, 1836, in Providence, R. I. and entered the 2nd Regiment of Dragoons, as a bugler, when he was 10. He was at the battles of Palo Alto and Resaca de la Palma, the siege of Veracruz and in the attack on Puebla. He was in numerous battles around Mexico City, including Contreras and Cherubusco, serving as an orderly to Gen. William S. Harney. At war's end, he enlisted in the Texas Rangers, serving with Captains Grumble and Rip Ford. In 1858, he was appointed deputy sheriff of Nueces County.

The obituary read: "It was while in the discharge of his duty as such, in aiding to secure and arrest the late John Warren, that he received at the hands of the latter the wound which resulted in his untimely death. On Thursday last, at five o'clock p.m., his remains were followed to the grave by the citizens of Corpus Christi, who showed their appreciation of his merit as an officer, by turning out en masse. Reared in arms, and educated on battlefields, the thunder of cannon and the whizzing of shells, shot or bullets, was familiar music to Thomas Nolan. A stranger to fear, he would go wherever duty called him; and a brave man, he was kind and generous to a fault." The obituary — signed "By One Who Knows" — was probably written by Sheriff Nolan.

When the Civil War broke out a year later, Mat Nolan raised a company of volunteers and served on the border in the command of "Rip" Ford, his old Ranger captain. Near the end of the war, Mat Nolan was re-elected sheriff of Nueces County. In the quiet of a descending evening, on Dec. 22, 1864, Sheriff Nolan was talking to

Confederate Maj. Mat Nolan was also the sheriff of Nueces County. He was shot to death on Mesquite Street at the end of the war.

a horse trader across from Nolan's house on Mesquite Street, just south of where the Caller-Times is today. Frank and Charles Gravis walked up and one of them shot Nolan with a shotgun.

In his final moments, Sheriff Nolan named the Gravis boys as the shooters and said he knew why they shot him, but he died before he could explain. Many believe the motive was Nolan's intent to arrest the young men's stepfather, H. W. Berry, a former sheriff, for treason. As the war ended and Union occupation authorities took power, the shooters were never tried for Nolan's murder. It was one of those things that happen in a war.

Five years after the death of his brother Tom, Mat Nolan became the second law-enforcement officer to be killed in the line of duty in Nueces County. The Nolan brothers were killed within a few blocks

179

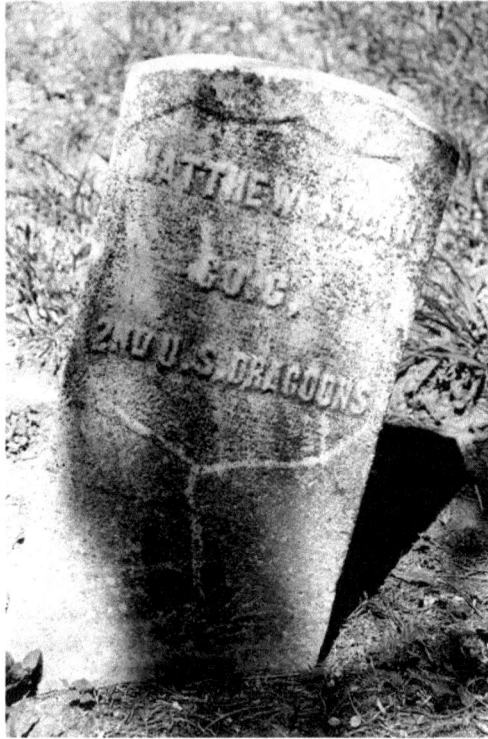

Matthew Nolan's tombstone in Old Bayview Cemetery. He and his brother Thomas served in Harney's Regiment of Dragoons in the Mexican War.

of each other and both were buried in Old Bayview. These Irish orphans grew up and died in war and violence.

Mat Nolan's tombstone is interesting. It reads: "Matthew Nolan, Co. G, 2nd U.S. Dragoons." It's interesting because it says nothing of his high rank as a Confederate officer or his position as high sheriff of Nueces County, but clearly indicates that he was most proud of his time as a young Irish bugle boy in the Mexican War.

— Oct. 24, 2012

CHARLES BRYANT'S UNION THEATER

When Zachary Taylor brought 4,000 U.S. soldiers to Corpus Christi in the summer of 1845, the small settlement of 200 people mushroomed into a population of more than 2,000, most of them all catering to the army.

The army brought the town's first water well, which was dug in what is now called Artesian Park, and it brought the first cemetery, Old Bayview, the town's first newspaper, the Gazette, and its first theaters, the Army Theater and Union Theater.

I don't know where the Army Theater was located, but it was built by army officers led by Capt. John B. Magruder. Lt. U.S. Grant, called "Beauty" by his fellow officers, was talked into playing a female role in one play at the theater, but the male actor kept breaking into laughter at the sight of Grant wearing a dress.

The Union Theater, at the corner of Lawrence and Chaparral, was built by Charles G. Bryant, an architect from Maine. It was a large building that could seat up to 800. When it opened in January 1846, admission prices were $1 for a box seat and 50 cents for the pit. In front of the theater, and connected to it, was a large saloon. Bryant, in an ad in the Jan. 1, 1846 Gazette, said, "Having been at great expense in fitting up accommodations for the amusement and convenience of the gentlemen of the Army and Town, he (Bryant) trusts the establishment will be generally patronized."

Bryant's great expense was soon wasted. A little more than two months later, Zachary Taylor moved the army to the Rio Grande, beginning in early March 1846, and Corpus Christi became virtually deserted, a ghost town. Both theaters sat empty. I don't know what happened to the Army Theater, but the Union Theater was later converted into a hotel by Bryant.

Charles G. Bryant was a famous architect in Bangor, Maine in the 1830s. He also conducted a military academy and organized a militia group, the Bangor Rifle Corps. Bryant became involved in a rebellion in Canada and talked of creating a second Texas "on the northern border of the United States." He crossed the border with a contingent of Maine volunteers. When the rebellion failed, Bryant was a wanted man in Canada and in his home state of Maine for violating the neutrality act, according to a book on Bryant titled "Flight of the Grand Eagle" by James H. Mundy and Earle G. Shettleworth Jr. In 1839, Bryant sailed for Galveston with his oldest son, Andrew Jackson Bryant.

Bryant moved to Corpus Christi in 1845, when the army was here, and built the Union Theater. After the army left for the Rio Grande, Bryant brought his family down from Maine. At Galveston, he designed and built St. Mary's Cathedral. In Corpus Christi, he began remodeling the Union Theater into a hotel, which he called the Union House. In 1849, Bryant was appointed mustering officer for three companies of Texas Rangers that were operating in the Corpus Christi district.

On a Friday morning — Jan. 11, 1850 — Bryant left Corpus Christi to visit Austin in connection with his Ranger duties. On Saturday morning the next day, at 8 a.m., 25 miles from Corpus Christi, at Wood's Ranch on the Chocolate Bayou, he was killed — speared in the back and the breast — and scalped by a band of nine Indians, believed to be Lipan Apaches wearing Mexican and American clothes. They took his horse, several hundred dollars in gold and banknotes, stripped him of his clothes and left his body in a pool of blood. They carried away everything but his hat. People at Wood's ranch saw the slaying, but were too few to intervene.

An account of Bryant's slaying in the New York Herald on Feb. 11, 1850 said, "Major Chas. G. Bryant, one of our citizens, was barbarously murdered near to and in sight of Wood's rancho, which is situated on the river called Chocolate, about five miles from the coast, 25 miles from Corpus Christi, on the high road to Victoria, and within 10 miles of the Mission del Refugio. The information given by a Mr. Welder, who lives at or near Wood's rancho . . . is that the Indians were disguised in the (clothes) of Mexicans and Americans, which doubtless threw poor Bryant off his guard and caused him to allow them to approach him . . . "

Ranger Capt. John Grumbles, stationed on the Nueces River above Corpus Christi, rode to the scene with a company of Rangers. He took a lock of what remained of Bryant's hair, buried him, then followed the trail of the Indians.

Charles Bryant designed St. Mary's Cathedral in Galveston, one of the oldest buildings still standing in that city.

In a report to the governor on Jan. 30, 1850, Grumbles wrote: "I have just returned from a long and unsuccessful jaunt that I have had after a small party of Indians that murdered Major (Charles) Bryant of Corpus Christi on the morning of the 12th. He had reached Chocolate Bayou journeying toward Goliad when he was ambushed and killed. They had taken some 60 or 80 horses from Wood's Rancho, which they succeeded in carrying off. Intelligence of these depredations did not reach me until the night of the 13th. On the morning of the 14th I, with a detachment of 23 men, gave pursuit, and followed them for six days, with the most untiring energy, but all my exertions to overtake them proved of no avail. I followed them over 300 miles, frequently coming upon horses that had been

183

abandoned and lanced, evidence of the rapidity with which their retreat was effected. They passed out near the Leona Station into the mountains, where I was satisfied that further pursuit would be useless. I am satisfied that if I could have gotten a fair start with these ruthless murderers, that the number of our foes would have been somewhat diminished. As it was, I was doomed to disappointment."

Bryant left a widow (Sarah Getchell Bryant) and six children and an estate of $1,500, town lots in Corpus Christi worth $1,100 and a case of architect's tools worth $5. Some years later, his family received 640 acres of land from the state of Texas in recognition of his services. Bryant's Union Theater was torn down to make way for the St. James Hotel, built in 1869, which, in turn, was torn down in 1937 and Lichtenstein's Department Store was built on the site.

— Oct. 31, 2012

BUYING VOTES

Leading up to the election, I thought about an old saying that politicians get elected by deceiving voters and they get re-elected by making them like it. I also thought about the 1914 election when a federal grand jury indicted Nueces County Judge Walter Timon and 42 prominent people for plotting to "corrupt the ballot."

Besides Timon, indictments were brought against County Clerk August Uehlinger, Sheriff M. B. Wright, County Treasurer Ed Oliver and others. The trial began in September 1915.

One witness, Fred Headley, testified that a meeting was held in Timon's office. He said the room was filled with county officials and they discussed how much it would cost to bribe voters "on the Hill" (meaning the Hispanic community). Headley testified that Timon said, "It will take $2,500 to $3,000 to carry the Hill, as the other side will spend money like water."

Other witnesses could not recall Timon saying that. Timon took the stand and with a voice that could dominate any room said, "I have lived in Nueces County for many years and God is my judge I can say that never has it been necessary to buy a single vote to keep Nueces County in the Democratic column."

The jury convicted five. Three were sentenced to a year in the penitentiary and two were sentenced to six months in the county jail. The jury could not agree that Judge Timon was implicated. (A good account of this trial can be found in Mary Jo O'Rear's "Storm Over the Bay.")

If Timon said (or didn't say) it would cost $2,500 or more to carry the Hill, it no doubt meant it would cost that much to buy the election whisky. It was through handouts of free whisky, cigars and meals that votes were bought and voters manipulated. An article in the Caller in 1936 interviewed an unnamed "old-timer" who described the practice.

185

Judge Walter Francis Timon

"The night before the election, there was plenty of free liquor and cigars and everybody got drunk and happy. The (Hispanic) population got plenty happy on that night, let me tell you. The candidates would get them as drunk as possible and pen them up in houses and not let them out until it was time to vote the next day. Then they would hand them marked ballots and lead them to the polling places, with stops on the way for more free liquor."

Chief Manteca Mucho

Several Comanche chiefs had colorful names, such as Chief Isomania, also called Chief Asa Minor. In 1849, when Jack Hays' Rangers attacked Isomania's camp, supposedly he was among those killed, but days later he was found alive and nursed back to health. Isomania claimed he had been dead for three days and came back to life. Another Comanche chief was called "Cut Arm" and Rip Ford had an encounter with one named "Carne Muerto" (Dead Meat). Names like these — Carne Muerto, Cut Arm — were likely bestowed by people who had grievances against them.

Several Karankawa chiefs also had unusual names given to them by mission priests. One with a missing ear was El Mocho (Crippled). One was Frazada Pinto (Spotted Blanket) and another was Manteca Mucho (Too Much Fat).

Tonkawa Joe

Indians, it was said, had no conception of private land ownership, but J. Williamson Moses, a surveyor in the Hill Country in the 1840s, wrote that Comanches targeted surveying parties because they understood what the surveyors were doing and why. They objected to surveying the land and blazing the trees because they knew it meant the land was being measured for white claimants.

John J. Linn told about an Indian called Tonkawa Joe who came into his store in Victoria. After a long silence, Tonkawa Joe asked Linn where he came from. "I told him Louisiana. He wished to know of whom I purchased my land. When I informed him, he said that white people were buying and selling the lands of Indians without regard to their claim. He said God gave this country to the Indians who peopled it, but they would soon be dispossessed of their inheritance.

" 'If I wish to buy something from your store,' Tonkawa Joe said, 'I must do so with your consent, and pay what you ask, but if a white man wants the Indians' land, he goes to another white man and a trade is made.' Such were the ideas of Tonkawa Joe in regard to the title of property. I confess that when he asked if I thought the course pursued by my countrymen was honest, I could only say that I had paid for all I possessed, but, alas, to a white man." Linn goes no further, but clearly he was not satisfied he had bought his property from those who rightfully owned it.

Chief Ten Bears

The pain of dispossession — the loss of their ancestral lands — was described in a speech at a peace council in 1867 by Comanche Chief Ten Bears. To quote a small part of Ten Bears' speech, addressed to an Indian agent:

"There are things which you have said to me which I do not like. You said that you wanted to put us on a reservation, to build our houses and make us medicine lodges. I do not want them. I was born on the prairie where the wind blew free and there was nothing to break the light of the sun. I was born where there were no closures and where everything drew a free breath. I want to die there and not within walls. I know every stream and every wood between the Rio Grande and the Arkansas. I have hunted and lived over the country. I lived like my fathers before me, and like them, I lived happily.

"So why do you ask us to leave the rivers and the sun and the wind and live in houses? Do not ask us to give up the buffalo for the sheep. If the Texans had kept out of my country there might have been peace. But that which you now say we must live on is too small. The Texans have taken away the places where the grass grew thickest and the timber was the best. Had we kept that we might have done the things you ask. But it is too late. The white man has the country we loved and we only wish to wander on the prairie until we die."

— Nov. 7, 2012

NORTH BEACH — 1

A stretch of land between Corpus Christi and Nueces bays was called Rincon, then Brooklyn, and finally North Beach.

After Henry Kinney founded Corpus Christi in 1839, he hired men to slaughter wild horses for their hides on the Rincon. One day Kinney's men hid in a thicket and watched Comanches spread buffalo robes on the bayou — usually more damp than wet — to keep their ponies from bogging in the mud.

A company of Rangers chased another Comanche war party to Rincon Point. It was sundown and the Rangers waited for morning to attack the Indians, penned up against the water. When the sun came up, the Indians were gone. The Rangers found tracks leading into the bay and discovered they escaped by riding across an oyster reef.

This underwater land bridge, which became the Reef Road, served horse and wagon traffic. It was three miles from Rincon Point to Indian Point and as crooked as a worm fence. It was marked with stakes to show the turns. To one unused to the sight, it was surreal watching wagons cross the bay. Although marked, it was easy to stray into deep water where horses could bog or get cut by sharp oyster shells.

On Aug. 1, 1845, Zachary Taylor's troops landed on the Rincon, cleared salt grass buzzing with rattlesnakes, and pegged out army tents. The encampment — Fort Marcy — was enclosed with earthworks. Taylor's engineers, looking for a way to transport supplies to a detachment at San Patricio, gouged out a cut in the reef so small boats could travel up the Nueces River to San Patricio. Afterwards, horses had to swim across the place where they gouged out a hole in the reef.

The first work ordered by the Nueces County Commissioners Court, on Jan. 11, 1847, was to stake the Reef Road.

During the Civil War, Taylor's Fort Marcy embankment was used for a Confederate gun battery. In the Battle of Corpus Christi on Aug. 16, 1862, Union ships landed 30 men with a howitzer on North Beach, to seize the battery. Confederates charged the landing party and forced them back to their ships.

After the war, one of the first acts of a reorganized county government was to order the stakes on the Reef Road be replaced. They had been removed during the war.

William Ohler bought much of the Rincon in 1870 and renamed it Brooklyn. A plat showed plans for streets, parks, and public squares. New homes were built and a man named Ziegler planted salt cedars at Rincon Point and opened a beer garden there.

During the beef packing era in the 1870s, three packing houses — packeries — operated on the Rincon. One was owned by John Hall, a former Union soldier and immigrant from England. Hall dumped rotten meat in the mud slough, which became known as Hall's Bayou. The packing houses gave off a fearsome stench.

The Morris and Cummings Cut across the bay, completed in 1874, brought deep water (and commerce) to Corpus Christi. The city granted monopoly rights to the owners of the Central Wharf, which led to high wharf rates. This prompted Norwick Gussett to build a competing wharf off North Beach, outside city limits, which put an end to the Central Wharf monopoly.

After a storm in 1874, tides were so high that Hall's Bayou was 12 feet deep and running like a mill race. Storm damage on the Rincon included the T-head of Gussett's wharf, which was swept away. Afterwards, a rickety bridge was built across the bayou at what was called the Brooklyn Crossing.

In 1886, the San Antonio and Aransas Pass Railroad — the SAAP — planned to build a trestle bridge across the bay, starting at White Point. Capt. Andrew Anderson, hired to make soundings, found such a depth of mud that the trestle had to be built near the old Reef Road. Afterwards, boys going duck hunting at Gum Hollow would cross over the bridge and if a train arrived they would drop down and hold onto the ties until it passed.

Sometime in the 1880s the name Brooklyn was dropped in favor of the old name, Rincon. In the 1890s, during the Ropes Boom, a fancy resort hotel was built by local investors on the Rincon. The Miramar was the pride of Corpus Christi. It opened on June 1, 1891 and registered 4,000 guests in the next three months before it burned

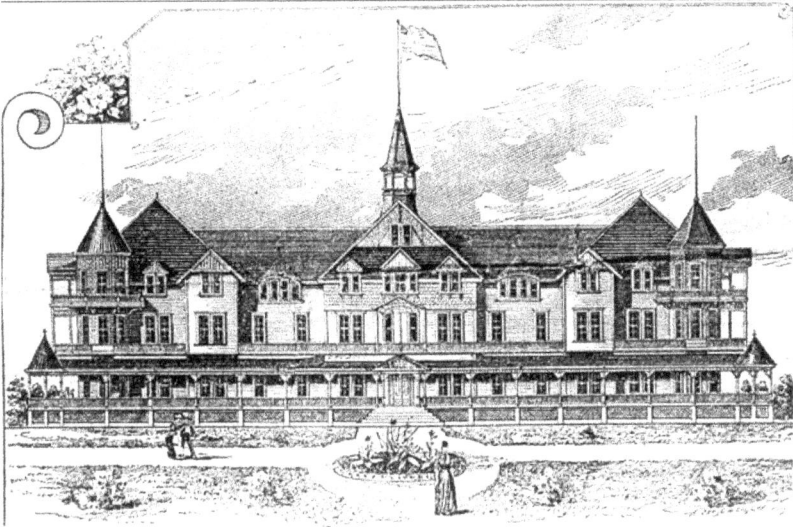

The Miramar Hotel on North Beach was built during a fever of speculation during the Ropes Boom. It opened in May 1891 and burned three months later.

in a spectacular fire on Sept. 11, 1891. The fire began in an upstairs room at 3 a.m. on Sunday. Twenty-eight people, employees and guests at the hotel, escaped with their lives, some jumping from the second floor to mattresses spread on the ground as, the Caller wrote, "the fiery-tongued destroyer sprang from room to room." No one was killed but the hotel was a total loss.

In 1895, heavyweight champion "Blacksmith" Bob Fitzsimmons opened a camp on North Beach to train for a fight with "Gentleman" Jim Corbett. F. E. Ring built tourist cottages to capitalize on the heavyweight boxer's presence. The Ring Villa tourist courts were the first in Corpus Christi. Fitzsimmons' pet lion would run with him when he did wind sprints on the beach. An alarm spread one day that the lion was missing. People loaded their guns and mothers kept their kids inside. The lion was found napping peacefully under a house.

During the Spanish-American war, Corpus Christi volunteers — called the Kenedy Rifles — were sent to Cuba while a volunteer unit from Longview — the Longview Rifles — were stationed on North Beach, in case Spain invaded Texas.

On Aug. 8, 1905, the Epworth Revival opened. Beginning that year, and continuing for a decade, North Beach was the scene each

Epworth-by-the-Sea, a Methodist revival encampment, opened on the north end of North Beach in 1905.

August of a Methodist revival called Epworth-By-The-Sea. Families arrived to attend religious services and have fun on the beach. SAAP Railroad built a depot — the Epworth — across from the Epworth grounds.

A.K. Ragsdale of Dallas, one of the Epworth League managers, said there wasn't much on North Beach before the Methodists arrived. "We put up 300 tents and built a 200-foot long box hotel." They found the air cooler because North Beach is sandwiched between two bays. Corpus Christi resident Roy Terrell remembered the encampment. "Preaching took place night and day, but there was time for games and bathing. There was a big tent where they served meals. The first time I tasted ice tea was at one of these Epworth meetings."

— Nov. 14, 2012

NORTH BEACH — 2

After the turn of the 20th Century, the Reef Road across Nueces Bay, discovered in the 1840s, still served as a unique underwater land bridge.

People coming in wagons to shop in Corpus Christi timed their trip to return before dark. If they stayed too late, they would try to see the marker posts on the Reef Road by the phosphorous glow kicked up by the horses' hooves. The Caller noted that R. K. Reed of Portland reported that a wagon belonging to D. C. Rachal "is stuck in the reef, the driver taking the wrong side of the stakes in crossing Nueces Bay."

In 1905, Spohn Sanitarium was built where the old Miramar Hotel had burned. Before the hospital was built, doctors performed surgeries in the homes of patients. Dr. Arthur Spohn raised money to build a hospital, a tract of land was bought on North Beach, and a two-story building erected.

On Oct. 22, 1909, President William Howard Taft delivered the dedication speech at the opening of Corpus Christi's first Country Club. It was on North Beach. Taft struck the first ball on a new nine-hole golf course and, as the rotund president bent over to strike the ball, a photographer couldn't resist taking a picture of the seat of government. For years, the Country Club displayed the golf club, ball, and photo of the president's rear end.

North Beach was the setting for the first airplane flights in the area. Eight years after the Wright brothers first flew over at Kitty Hawk, N. C., the Wright Brothers company gave demonstration flights over North Beach on July 3-4, 1911. A crowd gathered on the salt flats north of the Epworth encampment. Admission was 50 cents for adults, 25 cents for kids. Aviator Oscar Brindley flew a Wright Brothers' plane that had been shipped in crates and assembled here.

In 1912, John Dickensen built the Beach Hotel, a fancy resort surrounded by oleanders and palms. A streetcar stopped at the front

An old sailing ship was moved next to Pleasure Park Pier on North Beach and became a popular dancing place in the early 1930s. Photo taken by Doc McGregor on June 8, 1931.

door and the grounds ran down to the water. Room rates at this luxury hotel began at $3.50, three times the price of a room at the State Hotel downtown.

Nueces County, in 1915, dedicated a beautiful arched causeway across Nueces Bay which replaced the old Reef Road. Not long after it opened, the causeway was badly damaged in the 1916 hurricane.

Three years later, on Sept. 14, 1919, a Sunday, this area's worst hurricane ever swept across North Beach. On Monday morning after the storm, only three structures remained standing on North Beach: Judge McDonald's home, Spohn Hospital, and the Beach Hotel, which had been converted into an Army hospital. Hundreds of people were killed, their oil-coated bodies washed ashore at White Point. We can only guess at the tragedies that took place during that terrible storm.

Some of the finest homes in the city were destroyed, erased. Where homes had been was left as empty as an open field, littered

194

with ruined sewing machines in and the detritus of people's lives. "The only thing we found of our possessions," said one North Beach survivor, "was a cut-glass bowl that had been on the mantel. Daddy found this bowl, with three pennies still in it, in the sand. That's all that was left."

In the 1920s, North Beach began to rise from the ruins, beginning with an amusement park that was a joint venture of Bruce Collins Sr., and his cousin John Mosser. If anyone "invented" the North Beach of popular memory, it was Collins, and he did it without any public subsidies. He built the North Beach Pleasure Park, the Saltwater Pool, and purchased an old sailing ship abandoned in the port turning basin, moved it next to a pier on North Beach and had the side painted in capital letters, "Dance On The Ship." Dancing on the deck of "The Ship" under the stars became very popular.

When the USS Constitution — Old Ironsides — visited Corpus Christi in 1932, the wake of its destroyer escorts lifted "The Ship" from its base and it broke free of its moorings. The vessel was finally returned to its berth at the pier. "The Ship" and adjacent pier were destroyed in a hurricane in 1933.

The Saltwater Pool, built in 1926, was a popular place for youngsters to swim. The pool was filled with piped-in saltwater, filtered to keep out jellyfish. One swimming instructor at the pool was an Englishman known as Major Blake. Caller-Times bird columnist Phyllis Yochem once sent me a note recalling that she learned to swim at the pool. "I remember the smell of the water and that because of the salinity of the water you could float in it whether you could swim or not. The dressing rooms were not roofed. The teacher was a man named Major Blake, who had a strong British accent. I was afraid to put my head under water and was a poor pupil. At the end of the class, Major Blake said of me, 'Pretty punk, but pass.' "

The old Beach Hotel — the Army convalescent hospital during the 1919 storm — was remodeled and renamed The Breakers. Its Spanish village ballroom, designed to resemble a rose garden in moonlight, was famous. The Crystal Beach Park Ballroom and pier were built south of the bathhouse in 1929. The following year, a dance marathon contest was staged in the Crystal Beach Pavilion. The marathon, which attracted large crowds, lasted for 31 days. In 1931, the Crystal Beach Park Ballroom and pier were renamed the Bayside Park and Ballroom.

The roller coaster on North Beach was a popular attraction in the 1930s until a 13-year-old girl was thrown off and killed. Not long afterwards, the roller coaster was closed down and dismantled.

A top attraction in the early 1930s was the famous rollercoaster called Skyrocket near the pier for "The Ship." In 1931, a 13-year-old girl was killed; she stood up on a turn and was thrown out. In another fatal accident, a woman was killed when one of the cars jumped the track. The rollercoaster was closed and torn down.

During that era, net shrimpers would spend their evenings on the old Epworth Pier. They would put out a crab baits and wait for dark before lighting kerosene lanterns. After dark, they would throw cast nets and catch large white bay shrimp, which they sold to seafood buyers waiting in Model-T trucks.

— Nov. 21, 2012

NORTH BEACH — 3

From the middle of the 19th Century into the 20th, people crossed North Beach on the way to or from the Reef Road. After the port opened in 1926, they crossed North Beach to get on or off the bascule bridge. North Beach was a place of transit.

In 1925 and 1926, as the bascule bridge was being built, dredges worked behind it in the salt flats digging a turning basin for the port to be. The port and bascule bridge opened on Sept. 14, 1926. The new bridge was massive, compared to the little wooden bridge that once spanned Hall's Bayou. It often attracted a crowd to watch it go up and down. The bridge never got a formal name. Bascule — French for "seesaw" — describes the counter-balanced lifting action. It was built by Wisconsin Bridge and Iron at a cost of $400,000. It was 121 feet long, 52 feet wide, and one end could be raised 141 feet. It was painted black and coated with grease to protect it from the salt air.

In September 1933, a hurricane wrecked tourist courts and destroyed the pier and dance ship, the Bayside Park and Ballroom. The storm damaged the Yacht Beach Court cottages owned by race-car driver Barney Oldfield, the first man to drive a car 60 miles an hour.

North Beach soon returned to business as usual. On a good weekend, the North Beach Amusement Park, the carnival midway, the Ferris wheel, merry-go-round and other rides would attract as many as 4,000 visitors, or 20,000 on a holiday. A North Beach businessman said one tourist was worth one bale of cotton, and was easier to pick.

Linn K. "Doc" Mason, a gambler with Las Vegas connections, opened the Dragon Grill, a nightclub that gained fame for illegal gambling, in 1930. It later became known as the Beach Grill. In 1934, he opened another place, three blocks past the bascule bridge, called the Oasis Dinner Club. In 1937, he moved the equipment from the first place into the second and renamed it the Dragon Grill. It burned on Jan. 15, 1944. Mason then moved into the old Elks Building in downtown Corpus Christi.

After Corpus Christi annexed North Beach in 1935, some honky-tonks became a source of trouble. One, called the Kat's Meow, had frequent brawls and complaints of gambling. Mayor H. R. Giles in 1936 said he would push to close the worst joints, but not all. "We don't want an air-tight city," Giles said. "There are certain pleasures the citizens and visitors demand." The city also made a push to clean up a migrant camp of tents and tin shacks at Rincon Point. In 1939, when Corpus Christi won the battle for a new naval air station, the migrant camp was filled with workers looking for jobs building the base.

The boom years in the 1940s, when thousands of Navy cadets trained at the Naval Air Station, were prosperous times for North Beach. On Saturdays, the amusement park would be crowded during the day and at popular night spots, couples danced to Glenn Miller's "Moonlight Serenade" or the Andrew Sisters' "Boogie Woogie Bugle Boy." After the war, and by the end of the decade, the numbers of visitors began to decline, especially after the Padre Island Causeway opened up a new playground in 1950.

Bruce Collins Sr. blamed the bascule bridge for the decline. From the beginning, the bascule was a problem. The Corps of Engineers had opposed building that kind of bridge but the city, which was paying for it, opted for the cheapest bridge it could get, which was the bascule.

When a blast of the siren warned that the bridge was going up for an approaching ship, the moans of those caught on the wrong side of wherever they were going must have been almost as loud. Of all the causes of a traffic jam, a ship way out in the bay was hard to accept. The bridge would stay up for about 20 minutes, but the wait seemed endless. Bascule became an adjective for nuisance. For ships, the 97-foot opening was a tight squeeze, which captains called threading the needle. A Dutch captain said, "It scared the hell out of me."

The problem grew worse as the frequency of the bridge being raised increased and ships became larger. A hot debate in the 1950s was whether to replace the bascule bridge with a tunnel under the port entrance or a high bridge over it. North Beach businessmen preferred a tunnel. The debate was settled when the state agreed to

A Doc McGregor photograph shows North Beach in its heyday in the early 1940s.

The popular North Beach Amusement Park was crowded one day in the early 1940s when North Beach was one of the premier fun places on the Texas coast. Photo by Doc McGregor.

pay for building a high bridge, as opposed to the city paying for a tunnel with city-backed bonds and recouping the money through a toll.

When the Harbor Bridge opened in October 1959, it dealt a major blow to this once prosperous part of the city. North Beach was bypassed and soon became run-down, a victim of progress. The place of transit had become a cul-de-sac, a dead end. In quick succession in the late 1950s, the amusement park and boardwalk were torn down, the roller rink was razed, the Saltwater Pool was closed and removed to make way for the Sandy Shores. In 1959, Bruce Collins and other North Beach property owners urged the City Council to change the name to Corpus Christi Beach in the hopes that it might revive North Beach's glory days when it was called the Playground of the South. It didn't stop the decline.

In the half a century since, North Beach recorded some major successes, such as the Texas State Aquarium and the Lexington, a partial resurrection, but it will never be what it was when it was one of the premier tourist attractions on the coast.

Have you ever gone back to a place known to you when you were young and been disappointed? Well, North Beach can never be what it was, except in the memories of those who loved it. They say: You should have seen North Beach in the old days, when you could splash in the Saltwater Pool, or go dancing on The Ship, or lose money at the old Dragon Grill. So it is said.

— Nov. 28, 2012

THE KICKAPOO RAID

They called it the Kickapoo Raid. The raiders actually were a mixed band of 40 Mexican outlaws and hostile Indians — including Kickapoo and Lipan — and one Anglo American. They cut a violent trail across South Texas, stealing horses and killing for the sake of killing. It was the week before Easter 1878.

We know the details of this raid because witnesses made sworn statements in Corpus Christi and San Diego. Their affidavits were sent to Washington in an appeal for protection for rural ranches of South Texas. I used the affidavits to piece together a narrative of events.

On Sunday, April 14, 1878, the raiders crossed to the other side of the river — *el otro lado del rio* — at a regular crossing called Apache Hill, north of Laredo. On the Texas side, they killed two vaqueros who worked for ranchers Prospero and Justo Guerra and at a sheep ranch they killed rancher Jorge Garcia. A witness heard him pleading — *"No mi matan!"* (don't kill me) but they shot and lanced him to death, took his pistol, turned his pockets out, and stole his horse.

Fourteen miles north of Laredo, the raiders turned northeast toward the Nueces River and stole 30 horses at Dr. Henry Spohn's ranch. Dr. Spohn, a Laredo physician, came from Canada and like his brother, Dr. Arthur Spohn of Corpus Christi, he was known for his medical skills.

At sundown on Tuesday, the raiders wounded Tomas Solis at Rancho de los Machos, leaving him for dead. Dr. Spohn dressed his wounds. He said the man who shot him demanded his socks and when he refused, ordered him to run and shot him as he ran. When he fell, he heard one say, "That will finish him."

On Wednesday morning, the raiders reached a sheep ranch called Palo Alto, east of Fort Ewell, owned by William Steele. His ranch was on the south side of the Nueces River. Steele had gone to

Dogtown (Tilden). The raiders found a man and two boys tending sheep. The man was John Steele, William's brother, and two boys, Mrs. Steele's sons by a previous marriage. They killed John Steele, a religious man who didn't believe in carrying guns, and killed the two boys, scalped them and mutilated their bodies. Two shepherds, Martin Martinez and Florentine Leo, were killed, and another man, Venturo Rodriguez, was wounded and left for dead.

Jane Steele, the rancher's wife, climbed up on the roof of the house to get a better view and from that vantage point watched helplessly as her brother-in-law and her two sons were murdered.

"I saw two men running, about two miles off, on the high open country," she said. "They were on horseback and seemed to be running a man. A few minutes later, two other horsemen appeared, coming in the direction of the house. I saw three more men come into sight and they got between John (Steele) and the house, one of the three men after John, driving him away from the rancho. Directly I saw the man fire one shot, and John fell from his horse. Two men rode off in the direction of my children (boys, one aged eight, and the other 12), who were herding sheep, and one of them fired one shot before they went out of sight."

She gathered her other three children (the youngest was nine months old) and they crawled through tall grass to the river. "I put them on the branch of a tree and wading in water up to my arms pushed them ahead of me to cross the river." They hid in brush along the riverbank until the raiders rode away.

That afternoon, the raiders chanced upon E. C. Moore and his cousin Frederick Moore riding down the road. The Moore cousins had roasted pecans and were eating them when they saw a large dust cloud. "I thought they were cow-drivers," said E. C. Moore. "One was a white man, bull-necked, sunburned . . . next to him was a wiry little Mexican . . . Fred noticed their flanking movement and said, 'Here they come!' Those were his last words." He was killed, shot in the chest, while E. C. Moore, taking a bleak view of the situation, whipped his horse as he escaped with his life.

At noon Thursday, the raiders hit Rancho Solidad in Duval County where they killed Guadalupe Basan and gathered all the horse stock. They killed a shepherd and his wife, tied them together and swung them over a horse. Their bodies were never found.

The raiders next attacked the sheep ranch of Richard Jordan, well-known in Corpus Christi. In 1871, Jordan and William Rogers built the Market Hall, which served Corpus Christi as a marketplace and City Hall. Jordan's sheep ranch, 30 miles west of San Diego, was called Charco Escondido (Hidden Pond). The ranch was managed by his three sons. The raiders came upon and killed John, 19, the youngest son, and an old man named Antonio Valdez. Richard Jordon said, "John had three bullet holes and an Indian arrow in him. They cut the boots open on my son, took off his socks and hat, but did not mutilate him." His neck was broken when he was pitched headlong from his horse.

The raiding party took the Laredo road, killing people they encountered along the way. A posse led by Frank Gravis, who had a sheep ranch near Jordan's, chased them. The posse included Gravis' stepfather, H. W. Berry, a former sheriff of Nueces County, and E. H. Caldwell, who owned a sheep ranch at Borjas. Near Laredo, the posse caught up with the raiders with about 200 head of horses. There was a sharp skirmish but, said Gravis, being outnumbered he thought it expedient to fall back.

A few miles south of Laredo, as darkness fell, the raiders made rafts of dry wood to float their plunder and crossed to the other side of the river, *el otro lado del rio*. It was on the evening of Good Friday. The raiders killed at least 18 people — men, women and children; shot, lanced, and hacked to death — and left a dozen others badly wounded. It was the last major Indian raid in South Texas.

After the raid, a petition was sent to the Secretary of State in Washington seeking federal protection from bandit and Indian raiders crossing over from Mexico into Texas. The petition from Corpus Christi was signed by Judge John C. Russell of the 25th District Court, Nueces County Judge Joseph FitzSimmons, Corpus Christi Mayor John M. Moore, former sheriff Henry W. Berry, and John J. Dix, Duval County surveyor. Detailed affidavits of the raid were made by Frank C. Gravis, Dr. Henry Spohn, Calixto Rodriguez, E.H. Caldwell, and Charles F. H. von Blucher.

— Dec. 5, 2012

W. W. JONES

The story goes that the old man liked to sit in the lobby of the Nueces Hotel and talk. He chewed tobacco and when he had to spit he might hit or miss the spittoon. A guest asked a bellhop, "Why don't they throw that old man out?" The bellhop said, "They can't. He owns the hotel."

William Whitby Jones was known in his family as Big Daddy. To others he was Bill or W. W. He was one of the richest cattlemen in Texas and he was a banker, real-estate broker and hotel-owner.

W. W. Jones was born in Goliad in 1858. His father, A. C. Jones, was a prominent merchant who later moved to Beeville. Bill Jones went to a private school, the Covey Academy at Concrete in DeWitt County. A classmate, John Young, recalled when he and Jones went to Cuero to fetch a package for Professor Covey. They took a buggy pulled by an old mule who moved at his own pace. They bought a bottle of whisky and firecrackers at Cuero and on the way home drank whisky and lit firecrackers to make the mule run. "The sport was cruel," Young was quoted in 'A Vaquero of the Brush Country,' "but I doubt if Bill Jones or I enjoyed another ride more than we enjoyed that one."

Jones went east to school, to Roanoke College in Salem, Va., and Poughkeepsie Business College in New York. A motto on the wall at Roanoke proclaimed that "Labor Always Wins." Jones adopted it as his own. If circumstances were different, he would turn it into, "Love Always Win." At least, both have been attributed to him.

When W. W. returned to Texas, he trailed herds to Kansas. He bought a ranch near Beeville and ranchland in McMullen County. He married Louella Marsden and began a family. Around 1889, Jones bought the San Javier Ranch, of the old Las Animas grant, and much of the land that became Jim Hogg County. Alta Vista, headquarters of Jones' ranch, was 22 miles south of Hebbronville.

Neighbors were the Truitts on the 146,000-acre Wells Ranch in Hidalgo and Starr counties. Maude (Truitt) Gilliland wrote about the ranch in "Rincon." Her father, Alfred Truitt, managed the ranch for Jim Wells, the powerful political boss in Brownsville. Mrs. Gilliland wrote that W. W. Jones would come over in a cart pulled by mules. The cart had wide wheels to pull through the deep sand. She said that in crossing pastures, Jones would take down fences, then tell her father where the gaps were so the fence-riders could re-string the wire.

When Jones came to visit he showed no signs he ever intended to leave. His visits could last two or three days. He would sit on the porch, where he made his general headquarters, chew tobacco, and spit in the yard. Once, she wrote, he spat a stream of tobacco that hit their cat between the eyes. After much slapping and pawing and face-washing, Old Tom, as a matter of policy, kept his distance. Mrs. Gilliland said Jones carried an unusual walking stick, which was carved at the top with a steer's head and set in the eye sockets were two sparkling rubies.

Although he was one of the wealthiest men around, the Truitts regarded W.W. with amusement, laughing at his reputation for watching his pennies. He had special pockets, they said, that took money in but let nothing out. In Hebbronville, he once cut off his horse's tail and swapped it for chewing tobacco. At the cafe, he was known to stick his chewing gum on a saucer to be saved and re-chewed later.

W.W. was not so friendly with another neighbor, Ed Lasater, who built his own ranching empire. Lasater owned the largest herd of registered Jersey cattle in the world. The famous Falfurrias butter was produced by his diary. Lasater and Jones both came from Goliad — born within a few miles of each other — but there were few similarities between them, other than both were cattle barons and acquisitive land-buyers.

Jones could sit and talk for days. He was never in a hurry. Lasater, with long strides, was always moving. He traveled at night to save the daylight hours for work. Jones and Lasater became bitter political foes. All that each of them wanted, it was said, was for the other to stop breathing. Their ranches bordered each other. Lasater owned 300,000 acres and Jones had 250,000. In the book "Falfurrias," Lasater's grandson, Dale Lasater, said every gate between the two ranches was secured with double locks and double

W. W. Jones, pioneer rancher in Jim Hogg County, moved to Corpus Christi and helped build the Nueces Hotel, which he later owned.

chains and that no gate could be opened without a representative from each ranch on hand.

There were political differences between Lasater and Jones (and Manuel Guerra, who controlled the southern part of Starr County) and, at that time, in that place, political differences could end in gunfire. They did lead to the creation of Brooks County in 1911, where Lasater held the reins of power and usually got his own way. This led to the creation of Jim Hogg County, where Jones and his son, A. C. Jones, held power. Falfurrias was Lasater's power base and Hebbronville was Jones's.

The W. W. Jones house on the bluff later housed La Retama Library.

In 1905, Jones moved to Corpus Christi and rented the old Fullerton-Doddridge mansion on South Bluff. It was a small town of 5,000 then but a big city compared to Hebbronville. Jones built a home on Lower Broadway and turned to banking and real estate. He invested in building the 278-room Nueces Hotel, which opened in 1913, and later bought out the other investors. As sole owner, he became a fixture in the lobby and hotel employees learned not to notice his tobacco-chewing and errant aim. Besides the hotel, he bought the Jones Building (first called the Sherman Building) across the street.

Jones had one son, A.C. Jones, named for his grandfather, and three daughters. One daughter, Lorine Jones Spoonts, served as president of the Corpus Christi Chamber of Commerce in the 1920s. William Whitby Jones died in the Medical-Professional Hospital on July 17, 1942. An obituary noted that his favorite saying was, "Love Always Wins." It seems an unlikely motto for such a crusty old cattleman as W. W. Jones. Perhaps it was "Labor Always Wins" after all.

—Dec. 12, 2012

DRAGON GRILL — 1

No known link existed between three big-shot gambling operators in Texas in the 1930s and 1940s, but they operated with similar style, running high-class places that offered gourmet food and top-rate entertainment. They were Jakie Freedman of Houston, Sam Maceo of Galveston, and Doc Mason of Corpus Christi, all products of Prohibition.

Jakie Freedman was a bellhop at the Rice Hotel who made a lot of money hustling bootleg whisky during Prohibition and by the 1930s he had a colonial mansion just outside town that was an illegal casino called the Domain Privee. Marguerite Johnston in "Houston, The Unknown City" wrote that Freedman would allow no one in his place who lacked good manners or whom he considered a risk.

"The ones who can get inside can afford it," Freedman said. "A man comes to the gate and gives his name and if he is somebody I want to invite in, he is allowed in the gate and I meet him on the porch myself. If not, he's told, 'Mr. Freedman is not at home.' " One night, a wealthy Houstonian lost $200,000 and tried to settle for 20 cents on the dollar, to which Freedman said, "No, I'm a businessman just like you." Freedman eventually moved to Las Vegas, where he founded the Sands Hotel.

In Galveston, the Maceo brothers — Sam, Frank and Rose (Rosario) — controlled all kinds of illegal activities. They opened the Hollywood Dinner Club in 1926, during Prohibition. Guy Lombardo and his Royal Canadians were booked for the opening and drew 20,000 guests during a three-week engagement, according to Gary Cartwright in "Galveston." The club featured gourmet food, bootleg whisky, illegal gambling, and first-class entertainment. When a raid threatened, the band was trained to strike up "The Eyes of Texas" as a warning.

After Texas Rangers attacked the Hollywood Dinner Club with axes and left it in pieces, the Maceos opened another club called Sui

Jen on a pier, with a Chinese menu, pagoda-shaped bandstand, and a casino on the T-Head at the end of the pier. In 1941, Sam Maceo hired Virgil Quadri, store decorator for Marshall Fields in Chicago, and Oscar Nordstrom, to transform the Sui Jen into the Balinese Room, patterned after the Balinese Room in Memphis. It became one of the swankiest nightclubs in Texas and no doubt inspired the design and operation of the Dragon Grill in Corpus Christi.

The Volstead Act of 1919 — the legal enforcement of the 18th Amendment — encouraged all kinds of illegal activity, starting with the manufacture and traffic in illicit whisky. After Prohibition was repealed in 1933, illegal activity continued, to avoid heavy taxes or evade liquor laws. In Texas, it was illegal to sell mixed drinks, except in private clubs, so the problem was solved when bootleggers opened private dinner clubs. The years of public acceptance of lawbreaking during Prohibition created an amused tolerance for this kind of illegal activity.

Maceo's Balinese Room in Galveston, Freedman's Domain Privee in Houston, and Mason's Dragon Grill in Corpus Christi were all private clubs, requiring guests to become members (for a nominal fee) to skirt state liquor laws. Requiring membership also facilitated illegal gambling; law-enforcement officers or unfamiliar faces could be screened and denied entry.

If high-stakes gambling in the post-Prohibition years was controlled by Jakie Freedman in Houston and the Maceo brothers in Galveston, it was controlled in Corpus Christi by Doc Mason through his places on North Beach and in downtown Corpus Christi.

Linn Keys Mason, born on Dec. 3, 1902, one of six children, grew up on a farm in Pennsylvania, at Monongahela. His father, a railroad man, worked for the Pennsylvania Railroad until the family moved to Port Arthur, Texas and he went to work in an oil refinery. Doc left school after the 9th grade and later managed a nightclub, selling bootleg liquor, in West Texas.

Mason came to Corpus Christi in 1926 and opened a private club, where illegal liquor was sold, above the Manhattan Cafe on Peoples Street, conveniently across from the Nueces Hotel. In 1930, he opened the first Dragon Grill in the North Beach tourist section. One of his partners was Bob Shoop, who got his start selling bathtub gin, and others were F. Wilbert Garton and Clyde Jennings.

According to one of Shoop's customers, as told by Bill Walraven in a column in 1982, Shoop and his partner bought pure grain

Doc Mason's Dragon Grill on North Beach was a hot spot for entertainment and illegal gambling in the 1930s. Photo by Doc McGregor.

alcohol from Kansas City in five-gallon cans. "They did not deal in moonshine whisky, just quality gin. Regular customers never went to their place to pick up a jug. They delivered in person. Both were always immaculate and used briefcases to deliver their gin in. The man on the street could have mistaken them for Philadelphia lawyers. When Prohibition ended, Bob and his partner opened the first liquor store in Corpus Christi." Shoop later opened the popular Shoop's Grill.

In the mid-1930s, Mason built another place on Timon Boulevard called the Oasis Dinner Club, which was open during the tourist season. Eventually, he closed the original Dragon Grill, moved the equipment into the Oasis on Timon Boulevard, and renamed it the Dragon Grill. The second Dragon Grill became Corpus Christi's most posh nightclub. If one wanted to impress a date, make a big splash, or just celebrate a special occasion, the Dragon Grill was the place to go. As in "Casablanca," judges and politicians would have been shocked! shocked! to find illegal gambling going on — in the form of slot machines, poker, craps, and chuck-a-luck.

On June 28, 1940, Friday at midnight, an undercover Texas Ranger, A. L. Barr from Harlingen, dressed as a civilian, showed up at Mason's Dragon Grill on North Beach. He saw six men gambling at the blackjack table. He walked up and threw down his badge and said, "I'll play this."

The raid, conducted with a minimum of fuss and excitement, was organized by Sheriff John B. Harney and District Attorney Joe Hatchitt, with Ranger Barr assisted by Deputy Sheriff Bill Elliff, Deputy Sheriff George Connell, and Special Investigator Earl C. Dunn of the district attorney's office. A dice table and a blackjack table were confiscated in the raid.

Six men, including Doc Mason, were charged with illegal gambling. They all entered pleas of guilty and Mason paid their fines, which totaled $354. Mason posted a bond of $2,000 on felony charges of "keeping a gambling house."

It was the second time in four years that Mason was charged with running a gambling establishment. He had been arrested in 1936. The usual form for Mason was to pay the fine, get court continuances then wait until the charges could be quietly dismissed, which happened in this case. Getting raided and paying fines represented the cost of doing business.

—Dec. 19, 2012

DRAGON GRILL — 2

Linn K. "Doc" Mason controlled illegal gambling in Corpus Christi through the Dragon Grill, his nightclub on North Beach. Like other famous nightclubs of that era, the Dragon Grill was a legacy of Prohibition. When Prohibition was repealed in 1933, former bootleggers opened fancy nightclubs as respectable fronts for illegal gambling.

For seven years the Dragon Grill on North Beach was the city's top nightspot until the morning of Jan. 15, 1944 when it burned to the ground. Firemen were hampered by the explosion of cans of cooking oil stored in the kitchen. The place was a total loss.

Doc Mason leased the three-story Elks Lodge building in Corpus Christi at the corner of Starr and Water streets, with plans to transform it into an elite dinner club. Mason must have taken a close look at Sam Maceo's place in Galveston for he hired the same designers who converted Maceo's Sui Jen into the Balinese Room, one of most exotic nightclubs in the country.

Mason hired Oscar Nordstrom, Chicago architect and interior decorator, who designed the Hawaiian Century Room at the Adolphus Hotel in Dallas, and he hired Spanish artist Virgil Quadri, store decorator for Marshall Fields in Chicago. Nordstrom and Quadri designed the Balinese Room at the Hotel Claridge in Memphis.

Mason put Nordstrom and Quadri to work converting the Elks building into the new Dragon Grill. He wanted a richly decorated interior that would attract upper-bracket customers to drink, dine, dance, and otherwise spend their money. He told a reporter, "I intend to serve the same high-class food as was provided to patrons of the original Dragon Grill. It will be a properly operated place where everyone will enjoy going."

After 18 months work and an expense of $260,000, the third Dragon Grill was set for a grand opening on March 26, 1946. Some

213

450 ticketed guests had seen nothing like it. They came through solid hand-hammered copper doors. The main floor dining room, the Zodiac Room, could seat 450. It featured floor-to-ceiling Quadri murals that depicted the courtship and marriage of a Swedish couple. Between the murals were panels in coral and silver. There was a raised dance floor made of maple parquet and the orchestra stand was covered with silver sparkled cloth and gilded chairs. The orchestra performing that opening week was the Duchess and Her Men of Note.

The second floor included living quarters for the Chinese cooks and other workers and private rooms that were available for guests and gamblers. On the third floor was the Jalna Room, an elegant supper club which featured more seven-foot murals by Quadri, inspired by tales from the Arabian Nights. The Jalna Room could seat 220. It also had an orchestra stand and crescent-shaped bar. Access to the Jalna Room and gaming tables beyond was strictly controlled with a system of warning lights and buzzers that signaled when law-enforcement made an unwelcome visit. Cards, dice, roulette wheels could be concealed behind secret panels and moveable walls. Behind the walls on the third floor was a maze of sliding panels, hidden rooms, secret exits.

The Dragon Grill became an oasis of order, good food, and excellent manners, with flickering candles on white tablecloths, crisp linen napkins folded to stand at attention, champagne iced down in silver buckets, women wearing jewels and men in fancy suits. Waiters in Dragon Grill uniforms moved about like colonels on parade. The Dragon Grill would gain a reputation as one of the top nightclubs in the nation, famous for its food, its atmosphere, its entertainment, and its illegal casino gambling.

Doc Mason would permit neither cheap entertainment nor strong-arm tactics. If a gentleman should forget he was a gentleman, it was said, he would be ushered to the exit as quietly as possible without suffering any indignity and without any show of resentment by the management. If a man showed up without a tie, a polite waiter would get him one and help tie it on.

The Dragon Grill was known for its fine food and boasted of having one of the best-equipped and best-supplied kitchens in the country. Maine lobsters on ice and prime steaks from Chicago were flown in daily. The kitchen was run by a Chinese head chef named Joe Ming.

A fashionable group enjoys drinks at the downtown Dragon Grill in August 1947.

A former worker, Gilbert Garcia, once said — "We had beautiful floor shows and big-name bands. Doc and his wife Floy would go as far as New York and California to book the shows. We had dancing nightly, a hat-check girl and cigarette girls. People came in formal dress. The Dragon Grill was very prestigious." It was a place people went when they wanted to reward themselves and they would remember their visits with pleasure. Part of the Dragon Grill's excitement, its allure, was no doubt because of the taint of illegality, another legacy of Prohibition.

In August 1953, an enterprising policeman named Raymond Lamp'l gained access to the Jalna Room on the third floor. An account of the raid was printed in an 1989 article on the Dragon Grill by Gigi Starnes: "The story goes that some members of the local law enforcement (including Lamp'l) and FBI agents spent several months dating local girls who were known to Doc. They decided it was time to make the hit. Lamp'l and his date were,

215

Doc Mason in his office on July 30, 1947. His Dragon Grill was Corpus Christi's most famous nightclub.

decked out as party-goers. Because they had been in several times Pop Powers (the doorman) knew them and took them upstairs. Lamp'l watched as players threw down their chips. When it was his turn to play, he threw down his badge." Once again, Doc was charged with keeping a gambling house, but the grand jury returned a no-bill in the case.

That killed the Dragon Grill. Not long after the raid, Mason sold out to the Town Club, which occupied the place until 1988. Linn Keys "Doc" Mason died in Las Vegas when he was 85 years old. He was buried in Corpus Christi, where he had lived for 40 years and was known far and wide as the owner of the incomparable Dragon Grill, Corpus Christi's most famous and elegant nightclub and illegal casino.

— Dec. 26, 2012

THE BLUFF BALUSTRADE

Corpus Christi's high bluff — affording a panorama view of the great sweep of the bay — was where Henry Kinney built his trading post in 1839. This dominant feature later gave the city one of its nicknames, the Bluff City. Corpus Christi, a town on two levels, has a downtown and an uptown. The lower level was once known as the beach, while the upper level has always been called the bluff.

Six years after Kinney's arrival, Zachary Taylor chose Corpus Christi, rather than Live Oak Point, as the place to concentrate the army in part because of the flat tableland on the bluff where the army could drill.

Taylor's soldiers found "Mexican" families living in jacals in an area of the bluff called Little Mexico. A decade later, when another army unit was stationed at Corpus Christi, a fight broke out at a New Year's fandango on the bluff. One soldier was stabbed to death and four wounded. Next day, angry soldiers burned jacals as residents in Little Mexico hid in the brush. This was the fandango riot of 1854.

There wasn't much on the bluff then. Kinney's compound was about where the telephone building is now, near the home of Forbes Britton, known as Centennial House today. In 1857, the government built a lighthouse on the bluff (above where the Caller-Times is today) to guide ships across the bay. When it was closed in 1859, the editor of the Ranchero wrote that he was "sorry to miss the clear shining of the light in my window last night." In 1863, when Nathaniel Banks' Union forces invaded Texas, Confederates tried to blow up the lighthouse, but the charge only knocked off a corner of the white brick structure. Annie Marie Kelly passed the lighthouse on her way to school. "It was all open on one side, with a little ditch around it. We used to go inside the old lighthouse and look around."

Corpus Christi notified the U.S. Lighthouse Board in 1871 that the old lighthouse was a public hazard and the city planned to demolish it. Washington replied that it was federal property and could not be torn down by local authority. The city ignored that and soon afterwards a team with ropes and mules pulled down the lighthouse. At the same time, the old Meuly house on the bluff (where the Nixon Building was later constructed) was also demolished.

During the Nuecestown Raid in 1875, a wounded bandit was brought to town in a two-wheeled cart. Posse members escorting the cart, looking for a place to hang the bandit, tried to attach a rope to a sign that said "Zapateria" at a shoemaker's shop, but it was too low. They fixed a rope to the steeple of St. Patrick's Church, but cattleman Martin Culver told the men not to desecrate a house of worship. They found a gate on Leopard, with a cross pole high enough, where the bandit was hanged and his body left dangling until Easter morning.

During the 1870s and early 1880s, lumbering oxcarts loaded with wool came in by Leopard, the city's chief thoroughfare from the west, and traveled down the bluff to the stores of the wool merchants below. The side of bluff was like an ugly scar between the lower and upper sections of town. Gullies washed out on the side of the bluff and runoff carried mud onto the streets below. During a heavy rain, the streets in the beach section would be under water and the sidewalks passable only when planks were laid across them.

The bluff was steep in places. Mrs. Angie Westbrook recalled that when they came to Corpus Christi in 1900 they traveled in a wagon down the side of the bluff below Leopard Street. "We had to lock all four wheels and then we could hardly hold the horses, the bluff was so steep."

About that time, the Caller tried to start a contest to name the bluff, noting that Rome has Seven Hills, San Francisco has Nob Hill and Chattanooga has Missionary Ridge, but the contest fizzled and the bluff remained the bluff.

In 1912, during the administration of Mayor Clark Pease, the city decided something had to be done with the slippery slope. After Pease, Roy Miller was elected mayor in 1913 and it was during Miller's administration that bluff beautification work was undertaken and completed.

The city hired an engineer from New York, Alexander Potter, to develop a municipal water system. Potter was asked to make suggestions on how to convert the bluff eyesore into something the city could be proud of. Potter's plan called for terracing the bluff and building a balustrade. Conrad Blucher used Potter's design to make

Dirt roads trickle off the side of the bluff before the balustrade was built (above). The unsightly bluff was converted into an attractive feature with the bluff improvement project (below). Concrete walls reinforced with base anchors were built and the bluff terraced to prevent erosion.

detailed plans for the bluff improvement project, which was financed by a street bond issue.

Work began between Lawrence and Peoples. The bluff was terraced to prevent erosion and it was leveled, raised in places and lowered in others. Huge retaining walls, with reinforced concrete base anchors, were built and highlighted with an elegant balustrade and grand stairways leading from downtown to uptown. The first section was completed in 1915. A $150,000 bond issue in 1916 extended the work north. Property owners on Broadway financed the extension to the south. The project was carried from Peoples Street north to Mann Street and south to the juncture of Mesquite and Upper Broadway.

As the balustrade was being built, the Daughters of the Confederacy contributed funds to build a fountain at the bottom of the slope and at the top of Schatzel and Peoples streets. They hired sculptor Pompeo Coppini, who had moved to San Antonio, for $1,000 to design a Confederate memorial fountain. His fountain depicts Corpus Christi as a beautiful young woman flanked by Father Neptune and Mother Earth. Coppini's fountain was completed in 1915 and became the crown jewel of the bluff improvement project.

Alexander Potter's original plans called for a pedestrian tunnel linking downtown and uptown. The tunnel, built long after the bluff improvement project was completed, was opened in 1929. John G. Kenedy donated land at the south end of the bluff for a World War I memorial in what today is known as Spohn Park.

The bluff improvement project, with its white balustrade and grand stairways, was part of the city's dynamic growth surge during Roy Miller's tenure. Today, 100 years later, this distinctive border between the uptown and downtown is undoubtedly the city's second most dominant feature, after the seawall.

— Jan. 2, 2013

CONRAD MEULY

It was called a trade expedition to Santa Fe, but it was a scheme by Texas President Mirabeau Lamar to bring New Mexico under Texas control. Volunteers, adventurers and merchants calling themselves the Santa Fe Pioneers set out from Austin in June 1841 with 23 covered wagons and cumbrous ox-carts carrying merchandise valued at $200,000.

Among the traders was Conrad Meuly ("Miley"), a native of Switzerland who moved to Texas and invested $16,000 in the Santa Fe venture. His goods included silk hose, scarves and bolts of fine alpaca, valued at $15,792.

The expedition was an attempt to push the Texas border westward, to absorb New Mexico and the great trade route that followed the Santa Fe Trail. The flow of wealth to Texas would follow the control of that trade. From hindsight, we know the plan was ill-informed, badly organized and the Pioneers could scarcely conceive what they were in for.

From the start, they blundered around with no one knowing the way. They were harried by Comanches and, short of provisions, suffered hunger and thirst. They went from Brushy Creek near Austin to the Brazos River near Bee Mountain; from there to the Cross Timbers, then to the Wichita River, which they mistook for the Red, to the Llano Estacada and to New Mexico, where they expected to be greeted by friends and allies. Then the New Mexicans would be encouraged to revolt and the Texans would be on hand to lend their support — the best-laid plans and all that.

In New Mexico, they were captured by Mexican soldiers without a shot fired. The Texans, under guard, were forced to walk 1,400 miles to Mexico City and on the way were starved, beaten and those who fell behind executed, their ears cut off to prove they hadn't escaped. Those who survived were imprisoned in Mexico until a flurry of diplomatic action brought about their release in April 1842.

Conrad Meuly returned to Texas. Three years later, in the summer of 1845, he opened a bakery in Corpus Christi, a crude little trading post, anticipating the arrival of Zachary Taylor's troops. Meuly advertised coffee, hot drinks, pastry and bread for sale while roughly half the U.S. Army was concentrated at Corpus Christi.

In 1847, Meuly married Margaret Rahm in New Orleans and the couple returned to Corpus Christi. Meuly built a two-story home on Chaparral and bought another house on the bluff. The house on Chaparral was a showplace, with 14-foot ceilings and two-feet-thick walls. Bricks were made of shellcrete and the house was decorated with iron grillwork from New Orleans. The growing Meuly family lived upstairs while a general store occupied the lower floor.

About 1853, Meuly bought the 17,714-acre Rancho Puentecitas at Santa Petronila, which had been granted to Andres Fernandez de la Fuente in 1809. It was variously known as the Meuly Ranch or Puentecitas Ranch. Meuly also bought property in San Patricio and had scattered holdings around the state.

During the Civil War, Meuly became persona non grata with Confederate authorities who, rightfully enough, questioned his loyalty. Although he was a slave-owner (he owned a household servant named Martha), he publicly championed the Union cause and became "personally obnoxious" to the Confederates.

The Meulys had been close friends with Felix and Maria Blucher, but that friendship must have been strained during the war. The Bluchers were staunch Confederates; Felix was a major in the Confederate Army. In Corpus Christi, as tensions increased between Confederates and Unionists, a mob threatened to skin Meuly with a dull knife then hang him. Conrad closed the store and the bread-and-biscuit bakery and moved the family to the ranch on Pintas Creek, 30 miles west of Corpus Christi, near Banquete. This was in 1862 before Corpus Christi was bombarded by Union warships.

Confederate cavalry confiscated Meuly's beeves to feed the troops and the Meuly ranch became a way station for Union boys evading Confederate conscription laws. They would stop at Meuly's for food and information as they tried to avoid Confederate patrols on their way to Mexico.

In late 1863, after Confederate Gen. Hamilton Bee evacuated Brownsville, he and his staff stopped at Meuly's ranch near Banquete on their way to Corpus Christi. Bee called Meuly a traitor and threatened to hang him. Meuly, a brave if obstinate man, told

Conrad Meuly (left) dared Gen. Bee to carry out his threat to hang him. His widow Margaret shooed away a lynch mob with a broom at her home on Chaparral.

Bee, "General, issue your orders. I am here." Bee, always more talk than action, did not carry out his threat.

At war's end, Meuly agreed to supply beef to Union occupation troops in Brownsville. He was in Brownsville when he caught yellow fever and died on July 9, 1865. He was 55 years old and left a widow and 12 children.

During the occupation of Corpus Christi, Union soldiers ransacked Meuly's home on the bluff. They took the furniture and ripped out the fixtures, including doors and window sashes, to use for firewood. Margaret Meuly later filed a claim for damages and was paid $1,150.

On May 15, 1866, a lynch mob stopped at the Meuly home on Chaparral. The mob was dragging along a man named Jim Garner, who had shot and killed a storekeeper for refusing to sell him a pair of boots on credit. Members of the lynch mob tried to fix a rope to the fancy iron grillwork on the front of the Meuly home, but Margaret scolded them and ran them off with a broom. Down the street, at the arroyo, they found a mesquite with a limb high enough for the hanging.

Margaret Meuly continued to direct the affairs of the family ranch, assisted by sons Herman, Alex and Charles. One of Meuly's daughters, Mary Ellen, married Charles Blucher, the son of their old friends, Felix and Maria Blucher. Ursula, the oldest daughter, married William Daimwood. Two other daughters, Margaret,

Conrad Meuly's house on Chaparral, built in 1852, was known as the house with the iron front. It was one of Corpus Christi's oldest surviving structures when it was torn down in 1955. Arthur Stewart photograph, in 1936, from the Library of Congress.

known as Maggie, and Amelia, called Tudie, remained unmarried. Conrad Meuly's widow Margaret died on Oct. 29, 1912 when she was 83.

The Meuly home, built in 1852, was torn down in the 1950s for a Fedway store and that was remodeled to house the Education Service Center.

A lot of history passed by the old Meuly home, known for a century as the house with the iron front, built by a survivor of the ill-fated Santa Fe Expedition.

— Jan. 9, 2013

FRED GIPSON AND OLD YELLER

According to Fred Gipson's theory of life, a person comes into the world without his consent and leaves it against his will. In life he is misjudged and misunderstood. In infancy he is an angel, in boyhood a devil, and in manhood a fool. If he is a poor man, he has no brains; if he is rich, he has been lucky. When he comes into the world, people want to kiss him; before he goes out, they want to kick him. From the cradle he roughs it until the day he snuffs it.

Gipson penned that in 1939 when he wrote a regular column for the Caller-Times, before he became the most famous writer ever fired by the newspaper. He wrote "Old Yeller," one of the top dog books of all time, "The Hound Dog Man," and "Savage Sam." Like J. Frank Dobie, he was a writer who belonged to the old school of storytelling tradition and, like Mark Twain, he could tell a story from a boy's point of view. Walter Prescott Webb once called him the Mark Twain of Texas.

Gipson was born in Mason County on Feb. 7, 1908 and grew up in a struggling family in the Depression in the Hill County. He attended schools in Mason and worked as mule-skinner, cotton picker, and he raised turkeys, grew watermelons, and once built a ranch fence by hand-drilling postholes in solid rock.

In 1927, he took what he thought would be an easier job. It was to move a herd of goats from Mason County to Blanco County, some 90 miles away. Gipson wrote about the experience. There were three herders for 700 goats. One man on horseback took point, Gipson on foot took drag, and the third man took flank in a Model-T carrying provisions.

The first night a norther hit, with a cold sweeping wind and heavy rain. The goats sought shelter along a creek bed, shivering and trembling under every bush. The Model-T stalled when they tried to drive it across the creek. The men, slapped around the face by a bitter wind, waded through rising water to drag out the car. Next morning, they were all miserable and wet, including the goats. The goats scattered like quail and the men ran their tails off chasing them. They fought every goat over every inch of mud for three 18-hour days. When they reached Blanco County, the three herders were close to crying. They didn't want to talk to each other or even look at the goats. Gipson wrote about chasing wet goats in the rain in an article headlined, "Easy Money, This Goat Money."

After years of hard work, Gipson studied journalism at the University of Texas and in 1937 was hired as a reporter for the Caller-Times. Bob McCracken, longtime editor of the paper, wrote that Gipson came to work in a battered old Stetson and scuffed boots thoroughly down at the heels. He approached the daily grind of newspaper work with the same kind of avoidance of the devil toward holy water.

Send him out to cover an event, McCracken said, and they could expect a listless and garbled story. But send him out to do a color piece, and the result would be a masterpiece of clarity and reader interest. One day McCracken sent Gipson to write about the annual review of a dance class. Gipson treated it as if it were a rodeo. As McCracken related, "Students included tiny tots who were beginners to finished performers. He gave the same attention, maybe a little bit more, to those who muffed their routine as he did to those who didn't miss a step."

Next day, after the story ran, McCracken was besieged by the angriest, most unreasonable woman he had ever met. She was Bertha Lacey, the dance instructor, and she was there to make critical observations about Gipson's dance review story. McCracken said she didn't leave until she lost her voice from screaming about "that awful cowboy."

In January 1940, Gipson married Tommie Wynn of San Angelo and managed to combine his honeymoon trip to Monterrey with his newspaper demands, writing a series of columns from Mexico about his new wife and their honeymoon. When he returned, the honeymoon with the paper was also over. The editors wanted him to write closer to home, to make his stories less personal, and they planned to cut his salary by $5 a week, to $37.50. Rather than accept the cut, he demanded a raise and was promptly fired.

Gipson and his wife moved to Mason and he turned to writing articles for Reader's Digest and Collier's. His first book, "Fabulous Empire," was a biography of Zack Miller, who ran a Wild West

Fred Gipson wrote the novel "Old Yeller."

Show. His next book was "Hound Dog Man," followed by "Trail-Driving Rooster," then "Old Yeller," which sold three million copies and captured hearts around the world. "Savage Sam" was a sequel to "Old Yeller."

What Gipson learned growing up on Comanche Creek in Mason County nourished all his stories. He had once watched a turkey hen trying to protect her brood from a chicken snake, and he had seen buzzards pecking out the eyes of a live fawn trapped in a barbed-wire fence. He used both incidents in "Hound Dog Man."

Gipson went to Hollywood, turning his books into movie scripts, but became enraged with the treatment of "Hound Dog Man," when the producers refused to use the word "coon" for fear it might be misconstrued as a racial slur. Gipson never forgave them for changing coon hunt to possum hunt.

Gipson's life took a tragic turn. He had long suffered severe depression, followed by drinking bouts that were hard on his family. He was charged with assault after kicking a pig farmer and his sons found the family dog — the prototype for "Savage Sam" — beaten to death at their house. Mike, the oldest son, committed suicide days afterwards. After that, Fred and Tommie divorced and the old Gipson family home burned. He never published another major work.

Fred Gipson died on Aug. 14, 1973 in Mason County and was buried in the State Cemetery in Austin. Writing, for Gipson, was a hard slog and he was challenged in trying to meet the expectations demanded because of his earlier triumph with "Old Yeller." He had achieved fame and success, with his books translated around the world, but he was like that helpless fawn trapped in a fence, at the mercy of forces beyond his control.

— Jan. 16, 2013

NUECESTOWN RAID

In the last week of March 1875, a band of 33 bandits crossed the border below Rio Grande City and rode for Corpus Christi. They arrived on Thursday, March 25, and camped on the Oso nine miles from town.

Early on Good Friday, they stole horses at the Joseph Campbell ranch near Tule Lake, then went on to the S. H. Page ranch. At Page's, they swapped their worn-out saddles for better ones and took the men at the ranch hostage. They rode on to the Juan Saenz community. At Frank's store, they put on new boots and killed an old man who worked for Frank; he recognized one of the bandits.

Rancher George Reynolds, his two daughters, their governess Adele DeBerry, and ranch hand Fred Franks were captured on the road. The bandits ordered Reynolds to remove his clothes. He was indignant. "You're not going to make me take off my pants, before my daughters and this young lady!" The bandits relented, but made Franks take off his boots and trousers. They captured Henry Gilpin and Laura Allen in a buggy heading for Corpus Christi. Sidney Borden, Mrs. E. D. Sidbury and her daughter, were captured.

The bandits forced the captives to run. One who knew Gilpin shouted, "Andale! Don Enriquez!" Joe Howell complained about running in bare feet, so the bandits made him put on Laura Allen's slippers. When he refused to move, they cursed him and jumped their horses over him, but left him behind. Some captives were quirted to make them run, but since they did not shoot Howell, others refused to budge. The bandits argued about whether to shoot them, but left them behind.

Earlier that day, John Dunn was saddling his horse to go to Corpus Christi when a neighbor's boy brought the news that bandits had robbed the Page place. Dunn wrote a note to Sheriff John McClane and told the boy to show the note to his cousin "Red John" Dunn on the way.

Dunn was loading his guns as cousin "Red John" and brothers arrived. They rode to the Page house, where they saw the bandits' old saddles on the ground, then rode to Campbell's, where the women were crying. The men had been taken prisoner, except for "Old Man" Campbell who hid in the brush.

The Dunns rode on and saw the bandits ahead. They were forcing Sidney Borden to run while one bandit was riding Borden's gray racehorse. At Frank's store, the Dunns and bandits watched each other warily from a distance, but there were too many for the Dunns to attack and the bandits were not disposed to start the fight. Dunn recognized his brother Mike's horse and realized he had been taken. Someone said John Dunn should go to Corpus Christi for help. He didn't want to leave, with his brother being held, but "Red John" convinced him to go.

When the alarm reached Corpus Christi, Sheriff McClane lathered his horse riding the streets, warning people to stay inside. Women and children boarded the Aransas steamship, which moved out into the bay for safety, as men prepared to ride to Nuecestown to take on the bandits.

At Thomas Noakes' store in Nuecestown, Noakes was waiting for the mail rider when a man called "Lying" John came in to buy flour. As Noakes was getting it, he saw the bandits ride up. He got his Winchester and, as a bandit raised a pistol to shoot "Lying" John, Noakes shot the bandit in the chest.

Noakes' wife ran from the store with their five children while Noakes and "Lying" John scuttled through a trap door and hid under the store. The bandits plundered the store, then started a fire. Mrs. Noakes, who returned after seeing the children to safety, poured water on it. Several times a bandit started a fire only to have her put it out, before the flames took hold.

With the store on fire, "Lying" John ran for it and was shot. As the flames became intense, Noakes left his hiding place and had his rifle ready to fire when Mrs. Noakes yelled that the bandits were gone. She ran inside the burning store to save her featherbed.

As the store burned, the men from Corpus Christi rode up, their horses winded. Among them were George Swank, Pat Whelan, "Wash" Mussett, Clem Vetters and Jesus Seguira. Noakes was sitting on the ground with his Winchester. Swank demanded the gun, saying that all he had was a six-shooter to go up against the bandits. Noakes refused, fearing they might return. Swank levelled

Nueces County Sheriff John McClane rode up and down Corpus Christi's streets to spread the alarm.

his six-gun and said, "Hand over that rifle or I'll shoot you myself." Noakes gave him the gun.

The bandits were camped in the brush. As Swank and Dunn rode up, one shot was fired, killing Swank. As other shots were fired, the bandits rode away, leaving their plunder and captives. Sheriff McClane arrived and took Swank's body. They put the bandit Noakes had shot in a two-wheeled wool cart. "Lying" John had been hit four times, but was alive. He later claimed he was shot eight times.

On Saturday morning, Sidney Borden, who had been captured the day before, led a posse in pursuit of the bandits. Near the Borjas Ranch, they ran across and hanged two men. As they later learned, the men were from Laredo and had no connection with the raiders.

S. G. Borden, the founder of the town of Sharpsburg, was captured by the bandits in the Nuecestown Raid.

The wounded bandit was brought into Corpus Christi on the wool cart. On Leopard Street, they began looking for a place to hang him, and fixed a rope to the steeple of the Catholic Church, but cattleman Martin Culver stopped them. They found a gate with a cross pole where the bandit was hung. His body was left hanging until Easter Sunday.

Mrs. E. D. Sidbury and daughter and Miss Laura Allen were found Easter morning. They had escaped and hid in the brush for two days. Later, Thomas Noakes built a new store a mile from the old site and George Reynolds spent two years tracking down his stolen horses. He found them in Saltillo and got them back. The 1875 Nuecestown Raid, sometimes called the Noakes Raid, was only one episode in a long-running conflict, but it left a legacy of bitterness that lasted for a long time.

— Jan. 23, 2013

LIPANTITLÁN

The Rio de las Nueces, or River of Nuts, is shown on some old maps as Rio Escondido, the Hidden River, which seems more apt than nuts since the pecan trees on its banks vanished long ago.

In 1528-1535, Cabeza de Vaca, the shipwrecked Spaniard, who was a slave of Indians in the region, described a river of nuts, which could have been the Colorado or the Nueces; no one knows for sure. W. G. Sutherland, who was a scholar of local history, believed that Cabeza de Vaca visited a Lipan Apache village near today's Bluntzer community in Nueces County. Sutherland was surely wrong; the Lipans were not here for at least another century. But long after Cabeza de Vaca, there was a Lipan village across from where San Patricio is today, which gave the place its name, Lipantitlán, the land of Lipans. The Indians camped on the Nueces to hunt buffalo.

In 1685, French explorer Robert Cavelier, Sieur de La Salle, landed on Matagorda Bay and built Fort St. Louis on Garcitas Creek. LaSalle's men killed him in ambush and the French settlers were wiped out in an epidemic followed by an attack by Karankawas.

La Salle's landing goaded Mexico into action. Spanish authorities sent an expedition headed by Alonso de León to find and destroy the French colony. On April 4, 1689, De León noted in his diary: "We came upon a river . . . we called it the Rio de las Nueces because there were many pecan trees on its banks." Some claim he crossed the river at Santa Margarita, but more likely he followed an Indian trail that took him (using today's names) past Frio Town, Jourdanton, Cuero, then south to Garcitas Creek. De León found the ruins of La Salle's fort and collected French children who survived the massacre.

A few miles south of Lipantitlán was the Santa Margarita crossing, where the river widens, becoming shallower, with a rocky bottom that made an excellent ford. Traffic going to La Bahía (Goliad), the Atascosita road, and the Laredo branch of the Camino Real crossed at Santa Margarita.

In 1746, José de Escandón was commissioned to colonize territory from Tampico to San Antonio, which he called Nuevo Santander. Escandon sent Joachín de Orobio Basterra to explore the land and he discovered that the Nueces didn't empty into the Rio Grande, as thought, but entered the Gulf "at a place where a great bay is formed."

At this place, where the Nueces emptied into a great bay, was where Escandón planned to found a town called Villa de Vedoya, on the site of today's Corpus Christi. The families recruited to settle there never made it north of the Rio Grande. If Escandón's plan had succeeded, Corpus Christi would be 100 years older than it is. In 1766, Blas María de la Garza Falcón founded Santa Petronila ranch, one of many ranches that originated with the great colonizer Escandón.

Some believe a fort was built three miles west of the present site of San Patricio in Escandón's time; evidence is lacking, but a fort was built there after Mexico gained its independence. Manuel de Mier y Teran, on an official tour of Texas in 1828, marked it as a good place for a garrison. Fort Lipantitlán was built on his recommendation. The fort was built at the site where the Lipan Apaches were known to camp. They came to the area in the winter to hunt buffalo. After the fort was built and was under the command of Capt. Enrique Villarreal, the Indians still congregated nearby, according to Jose Maria Villarreal, who was at the fort with his father from 1828 until 1835.

In 1835, with Texas restive, Gen. Antonio López de Santa Anna vowed to drive all Americans from Texas and fielded an army of operations against the rebellious province. On Sept. 20, Gen. Martin Perfecto de Cós landed at Cópano Bay and ordered reinforcements for Fort Lipantitlán.

On Nov. 4, Texans under the command of Ira Westover captured the fort while 80 Mexican soldiers from the garrison were out looking for Westover's men. About sundown, a San Patricio man, James O'Reilly, was sent into the fort to tell its defenders, some 30 militia, including San Patricio men, that if they surrendered they would be treated with leniency. They marched out with hands raised and Westover's men took possession of Lipantitlán, which one

Fort Lipantitlán was built on the recommendation of Manuel de Mier y Terán. It was located on the Nueces River.

described as looking more like a hog pen than a fort. They captured two four-pounder cannons, eight escopets (old Spanish guns) and several pounds of gunpowder.

Next day, Capt. Nicolás Rodriguez, the fort's commander who had been out searching for the Texans, arrived with his men and a battle was fought on the river. Sgt. William Bracken, of the Lavaca River, lost three fingers of his right hand, shot off while he was loading his rifle. He was the only Texan wounded, while the Mexicans suffered 28 casualties, killed and wounded. One Texan said they had met the enemy and "flogged them like hell." Capt. Rodriguez and men retreated to Matamoros.

For the Mexican army in Texas, the loss of Lipantitlán removed a strategic link in the line of communications between Matamoros and San Antonio. The following April, after the battle of San Jacinto, the Mexican army under Gen. Vicente Filisola began its long retreat to Mexico and crossed the river at Fort Lipantitlán. Filisola ordered the old fort destroyed and dumped the two cannon into a nearby lake or the river.

In 1839, during Mexico's federalist-centralist civil war, a federalist army under Gen. Antonio Canales camped at the site of the old fort. In 1842, Texas volunteers were stationed at Lipantitlán when Texas was threatened with renewed hostilities from Mexico. Some 700 Mexican militiamen under that same Antonio Canales attacked Lipantitlán on July 7, 1842. In the battle, five Mexican soldiers were killed and Canales' force retreated to Matamoros.

In March 1846, when Zachary Taylor's army began its move to the Rio Grande, the army marched west to just below Santa Margarita, then turned south on the old Camino Real, known today by the more prosaic designation of County Road 666.

235

Early ranchers in the area, beginning in the 1850s, included James Durst and Nicholas Bluntzer. In 1849, Bluntzer established his ranch near the ruins of the old fort Lipantitlán. Samuel Reed Miller built a ferry a little north of the rocky crossing at Santa Margarita.

During the Civil War, wagons traveling the Cotton Road crossed at Santa Margarita. In 1863, after Corpus Christi was bombarded by Union warships, the town's newspaper and county government moved to the village of Santa Margarita and stayed there, out of harm's way, for the rest of the war.

From Cabeza de Vaca to the Texas Revolution to the Cotton Road in the Civil War, a lot of history passed the site of Fort Lipantitlán and the Santa Margarita crossing on the lower bend of the River of Nuts.

— Jan. 30, 2013

RADAR ISLAND

Corpus Christi was booming in 1892 when Elihu Ropes was building a deepwater port and buying and selling property. During the Ropes Boom, land was selling for grotesque prices, with such a frenzy of buying there was no time to haggle; one paid the asking price or someone else did.

John Ward bought a triangle of land wedged between the Cayo del Oso and Corpus Christi Bay called Island A. He paid Ropes $1,448 for the island (or peninsula) containing 250 acres. Ward planned to develop it into an exclusive resort.

A year later, in 1893, the grotesque land prices turned into grotesque losses. We would call it a depression today; they called it a money panic. It brought the economy to its knees and in Corpus Christi the boom collapsed. When Ropes left, the whole town became seriously broke. John Ward moved to Beaumont. All he left behind was a name: Ward Island.

With the Ropes collapse, Corpus Christi returned to the sleepy little place it had been before the Ropes dynamo arrived, a town without ambition, and Ward Island returned to what it had always been, a good place to hunt ducks and a favorite fishing spot.

In 1914, after 22 years of unrecorded fishing and duck hunting, Ward Island was in the news. Investors planned to build an amusement park on the island. Papers of incorporation were filed with capital stock of $40,000. Local investors included J. H. Caswell, W. G. Blake, and W. E. "Uncle Elmer" Pope, the later legislator and candidate for governor. Caswell said Ward Island would be "the greatest amusement park of its character in the South."

The plans called for building an electric trolley line from uptown to the island, a distance of eight miles. Construction of the Ward Island line began on July 6, 1916 on Chamberlain Street (now

Alameda) and by the end of July, the tracks had progressed to the city limits; grading work had been completed for five miles outside the city.

On Aug. 18, 1916, a hurricane caused widespread damage and destroyed most of the structures built on piers along the shore. Workers building the Ward Island Interurban were diverted to clean up storm debris from downtown streets. The work on the line never resumed, which may or may not have been connected to the storm.

At first, the newspaper said boxcars of rails and ties had been delayed and that work would begin when they arrived. Then the newspaper ceased to mention anything about Ward Island. I couldn't find a word about the unraveling of the Ward Island project. It had been big news for two years, then nothing.

Perhaps it was bad economic timing again, like in 1892. Absent any other rationale, I suppose that Eastern investors pulled out because of general economic conditions or perhaps because of the storm. But the project went under, like Ward's went under with the demise of the Ropes boom and no more was heard of the greatest amusement park in the South.

On Ward Island, it was back to duck-hunting, and farming. Martin Pearse, who was born in New Zealand and emigrated to the U.S. with his parents when he was 17, owned a farm north of the Oso. In 1926, he bought about half of Ward Island and farmed it. By 1942, there were a dozen summer cottages on Ward Island where people stayed to fish, swim and sun-bathe on one of the most beautiful sites on the Texas coast.

In his time, John Ward imagined turning the island into a tourist resort. "Uncle Elmer" and fellow investors envisioned turning it into a big amusement park. But no one could have guessed what the U.S. government had in store for the island.

In 1942, after the Naval Air Station was built, the government condemned Ward Island and paid the property owners $143,406 for 23 parcels of land. The summer cottages were moved or torn down. A high wire fence was erected around the island, excluding Ocean Drive, and Navy and Marine sentries patrolled the fence and manned the gatehouse. A sign warned that it was a restricted military zone.

What was going on out on Ward Island? It was a big secret, hush-hush. There was plenty of news coverage of the Naval Air Station, under rules of wartime censorship, but of Ward Island there

Aerial view of Ward Island in March 1965 when it was occupied by the University of Corpus Christi.

was not a peep. People in Corpus Christi only learned after the war what the big secret was.

Beginning in 1942 the Navy operated a radar training school on Ward Island. Even when supplies arrived with a bill of lading addressed to "Radar Island," people in town didn't know what it meant. Where was Radar Island? After the base was commissioned on July 1, 1942, until the end of the war, 10,000 Navy personnel were trained on "Radar Island." In 1947, the school was closed, the base deactivated, and the Navy moved its operations to the Memphis Naval Air Station at nearby Millington, Tenn.

With the Navy's departure, Ward Island was leased for $1 a year by the Baptist General Convention to establish the University of Corpus Christi. Classes began in January 1948 in the wooden buildings that had been used for radar and electronics training. Of all the possibilities for Ward Island — a tourist resort, an amusement park, a military base — this was the best outcome.

In fairness, you can't summarize what happened to Ward Island since then, but I will try. The University of Corpus Christi was acquired by Texas A&1 in 1972 and in 1993 Corpus Christi State University became Texas A&M University-Corpus Christi. Ward

Island was clipped and styled and transformed into the modern university campus we know today.

There was a misguided effort in 1953 to change the name of Ward Island to University Island or to University Heights (funny, when you consider that Ward Island is as flat as a floor). Today, everything that was Ward Island has been made over, built over and took over by the university for purposes that we all endorse. What once had been a duck hunter's paradise is covered with a complex of modern buildings and the most exotic creatures seen today are pink-haired back-packing students on skateboards. The university holds complete sovereignty of Ward Island. Only the name remains.

— Feb. 6, 2013

END OF THE LINE

Horse-drawn cabs operating in Corpus Christi in the 1880s were called Herdics, after Peter Herdic, a wealthy Pennsylvania lumber baron who invented them in 1881. The St. James Hotel advertised that "Herdics pass the house to and from the depot." The four-wheel cabs carried 10 passengers and featured side seats and a rear entrance.

Corpus Christi got a steam-powered railway in 1890 during the Ropes boom when Elihu H. Ropes, a land speculator from New Jersey, was trying to develop a deepwater port on Mustang Island. Among his many projects, he built the Alta Vista Hotel at Three-Mile Point and constructed his own transit system to carry passengers from downtown to his luxury hotel.

In May 1890 a shipment of rails arrived and workers started grading the route from Tiger Street near the Courthouse down Chaparral. When completed, the track stretched from the Miramar Hotel on North Beach to the Alta Vista Hotel six miles away. In June, a trial run was made. The coaches were pulled by a steam locomotive called a steam dummy railway. The steam engine was enclosed to make it look like a railroad passenger coach. Reporting on the trial run, the Caller said no horses were frightened and no one's eyes were filled with cinders. When the Ropes' line opened on a Sunday, the Caller reported that "it was simply impossible to accommodate everybody, so large and unexpected was the rush."

After the Ropes boom collapsed in 1893, the railway was sold at a sheriff's sale, ending up in the hands of Norwick Gussett. He replaced the steam engine with mule teams, finding hay cheaper than coal. The Gussett Street Railway had six miles of track, 16 mules and six cars. When the cars reached the end of the line at Three-Mile Point or North Beach, the driver would unhitch the mules and re-hitch them on the other end.

In 1898, Gussett sold the line to P. A. Graham, who cut it down to one car pulled by two mules, one white and one yellow, and on some days Graham ran the mule car on Chaparral, but he would disappear for days at a time. He was out of business by 1900.

For the next decade, Corpus Christi had no public transit system, until the arrival of Daniel Hewitt, a railway promoter from Tyler. He founded the Corpus Christi and Interurban Railway Company, the city's first electric trolley line. Local electric railways were called "interurban" at the time.

Hewitt laid tracks on wooden blocks on the unpaved streets with copper wires strung above. The line began operations with four cars and electric power purchased for three cents per-kilowatt hour, from the Peoples Light Co. The first run was made on March 28, 1910.

A year later, Hewitt moved to Cleburne and sold his Corpus Christi line to the Heinley brothers of Denver, who had achieved some success with a street railway in Salina, Kansas. V. S. (Vinton Sweet) Heinley ran the operation while his brother Earl, a wholesale grocer, would visit to check on his investment. V. S. Heinley built a power plant that ran on Mexican oil and added three cars. The seats ran down the sides, except for one open car that had rows of vrtical seats, which was used in the summer on the North Beach run.

Four years later, the Heinley brothers sold out to a Philadelphia syndicate. The new owners changed the name to the Corpus Christi Railway and Light Company, added eight cars and extended the lines. One major change was to install coin boxes which eliminated the job of conductor.

One line in 1915 ran from the City Drug Store at Mesquite and Starr to North Beach. The South Bluff ended at Third and Booty. One line ran to the Segrest and Rabbit Run area. Another was the Paul Court run, at Lipan and 13th. A fifth line ran to the Nueces Bay Heights, now known as the Hillcrest area. After the Epworth League moved to Port O'Connor, they changed the name of the Epworth run to the North Beach run.

There were plans for a second streetcar line in 1916 when local investors planned to develop Ward Island into an amusement park and the plan called for building a streetcar line. The construction of the Ward Island Interurban Line was well underway when the 1916 storm hit and soon afterwards the Ward Island project went under.

Corpus Christi's streetcar system was a losing venture until an Army training post was established in the Del Mar area in 1916.

V. S. and Earl Heinley of Denver, who had started a successful street railway project in Salina, Kan., purchased the Corpus Christi and Interurban Railway Company from Daniel Hewitt in 1911. The Heinleys added three new cars to the line and built their own power plant.

With thousands of soldiers stationed at Camp Scurry, the trolley business took off. Between the summer of 1916 and March of 1917, the number of riders exceeded one million. It was the golden age of streetcars in Corpus Christi.

That golden age ended with the 1919 storm. After the storm, the railway was virtually destroyed, with damaged cars, the car barn all but destroyed, and the power plant knocked out. With streetcars out of operation, a Jitney service was established, with Model-Ts, Buicks and Overland touring cars used along the street railway's fixed routes. It cost 10 cents for adults and five cents for children under seven to ride the Jitneys.

By Nov. 19, 1919, the streetcars were put back in operation and the Caller rejoiced. "The clang of the gong as the cars sped down the street brought smiles to the faces of many and remarks could be heard that the city seemed to be getting back to old times."

The old times didn't last long. Within two years, the system went receivership and the electrical plant caught fire. The streetcar system was reorganized, but the golden age was over. It wasn't the storm or the destruction of the electrical plant that killed the trolley system, but the growing love affair with the automobile, as more

243

In the 1920s, a streetcar was traveling south on Mesquite between Peoples and Schatzel. On the left was City Hall and on the right was the State National Bank.

people acquired their own means of transportation. Various attempts to revive the system failed and on Jan. 31, 1931, the last trolley car reached the end of the line in Corpus Christi. The streetcars were sold to Laredo. The clackety-clack as wheels hit rail junctures and the clang-clang of the warning bells were heard no more.

— Feb. 13, 2013

THE NUECES HOTEL

Of Corpus Christi's famous hotels, like the St. James and Seaside, the most famous was the Nueces, the city's pride and glory when it opened 100 years ago in 1913. It was too big, too ambitious, too much hotel for a town of 10,000, but local investors believed the city was being held back because it lacked a first-class hotel.

The Nueces Hotel was certainly first class when it opened in 1913. The six-story building, the tallest south of San Antonio, was built at Chaparral and Peoples for $413,000. The hotel boasted more than 200 rooms, an elegant ballroom, Sun Parlor and Tropical Gardens. In the foyer were imitation marble columns finished with a process called Scagliola. Italian specialists used Egyptian reeds and exotic oils to polish the columns which were similar, I have read, to those in the courthouse at Corsicana.

The Sun Parlor featured Victorian decor and wicker furniture. Later, in winter seasons, the Sun Parlor was converted to the Palm Room with its own dance floor and "Sphere of Fire," a revolving globe made of tiny mirrors reflecting light. Besides the Sun Parlor and Palm Room, the hotel was known for its Peacock Alley, with colorful draperies and period design chairs, and the Tropical Garden, enclosed by a lattice fence overgrown with vines.

A year after it opened, room rates were listed at $1 and up. In 1919, W. W. Jones bought out the other investors. It was also the year of the most destructive hurricane in the city's history.

Lucy Caldwell, a schoolteacher from Ennis, described the storm from the hotel, one of the few safe places below the bluff that night. It was dark inside and outside the hotel Sunday evening, Sept. 14, as survivors rushed in, their clothes ripped away by the force of the storm. "Each had a more horrible tale than the preceding one, of floating on doors and mattresses, of helping rescue women and children, of seeing bodies swept into the bay." As the storm raged, doors and windows were crashing in and dark waters were rising in the lobby. At the height of the storm, between 10 o'clock and 2:30 a.m., "the water on Chaparral stood 10½ feet and in the hotel lobby it stood even with the top of the desk."

Three years later, in 1922, Clarence O'Rourke, called the human fly, scaled the side of the hotel. At the top, he dangled, seeming to lose his grip, before catching hold and stopping his fall. The performance was repeated at night with a searchlight playing on him as climbed the walls.

Theodore Fuller in "When the Century and I Were Young" wrote that the Nueces provided comforts suitable for visiting millionaires and a gathering place for the local elite. "St. Cecilia's Orchestra played for dancing every evening in the summer and once a week the rest of the year. The Nueces couldn't depend on the local power plant to furnish its electricity. Nobody thought it strange that it had its own power plant because it was the Nueces."

A well-known bootlegger during Prohibition was a bellhop at the Nueces called "Old Dan." When he was tried for bootlegging, the judge lectured him for charging $6 for a bottle of tequila. "But, Judge," Dan pleaded, "everybody is getting six dollars for tequila. You know that."

After the port opened in 1926, a new hotel was built on the bluff, the Plaza, later renamed the White Plaza. To compete, the Nueces added a 103-room wing. When the Plaza site was cleared, three palm trees in the yard of the Redmond house were moved to the lawn of the Nueces Hotel garden. The stately palms became the emblem on the hotel's menu cards and stationary. Someone called them Faith, Hope and Charity. The hotel called them Tres Palmas.

Over the years, famous guests at the Nueces included Gen. "Black Jack" Pershing and, supposedly, though details are scarce, Bonnie and Clyde once stayed there, incognito of course.

About 5 p.m. on Nov. 17, 1932, a hotel barber, Henry Rudd, was shaving W. W. Jones when they heard gunshots. Jones, owner of the hotel, ran through the lobby up to the mezzanine where the hotel manager, Arthur Dowd, had been shot to death in his office. The killer, Isaac Davis, was the husband of a maid who had been fired. He shot Dowd eight times. Less than two weeks after the shooting, on Nov. 26, Davis was found guilty after a two-day trial and assessed the death penalty.

When the Naval Air Station was being built and hotels were packed, the Nueces put up extra cots in its famous Sun Parlor.

The lobby of the Nueces Hotel in the 1930s. Columns in the foyer were imitation marble finished with a process called Scagliola.

During the war, one of the more serious fights occurred at a Junior Coed dance in the Tropical Garden of the Nueces. About 150 civilians and sailors clashed in a brawl when a sailor was refused admittance to the dance. Several people were injured and a sailor received a bad cut on his neck from a broken bottle. After the incident, city police and Navy Shore Patrol stepped up their presence downtown.

A 1952 ad listed a week's menu at the Nueces. On Sunday, there was roast hot house baby lamb with mint sauce; Monday, casserole of chicken and dumplings; Tuesday, corned beef and cabbage; Wednesday, old-fashioned chicken-pot pie; Thursday, American pot roast with Jardinière Sauce; Friday, redfish steak with Maitre d' Hotel; and Saturday, veal cutlet with Noodles Polonaise.

The hotel fell on hard times. In 1961 it was sold for $501,000 and later converted into a retirement home. The final blow came on Aug. 3, 1970. The hotel, which sheltered survivors in the 1919 storm, was damaged by Hurricane Celia and condemned by the city. Reportedly, there was a danger of falling brick, but they were ready to pull the old building down and perhaps storm damage provided a useful fiction.

247

The enlarged Nueces Hotel, about 1930, showing the "Tres Palmas" in the garden. The hotel was enlarged to compete with the new Plaza hotel on the bluff.

The Nueces was razed in 1971 and its contents auctioned. People bought bits and pieces of the famous old hotel. Dick Swantner paid $2,600 for the marble-faced clock from the lobby and donated it to the Museum, where it is today. Time caught up with the grand old Nueces, once the pride of Corpus Christi. We can visit it now in the only place left — the pages of history.

— Feb. 20, 2013

STREET NAMES — 1

Ever wondered about the background of some of Corpus Christi's street names, like why is it called Cooper's Alley? Who were Peoples, Schatzel, Belden, and Mann?

Cooper's Alley was named for J. M. Cooper, a well-digger from Alabama who arrived in 1848 to dig artesian wells on Henry Kinney's Rancho del Oso and for the town. The story of how Cooper's Alley got its name reminds us, if we needed a reminder, that Corpus Christi has struggled with droughts throughout its long history.

As Maria Blucher wrote in a letter to her parents in Germany in 1852, "Drought has depleted the grass and our pond is half dried out. The town's artesian well is always being dug, dug, dug. The digger, however, gets $2 a day and free board in Kinney's house. This fellow has plenty of time, has been digging four years already, and always says, 'In a fortnight there will be water!' "

J. Williamson Moses told a story about Cooper, described as a God-fearing church deacon who did not smoke, gamble or drink. A no-account gambler named Wash Foster convinced Cooper to lend him $50. Foster promised to repay him the next Saturday. Weeks passed, then Cooper demanded that Foster repay the debt. Foster said there was only one way he could get $50. Some ranchers were in town and there would be a game of three-card monte. Foster asked for $25 to stake him to the game. Cooper, reluctantly, gave him the money.

Next day, Foster saw Cooper go into the post office. As the deacon was talking to a member of his church, Foster walked up and said: "Our partnership was in good feather last night. We won $100 clear. Without counting expenses, such as liquor and cigars, that leaves $100 and these five decks of cards. But knowing you don't have any use for the cards, you're entitled to half the money." Moses said it took Cooper a long time to live down the scandal.

Gen. David E. Twiggs, from about 1860 to 1862. Twigg Street was named for the general, who was with Zachary Taylor's army in Corpus Christi in 1845-46. (From the Library of Congress.)

Henry Kinney, the town's founder, laid out the town's early streets. On an 1852 street map, Kinney spelled Broad Way as two words and added the proud notation that it was 166 feet wide. Kinney named streets for friends, relatives, important generals, and a man who loaned him money. Two cross streets were named for Zachary Taylor and David Twiggs, generals here before the Mexican War when half the U.S. Army was camped at Corpus Christi. The city misspelled Twiggs' name by dropping the "s."

Kinney named Chipito Street for his faithful spy, Chipito Sandoval. When Taylor's army was at Corpus Christi, Gen. Taylor relied on Sandoval for news of Mexican army movements. One of Taylor's senior commanders, Ethan Allen Hitchcock, noted in his diary that he visited Kinney with Taylor. "As I left I met Chepeta, Kinney's spy, just in from the Rio Grande. He heard that Mexican troops are approaching Matamoros."

Kinney named Schatzel Street for John Peter Schatzel, a wealthy merchant engaged in the Mexican trade who was the honorary U.S. consul at Matamoros. When he was in Mexico, Schatzel loaned money to the Mier prisoners, survivors of the black bean drawing, when they were released. Schatzel's loans allowed them to buy clothes and pay for their passage back to Texas. He was tireless in his efforts to have them freed and then paid for their return. He never collected on his Mier debts.

After Schatzel moved to Corpus Christi, he loaned Kinney $45,000 to put on the Lone Star Fair. Schatzel wasn't here long, from 1850 until he died in 1854, but his name survives in local usage because of the street.

Next to Schatzel, running to the bay, is Peoples Street. It was named after John Peoples, a former Mexican War correspondent who became editor of the Corpus Christi Star. In February 1849, Peoples joined a party of 49ers going to the California gold fields. He drowned crossing the Gulf of California.

Starr Street was named for James Harper Starr, treasury secretary of the Republic. Some old street maps show it as "Star." Mann and Belden streets were named for William Mann and Frederick Belden, wealthy merchants involved in the Mexican trade. Mann was a former customs inspector at Aransas City who moved to Corpus Christi in 1845. He built a store, residence and warehouse complex on Water Street called Mann's red house, for the red clay used in making the shellcrete bricks. Belden moved to Corpus Christi from Matamoros in the 1840s. During Zachary Taylor's encampment, Capt. W. S. Henry dined at the Beldens where he ate a dish he called "themales, made of corn meal, chopped meat, and cayenne pepper wrapped in a corn husk, and boiled. I know of nothing more palatable."

Kinney named Brewster Street for Dwight Brewster, who married his sister, Emily Catherine Kinney. Kinney's other sister in Corpus Christi was Anna Lucy Kinney, who married attorney Walter Merriman. Aubrey Street was named for William Aubrey, Kinney's partner when they established the trading post in 1839, and he named Lawrence after his doctor, D. H. Lawrence; Buddy Lawrence Drive was named for his grandson.

Chaparral, Corpus Christi's main street, was often called Front Street. This photo from the 1890s, looking north, showed the Corpus Christi National Bank on the left, at the corner of Schatzel and Chaparral.

One of Kinney's original street names, Laguna, was named for the arroyo that drained from Kinney's Tank on the bluff down to the bay. The name was changed to Sartain after policeman John Sartain, who was killed in 1971 by a sniper at the old police station. The sniper was 16-year-old Richard Ridyolph who boasted to friends, "I got me a cop." He was sentenced to 50 years in prison and paroled in 1984.

Among the first streets Kinney named were Leopard, Buffalo, Antelope, Lobo, Oso, and Mestina. Tiger Street was later changed to North Broadway. Kinney named streets after Indian tribes, including Carancahua, Tancahua, Comanche, Lipan, Waco, and even a Lake Michigan tribe, Winnebago. He named streets Carrizo, Mesquite, Chaparral. For a time, Carrizo, Mesquite and Tancahua were spelled Carisa, Mezquit and Tankhua.

Eli Merriman once noted that when he was a boy there were three main streets in Corpus Christi, Chaparral, Mesquite and Water streets, but people rarely used the names Chaparral and Mesquite. They were mostly called Front and Back streets.

— Feb. 27, 2013

STREET NAMES — 2

Corpus Christi's downtown streets were named by Henry Kinney, who laid them out in 1852, and after Kinney's time city officials named streets for mayors, businessmen, and other civic leaders.

Doddridge was named for Perry Doddridge, who came to Texas from Lower Peachtree, Ala. He was a wool merchant who opened the first bank in Corpus Christi in 1871 and was elected mayor on the People's Ticket in 1873. Mitchell Street was named for Mayor J. B. Mitchell and Neal Street was named for Benjamin F. Neal, lawyer and newspaperman who was the city's first mayor, elected in 1852. During the Civil War, he presided over the Chipita Rodriguez trial and sentenced her to be hanged.

Born Street was named for E.A. Born, who developed the city's electric system and was one of the first to use crude oil to generate power. Staples Street was named for Wayman N. Staples, who owned a store and packing house at Packery Channel and served a term as major. Like Doddridge, he was also a native of Alabama. After Market Hall was built and gave him too much competition, Staples sold out and moved to Alice.

Staples Street past today's Six Points was officially named Colorado but was called Dump Road. During the Ropes Boom in the 1890s, capitalist developer E. H. Ropes planned to build a railroad to Brownsville and rails and ties were dumped at the end of Staples; hence Dump Road.

Alta Vista Road led to the Alta Vista Hotel, another product of the Ropes Boom. Fourth Street, which turned into Alta Vista Road, became Santa Fe. Ropes named streets in his Ocean Drive development for states, including Louisiana, Indiana, Ohio. Popular myth held they were named for National Guard units at Camp Scurry in World War I, but they were named by Ropes two decades before. Ropes Street, named after the promoter, was first called Scott.

The promoter E.H. Ropes in the early 1890s named streets in his Ocean Drive development for states, including Louisiana, Indiana and Ohio. They were not, as popularly believed, named for National Guard units stationed at Camp Scurry.

Chamberlain was a major street leading out of town to the south, but at some point the name was changed to Alameda. The names of pioneer families can be found in Dunn, Blucher, Bluntzer, Ayers, Bagnall, McBride, Kaler, and Furman streets, among many others. Cole Street was named for E. Barnes Cole, real estate dealer who bought and sold the land that became the Del Mar and Lindale subdivisions. Cole donated the land for our premier bayfront park.

Kostoryz was named for Stanley Kostoryz, who bought the Grim Ranch in 1904 and resold the land to Czech farmers. Gollihar, Weber, Everhart and McArdle were named for farmers and prominent landowners in the area. Ennis Joslin Road was named for Ennis Joslin, chairman of Central Power & Light and one of the developers of Padre Staples Mall. Joslin joked that he got a lot of ribbing about "that crooked road named for me."

Rand Morgan was named for Randolph Morgan, a farmer in the Saxet area. I don't know the origin of the name for Morgan Street. It might have been named for Col. James N. Morgan, a local Confederate officer who owned a livery stable in Corpus Christi after the Civil War. Or it might have been named for shipping tycoon Charles Morgan, whose Morgan Line ships made Corpus Christi a port of call. But if Morgan Street was named for the shipping tycoon, I doubt he was impressed, since a thriving port city in Louisiana, Brashear, changed its name to Morgan City in his honor.

City Council members have always been a threat to historic street names. They were in 1912 when they changed Tancahua Street to Pleasant Street and Carancahua to Liberty. You can still find tile insets with the Liberty Street name on Carancahua. The names were changed on April 5, 1912 then changed back on Sept. 12, 1913.

Several of the 1912 changes remained, including Bluett to Mary Street, Rogers to Marguerite, Ladd to Agnes. Other names were changed later. Gussett Street, for wool merchant Norwick Gussett, became 10th Street. Lott Street, for railroad builder Uriah Lott, became 12th Street. About the same time, the City Council changed Chatham Street, an old name that came from Chatham's Ravine, to Blucher Street. Railroad Avenue was changed to Kinney Street.

World War II gave us several street names. Davis Street, named for Reconstruction Gov. E. J. Davis, was changed to Brownlee for Billy Jack Brownlee, killed at Pearl Harbor. Langley was changed to Rodd Field Road to honor Herbert Rodd, a pioneer naval aviator. Waldron Road was named for John Charles Waldron, commander of a Navy torpedo squadron that led the attack on the Japanese fleet at Midway. Waldron, who was part Sioux, was killed in the attack.

Many names have traceable origins, while others are obscure. Why is there a Calamity Drive? An Arctic Circle? Others are clear enough. A pandering City Council gave us Corn Products Road, Southern Minerals Road, Whataburger Street and Shopping Way. The road from Corpus Christi to the Naval Air Station was designated Lexington Boulevard, after the aircraft carrier, in 1941. The name was changed to South Padre Island Drive in 1966 to emphasize the link to the new Padre Island National Seashore.

Aberdeen Street was named for the Aberdeen community, out past the area once known as the Chautauqua Grounds. Don Patricio Drive was named for Patrick Dunn, the Duke of Padre Island, and

Mesquite Street, often called Back Street, looking south about 1895. Uehlinger's Bakery was on the right. The two-story building with the buggy in front was Ritter's Bazaar.

Bascule Drive was named for the old bascule bridge which was replaced by the Harbor Bridge.

Timon Boulevard on North Beach was named for Walter Timon, longtime county judge. There was a Garner Street on North Beach, named for Vice President John Nance Garner, who once represented Corpus Christi in Congress and was instrumental in getting a deepwater port for the city. As I have written before, no member of Congress did more for Corpus Christi than "Cactus Jack" Garner, yet, at some point, the name of the street in his honor was changed. I don't know when or why.

Street names give us an insight into the past. Corpus Christi's history is recorded in shorthand in the name of its streets, which is why city officials should be very reluctant to change old place names. Wiping out historic names that belong to the city's rich history make us all poorer.

— March 6, 2013

PADRE ISLAND — 1

The recorded history of Padre Island began with a real tragedy. A fleet of Spanish galleons sailed from Veracruz on April 9, 1554 for Seville loaded with gold and silver from the mines at Zacatecas. It was a treasure fleet, Plata Flota, the silver fleet. Caught in an early storm, the Santa Maria de Yciar, San Estebán, and Espíritu Santo wrecked on the long white island, Isla Blanca. One ship made it back to Veracruz to tell of the loss of the treasure fleet.

When the ships ran aground, 300 crewmen, soldiers, priests and passengers, including women and children, struggled ashore. Some swam to the San Estebán and brought back arrows and two crossbows. They agreed to walk to a Spanish settlement, thinking they were three days from Tampico, but they were about 40 walking days instead of three.

On the seventh day, Karankawa Indians attacked. Soldiers with the crossbows killed three Indians and wounded more. When the Karankawas retreated, the ship survivors began their walk down the island. They didn't carry much food.

After five days, they ate shellfish on the beach and licked dew from island grasses, not knowing an elementary fact that fresh water could be found by digging in the sand two or three feet below where a layer of freshwater rests on the saltwater. The Indians returned to the attack and many of the Spanish were killed. Children cried, but their mothers were too weak to carry them. The blazing sun aimed daggers at them.

The Karankawas captured two stragglers, made them undress, then let them go. The Spanish thought it was their clothes the Indians wanted, so they undressed and piled their clothes on the sand. Women and children were sent ahead for safety, since the attacks came from the rear, but the Indians went around and killed them all.

At Brazos Pass, the men made rafts of driftwood to get across. One man, tired of lugging his belongings, meant to throw them away but he threw the bundle overboard that held the crossbows. Without protection, almost all the men were slain. Of the 300 who began the flight of terror, two survived. One escaped and returned to the shipwreck and another badly wounded man made it to Tampico.

A salvage fleet anchored at the site of the shipwreck and divers brought up the silver and gold bullion from the San Estebán, which was easily found with its masts above water. The Santa Maria de Yciar and Espíritu Santo were found by dragging a chain between two ships. Most of the treasure was recovered and sent to Seville.

Centuries passed and in 1804 Padre José Nicolás Ballí received a grant for 51,000 acres, a third of the island, for about $40. Padre Ballí established Rancho Santa Cruz 27 miles from the southern tip of what was called Isla de Corpus Christi. Padre Ballí left running the ranch to his nephew, Juan José Ballí II. The Ballís had a thousand head of cattle on what was called Padre Ballí's island. After the padre died in 1829, his nephew ran the ranch until it was destroyed by a hurricane on Aug. 4, 1844.

When Zachary Taylor's army was concentrated at Corpus Christi, the general sent several reconnaissance patrols to explore the island in search of the best route to the Rio Grande. One patrol was led by Capt. William J. Hardee of the 2nd Dragoons and he was accompanied by Lt. Jacob E. Blake of the Topographical Engineers.

Capt. Nathan S. Jarvis, a surgeon, noted in his diary for Feb. 21, 1846 that Capt. Hardee's detachment in "proceeded as far as Brazos Santiago at the foot of the island and described the road the whole distance along the seashore as delightful, being perfectly smooth and hard and nearly in a straight line. They saw numbers of wild cattle on the lower part of the island (left from Padre Balli's ranch). On their march down they came across several skeletons that marked the spot where an encounter took place between some Mexicans and Caronkaway Indians . . . They also came across two skeletons lying on a ship's hatch to which they evidently had been lashed, as part of the lashings remained, and were doubtless the remains of shipwrecked persons."

In 1847, a schooner wrecked on the island carrying John V. Singer and family. He planned to establish a shipping business at Point Isabel when Singer, his wife and two children were caught in a storm and washed ashore on Isla del Padre Ballí. They built a house of driftwood and became a Crusoe-like family, growing vegetables, running cattle, and combing the beaches for salvage. The Singer homestead was on the site of Padre Ballí's Rancho Santa Cruz, which they called Las Cruces Ranch.

Lt. Blake, of the Topographical Engineers, noted in his report of the reconnaissance that there were two good fording places across the upper Laguna Madre, that the depth of water was not over a wagon axle tree, that the beach was hard and well adapted to transportation by wagon, but that there was little grass on the island and no good ford on the lower Laguna Madre. He said in his report, "Owing to lack of grass and difficulty of getting off at the southern end, the route is not desirable for horse or artillery."

Because of the scarcity of grass as forage for horses, Taylor took Blake's advice and chose to send his army down the inland route.

Helen Chapman, wife of an Army major, described her visit to the Singers. "Their house had been built by joint labor of their hands and all their furniture consisted of wood thrown upon the shore. The children are beautiful and perfectly healthy. The wife is a great, strong, muscular looking, good-humored woman; she helps him with his outdoor work."

On a trip to New York, Singer loaned his brother Merritt $500 to market his sewing machine. John later got a shipment at Brownsville, a Singer Sewing Machine, reputedly the first to arrive in Texas.

In the same neighborhood of Singer's Las Cruces Ranch, Richard King in 1854 bought more than 13,000 acres from a niece of Padre Ballí, though King never ran cattle on the island or made it an active part of his working ranch.

At the outbreak of the Civil War, Confederate authorities invited Singer, a Yankee of uncertain allegiance, to leave the island. He buried a clay jar filled with jewelry, gold and silver worth $60,000 to $80,000 and moved to Flour Bluff. Like others there, the Singers engaged in the salt trade. A salt works was located at Flour Bluff near the Laguna Madre.

Because of the blockade, salt became a valuable commodity. The South suffered for lack of salt, not only to season food but to preserve it. Salt was gathered on the shores of the Laguna Madre and Baffin Bay and transported on flat-bottom scows. Salt could be sold inland for $8 a bushel or traded for food. It was better than

In a timeless scene, lace-like waves lap at the long curving tide line on Padre Island in the 1930s.

Confederate dollars. After federal troops captured Mustang Island, efforts to stop the salt traffic intensified, with Union forces under orders to "dissolve the cargo if you cannot capture it." When the war ended, Singer tried to reclaim his buried treasure, but storms had changed the landscape and erased his landmarks. After his wife died and another hurricane in 1867 covered the ranch with sand, he gave up and left for Honduras. It may be that a storm one day will unearth an old clay jar filled with Singer's lost treasure.

— March 13, 2013

PADRE ISLAND — 2

After the Civil War, a Baptist preacher from Alabama named Carey Curry founded a community on Padre Island 17 miles below Corpus Christi Pass. Curry had two sons, Joe and Uriah ("Coot") and two daughters with husbands and families. Their place was called the Curry Settlement or the Settlement.

Curry was resourceful. "Not a piece of machinery was in the Settlement, not a manufactured tool, yet Mr. Curry made flues, mixing the mortar of sand and lime, contrived home-made implements, and made his own ox-carts," according to the book "Padre Island." Other families at the Settlement included the Woods, Dinns, Griffins and Chapas.

Wild cattle left from Padre Ballí and John Singer ranches grazed on sedge grass and foraged in the surf. W. N. Staples and John King built a beef packing house that shipped out hides, tallow and horns while the meat was dumped in Packery Channel. About this time, J. T. Lyne established a community above the Curry settlement, seven miles below Corpus Christi Pass. Lyne ran cattle on Padre and Mustang and managed the packing house at Packery Channel.

During Lyne's time, in 1876, a Corpus Christi man walked the length of the island. A. M. French, a surveyor, was working on a railroad in Mexico that went bankrupt and he and a man named James Hayes started walking home. In Brownsville they were told it would be an easy trip up the island, where they could get food and shelter at ranch houses on the way.

French wrote in his diary that when they started up the island on Friday, Feb. 4, a norther blew in and it turned very cold. That night, they built a fire. On Saturday, they found water and camped at an old corral (Singer's or Ballí's). They met a fellow traveler who had no blanket and they took him in.

On Tuesday, they ate a dead fish and on Wednesday killed a half-dead water turkey, which they consumed with relish. They killed a possum, which French described as good eating. On Thursday, they reached a house, which was unoccupied, and at the next house a woman cooked a meal for them. After breakfast on Saturday, they waded the Laguna Madre then sat on a log to dry out. They reached Kenedy's packing house at Flour Bluff and from there made it the last easy stage to Corpus Christi. After spending eight days walking up the island, almost perishing from cold and hunger, French decided Padre Island was a good place to stay away from.

Three years later, Patrick F. Dunn was 21 when he and his brother moved their cattle to the island, which Dunn said was the best ranch in the world. Dunn explained why he moved to the island. "In the early days, the range was free, there were no pastures, then people commenced building fences and buying land. My brother and I had some cattle and we had to go somewhere, so we went to Padre. At that time, a man named Healey had cattle on there."

In 1880, Dunn bought 400 head of cattle at White Point, trailed them to Flour Bluff and took them across the Laguna near Pita Island. Padre Ballí took his first herd across the Laguna on the lower end. Dunn's wading cattle were spooked by jumping redfish flashing silver in the sun.

After Dunn moved to the island, trail boss Hub Polley was hired to drive Healey's herd from Padre Island to Kansas. Polley traveled to Galveston, Indianola, and on to Corpus Christi where he bought supplies and arranged to have them delivered to Padre Island. His drovers crossed the Laguna on horseback. When food supplies were late in arriving, Polley's cowboys ate bird-egg omelets sprinkled with salt scraped from driftwood. It took them several attempts before they forced the herd to wade the Laguna and start up the long trail to Kansas.

It was also in 1880 when Will Anderson and Henry Palmer converted the abandoned packing shed at Packery Channel into a taxidermy plant to skin and cure birds. Plumes from roseate spoonbills were sold to New York fashion houses to decorate women's hats. Stuffed spoonbills, gulls, terns and pelicans were sold for mantel decorations. The business collapsed after Edward Bok, editor of the Ladies Home Journal, led a campaign to stop the slaughter of birds for fashion plumage. "I am absolutely opposed," he wrote, "to the use of egret feathers for millinery purposes." Women became ashamed to be seen dressed up in bird feathers and egret plumes.

Pat Dunn, known as the Duke of Padre Island, was the owner of a unique ranch on the island until 1926, when he sold out and moved into the Nueces Hotel.

The main focus on the island was ranching. Pat Dunn established four cattle stations on his ranch, with corrals and holding pens. Number one, at the head of the island, was Owl's Mott, number two was Novillo, three was at Black Hill, and four was at Green Hill, the highest elevation on the island. The white-faced cattle grew fat from sedge grass and whatever they could find in the surf. Their hides showed spots of tar from the tar blobs that wash up on the beaches.

After Dunn began his ranch, families at the Curry Settlement began to drift away; hardly any traces were left of the Settlement by the end of the 19th Century.

In the 1916 storm, hands on Dunn's ranch rode out the storm on Green Hill. "We lay there flat and watched all that water, and prayed," one ranch hand remembered. "It was like the whole ocean crashing in."

Pat Dunn's ranch house and corral on Padre Island in 1950. After the 1916 hurricane destroyed his two-story home near Packery Channel, Dunn built this ranch house at the head of the island.

Pat Dunn still spent most of his time on the island, except during legislative sessions when he was obliged to live in Austin. In 1926, a tourist resort. Dunn moved to town and stayed at the Nueces Hotel. To the end of his days, he regretted selling the island, explaining that life on the island meant freedom, as defined by the lack of alternatives, and he wished he had it back. He died on March 25, 1937. The death of the man called the Duke of Padre Island marked the end of a chapter in the history of the long white island and the beginning of another.

— March 20, 2013

PADRE ISLAND — 3

Sam Robertson, an engineer from Missouri, got the contract to lay tracks and build trestle bridges from Robstown to the border for the St. Louis, Brownsville & Mexico Railroad, the "Brownie," because he was known as a tough man who finished tough jobs.

Robertson showed how tough he was. In a derailment at Santa Gertrudis, he broke both legs and several ribs, but stayed on the job, learning to use crutches with such agility he could catch a moving train. He taught his horse to kneel like a camel so he could get in the saddle with crutches. He was still hobbling when the railroad was completed to Brownsville in 1904. Robertson went on to found San Benito, served as a scout for Army forces chasing Pancho Villa, and enlisted in World War I, where he went to France as a colonel in command of the 22nd Railroad Engineers.

Back home after the war, Robertson had plans for the last frontier in Texas, Padre Island. He was one of the first to understand the island's great appeal. With three investors from Kansas City, he bought the island from Patrick F. Dunn with plans to develop both ends of the island. He planned to build a 110-mile toll road down the length of the island, called the Ocean Beach Driveway, and he built the Don Patricio Causeway from below Flour Bluff to the island, named in honor of Pat Dunn.

The wooden causeway built on pilings opened on July 4, 1927. Robertson drove the first automobile across. For the first time, the mainland was joined to the island and a steady stream of traffic crossed the causeway, 1,800 cars the first month and 2,500 the next.

During this time, when Prohibition was the law, jettisoned cargoes of whisky washed ashore on the island. In the Civil War, salt was the contraband on the island; now it was whisky. Louis Rawalt, who lived in a shack on the island, wrote about an incident when a smuggler was chased by a Coast Guard cutter and the captain dumped his cargo overboard.

Sacks filled with tin cans labeled insect spray, which contained bottles of "Old Hospitality" Bourbon, washed ashore. Rawalt hid 110 sacks in the dunes, then took a duffle bag with 72 bottles to Port Isabel, where he sold the whisky. On his way back home he saw the ferry captain driving back down the island in a pickup truck and Rawalt realized he had followed his tracks into the dunes and found the hidden whisky. It was all gone.

Besides the Don Patricio Causeway, Sam Robertson operated ferries at both ends of the island, built the first 12 miles of the toll road, built the Sportsmen's Hotel and the Twenty-Five-Mile Hotel. In 1931, a Brownsville man was staying at Robertson's Twenty-Five-Mile Hotel when he found a site 27 miles up from the lower end. Buried in sand were pieces of timber held together with ship hardware, a box stuffed with Spanish doubloons, Belgian coins, U.S. Army sword handles, and bullets from muzzle-loading guns. This, it was supposed, was the site of Padre Ballí's Rancho Santa Cruz and John Singer's Las Cruces Ranch.

Sam Robertson was wiped out by the Depression, followed by a hurricane in September 1933. The storm destroyed the Twenty-Five-Mile Hotel and demolished the Don Patricio Causeway; only the pilings were left. Robertson died five years later, on Aug. 22, 1938.

The Kansas City investors — Albert R. Jones, his brother Frank and J. M. Parker — acquired Robertson's holdings, taking possession of the colonel's land and dreams. The principal investor was Albert R. Jones, who bought out the other two.

Jones, a wealthy Kansas City oilman, believed Padre Island was a natural site for a multi-million dollar tourist resort, a Texas version of Miami Beach. He struck it rich by finding and developing oil and gas fields in Kansas, Oklahoma and Texas. He was an avid collector of famous paintings; he built a wing on his home in Kansas City for his world-class collection of art works. Jones became interested in Padre Island in the 1920s. He was a principal backer, if not the major backer, behind Sam Robertson's efforts to develop the island. It was largely Jones' money that built the Don Patricio Causeway and when Robertson ran into financial difficulties brought on by the Depression, Jones stepped in and bought his island holdings. Jones owned almost 90,000 acres on Padre Island.

In 1936, A.C. McCaughan, mayor of Corpus Christi, was among those lobbying to turn Padre Island into a state park. It was pushed

Col. Sam A. Robertson planned to build a world-class resort on Padre Island.

through the Legislature by W. E. Pope. Albert R. Jones offered to sell the state his 90,000 acres on the island for $4.50 an acre, $405,000 total. The bill was vetoed by Gov. James Allred, who spelled out his reasons: (1) He thought the state owned much of Padre Island and should not buy land it already owned. (2) He objected to buying land without acquiring the mineral rights. (3) The bill included plans for toll-financed causeways at the north and south end of Padre and he considered this indirect taxation. Allred's opposition killed plans to turn the island into a state park.

During the war, the island was off limits to visitors. Three large circular areas on the Gulf side, beginning near Packery Channel,

The Don Patricio Causeway to Padre Island opened on July 4, 1927. A round-trip crossing cost $3.00, before the causeway was destroyed by a hurricane in 1933.

stretching to the south, were used for aerial bomb practice. A fourth area reserved for gunnery practice was on the Laguna Madre side. It was said cattle from the late Pat Dunn's ranch, still grazing on the island, became so used to bombing sorties they would run in the opposite direction when they heard the drone of planes overhead.

The island was patrolled by the Coast Guard, which maintained observation stations every six miles, all linked by phone. Survivors from ships torpedoed by U-boats often washed up on the island and were rescued by the Coast Guard units. There's another story about Padre Island in World War II. In a test, the first atomic bomb was exploded near Los Alamos, New Mexico, on July 16, 1945. One of eight sites considered for that first atomic blast was Padre Island.

— March 27, 2013

PADRE ISLAND — 4

After the Don Patricio Causeway was destroyed by a hurricane in 1933, getting to the island on wheels meant a long trip, from Aransas Pass to Harbor Island to Port Aransas then driving down Mustang.

A rickety wooden causeway connected Aransas Pass to Harbor Island. From there, the ferry operated across the channel to Port Aransas. Corpus Christi Pass (Packery Channel now) separated Mustang and Padre. It was shallow enough to drive across, but at times of high water a man with a hand-poled ferry took cars across for a fee. Storms would open up the passes between Mustang and Padre, making it impossible to drive across.

After the war, Nueces County began planning to build a toll-financed causeway to the island, which, county officials believed, would jump-start growth on the island. The Don Patricio Causeway was the first to link the mainland to the island. The new Padre Island Causeway was the second. It was an elevated highway filled with sand dredged from the Laguna Madre. Construction included 3.8 miles of causeway, two swing bridges, one trestle bridge, five miles of highway on the island and one mile on the mainland.

On June 17, 1950, a brilliant summer day, the causeway was opened, with dignitaries as well as tourists from all over, in attendance. The first to pay the $1 car toll was Frank Morris, a cotton farmer from Portland, with a shell collector from Fort Worth in the second car.

In conjunction with building the causeway, Nueces County purchased the privately owned Port Aransas Causeway and built new ferry landings on Harbor Island and Port Aransas. With the cost of the causeway at $1.7 million, the county invested $3 million to spur growth on the island, and that was when $3 million was real money. (The state took over the renamed JFK Causeway and Port Aransas ferry operations in 1968).

While one million cars crossed over the causeway by Feb. 24, 1955, the county expected more visitors and more development. Some blamed bankers for refusing to extend credit to build on the island for fear of hurricanes. W. R. Swan, who represented Albert R. Jones and his partners' interests on the island, pointed out that Florida was hit by more destructive hurricanes than Texas but that had not stopped development on Florida's coastlines. But bankers in Texas could put their money on less risky ventures on the mainland, and they did. Why this rationale didn't prevail on South Padre was a mystery.

When Cameron County built the first Queen Isabella Causeway in 1954, development on South Padre quickly followed. A Corpus Christi real estate man, John L. Tompkins, frustrated by his inability to get anything accomplished on the northern end, turned to the southern tip, where he led the way in developing South Padre. In 1974, a new Queen Isabella Causeway was built to carry the ever-increasing volume of traffic between Port Isabel and the fast-growing resort on South Padre.

What was the difference between South and North Padre? A spokesman in 1956 attributed it to attitudes. "Up here, old-timers have not realized the tourist trade is big business. In the Valley, they are resort-minded and give it priority." Another explanation was linked to the Korean War. "The northern end of the island was the victim of a national situation which set it back before it got going. Seven months after the causeway opened, when enthusiasm was high, the government clamped down on all but essential construction, not knowing how long the Korean War would last. By the time the ban was lifted, the spirit of island enterprise was deflated."

Seven years after the causeway opening, development languished. Albert R. Jones had divided his holdings, selling off a half interest to four corporations organized by county boundaries. Of the four, the closest to Corpus Christi was the Padre Island Development Company, founded by M. E. Allison Sr., who purchased a big part of the island from Jones in 1946. The other three included the Laguna Madre Corporation in Kleberg County, the Baffin Bay Corporation in Kenedy County, and South Padre Inc. in Cameron County. Jones also gave some land to Nueces County for public parks in return for the county's investment in building the causeway. A year later, Jones died in Kansas City, at age 83.

Cars waited in line on June 17 for the opening of the new $1.7 million Padre Island Causeway (later renamed the JFK Causeway). A total of 4,800 cars passed the Flour Bluff toll gate in the first 36 hours.

In the 1930s, Jones offered to sell most of Padre Island to Texas for $400,000, or $4.50 an acre. After Congress passed legislation creating the Padre Island National Seashore and President Kennedy signed the measure in 1962, the government received 33,000 acres from Texas. It expected the remaining 100,000 acres to cost about $5 million.

However, with condemnation proceedings, it was left to Texas juries to set the per-acre value. Once the legal dust settled, the government paid $22 million for the land to Jones' heirs, M. E. Allison Sr., and other owners of the Padre Island Development Company, the Laguna Madre Corporation, the Baffin Bay Corporation, and South Padre, Inc.

This higher-than-expected price raised charges in Congress that greedy Padre landowners, abetted by Texas jurors, were ripping off the government. Rep. John Young, who represented Corpus Christi in Congress, explained the high land price. "The government does not pay for the land until four or five years after the legislation is passed; by that time the values have skyrocketed." Land the state was offered for $400,000 in 1936 ended up costing the federal government $22 million three decades later.

271

Once-remote Padre Island was a crowded scene on July 4, 1950 two weeks after the causeway opened. Tolls were collected as one million cars crossed over the causeway in its first five years.

Uncle Sam did not get as good a deal as Padre Ballí when he paid the Spanish crown the equivalent of $40 for 51,000 acres, a third of the island, but still it was a bargain. Maybe not a bargain for real estate — I wouldn't know — but a bargain for a wild place, the last frontier of Texas, where the sea answers every question the same way, where the waves wash up on the sand, as they have since the beginning of the world, and with the lacy fingers of a lady at tea grasp at the biscuit-colored sand. Backwards and forwards, reminding us that every beginning and every ending is arbitrary, something caught in motion that is already past. What scales can measure a bargain? The future will have a better answer to this question than we do.

— April 3, 2013

ANNA MOORE SCHWIEN

I have long been intrigued by Anna Moore Schwien, daughter of a slave, who related the events of her life before she died in 1946. She harbored no hostility about slavery, saying, "You can't go to heaven with bitterness in your heart." But who was she? There is a mystery about her. I have searched for the answer, reading through the files, looking for some evidence. But let's not get ahead of the story.

Her mother Malvina arrived in Corpus Christi in 1849. She was 29 years old, the slave of John Baskin. Baskin was in business with William Mann and Forbes Britton, who owned several ships carrying hides from Corpus Christi to Galveston. When the Baskin-Mann-Britton business dissolved and the assets were divided, among those Britton received, as property of the partnership, was the attractive slave Malvina.

Forbes Britton, a retired army officer, came to Corpus Christi in 1850. After West Point, he had been assigned Trail of Tears duty moving Cherokees and other Indians from Georgia and Alabama to Indian Territory. He married Rebecca Millard and they had twins; Britton called them his "dabs of fat." He was with Zachary Taylor at Corpus Christi in 1845. During the war in Mexico he was a friend of war correspondent George Wilkins Kendall. They would drink warm champagne from an army canteen. Britton resigned from the army in 1850 and moved to Corpus Christi, where he began a shipping and mercantile business linked to the Mexican trade.

Britton established a ranch on the Oso called Britton Motts, where Malvina was a maid. Anna in her recollections said, "Mother was fond of speaking about the days she spent at the Britton Ranch. Mr. Britton would serve sherry when company came and mother was always pleased to put on a fresh apron and carry in the tray with the wine."

Three years later, Malvina was pregnant and Britton sent her to a sheep ranch near New Braunfels owned by his friend Kendall. This

273

was unusual, to send a house servant far away to live on a rural ranch. Malvina gave birth to a daughter. In her recollections, Anna said, "I was born on May 15, 1856. Mrs. Georgina Kendall Fellowes, daughter of Mr. Kendall, verifies this date, as it was just after the Kendalls arrived at the ranch."

Britton then sent Malvina and baby to various ranches and they lived for a spell with Capt. Samuel Plummer's family at Fort Merrill. Anna said these were lonely times for her mother because the fort was isolated "and there were no friends with whom she could visit."

The story takes another twist. After 1858, when he arrived in Corpus Christi, John M. Moore purchased Malvina to be a wife for his slave Sam. This was unusual, but Moore was an unusual man. The kind slave master was mostly a myth made up by apologists of slavery, but for Moore it was no myth.

Before he came to Corpus Christi, Moore owned iron works near Birmingham; he shipped the first iron from Alabama to Pennsylvania. While he abhorred slavery, he had inherited slaves from his family, except for a few he bought out of compassion. One was a blind man who begged him to buy him. Another was an abused slave who had run away, but on hearing of his sale to Moore came out of hiding and remained a faithful servant. Moore moved to Corpus Christi to dredge a channel across the bay. Among the slaves who came with him was Sam. Moore and Sam had been together since they were children and were very close. So Moore bought Malvina Britton to be Sam's wife, long after the birth of Anna. In her memoirs, Anna said Sam Moore was her father. And yet . . .

When John M. Moore began dredging a ship channel across the bay in 1858, many of his slaves, including Sam, worked on a dredge boat. The work ended with the Civil War. Malvina took in laundry and was known as an excellent midwife. She had three daughters, including Anna, who were so well-behaved they were called Malvina's convent girls. They lived near the Bluchers on the bluff. "Büsse was an old German who lived on the Blucher place," Anna recalled. "He had a lovely garden. My mother's calves would stray over to his place and when I would go after them I would look through the gate at the beautiful flowers. Mother taught me it was all right to look at people's flowers through the fence, but that I must never reach my hand through to pick one."

Anna Moore Schwien in 1936 when she was 80 years old, photographed by Dorothea Lange, from the Library of Congress.

Anna attended a Freedmen's Bureau school, a school conducted by Mrs. John Dix, and a public school for colored children held in the old Mann home. She became a teacher of primary grades for black children and later in life turned to laundering. In 1881, Anna married a German, C. W. Schweine (also spelled Schwien), a waiter at the St. James Hotel. After being threatened for marrying what the newspaper called a mulatto woman, he skipped town. She never remarried and kept her husband's name for the rest of her life. She died at age 89 on April 19, 1946.

I suspect that Anna Moore Schwien was the daughter of Malvina and her master Forbes Britton, a state senator and one of Corpus Christi's most prominent citizens. It doesn't say this in any files or old letters that have surfaced, but it wouldn't. The lives of slaves and relations between masters and slaves were not recorded, were not even the subject of gossip. But isn't it curious that Britton would send a valuable house servant to a sheep ranch to have her baby? Isn't it curious that he kept the mother and baby away from his own home for several years? And isn't it curious that the woman

275

A young Forbes Britton in the early 1830s from the Fenwick Collection of the St. Mary's County, Md., Historical Society.

described as a mulatto was as proud of the Britton family as if it were her own? And perhaps it was.

We don't know for a fact that Forbes Britton was Anna's father. Another local historian suggests that Anna's father may have been one of Forbes Britton's sons. They would have been young teenagers at the time. Unless some evidence surfaces — and the truth about events in the gray world of the past is elusive — I have to settle for not knowing and leave the case of Anna Moore Schwien open. One thing we know for sure. She was a child of slavery.

— April 10, 2013

MIER Y TERÁN: TEXAS IN 1828

Seven years before the armies came, the government in Mexico sent one of its most promising officers to assess the problems in Texas, especially the problem of illegal immigration. The promising officer was Manuel de Mier y Terán, a perceptive man who wrote about Texas with intelligence and insight.

In early 1828, Mier y Terán traveled from Laredo to San Antonio to Nacogdoches and back to the coast with a large entourage and military escort. He kept a diary, published a few years ago — "Texas by Terán" — which I relied on. His diary doesn't begin until after San Antonio, but José María Sánchez, a member of the entourage, described the town in his diary.

San Antonio in 1828 had unpaved streets and buildings that showed no beauty, noted Sánchez, with two public squares, neither worthy of notice. What little commerce there was, he wrote, was carried on by foreigners (North Americans) and two or three Mexicans. From San Antonio, Terán wrote the president of Mexico, Guadalupe Victoria, advising that North Americans were flooding into Texas, with their families, their slaves, and their own ideas of what was politically acceptable. He warned that if Mexico did not stop the flow of illegal immigrants and if it could not satisfy these immigrants politically, the logical end would be the loss of a rich province.

Terán estimated the population makeup of Texas as composed of 25,000 Indians, 8,000 North Americans and 4,000 Mexicans (how he came by his numbers is not explained). He described North Americans as rapacious, profane, hard-working, and hard-drinking. He said they were haughty, shunning society by inclination, and while he admired their ability to get things done he feared their unquenchable vitality. As he understood it, what he admired most about the North Americans — their stubborn independence — was a serious threat to Mexico.

Of his fellow Mexicans, Terán displayed the prejudices of Mexico's ruling class, writing that Tejanos congregated in the towns of Béxar, La Bahia (Goliad), and Nacogdoches, that their livelihood depended on soldiers' pay, that they were underpaid, undereducated, and belonged to the "indigent and wretched class." While his prejudices were severe, they revealed the thinking prevalent in Mexico City about Tejanos and North Americans.

After leaving San Antonio, Terán's party camped on Salado Creek where they heard bullfrogs that night. Next day, they rode through sandstone hills. Fifty miles from San Antonio, they came across two carts loaded with pecans pulled by oxen and driven by North Americans. They stopped at the Guadalupe River, where the beauty of the country, Terán wrote, surpassed all description. At Gonzales, there were six log cabins "whose construction shows that those who live inside them are not Mexicans." The families raised corn and cotton and they had a few cows and oxen.

On the Colorado, they visited the home of Benjamin Beeson, who ran a ferry, had 60 to 80 head of cattle and cultivated a large field of corn. Terán ate cornbread, which he said resembled a thick tortilla.

At San Felipe de Austin, the land was cleared to grow cotton. The colonists told Terán they wanted to bring in slaves for the hard work cutting down trees and clearing the land. Since there were lawyers in the settlement, Terán observed, there was no lack of disagreement.

When they crossed the Neches, Terán noted that the river flowed in the same direction as all Texas rivers, northwest to southeast. They arrived in Nacogdoches, one of the trouble spots on the frontier, where they remained for several months.

In Nacogdoches, Terán found that the foreigners (North Americans) outnumbered the Tejanos 10 to one. Many of the foreigners, he wrote, were vicious men with evil ways, some fugitive criminals, and all of them were ambitious, aggressive and quick to claim the land by rights of first possession. The foreigners had great advantages over the Mexicans, which was a cause of growing friction. Commerce was controlled by North Americans while legal authority was in the hands of the Tejanos. The North Americans ran an English school and some sent their older children north for an education while "the poor Mexicans neither have the resources to create schools nor is there anyone to think about improving their institutions."

Manuel de Mier y Terán in 1828 warned Mexico about the threat posed by illegal immigrants from the U.S. Photo from "Texas by Terán."

"From this state of affairs an antipathy has emerged between Mexicans and foreigners that is not the least of the volatile elements I found," Terán wrote. "If timely measures are not taken, Tejas will pull down the entire federation."

On his way home, he stopped at the Groce plantation, with 105 slaves, and visited the colony of Martín de León (Victoria) where he found 42 "well-behaved" families from Tamaulipas, who raised cattle and tilled fields, but did not produce exportable products. Unlike the North Americans, Terán noted, they lived in town and traveled to and from their fields.

He found 300 people at La Bahia (Goliad) living "on a barren hill that lacks even firewood" and troops in the town reduced to abject poverty. He crossed the Nueces River, which he noted dried up in drought years, passed Agua Dulce and camped near the Santa Gertrudis creek. In this country, Terán said, he had to post sentries to keep watch or their pack horses would run off and join the herds of wild horses. They halted at the Arroyo Colorado where Terán bought a cow from a ranch for the soldiers, and later crossed the Rio Grande to Matamoros, a large town of 6,000 people.

After his tour of Texas, Terán outlined steps he thought should be taken, urging Mexico to stop all North American immigrants from coming into Texas, legal and illegal. He encouraged immigration from the interior of Mexico, especially from Yucatan, whose inhabitants he thought were as energetic as North Americans. He urged the establishment of penal colonies in Texas, offering free land to Mexican convicts on their release. Based on Terán's recommendations, Mexico closed the frontier to Anglo-Americans and no one from the U.S. could enter Texas without a visa, but it was too little too late.

Terán ended his life in 1834. A year later began the well-known cycle of revolutionary events that ended in the battle at a place called San Jacinto and Mexico's loss of Texas, which Mier y Terán warned about eight years before.

— April 17, 2013

KING RANCH BOURBON

Retired District Judge Max Bennett, who now lives in Weatherford, sent me the story of how King Ranch acquired its own supply of very special bourbon. This is the story. An interview was arranged with Robert J. Kleberg Jr. for the Caller-Times' book in recognition of the 1953 Centennial of King Ranch. James Rowe, an outstanding reporter, was assigned to do the interview. He told the story later to a group that met regularly at Price's Chef.

"Rowe said he drove over to the Big House and Mr. Bob met him at the door and took him into a large den. Mr. Bob asked him if he would like a drink. Rowe said yes. He told us he intended to have just a couple of sips and not jeopardize the interview.

"Mr. Bob rang a small bell and told a male servant that he and Rowe would like a drink. The servant returned with a tray with a cut glass decanter and glasses and Mr. Bob poured bourbon into Rowe's glass then completely filled his own.

"The interview went well. Mr. Bob emptied his glass more than once. Rowe took a few sips before the interview concluded and both were exchanging small talk. Then Rowe said he took a large swig of the bourbon and realized how good it was. He said, 'Mr. Kleberg, that is very good whisky. I was wondering where a fellow could buy a bottle.'

" 'Oh, Mr. Rowe, you couldn't buy a bottle of that bourbon. I bought it all.' "

Bennett later told the story to a Corpus Christi liquor store owner who said it was true, that a friend of Kleberg's introduced him to the bourbon that came from a small distillery in Kentucky and Mr. Bob contracted with the owner of the distillery to take the entire yearly production. To comply with existing laws, the bourbon had to come to Texas through a licensed liquor dealer.

Sometime ago, Bennett and J. P. Luby visited the King Ranch museum in Kingsville. "I was surprised to see an empty bottle of

281

James Rowe, a reporter for the Caller-Times, took a long sip of the King Ranch bourbon.

bourbon with a large Running W label on it. I told J. P. the story and another I had heard or read, that Mr. Bob wanted a large reception after his funeral and wanted his liquor and wine collection completely consumed by his friends who came to his funeral.

"Being raised in Kingsville, residing on King Street, attending King High, and living in the shadow of the great King Ranch, made for an interesting childhood," said Bennett. "Mr. Bob and I went to the same barber, a Mr. Filla on King Street, and on occasion I would see him there but he had little to say to Mr. Filla or anyone else. He wore his khakis stuffed into his worn boots when he was seen about town."

Robert J. Kleberg Jr. showed the art used for the Dec. 15, 1947 cover of Time Magazine.

Goliad Tornado

We are approaching the 111th anniversary of the tornado that struck Goliad on May 18, 1902. It killed 115 people, injured 230, and destroyed more than 100 buildings. I ran across an account of this terrible storm in the Corpus Christi Crony of May 24, 1902.

"Goliad's Calamity: Dozens of prominent Corpus Christi people were born in Goliad, hundreds have lived there, and many more possess relationships in the historic old town. So there was keen anxiety in Corpus Christi when, last Sunday afternoon, it was learned that a terrific wind had stricken many people and destroyed much property in Goliad.

"As usual in time of need, the Western Union telegraph wires did not operate. Not because of the storm, but because of the horribly bum equipment of the line for a hundred miles north of Corpus Christi. The Western Union telegraph wires running out of Corpus Christi are maintained in a way which would disgrace a razorback hogpen fence on a tenth-class ranch. At last, on Monday afternoon, by the kindness of the San Antonio Light, the Crony was enabled to publish a list of the dead and wounded as far as it was then complete.

283

Rev. J. J. Donaldson of the colored Congregational Church here was in Goliad during the storm. He was not in the devastated portion of the town at the time, but he saw it strike. Like everyone who witnessed it, he is not able to describe it. About all he remembers after the great cloud from the northwest met the stiff southeast gale, is a sight of broken timbers and flying rocks, a sound of agonized shrieks and crashing solids, all overwhelmed by the mad voice of the elements like the noise of escaping steam. He took part in the work of succor to the stricken, and he testifies that any rumored idea that even the humblest corpse was neglected in its turn is all without foundation. Whites and blacks and everybody worked together for the relief of suffering humanity or the decent bestowal of the dead. . . .

"Professor A. A. Brooks of this city was proprietor of the Goliad College, which for years was the educational center of South Texas. The only residence left standing in the wrecked portion of Goliad was one built in 1855 by Judge John S. McCampbell, now of Corpus Christi. Such facts make Corpus Christi particularly interested in Goliad."

— April 24, 2013

LAND FRAUD — 1

The first ranch in today's Nueces County went back a long way. It was established between 1762 and 1765 by Blás Maria de la Garza Falcón, founder of the Mexican town of Camargo.

Garza Falcón's ranch on Santa Petronila Creek was about 13 miles from the mouth of the Nueces River. He called it Rancho Real de Santa Petronila, stocked it with horses, cattle, sheep and goats, and moved his family from Camargo. This was part of José de Escandón's effort to colonize the territory from Tampico to San Antonio.

The ranch served as a jumping off place for exploring expeditions. On one, Garza Falcón's son Jose named Santa Gertrudis Creek for his daughter, Gertrudis de la Garza. A second expedition left the ranch in 1766 to look into rumors the English had landed on Padre Island. Diego Ortiz Parrilla led the expedition to explore the island. They found no trace of English intruders. His report refers to "the bay named Corpus Christi," the first reference to Corpus Christi Bay by that name.

Garza Falcón's ranch failed because of persistent Indian attacks. He moved his family back to Camargo, where he died in 1767. Six decades later, his great grandson, Blás de la Garza Falcón, returned to stake his claim to the family's old holdings.

In 1834, Blás de la Garza Falcón received a land grant from the governor of Tamaulipas for five and half leagues, or 24,000 acres, called the El Chiltipin grant. (The Spanish square league equals 4,428 acres. Land grants issued by the King of Spain, who personally owned all the land in Texas, were called Spanish land grants, dating from 1758 to 1829. Those issued by the Republic of Mexico, from 1829 to 1836, were called Mexican land grants.)

After Santa Anna's defeat at San Jacinto in 1836, Blás Falcón, like many Mexican ranchers in Texas, followed the retreating army to the other side of the river. Four years later, when things settled down, he returned to his ranch and visited Henry Kinney's new trading post at Corpus Christi.

In 1845, Blás Falcón signed a deed conveying his ranch to Henry Kinney and William Mann. (A detailed account of this can be found in Paul Shuster Taylor's book, "An American-Mexican Frontier: Nueces County, Texas," published in 1934.)

Blás Falcón, who could not read or write, signed what he thought was a mortgage in return for $500 in cash and goods. What he signed was a deed conveying his ranch to Kinney and Mann. Blás Falcón then went to work as a hired man on one of Kinney's ranches.

After Mann died in 1855, his heirs sued Blás Falcón for trespass and to try title. During the trial in 1858, a witness, Fermin Salas, testified that Blás Falcón told him he pawned his Chiltipin title papers for merchandise from Kinney and Mann. "I heard Kinney advise Blás Falcón that it would be better for him to give him the ranch as the Texans did not like him and were going to kill him. Kinney said he would be better able to defend Blás Falcón's property if he had the land." Salas said that once in 1852 he was with Mann receiving some cattle "when I heard Mann in conversation with Blás Falcón. Mann told Blás Falcón he was willing to give back his lands upon his paying what he owed, in horses or mules." Salas said he was present several times when Blás Falcón asked Kinney to give him back his title papers, but Kinney always had some excuse.

On June 25, 1858, the jury ruled that Kinney and Mann obtained Blás Falcón's ranch by fraud. The victory cost Blás Falcón more than a third of his 24,000 acres to pay his lawyer. Still, the victory in court did not end the attempt by Kinney to take away Blás Falcón's El Chiltipin grant.

In 1861, Kinney was broke and his attorney Simon Jones was pressing him to pay him what he owed. Kinney sent Jones, an interpreter and two witnesses to see Blás Falcón. Both witnesses — Martin Hinojosa and Chipito Sandoval — were Kinney's friends, longtime allies. The arrival of a lawyer, with an interpreter and witnesses, all bent on getting a signature or X on a legal document, should have been enough to set the dogs to running, but Blás Falcón still trusted Kinney.

The interpreter, speaking Spanish, said Kinney sent the paper for Blás Falcón to sign, that he should sign it so he would not lose his

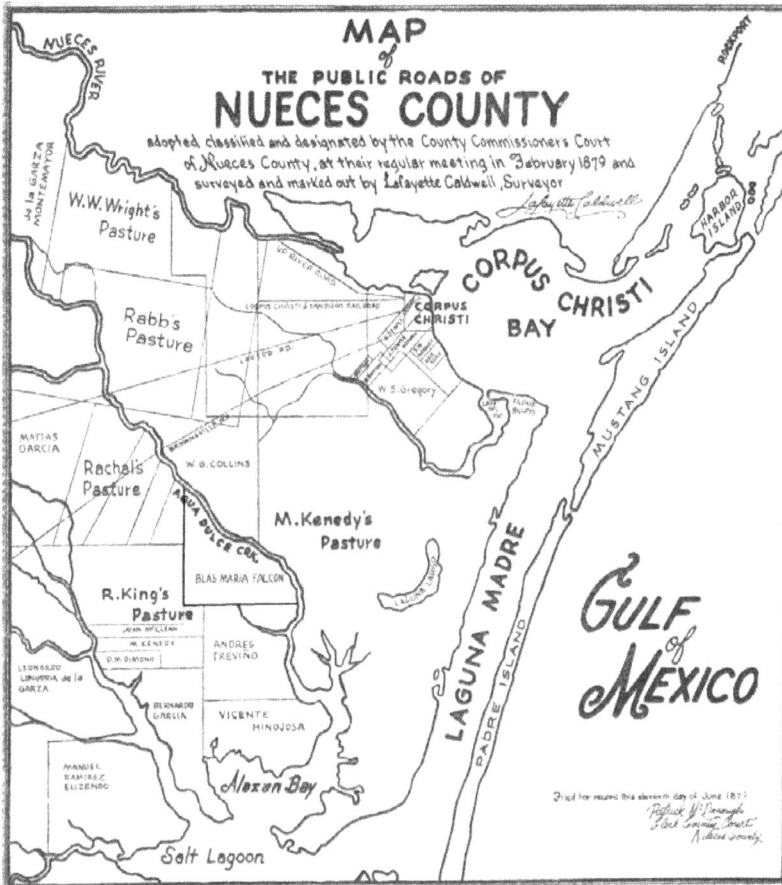

An 1879 map shows Blás Falcón's land grant of 24,000 acres called El Chiltipin, southwest of Agua Dulce Creek, between Richard King's ranch and Mifflin's Kenedy's ranch.

ranch, and Blás Falcón said if Kinney wanted him to sign it, to save his land, he would sign it. He made his mark conveying El Chiltipin to Kinney's attorney Simon Jones.

This case also went to court. Hinojosa, one of the witnesses, said he saw the interpreter give Blás Falcón one dollar and a half after he signed the paper. The deed was in English and Blás Falcón could not read or write. The witnesses said he thought he was signing a document giving power of attorney to Kinney, but he was signing over the deed to his ranch. The interpreter and the lawyer told Blás

287

Falcón that it was not safe to stay here, that he had better go across the Rio Grande.

Blás Falcón was lucky for a second time. The jury found for him and the court ordered the deed cancelled as fraudulent. Though it did not work in either case, the technique used by Kinney and associates — relying on feigned friendship and intimidation — shows how tracts of land owned by Spanish-speaking ranchers were stolen by land-grabbers, a curse of early Texas. Spanish-speaking citizens did not often get a fair hearing, and maybe this is one of those rare examples when they did, but Blás Falcón's victories in court demonstrated that Mexican-American holders of original Spanish and Mexican land grants could sometimes receive justice in Texas courts.

— May 1, 2013

LAND FRAUD — 2

For a time in the 1870s, the most hated men in Corpus Christi were Levi Jones, J. Temple Doswell and Henry Kinney because of a land suit that caused distress for property owners.

In 1839, when Kinney built a trading post in what would become Corpus Christi, he did not own the land; he was a squatter. The owner, or so Kinney thought, was a Mexican cavalry officer named Enrique Villareal.

In 1810, Villareal received a Spanish grant for lands stretching from Corpus Christi Bay inland for 28 miles. His title papers were lost in a flood in 1812. He returned to below the Rio Grande in 1817 and did not come back to the Corpus Christi area until 1829. He obtained title to 10 leagues of land — the Rincon del Oso — in 1831 from the alcalde at Matamoros. He paid 460 pesos for the 44,420 acres.

In 1840, the year after Kinney founded his trading post, Villareal showed up with an army escort to reclaim his land. Kinney convinced Villareal that he had booby-trapped the place with hidden bombs, but he also agreed to pay Villareal for his land.

On July 16, 1842 in Matamoros, Kinney bought one league (4,428 acres) of Villareal's 10 leagues. He paid $2,500 — 56 cents an acre. The transaction was signed by "Henrique" Villareal and "Henrique" Kinney. After Villareal died in 1846, Kinney bought the other nine leagues from his heirs, paying $4,780, or 13.5 cents an acre, for eight leagues and $1,000, or 22.6 cents an acre, for the other league.

Soon afterwards, in 1849, questions arose about Kinney's title to the Rincon del Oso.

Levi Jones was a physician, lawyer and land speculator. He was the physician who treated Stephen F. Austin when he died of pneumonia. As a land speculator, Jones was called "cunning as a weasel." He would secure title to lands in anticipation of their settlement and increased value. Before Kinney set up his trading post, Jones found two certificates issued by the Republic of Texas for two leagues of land stretching southwest from Corpus Christi Bay issued to Jose Bargas and Miguel Bosquez. Jones bought those certificates for a few dollars, had the tracts surveyed by William Manning and patents issued. In 1849, Jones sold part of these holdings to J. Temple Doswell for $21,285. The tract sold to Doswell included the site on which the city of Corpus Christi was located. Suit was brought for trespass and to try title.

As the case was shunted around Texas courts, Kinney continued to sell Rincon del Oso land, but the problem of "unquiet" land titles was always there. The case that started in 1849 was not resolved until 1873, long after Kinney was shot dead by his paramour's husband. Jones, however, was very much alive and acting as attorney for himself and Doswell. The case went to the U.S. Supreme Court, which sent it back to the U.S. Circuit Court in Galveston.

The defendants, who bought their land from Kinney, claimed title under a Mexican grant of 10 leagues from Tamaulipas to Villareal in 1831 and showed conveyance from Villareal to Kinney. The question was whether the Villareal grant was perfect or needed further acts to make it so. The charge of the judge was that the title, to be complete, required a final grant of possession from the alcalde of Camargo, as required by the governor of Tamaulipas.

The plaintiffs, Doswell and Jones, contended that if Villareal's title had been perfect, it would not have passed to his heirs since he was an enemy alien during the time of the Republic. The plaintiffs argued that the surveys of Levi Jones, with no public record of the Villareal title existing, became the better title.

After a five-day trial, the jury returned a verdict on Feb. 14, 1873, finding for the plaintiffs, ruling that the Kinney-Villareal title was imperfect. This was bad news for Corpus Christi; with this ruling, many people no longer owned their own land. Since most of the town's homeowners and landowners bought their land from Kinney, they had to re-purchase their property or lose it. Jones and Doswell established a firm — the Corpus Christi City and Land Company — to resell property, lot by lot, to the erstwhile owners. A great deal of Corpus Christi money was transferred to Jones and Doswell.

Anna Moore Schwien, daughter of a slave, said her friend "Uncle Dempsey" owned two lots on Tancahua Street but as a result of the Jones-Doswell victory in court, he was told he would have to pay

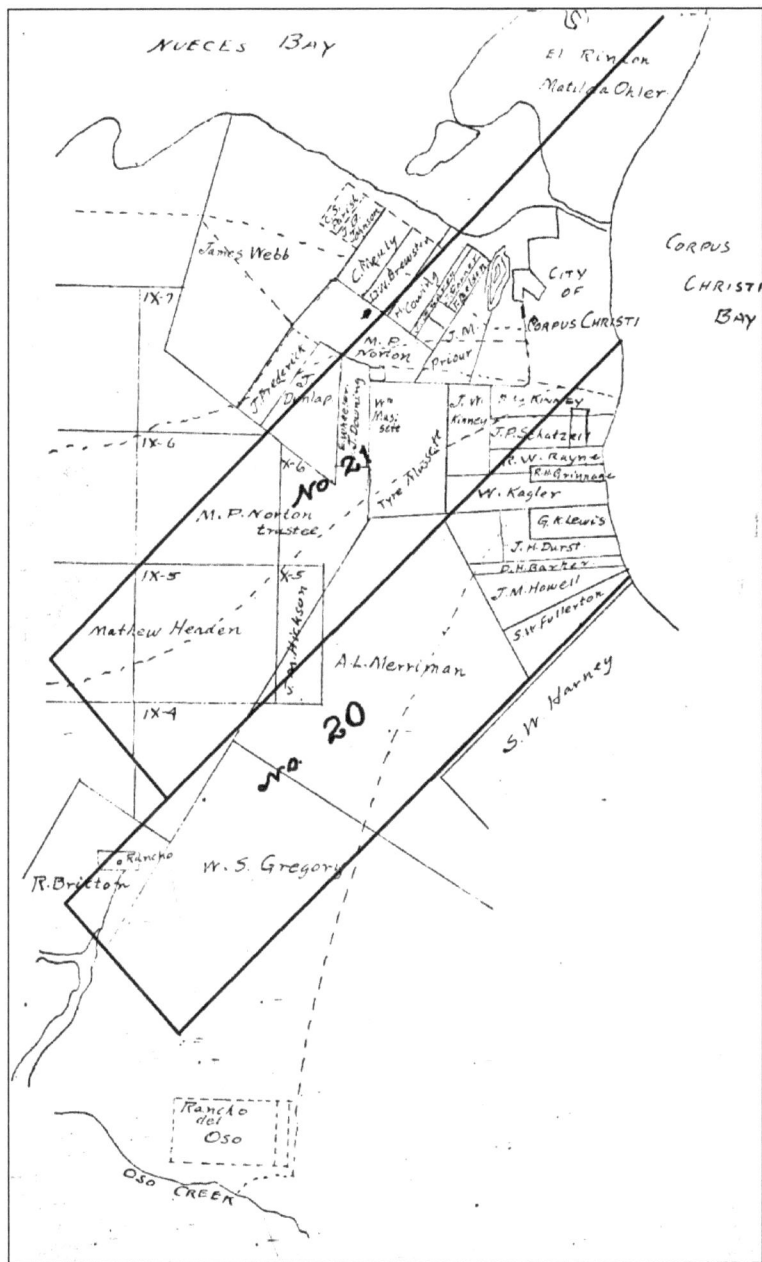

A map by surveyor Felix Blucher in 1868 showed surveys No. 20 and 21 in the names of Jose M. Bargas and M. Basques, which were assigned to Levi Jones. The tracts at that time took in all the city of Corpus Christi.

291

$20 for the corner lot and $15 for the other one. "His friends counseled him not to pay, as he had already bought the lots once, but he thought he had better pay. He did and later events showed his wisdom, as many other people had to pay many times what he did to secure title to their property."

James Ranahan bought a lot from Kinney for $150, but he had to pay Jones $60 in gold for the same property. Such stories were repeated all over town.

Levi Jones, the cunning land weasel, died a few years later, a wealthy man from reselling the land of Corpus Christi. People in Corpus Christi developed a fierce hatred not only of Jones, but also of Kinney. Even though Kinney's original purchase of land from Enrique Villareal may have been entirely in good faith on his part, it turned out to be a huge and costly mistake for many people.

During his lifetime, Corpus Christi overlooked, at least without any overt censure, Henry Kinney's salacious womanizing, his filibustering dreams of empire (he tried to set himself up as the emperor of the Mosquito Coast of Nicaragua), and his penchant for trimming his political beliefs to fit any occasion (he once offered his services to Abraham Lincoln, then Jefferson Davis). But when people had to re-buy land they thought they owned, what they said about Kinney must have caused him to blush in the grave. Which explains why, for a long time, there were no streets named in his honor and no statues of his likeness in the town that he founded.

— May 8, 2013

DRY SPELL

Another long hot dry summer threatens in what is probably the worst drought in a generation. While a hot summer during a bad drought is a more miserable season altogether, the drought on the land reflects in a drought on our spirits, we should be used to it.

Dry spells are certainly nothing new to South Texas. One of the earliest was in the time of Cabeza de Vaca in 1534 when Indians begged him to tell the sky to make it rain. There had been no rain for two years. Closer to our time, every decade of the last half of the 19th century recorded crippling dry spells. There was a drought in 1856-1857 and again in 1861, when livestock perished for lack of grass and water. During the Civil War, a drought compounded the war's miseries.

George Wilkins Kendall, who owned a sheep ranch in present Kendall County, wrote 150 years ago — "The past summer was unprecedentedly hot and dry; during the months of June, July and August we had hardly enough rain to lay the dust."

Thomas Noakes of Nuecestown wrote in his diary on Jan. 24, 1864 — "No rain worth mentioning since last July. Dead animals meet your gaze in every direction . . . the atmosphere is quite oppressive on account of decomposition." He saw a team of steers yoked together, one dead and the other standing quietly by its side.

Maria von Blucher of Corpus Christi wrote her parents — "To add to the calamities of war, we have had a drought such as I have never experienced. Cattle and sheep are dying of hunger in such masses that it is not difficult to count 10,000 a day on the Nueces River . . . The animals are so worn out that when they go to the water they get stuck in the swampy banks and slowly die there."

Dry summers followed by cold winters were called "die-up" years. Cattle died by the thousands. South Texas recorded die-ups in droughts of the 1860s and 1870s. In the winter of 1872, a drought year, cattle drifted south from the norther and bogged down along the creeks where they died, too thin for buzzards to eat. It was said one could walk a mile without stepping off the carcasses. The Corpus Christi Gazette in January 1873 reported great numbers of cattle dying. Many thousands had died the summer before. "Last season," the Gazette reported, "from animals found dead on the prairies, upwards of $500,000 was distributed from hides taken in this section."

In another bad drought in 1876, ponds and wells dried up and rivers slowed to a trickle. Maria von Blucher wrote on Nov. 16, 1876 — "The drought has been terrible; there has never been one here to equal it . . . The cattle die by the thousands, and deer come into town searching for water."

In die-up years, outlaw skinners worked the ranges, taking hides from dead cattle and often killing live cattle, which led to the Skinning War between ranchers and hide thieves. The great die-up of 1878-1879 ruined many small ranchers in South Texas. There was another drought in 1885 and 1886, when cattle shipments dwindled to nothing. The hurricane of 1886, the second great storm that wiped out Indianola, ended this dry spell, but another one plagued South Texas beginning in 1891.

J. Frank Dobie recalled dry times in Live Oak County. "No cattle ever died on our ranch for want of water, but they died on Tol McNeill's ranch west of us and on the Chapa ranch at the head of Ramireña Creek . . . They died on other ranches. I have heard them bawling all night long and all day long for water. No more distressful sound can be made."

The 1891 drought led to an unusual experiment based on a book, "War and the Weather," which theorized that artillery shelling in the Civil War would bring rain. A cloud-bombarding experiment was conducted in Corpus Christi in 1891. Howitzers were fired with shells exploding at 500 feet. After the barrage, rain began to fall. Skeptics noted that thunderclouds were over the city and it had rained the day before.

Similar experiments were conducted in San Diego, where it rained, and San Antonio, where concussions from cannon shots shattered hotel windows. No rain fell in San Antonio, but there was a violent downpour in Laredo, which sent a telegram to the man in charge thanking him for the rain.

South Texas experienced a severe drought in 1901 and 1902. A drought in 1915 was relieved by the 1916 hurricane, but drought

During a drought, when cisterns ran low, residents would buy water from "barreleros," water carriers who sold water door to door. In 1895, barreleros fill their barrels at a city stand pipe.

conditions returned after the storm. Between January and March 1916, Corpus Christi received .38 of an inch of rain. The following year for the same period, it received .37 of an inch. This drought, coinciding with World War I, lasted until 1918.

The Dust Bowl and Great Depression in the 1930s brought years of dry weather and hard times. Then came the terrible drought of the 1950s when pastures looked like a desert, with blowing sand drifted against fences. Elmer Kelton called this drought, in the title of his book, "The Time It Never Rained." It lasted mainly from 1953 to 1957 but really wasn't over until Hurricane Carla brought torrential rains in 1961.

There were many times when it never rained. Any reading of Texas history confirms the cyclical nature of the droughts. Roy Bedichek in "Karankaway Country" wrote of German colonists at New Braunfels who wanted to give up and go back to Germany during the drought of 1856-1857. A scientist among them cut a cross section from an old post-oak tree and showed the variation in tree rings, explaining that they were caused by dry years and wet years and convinced them the rains would return.

The trees today will have their own story to tell. We are in another historic drought cycle, one of the worst ever, which we think of as being unusual, like some Biblical affliction in Leviticus,

A "barrelero" with his water cart passed by the 1914 Nueces County Courthouse. Photo by Karl Swafford.

but prolonged dry spells have always been part of the natural order of where we live. They remind us, as J. Frank Dobie wrote, why thunder was the voice of hope and why ancient Indian tribes worshipped rain.

— May 15, 2013

FROM A DEEP WELL

An old photo shows Robert Kleberg Sr., who took over King Ranch operations after the death of Richard King, with Henrietta King, matriarch of the ranch, looking at the comforting flow of fresh water from the first artesian well drilled on the ranch. This was on June 6, 1899, an event of considerable importance in dry South Texas.

That first artesian well — Palo Alto Number 1 — was five miles northwest of the present site of Kingsville. It was drilled to a depth of 532 feet and its flow measured 75 gallons a minute. It was followed by Palo Alto Number 2, drilled to a depth of 704 feet. Both were free-flowing artesian wells, meaning the water rose to the surface without the aid of a pump.

It was a happy occasion when that first well came in. Kleberg was so overcome that tears rolled down his cheeks as he watched the water splashing from the well pipe, according to Tom Lea in "The King Ranch." This would solve the complaint of the ranch founder, Richard King, that where he had water there was no grass, and where he had grass there was no water.

The men standing near Kleberg wondered why he was crying, but he said, "I knew that once a definite source of water was available, I could induce railroad construction, which in turn would lead to the development of South Texas."

The shortage of water had always been a problem for the region. Ranchers relied on ponds and streams, which would dry up during droughts. In 1853, W. G. Freeman, an army engineer, in a report on the Eighth Military District, said the major obstacle to settling the region around Corpus Christi, besides the fear of Indians, was the lack of water. He pointed out, however, that water could be obtained by drilling artesian wells.

Nobody was listening to Freeman's advice until the 1880s when Dennis O'Connor in Refugio County brought in rotary drilling equipment and began drilling artesian wells. His drillers often hit oil sands, which was a nuisance, since O'Connor wanted water, not oil. That meant they had to find another site and start over. In time, the O'Connor family would be more than compensated for their trouble when the great Tom O'Connor oil field came in.

Dennis O'Connor soon had three artesian wells on his ranch, flowing at the rate of 100,000, 200,000, and 500,000 gallons a day. These were said to be the first artesian wells in South Texas. O'Connor's success led the Coleman-Fulton Pasture Company (later the Taft Ranch) to begin its own search. In 1892, the ranch bought a drilling rig and well casing and set up the equipment at the Doyle Water Hole a mile west of Portland. Drilling began on Jan. 12, 1893. The drilling crew hit cap rock at 1,340 feet.

They drilled through the cap rock then struck gas, according to Keith Guthrie's "History of San Patricio County." G. W. Fulton Jr. got his whiskers burned when he lit a match to test the gas. The burning well was put out by plugging the hole with dirt. Like Dennis O'Connor's oil, it was useless. The work was abandoned after one of owners of the ranch, David Sinton, objected to the huge expense of drilling for artesian water.

After the drought of the 1890s, Robert Kleberg Sr. hired Theodore Herring, famous for the wells he drilled around New Braunfels, and Kleberg bought a heavy well-drilling rig made by the Dempster Mill Company of Beatrice, Neb. On Jan. 8, 1900, Kleberg wrote the Dempster Company to express his satisfaction with the equipment. "Gentlemen, about 10 months ago I first began the use of your Hydraulic No. 6 well boring machine on this ranch . . . all of my trouble for water is rapidly being dispelled by the use of your machine. I have now 10 flowing wells made by your machine, the last just finished by Mr. Thomas Leary flows over 500,000 gallons per day."

By December 1900, the Corpus Christi Caller reported that, "Flowing wells of good water in this part of Texas means a great deal, because of this section's rich soil, and the early and late seasons, making it a popular garden spot of the Lone Star State." E. H. Caldwell, whose hardware store sold artesian well equipment, wrote in his memoirs, "One of the most important things for this country was the finding and development of artesian wells."

By March 1903, King Ranch had 52 artesian wells. Some were non-flowing — the water rose to within 30 feet or so of the well-

In 1899, Robert J. Kleberg Sr and Henrietta King look over water flowing from the first artesian well on King Ranch.

head and had to be pumped to the surface. Windmills became a feature of the ranch landscape.

Windmills were in use long before artesian wells were drilled. From the early wells, dug by hand, water was pulled up by man-power or horse-power, an almost impossible task when large herds of cattle had to be watered. Windmills were set up over the old wells to do the heavy lifting, at least when the wind was blowing. In 1876, S. G. Miller of the Miller Ranch near Lagarto bought an Eclipse windmill at Goliad to pump water from the well.

After the success on King Ranch, others ranchers were soon drilling deep wells to tap into the artesian stream. Mifflin Kenedy's La Parra Ranch had 22 producing artesian wells by 1903; the Texas Land & Cattle Company's Laureles Ranch had six; the Driscoll and Armstrong ranches had three each.

Drilling artesian wells at the turn of the 20th Century was one of the prime factors in bringing the farm settlers and the railroads. The availability of water made the land considerably more valuable. J.

In 1902, wagonloads of well casing pipe leave Chaparral Street for King Ranch

Frank Dobie in "Vaquero of the Brush Country" wrote, "The enormous importance of drilling machines and windmills to the range industry has never been realized by historians." It is a book still waiting to be written. The artesian wells allowed for irrigation, the subdivision of ranchlands into farm plots, which brought railroads and the towns that followed. That realization was why Robert Kleberg Sr. cried when water came gushing up from the first artesian well on the King Ranch. It was a milestone, not only in ranch history but in the history of South Texas.

— May 22, 2013

THE PEÑASCAL RAID

During lawless conditions that terrorized South Texas following the Civil War, bandits robbed, killed and burned ranch houses and attacked travelers on the roads. The bandits were outlaw vaqueros, former Confederate and Union soldiers, and bad men on the run who found freedom to pillage and plunder in the chaotic times of Reconstruction Texas.

Corpus Christi's newspaper, The Nueces Valley, reported on Sept. 24, 1870 that "soldiers returned from four years schooling in vice are ready for a life of crime." A letter noted that, "The situation is truly deplorable. There is no security for person and property between the Nueces and Rio Grande." The Galveston Daily News on May 9, 1873 reported that "the road between Corpus Christi and the Rio Grande is too dangerous to travel." It also noted that 27 desperadoes were operating near Piedras Pintas (Painted Rocks, near today's Benavides in Duval County), that a wagon train was held up at Lake Trinidad (near Ben Bolt), and a man was found hanging on a tree near Nuecestown.

At Brownsville, rustlers drove cattle across the border for sale at $2 to $4 a head, compared to $12 to $18 a head in Texas, while hide-peelers skinned the cattle and left the range dotted with carcasses for coyotes and buzzards. It was a lawless time.

On May 9, 1874, almost a dozen bandits attacked the Morton store in the community of Peñascal, 60 miles south of Corpus Christi on Baffin Bay.

A cook getting water from the well hid and watched as 11 bandits rode up and entered the store. It was dusk. He heard shots and saw Herman Tilgner, a customer in the store, run out vomiting blood, and then he watched as the killers finished him off.

The cook from his hiding place watched the bandits shoot Michael Morton, brother of the store owner, four times in the head. They tied up a customer named F. M. Coakley and executed him.

They shot the store owner in both arms and forced him to carry out their plunder. They shot him six more times. His body was found behind the counter, one leg bent under him, and a prayer book by his side. The Morton brothers were Irish; they had not been long in this country.

All the merchandise nearby was covered with blood. The killers stayed all night, drinking whisky and trying on store clothes. They packed up their plunder and left at dawn, wearing new store clothes and leaving their own clothes in the blood-splattered store.

When the news spread, a posse arrived at Peñascal and quickly struck a trail. In tracks outside the store, a man noticed a fine brown powder, which turned out to be brown sugar that had leaked from a bag the bandits had taken. The sugar trail told them the bandits were not heading toward the border, but toward Corpus Christi.

When the posses returned from Peñascal with no success in finding the killers, "Red" John Dunn, a former Ranger, helped form another posse to join the search. Based on a tip, they found two suspects in a sheep pen in San Patricio County near Meansville. Dunn wrote in "Perilous Trails of Texas" that — "The hard south wind had blown the big gate open and we charged right in among them. John Dunn (a cousin) and I happened to dismount beside a blanket where two men were asleep. One of these, as it was found out later, was Hypolita Tapia and the other Andres Davila, the two murderers. When we jerked the cover off Tapia's head, he jerked out a morral (knapsack). I struck him across the forehead with my pistol and jerked the morral out of his hand. His pistol was in it.

"We took them to Meansville and placed the prisoners in a room under guard. We took Hypolita out and told him we wanted him to tell us all about the murder, but he stated he would confess nothing. We took him to a mesquite tree and let him kick a few chunks out of the horizon, after which he stated that he was ready to divulge everything."

Tapia told them that a Corpus Christi policeman named Tomas Basquez had been in Buckley's store and overheard there was a large consignment of goods and money going to Peñascal. Basquez wanted to raise 10 men to go get it. Tapia said he agreed to do it and enlisted 10 men to go with him, including Davila, an American named Joe, and several others.

Once at Peñascal, Tapia said, they saw that the boat was some distance from shore and they assumed the shipment of money and

On Aug. 7, 1874, two men convicted of the slayings at the Morton store on Baffin Bay were hanged from a scaffold build out from the veranda of the original Nueces County Courthouse (left) next to the Hollub Courthouse.

goods had been delivered, but it had not. The raiders found only $12 or $13 in the cash drawer. Tapia told how the men were killed and said John Morton was killed while kneeling in prayer. D. C. Rachal, a cattle rancher and member of the posse, wrote down the confession.

While the suspects were being questioned, nearby ranchers showed up and wanted to hang the two men, but Dunn convinced them that if they lynched them, it would destroy the evidence against the policeman Basquez. Tapia and Davila were tied up and delivered to Nueces County Sheriff John McClane.

During the trial, Tapia and Davila changed their stories. They said they were with the gang, but held back when it reached Peñascal and arrived after the shooting was over. The prosecutor said Tapia made a voluntary confession, but Tapia jumped to his feet, pointed to rope marks on his neck and shouted, "That's the voluntary confession!"

Both men were found guilty and their hangings set for Friday, August 7, 1874. Two days before his scheduled hanging, Tapia asked to marry his common-law wife and the day before the hanging Tapia's friends and relatives attended the wedding at the jail. The bride wore a calico dress and black shawl. The ceremony was performed by Father Claude Jaillet.

303

Next day, Father Jaillet escorted the two men to the scaffold for the 1:50 p.m. hanging. The scaffold was built out from the balcony of the 1854 courthouse. Tapia and Davila were still wearing their fancy wedding clothes. Tapia's last words were — "My friends, I am here today to die by hanging. I have killed no person nor helped kill anyone. The people forced the party that was guilty to swear against me, but it is all right. Goodbye." Davila said nothing. Screams were heard from the crowd when the prisoners dropped to their deaths.

A third suspect, identified as the man who shot the storeowner Morton, was taken out of the San Diego jail and lynched. A fourth suspect, the American named Joe, was identified as a man named Joseph Delera. He had served in the U.S. Army under the name of Joseph Shane and was known on the border as "Jose el Americano." He was arrested in Matamoros by the Brownsville police and "met some sort of accident" on the way to Corpus Christi. The Corpus Christi policeman named Basquez, who supposedly instigated the attack, was never brought to justice.

— *May 29, 2013*

PERILOUS TRAILS — 1

Matthew Dunn, a native of Ireland, came to Corpus Christi in 1845 with Zachary Taylor as a sutler, a storekeeper who sold supplies to the army. After the battles at Palo Alto and Resaca de la Palma, he became a teamster so he could travel with the army into Mexico. He survived the massacre of an army supply train ambushed on the road to Saltillo.

After the war, Matthew Dunn returned to Corpus Christi and Henry Kinney gave him 100 acres on the old San Patricio Road five miles from town. Dunn married Sarah Pritchett and, over the next few years, they had three sons — John, born in 1851, Matthew, and James.

The father Matthew suffered a sunstroke in 1855, which affected his mind. He was sent to New Orleans for treatment and he became lost and was never found.

At the outbreak of the Civil War, Sarah Dunn took her three sons to Gonzales to be near her relatives. In his memoirs, Dunn said their Irish brogue amused the neighbors, that they would come visit "and one would say, 'Stir them up, make them say something' and when we responded they would let out yells that would cause a Comanche to turn green with envy."

While living at Gonzales, Dunn recalled the arrival of a showman with a white moose. A sign on the tent said, "Whole Families Admitted for $1." A farmer with a crowd behind him paid his dollar. When the ticket-seller counted 22 people following him, he stopped the farmer. "Is this all your tribe?" "Yes, sir," said the farmer. "Go ahead," said the showman. "It will be as big a treat for my moose to see them as it will be for them to see my moose."

At the end of the war, the Dunns returned to the homestead on the San Patricio Road. In a yellow fever epidemic of 1867, John Dunn came down with the fever and sweated it out by sleeping between two sick cousins. "I threw myself down between the two cousins I was nursing," he wrote, "and threw my arms across them to keep the covers on. I went crazy. I crawled across the room, struck my head on a table hard enough to make it bleed. That let the hot blood out. It saved my life."

After the epidemic, he went to Rockport looking for a job. He arrived at night and slept under a live oak. Next morning, he asked a man where the town was. "You're in the middle of it," he said. Dunn asked if the house at the end of the wharf was the only one in town. "No, there's another one." Dunn found a job hauling lumber for a man named Powell, then worked as a fireman on the old side-wheel steamer "Reindeer."

After a trip to St. Louis, Dunn returned to Corpus Christi where he found three new beef packing houses operating on North Beach. "Instead of shipping cattle across the Gulf, they built slaughter houses all over the country and commenced killing the cattle for their hides and tallow."

Dunn got a job in a packing house owned by Bill Brunwinkel and Henry Ball. As a fireman, Dunn's job was to keep fire going in the steam boiler to heat the tanks where the meat was boiled for its tallow. The tallow, or fat, was poured into barrels and the hides were salted down to cure and fastened into bundles for shipment. Some of the meat was packed in salt and shipped as "mess beef" but most of it was dumped to rot outside the packeries.

"I had seen other firemen throw shin bones of slaughtered cattle into the furnace to raise steam quickly, as the bones were full of oil and would make a very hot fire," Dunn wrote in his memoirs. "I followed their example and in a short time everything was sizzling." He got the fire so hot he almost exploded the boiler. "Young man," the engineer told him, "in a few minutes you would have been sailing through space."

John Dunn generally became known as "Red" John to distinguish him from a cousin by the same name. He quit the packing house job and joined the Texas Rangers. There were 60 men in the Ranger company who were, Dunn wrote, "the worst mixed lot of men that ever came together in one organization." One rode with Quantrill and another, called Three-Fingered Jack, was wanted for murder in California. This and other Ranger companies were disbanded when Gov. E. J. Davis established the State Police in 1870.

Dunn said they camped outside Austin, where they got drunk, then marched to the old Capitol to be discharged. "Some of the boys

Texas Ranger and vigilante John Dunn. He was known as "Red" John to distinguish him from a cousin by the same name.

were so drunk it took two sober ones to hold each of them up while waiting for the discharge." The Rangers were replaced by Davis' State Police, which lasted until 1873 when the Rangers were re-commissioned.

They were promised their back pay and commissions in the new State Police force, Dunn said, but they never received the commissions or back pay. While they were waiting in camp on the Santa Gertrudis on cold nights they would build a bonfire and Dunn noticed that after the men went to asleep an old bull would slip into camp and settle down by the fire. One night the bull came in and stretched out within a few feet of where Dunn and another man had their bedrolls.

The bull got too close to the fire. During the night he got burned and went up like a rocket, snorting and bellowing. With the bull in panic, the Rangers, startled from sleep, began shooting in all directions, thinking they were under attack. The bull scattered the coals of the fire and some of the bedrolls went up in flames. At daylight, they took inventory. There were two wounded men, several burned blankets, a broken bridle bit, a broken wagon tongue, and a saddle shot full of holes. Dunn wrote that they saw the old bull later that morning, three miles from camp. Dunn thought he must have been a sensible animal who learned from experience, for he never came back to claim a warm spot by the fire.

— June 5, 2013

PERILOUS TRAILS — 2

When Texas Rangers were disbanded during the administration of Gov. E. J. Davis, John Dunn was discharged. He worked at King Ranch for three months, cut hay for U.S. troops in San Antonio, and went up the trail with a cattle herd to Hays, Kansas.

Back in Corpus Christi, he joined vigilante groups after George Hatch was killed at the north end of the Reef Road on Sept. 5, 1872. The murderers cut out his pockets, robbed him, took his horses and fled.

"Outside of five or six persons, no one knows whether they were caught or not," Dunn wrote in "Perilous Trails in Texas." He said the names of the killers, made known to them, were written down for future reference. "It is amusing to hear people say the murderers were never caught. Well, ignorance is bliss."

When the Rangers were re-commissioned in 1873, Warren Wallace led a company chasing rustlers and hide thieves. From this time, Dunn related a shootout between Rangers Joe Osgood and Buck Harris.

"Osgood was industrious and hardworking while Harris was exactly the reverse. One morning Harris was detailed to bring in a beef for meat. He pretended to be sick and refused to go. Osgood did the job. When the beef was skinned, Harris came up to take a piece of meat. 'No, you are not,' said Osgood. 'It was your day to bring in the meat and you refused.' "

Both men pulled their guns and fired. Harris was shot in the hand while Osgood, hit in the stomach, died within minutes.

Dunn wrote in Perilous Trails that if the tales told by one man on Buck Harris were true "then he was certainly coldblooded. This man said that Harris had gone up the trail to Kansas the year before, there being a youngster along of not over 14 or 15 years of age. One day while in camp the boss of the herd sent Harris and the boy to a pond for a bucket of water. Sometime later they heard a shot in the direction the two had gone. They paid little attention, thinking they were shooting at prairie dogs.

On May 9, 1874, bandits killed four men at a store at Peñascal on Baffin Bay. In looking at tracks near the store, a man in a posse noticed brown sugar that had leaked from one a bag taken by the bandits. The sugar trail indicated the bandits were heading not for the border but for Corpus Christi.

Dunn gathered a posse of cousins and brothers to join the search. They found two suspects, Hypolita Tapia and Andres Davila, in a sheep pen. "We took them to Meansville and placed the prisoners in a room under guard. We took Hypolita out and told him we wanted him to tell us all about the murders, but he would confess nothing. We took him to a mesquite tree and let him kick a few chunks out of the horizon, after which he was ready to divulge everything."

Tapia and Davila were tried and hanged at Corpus Christi. After two of Tapia's brothers swore to get even, Dunn began sleeping in his cornfield. One night, when he went back to the house to get water and lit a lantern, shots were fired at him from the darkness. After that close call, after losing one of his nine lives, he rejoined the Rangers.

In March 1875, bandits rode in on Thursday, March 25, and camped on the Oso. On Good Friday, they stole horses and took men captive at two ranch houses. They killed an old man in the Juan Saenz community, captured travelers on the roads, and went on to Nuecestown. After some shooting and plundering at Noakes' store, the bandits took captives and plunder and camped in the brush.

"Red" John was with a posse pursuing the bandits. His cousin, the other John Dunn, was in the same posse. As they approached the bandits' camp in the brush, shots were fired and the bandits decamped, leaving behind their hostages and plunder. A wounded bandit was captured and taken to Corpus Christi, where he was hanged. All the others got away.

After the Nuecestown Raid, Dunn joined a militia group headed by Hines Clark, a cattle rancher at Banquete, that chased thieves who killed cattle for their hides. At many of the ranches in the Big Sands, Dunn wrote, "were large buildings packed full of dried hides in addition to pits dug in the sand that were also filled with dry hides."

Dunn's book "Perilous Trails in Texas" reveals the viral prejudice and vigilante violence of South Texas in the rough times after the

"Red" John Dunn, who collected firearms and artifacts, in front of his museum at his home on Shell Road. His memoirs — "Perilous Trails of Texas" — tell of bandit raids and pioneer times in South Texas.

Civil War. The militia groups, the Minutemen, and some Rangers were not known for their restraint or observance of legal formalities. While Dunn was with Wallace's company of Rangers stationed at Concepcion, in Duval County, the Rangers caught a man they called Moss Top for his head of unruly hair. They believed he had shot a fellow Ranger, Mark Judd, in the eye. The captain freed Moss Top, but the Rangers later found him and lynched him in a brutal fashion.

After a deaf sheep rancher named Thad Swift and his wife were murdered, a company of vigilantes rode up. This was a rough bunch from Refugio. Dunn rode out to meet them. They asked Dunn if he knew several people. Yes, he said, they lived on the Hill in Corpus Christi. Dunn rode with the vigilantes into town, pointed out the men, and the posse captured them, tied their arms and legs, and rode away. The men they took, Dunn said, he never saw again.

311

This was like a black hole in history — names, details, even the numbers were swallowed in darkness. What were the vigilantes doing? In Dunn's point of view, as he described it, they were making the country safe for Americans.

Dunn settled down to become a dairyman, married a woman named Lelia Nias, and in time opened a private museum at his place on Shell Road to display his collection of curiosities. Among other items, he had hundreds of guns from frontier times, including the pistol found on Henry Kinney when he was killed in Matamoros and the pistol Dunn took from Hypolita Tapia when he was captured in the sheep pen. John B. "Red" Dunn died on the last day of September 1940 when he was 89. The old Ranger and vigilante had ridden perilous trails in perilous times.

— June 12, 2013

COTTON ROAD

When Union warships blockaded Texas ports in the Civil War, bales of cotton were hauled down the Cotton Road to be sold in Matamoros, then one of the world's great cotton markets. This was the back door of the Confederacy.

The Cotton Road followed the old Matamoros Road, also known as Taylor's Trail. From the Santa Margarita crossing on the Nueces River (near today's community of Bluntzer), the road traveled to Banquete, then to the King Ranch headquarters. South of the King Ranch the route entered the Big Sands, also known as the Desert of the Dead. At the Rio Grande, the cotton was taken downriver to the Mexican port town of Bagdad, where ships waited to receive cargoes of cotton.

Throughout the war, a river of cotton flowed down the Cotton Road to be sold in Mexico to foreign buyers for gold, which bought military supplies for the Confederacy. These were boom times on the border called Los Algodones — cotton times.

Wagons and oxcarts from East Texas, Louisiana and Arkansas converged at Santa Margarita on the Nueces, south of the town of San Patricio. The cotton came down in a constant stream with hundreds of wagons hauling thousands of bales. The traffic never stopped.

John Warren Hunter was 16 when he hauled a load of cotton to Brownsville. He described the Santa Margarita crossing, with long caravans waiting to cross. As they passed through San Patricio, they saw few people but when they approached the river an animated scene came into view. Several wagon trains loaded with cotton were going to Brownsville and on the opposite bank were trains of pack mules returning from the border with supplies of guns and ammunition. It was sundown when Hunter rode into the encampment "with its bright fires and incessant din of oxen and horse bells and shouts of the herdsmen."

The next major stop was Banquete, where trains of wagons and oxcarts passed day and night. A detachment of Confederate troops under James Ware and Mat Nolan camped on San Fernando Creek to guard this important way station. Banquete was a busy, clamorous place with a saloon, stables, and supply stores on the south side of Banquete Creek.

The next major stop was King Ranch headquarters on the Santa Gertrudis. Richard King was one of the organizers of the Cotton Road and the ranch was a receiving depot for the Confederate government. Teamsters could buy supplies at the ranch commissary and replenish their fresh water before they hit the Big Sands, a sand belt 65 miles wide and 100 miles long. For the slow-moving wagon trains, getting through the Big Sands was an ordeal of searing heat, with no shade trees and no good water.

Brothers Robert and William Adams, who were 16 and 17 years old at the time, were drafted to haul cotton to Brownsville. Each had a wagon to drive and four yoke of oxen to handle. At night, their oxen were turned loose to graze. Because of a drought and the heavy traffic on the Cotton Road, the oxen had to wander far off to find grass. In the morning, they had a horse to use to hunt their oxen. Finding and yoking the oxen could take half the morning. The horse would be tied behind the wagon as it moved along. The wagons loaded with cotton usually made from eight to 10 miles a day, but they were lucky to make four or five miles a day when they reached the arid sand belt.

Sally Skull, a woman gunslinger, bought a fleet of wagons and became a cotton trader and teamster on the Cotton Road. It was said that it was more profitable for those hauling cotton to the border than for those who grew it. When John Warren Hunter saw her at the Las Animas water hole on the Cotton Road, she was wearing a black dress and sunbonnet, with a six-shooter hanging at her belt, and sitting on a black horse like a cavalry officer on parade.

A British military attache, Lt. Col. James Arthur Lyon Fremantle of the Coldstream Guards, traveled through the area on his way to join Robert E. Lee's army as an observer. When his ship arrived at the mouth of the Rio Grande, on April 2, 1863, he saw some 70 ships waiting to take on their cotton cargoes. Fremantle wrote in his diary that endless bales of cotton could be seen at Bagdad.

Fremantle left the border in a four-wheeled carriage pulled by mules. His party followed the Cotton Road and saw many wagons

Drawing of a cotton press at Piedras Negras on the Rio Grande, across from Eagle Pass, that appeared in Frank's Illustrated Newspaper in 1864. After Union forces captured Brownsville, the Cotton Road shifted west to Eagle Pass, Laredo and Rio Grande City.

loaded with cotton. "Generally," Fremantle wrote, "there were 10 oxen or six mules to a wagon carrying ten bales. They journey very slowly towards Brownsville."

After six days, the party reached King Ranch. For several days, wrote Fremantle, "I had heard this spoken of as a sort of Elysium, marking as it does the termination of the sands, and the commencement of comparative civilization." They camped at the ranch. Richard and Henrietta King were in Brownsville. Two days after King Ranch, they reached Casa Blanca, where they bought a goat, some corn, and two chickens. At Oakville, said Fremantle, all the women were anxious to buy snuff.

Fremantle traveled up the Cotton Road at the high tide of the Confederacy. He was with Lee and Longstreet at Gettysburg, where he climbed a tree to watch Pickett's fateful charge, the beginning of the end for the Confederate cause.

After Gen. Nathaniel P. Banks' Union forces captured Brownsville in November 1863, the cotton trains were diverted to Rio Grande City, Laredo, and Eagle Pass. At Eagle Pass, where cotton was crossed over to Piedras Negras on the Mexican side, it was said "the whole river bottom from the bank of the river to the end of town was covered with cotton." Matamoros and the port of Bagdad continued to funnel Confederate cotton to waiting ships.

Matamoros, the capital of Los Algodones, was full of Union and Confederate agents, cotton brokers, commission agents, soldiers of

315

The old steamboat landing at Brownsville in 1864 during the Cotton Road times. Photo by Louis de Planque.

fortune, draft evaders and Texas refugees. From Matamoros, the cotton was transported 25 miles east to the Mexican fishing village of Bagdad, a shanty boomtown made of tent hotels and tarpaulin restaurants. Cotton was piled everywhere waiting to be lightered to hundreds of ships riding at anchor at the mouth of the Rio Grande. French and British warships patrolled the Gulf to protect the merchant ships flying their national flags.

The end of the war spelled the end of Los Algodones and the boom times on the border. But for many years afterwards it was said that the route of the Cotton Road was marked by small sprigs of cotton that had snagged on the brush and prickly pear and waved in the sun like small white flags.

— June 19, 2013

E. J. DAVIS

Edmund Jackson Davis, a Union general in the Civil War, became the most despised governor in Texas history. Confederates called him the devil with red whiskers. They came close to hanging him during the war.

Davis came to Texas with his widowed mother when he was 11. He later moved to Corpus Christi, studied law, and was appointed federal judge. His circuit stretched from Corpus Christi to Laredo to Brownsville.

Davis married Anne Elizabeth (Lizzie) Britton on April 6, 1858 at the bride's home in Corpus Christi, which is still standing (Centennial House). Lizzie was the daughter of Sen. Forbes Britton.

When secession was a hot issue in early 1861, Davis spoke against Texas leaving the Union. When the war broke out, he went to Matamoros to organize the First Texas Cavalry, made up of Unionists like himself. He was commissioned a colonel of volunteers.

Confederates learned that Davis and his aide Capt. W. W. Montgomery were in Bagdad on the Mexican side. In a raid from Clarksville, across the river, Davis and Montgomery were captured and taken to the Texas side. Montgomery was promptly hanged and the Confederates were putting a rope around the neck of Davis when Confederate Gen. Hamilton ("Hamp") Bee ordered him returned to the Mexican side, with apologies to Mexico for the violation of its territory. Matamoros, as a transit point for Confederate cotton, was too important to risk any rupture in relations.

When Union forces captured Brownsville in late 1863, the Cotton Road traffic shifted upriver to Eagle Pass, Laredo, and Rio Grande City, then went downstream on the Mexican side of the river. Davis led an expedition to capture Laredo and put a stop to the cotton traffic. Davis and his forces left Brownsville in March 1864. Some were transported on the steamboat Mustang while the cavalry rode along the river. When the steamboat ran aground, Davis sent an advance guard of 200 men on to Laredo, with the main body following. The advance guard was supposed to seize 5,000 bales of Confederate cotton in Laredo's main plaza. Laredo was lightly defended, since the Confederates thought it unlikely that Union forces would venture so far from their home base at Brownsville.

Confederate Col. Santos Benavides, the highest ranking Mexican-American in the Confederate Army, dispersed his regiment to protect the cotton routes. Davis' advance guard was almost to Laredo when the alarm was sounded. With Benavides' regiment scattered in other places, Laredo citizens prepared to defend the town.

Col. Benavides took 42 men to the outskirts of Laredo and posted them in houses. When the skirmishers in Davis' advance guard drew near, Benavides' men began firing, forcing the federals back. "My men maintained a steady fire," Benavides later wrote Gen. Rip Ford. "The firing was kept up until dark when the Yankees thought it best to skedaddle in their own peculiar style." Laredo celebrated with the ringing of church bells as Davis retreated back to Brownsville.

At war's end, Davis returned to Corpus Christi and opened a law office. In the dog days of 1867, during a yellow fever outbreak, he brought a doctor from Havana at his own expense after the town's two doctors died. One Corpus Christi resident wrote that mean things were said about Davis "but he deserved credit for what he did for Corpus Christi" during the epidemic.

Davis was elected to the constitution convention of 1868-69, where he proposed dividing Texas into three separate states to weaken its political power.

In November 1869, with Texas under military rule, Davis was elected governor by beating Andrew Hamilton by 800 votes out of 78,993 cast. Nueces County voters — mostly Republican because of the disenfranchisement of Democrats — backed Davis. After the election, the ballots of some counties disappeared, dumped somewhere in the swamps of Louisiana it was claimed. It may have been the most fraudulent election in state history but, fraudulent or not, Davis took office on Jan. 18, 1870.

When Davis and his wife left Corpus Christi for Austin, their coach stopped at Mrs. Eliza Sullivan's home at San Patricio and the

E. J. Davis was the only Texas governor from Corpus Christi.

newly elected governor sent in his respects. The reply came back — "Mrs. Sullivan is not at home to the traitor."

In office, Davis was a virtual dictator, empowered to appoint more than 8,000 state, county and local officials, including judges and sheriffs. Through state printing contracts, he rewarded friendly newspapers and he forced the Legislature to give him a State Police force under his personal command. Davis' State Police broke up political meetings of his opponents, entered homes without warrants, made false arrests, and carried out summary executions.

During Davis' tenure from 1870 to 1874, a corrupt Legislature plundered the treasury, officials sold votes and stuffed ballot boxes, and the State Police terrified law-abiding citizens. A Victoria resident said that Texas with Davis as governor "was an incipient hell, with promise of full and intense development."

The man former Confederates called "the devil with red whiskers" ran for re-election in 1873 against Richard Coke, a former private in the Confederate Army. Despite widespread voting irregularities, the ex-Confederate private beat the ex-Union general by more than two to one.

Davis barricaded himself in his office and sent a telegram urging President U.S. Grant to send federal troops to keep him in power. Grant wired back — "Would it not be prudent, as well as right, to yield to the verdict of the people as expressed by their ballots?"

Grant's refusal to intervene so infuriated Lizzie Davis that she took Grant's portrait down from a wall and put her foot through it. Davis had to vacate the governor's office, but in a fit of petulance he locked it and threw away the key. Coke, the new governor, had the door broken down as Austin celebrated with a 102-gun salute.

This marked the end of Reconstruction. It also marked the end of Davis' political career. Former Confederates rewrote the state Constitution so that no other governor in Texas would ever again wield as much power. Davis died in Austin on Feb. 27, 1883. His monument, an obelisk, was the tallest in the State Cemetery. A former Confederate said the size was just about right since E. J. Davis was "the biggest son of a bitch Texas has ever seen." Not even death squares some accounts.

—June 26, 2013

TEXAS INVADED

When Vicksburg fell on July 4, 1863, it freed a Union army to invade Texas. The invasion was assigned to Gen. Nathaniel P. Banks, a former governor of Massachusetts known as the Bobbin Boy because, as a child, he worked in a cotton mill. In the Virginia campaign early in the Civil War, Banks' supplies were captured so often by Stonewall Jackson that Confederates called him "Commissary Banks."

The main reason for invading Texas was to stop the traffic in cotton going to Mexico, which provided the Confederacy with gold to buy military essentials. As long as the cotton road stayed open, it was harder for the Union blockade to starve and squeeze the South into submission. A secondary purpose was to discourage any alliance between Texas Confederates and Maximilian's French forces in Mexico.

Banks sent an invasion force of 5,000 men on 20 vessels steaming for Sabine Pass. When Union gunboats approached a fort guarding the pass, the Confederate battery opened fire, two Union gunboats surrendered and the invasion fleet limped back to New Orleans.

Banks tried again, but this time aimed at the mouth of the Rio Grande. His 7,500-man force was made up of veterans from the Vicksburg campaign under the command of Gen. Napoleon Jackson Tecumseh Dana, who had served in Zachary Taylor's army at Corpus Christi in 1845.

In a pouring rain, the army units boarded 13 transports, escorted by gunboats, on Oct. 23, 1863. At noon on Nov. 2, 1863, Banks' forces landed without opposition on Brazos Island at an abandoned salt works. Soldiers of the 15th Maine raised an American flag and fired a volley in salute. Banks wired Abraham Lincoln — "The flag of the Union floated over Texas today at meridian precisely."

A colonel in the 13th Maine ordered his men to take off their boots, to keep them dry, and wade the Laguna Madre. As a result, their feet were cut up by sharp oyster shells. At Brownsville, they quartered in Fort Brown, the Mexican War fort. Union soldiers had met no opposition. Gen. Hamilton P. Bee, in charge of Confederate forces in South Texas, almost burned Brownsville in his haste to destroy cotton and get out of the city. Bee withdrew to Banquete, pondering where the Yankees would strike next.

Banks' next objective was Mustang Island. The 13th and 15th Maine and 20th Iowa under the command of Gen. T. E. G. Ransom landed at Corpus Christi Pass on Nov. 16 and began marching to the head of the island, the men carrying 100 rounds of ammunition, guns, and rations for three days. Some of the soldiers' feet were sore from oyster-shell cuts and they were dragging two siege guns through the sand.

At daybreak, Union soldiers fired on Confederate sentries at Fort Semmes, driving them back as a gunboat in the pass shelled the fort. Confederates in the earthwork fort quickly raised a white flag. One man came out, waving in a friendly way, and was shot; his arm had to be amputated. The attackers captured three cannon, 140 horses, nine officers, and 89 men.

While Fort Semmes was under attack, Gen. Bee arrived from Banquete and sent a lieutenant under a flag of truce to find out what happened to the men at Fort Semmes, but the man was held prisoner. Expecting an attack on Corpus Christi, Gen. Bee withdrew his forces to safety north of the Nueces River.

A Union garrison was established in Fort Semmes, renamed Post Aransas. The 20th Iowa was assigned garrison duty under Maj. William G. Thompson. The 20th, composed of farm boys from the Marion, Iowa, area had fought at Pea Ridge and Vicksburg. As they settled in, they became industrious in obtaining wood to build their winter huts. They roamed far down the island in search of wood and made "furniture raids" in Corpus Christi. The regimental historian wrote — "Most of the men built comfortable quarters and furnished them with comfort, even luxury. The little frame huts contained mahogany and rosewood furniture of the richest description, procured during scouting expeditions, by confiscation from houses abandoned by rebels."

The remainder of Banks' forces moved toward Fort Esperanza guarding Pass Cavallo. As a norther blew in on Nov. 19, 1863, Union troops were ferried across Aransas Pass to St. Joseph's Island. They reached Cedar Bayou, separating St. Joseph's from

Union soldiers were busy digging a trench on Brazos Island after Banks' invasion in 1863. In the background were steamboats in Brazos Santiago Pass and the Point Isabel Lighthouse. Sketch by C. E. H. Bonwill in Frank Leslie's Illustrated Newspaper.

Matagorda Island, four days later. A Confederate major carrying a white flag appeared across Cedar Bayou, seeking to learn what happened to the men captured at Fort Semmes.

A sergeant from the 15th Maine swam across to talk. After an angry exchange, the Confederate major shot the sergeant and from across the bayou Union troops shot the major. His body was found in the sand dunes. The sergeant was wounded.

Union troops crossed Cedar Bayou on flatboats and marched 20 miles. On Nov. 27, they reached Fort Esperanza, a huge earthworks fort on Matagorda Island near the town of Saluria. The fort was armed with eight 24-pound cannons and one behemoth, a 124-pound "Columbiad," to guard Pass Cavallo.

Union troops fired on Confederate pickets, driving them inside the walls. Banks' soldiers prepared for a siege, digging rifle pits and trenches. Batteries were placed and cannon fire exchanged. A Union soldier stuck out his foot to stop a Confederate cannonball rolling in the sand, which caused such damage the foot had to amputated.

Inside the fort, Confederates spiked their guns, set powder magazines on fire, and evacuated before Union troops could block their escape. That November, the weather turned bitterly cold and Union troops on Matagorda sheltered in rifle pits covered with the hides of slaughtered cattle. Raids were made to Indianola and Port Lavaca.

In February, Banks was ordered back to New Orleans. He left garrisons at Pass Cavallo and Aransas Pass, but they were pulled out two months later.

Union Gen. Nathaniel P. Banks led an invasion of Texas in 1863. From the Library of Congress.

In the invasion, Banks captured Brownsville, two island forts, terrified the coast, and sent a cautionary warning to French forces in Mexico. But the invasion changed nothing strategically. It did not even stop the traffic in Confederate cotton going to Mexico. The cotton shipments simply bypassed Brownsville while it was under Union control. As the final battles were fought in the East, South Texas was virtually left alone.

— July 3, 2013

BORDER COMMISSION — 1

A government commission, a wit once said, is like a dog with four tails. In the case of the South Texas border commission, it was a dog with three tails — impressive but useless.

The Civil War was long over in 1872, but in the ragged bottom edge of Texas fighting didn't stop. Cattle rustling became an industry and danger lurked on the roads and at every river crossing. Predatory raiders were well-armed, violent and not inhibited by laws or lawmen. It was so dangerous that people didn't travel unless they had to.

After an outcry about cattle rustling and violence in South Texas, President Grant appointed a commission to investigate the situation. Commissioners appointed were Thomas Robb of Georgia, Richard Savage and Fabius Mead of Mississippi.

The commissioners arrived at Point Isabel in July 1872 and traveled to Rio Grande City. They took depositions and heard sworn testimony from July 30 to Oct. 3, 1872. They returned to Washington and then came back to Texas in 1873. They heard from many witnesses that South Texas was a dangerous place where neither person nor property was safe.

Witnesses called were ranchers, border residents, officials, state police members, cattle and hide inspectors. Prominent citizens who appeared before the commission included Adolphus Glavecke, Thaddeus Rhodes, Rip Ford, and the Champion brothers at Point Isabel. Richard King and Mifflin Kenedy appeared before the commission and so did Tejano ranchers Carlos Esparza and Pedro Vela. Ranchers in Nueces County and the Nueces Valley submitted claims for losses.

On Aug. 26, 1872, Richard King told the commissioners of an incident on July 31 when he was leaving his ranch in a coach to appear before the commission. His coach was ambushed at San Fernando Creek. Some 25 to 30 shots were fired and a traveling companion, Franz Specht, was killed. King told the commissioners he believed the dozen or so attackers were bandits from Mexico.

"I have been obliged for a number of years," King told the commission, "to keep a number of men, for my protection, at my own expense . . . and in traveling I am obliged to have an escort of those men." King said the guiding hand behind the rustling and raids in South Texas was that old enemy of Texans, Gen. Juan "Cheno" Cortina, who led a violent border revolt in 1859 and since then had carried on a private war against Texas.

William Thomas, a rancher known as "Red Thomas," said he saw a captain in the Mexican army with a herd of 400 stolen cattle. The captain, one of Cortina's men, said, "The gringos are raising cows for me."

William Burke, a lieutenant in the State Police (which replaced the Rangers during the E. J. Davis administration), testified that he saw men who worked for Cortina driving herds across the river at Rancho Prietas near Brownsville.

Rancher Antonio Tijerina testified that in February 1872 cattle thieves from Mexico gathered a herd of stolen Texas cattle near his ranch, 12 miles from Brownsville, and that he and several neighbors followed the thieves to Matamoros, where he found them selling the cattle to two butchers. He and his friends fired on the thieves and recovered the stolen cattle.

Carlos Esparza, another Tejano rancher, called Cortina "a bad and dangerous man" who was in charge of "all the murderers, robbers and thieves" on both sides of the Rio Grande. Esparza said he and Ignacio Garcia captured, near the Calabosa Ranch, 20 head of cattle from armed thieves out of more than 100 that had already been taken across the river.

Anaclito Padron, a soldier in Cortina's command, testified that he was sent by Cortina to protect the crossing of stolen cattle at Tahuachal rancho, on Mexico's side of the river, in June 1871. He said 200 cattle were crossed and personally appropriated by Cortina. And so it went, with hundreds of witnesses relaying names and details of cattle stolen in Texas and sold for a fraction of their value in Mexico. Some names of cattle rustlers given to the commission included the Holguines brothers; Antonio Blangel; Capt. Sabas Garcia; Segundo Garza; Juan Garcia; Librado; the notorious Lugo brothers; Francisco Villareal; and the Perales brothers, Pedro and Sylverio, among others.

Richard King told the Robb Commission of an ambush on his coach as he was on his way to testify.

Surprisingly, on a trip up the Rio Grande on the riverboat San Juan, the commissioners, on the morning of Sept. 6, 1872, saw a herd of stolen cattle being taken across the river at Las Cuevas, a notorious ford for rustlers. The thieves were naked to keep their clothes dry as they swam the cattle across the river. One of the witnesses, besides the commissioners, was rancher Mifflin Kenedy who was on board the San Juan that morning.

327

After Thomas Osborn replaced Mead, one of the three commissioners, the Robb Commission returned to Texas in February 1873. They traveled along the border, visited Corpus Christi, San Diego and the King Ranch. On their two trips to South Texas, they took 1,090 depositions and accepted 423 petitions of claims. The amount of losses from the theft of cattle and horses — mostly attributed to raiders from Mexico — totaled $48.4 million. Many of the claims, if not all, were no doubt exaggerated.

The Robb Commission was a political palliative, Washington's way of seeming to address a problem without spending much money or exerting much effort. The commission conducted its investigation and issued a scathing report, blaming Mexico for the outrages, and then waited for matters to run their course. Washington then, like now, loved reports, the longer the better. They could be printed, pointed to, quoted and then forgotten. As this one was.

Texans realized that they would have to take matters into their own hands to protect the frontier. As one Texas rancher said, "God help us — Washington won't." After the Rangers were reinstated, replacing the ineffective State Police, Capt. Leander McNelly and a company of Rangers were sent into the Nueces Strip to put a stop to cross-border raids. That wasn't the end of the cattle-stealing bandit era, but it was the beginning of the end.

— July 10, 2013

BORDER COMMISSION — 2

In 1872, the Robb Commission was dispatched from Washington to investigate the violence and cattle rustling in South Texas, to evaluate the state of affairs along the border. The result was a report blaming Mexico for instigating or tolerating cross-border raiding and providing a refuge for outlaws. The report accused Mexican officials of being corrupt and complicit in the lawlessness and tolerant of the criminals in their midst.

While impressive in detail, the Robb Commission report was useless in effect. It did have one result, though, in prompting Mexico to appoint its own border commission to investigate the situation on the Rio Grande and in the Nueces Strip. Not surprisingly, the commissioners in Mexico took a polar opposite view of the situation.

While the U.S. report blamed Mexico for the banditry in the border region, the Mexican report blamed "undisciplined and lawless men" of Texas, which it characterized as a godless and immoral land. It also said, in essence, that the American report did what Americans always do — blame the Mexicans.

The Northeast Border Investigating Commission — Mexico's equivalent of the Robb Commission — spent months listening to testimony and issued its first report on May 15, 1873. Other reports followed. About cattle stealing, the Mexican report said "each side of the border assumes that the ones who perpetrate or protect this rustling are neighbors or authorities of the opposite side." Then it proceeded to blame the other side. According to the Mexican report, the raiding parties were Texas bandits, Mexican outlaws living in Texas, and other bad hombres.

The Mexican commission disparaged the Robb Commission report and questioned the impartiality of its witnesses. The report accused Richard King of employing "a large band of men running constantly in all directions marking (branding) calves that did not belong to him." The report said King and Mifflin Kenedy testified that cattle thefts were committed by armed robbers from Mexico when they knew that the specific thefts were committed by a Texas rustler named Patrick Quinn. The report offered no testimony to confirm those accusations.

The Robb Commission report quoted William Thomas, a Rio Grande rancher, who said he saw a captain in the Mexican army, one of Cortina's men, with a herd of stolen cattle. The Mexican report said Thomas was an unreliable witness because he and an accomplice, Juan Lopez Arenas, were known to steal horses in Mexico.

The Robb Commission heard from Tejano rancher Antonio Tijerina, who said he witnessed herds of stolen Texas cattle being crossed over into Mexico. The Mexican report said Antonio Tijerina and his brothers were notorious horse thieves who built a corral on their ranch to hold horses stolen in Mexico.

Adolphus Glavecke told the Robb commissioners about outrages committed by Cortina and his men. The Mexican report called Glavecke "one of those who have most actively engaged in horse stealing in Mexico since the Rio Bravo has been the dividing line between the two countries." The report said Glavecke married Juan Cortina's cousin, that Glavecke and Cortina had a falling out, and that Glavecke held a personal grudge against Cortina.

The U.S. report quoted Thaddeus Rhodes about specific outrages committed under Cortina's protection. The Mexican report said Rhodes, known as Teodoro, "is a resident of Rosario, in the county of Hidalgo, and under his authority and protection a band of robbers dwelt, who pillaged the farms of Reynosa and villages of Nuevo Leon." The report said Rhodes, as a judge, presided over sheriff's auctions at which Tejano land holdings were sold at a low price to Anglos.

To demonstrate that Mexican ranchers suffered at the hands of Texans raiding into Mexico, the commission cited the case of Mexican rancher Leonidas Guerra, who tracked his stolen horses to Beeville and found them in the possession of Thomas Marsden, sheriff of Bee County. Marsden bought them for a fraction of their real value, which, said the Mexican report, proved he knowingly bought stolen property.

While the U.S. report blamed Cortina and his associates with launching cattle-stealing raids in Texas, the Mexican report

Gen. Juan Cortina. The U.S. report blamed him for instigating cattle raids while the Mexican border commission report defended him.

dismissed the complaints against Cortina as being based on Texans' hatred for Cortina going back to his border revolt of 1859. That was when Cortina and followers captured Brownsville, shouting "Death to the Americans" and "Viva Mexico." Because of the animosity against Cortina, the Mexican report said, "No crime was committed on the Texas side in which General Cortina's influence was not seen . . . Not a cow was stolen in Texas but Gen. Cortina's hand was not discovered in it . . . When a fact really occurred, it was disguised under the darkest colors, and when there were no facts, these were invented." The report said Cortina's influence was not understood by Americans in the context of Mexico's political history.

The Mexican report said the problems originated in Texas, which it described as a place with "great centers of corruption and unprecedented immorality." It found South Texas to be the refuge of criminals who fled from justice in Mexico. It was a refuge for criminals from the United States who sought a fortune and "were unscrupulous of the means of procuring it." It said South Texas was a haven for vagrants hoping, "in the shadows of disorganization and lawlessness, to escape punishment for their crimes."

By contrast, the report described Mexico along the border as a place of wonderfully peaceful and law-abiding citizens and concluded that "the moral condition of our frontier is far superior to that of Texas." You can almost sense (at least I can) that the Mexican commissioners must have taken no little pleasure in redirecting the accusations from Mexico to Texas.

While grievances on both sides were deep and the dueling reports hurled insults across the border, both sides agreed that cattle and horses were being stolen, that raids across the river were being conducted, and that murders were being committed. But for Mexico, they stemmed from Texas; and for Texas, they stemmed from Mexico. Neither report led to any policy changes, but they did present a detailed picture of the chaotic and lawless times in South Texas that followed the Civil War.

— July 17, 2013

HURRICANE — 1

On the last day of August 1919, a tropical storm crossed the Atlantic, hit the Florida Keys on Sept. 10 and churned across the Gulf with the sea in front of the storm rising as much as 15 feet.

On Saturday Sept. 13, people in Corpus Christi noticed that flounder were crowding in close to shore. Kids diving off Loyd's Pier found the water filled with crabs. Lucy Caldwell, a teacher on vacation staying at the Nueces Hotel, decided not to go bathing in the bay. "The water gave one the impression of a child denied something and chafing in a suppressed manner."

When the hurricane hit the barrier islands, people at Port Aransas sheltered in the sand hills, scooping out holes in the dunes in which to crouch while the fierce wind lashed them with wet sand. On Harbor Island, the storm ruptured oil tanks and turned massive timbers at the port facilities into dangerous battering rams.

At the Nueces Hotel, the rain was so thick guests could hardly see across Water Street. Lucy Caldwell said the wind threw the water of the bay "exactly as you would dash a bucket of water onto a fire." But there was no alarm. The Weather Bureau advised there would be a 40 mph gale with rain but no real danger. A few hours later, it revised its warning and urged an evacuation of North Beach.

As storm waters filled the lobby of the Nueces Hotel, Lucy Caldwell said the staff put on bathing suits and dove under the water to see if bodies of storm victims had washed in. A few blocks away, at the 1914 Courthouse, a place of refuge, two women gave birth during the storm.

On North Beach, the former Breakers Hotel had been converted into a government hospital for soldiers wounded in World War I. The roof was ripped off and the basement flooded, but the building was standing and refugees huddled on the upper floors.

At Spohn Hospital on North Beach, run by Sisters of the Incarnate Word, patients and nurses huddled in the main building, praying as the storm ripped away one wing. Sister M. Thais went to rescue a paralyzed patient; her body later washed ashore at Portland.

When the Bob Hall home was pulled apart by the storm, Hall, his wife, and parents escaped through a window into crashing water 15 to 20 feet deep. They clung to wreckage in a raging turmoil. "My husband's parents, being feeble, were the first to drown," Mrs. Hall said. "They were swept off a piece of a house and drowned, with us helpless to save them."

At the highest pitch of fury, Percy Reid, his wife, and five-year-old son jumped from the second story of their home on North Beach. When Mrs. Reid scrambled on to a piece of driftwood, she saw the family collie "Scotch" on another raft. He left his and swam to hers. Her clothes were ripped away by the fury of the storm as waves crashed over the raft and the horizontal rain, driven by the wind, stung like birdshot. It was darker than the darkest night. When the storm washed her overboard, the collie got a grip on her hair with his teeth and pulled her back to safety.

Ted Fuller, 10, his aunt and sister, took refuge in an empty house. As houses around them were toppled by the subversive force of the storm, walls crashed and roofs fell flat. As the house of refuge began to collapse, the Fullers tried to escape through a hole in the ceiling. Others struggled to get out first. Esther yelled, "Let Ted out! He's just a little boy!"

Ted squeezed out as the building collapsed. He and his sister fought to hold on to a makeshift raft in a violent maelstrom of rain, wind and water. Ted heard screams in the night and in a flash of lightning saw his aunt drown as waves swamped their raft and storm-tossed timbers crashed into them. When Ted passed out, Esther held his head out of the water.

On Monday morning, the storm was spent, the air still, the bay calm. Guests at the Nueces Hotel found two feet of water in the lobby. The scene outside was a mass of wreckage. Lucy Caldwell said pitiful people showed up looking for lost relatives. A man came to the hotel who had floated with his wife and baby for hours and finally lost them. A boy came in who had seen his mother, father and sisters drown.

Many who drowned and many who survived washed up around White Point. Rescuers found one woman's body hanging by her hair in a mesquite. Another woman was found dead on a roof, her hair tangled in nails. They found a dead cow with a rope on it

By 5 p.m. on Sept. 14, floodwaters were rising on Peoples Street (top photo) in the downtown area. Five days after the storm a trolley car was still stranded at Mesquite and Laguna.

floating in the bay; as they pulled it in, they saw a woman's body at the other end. They cleaned oil-covered bodies with gasoline and stacked them up for burial.

Ted Fuller and sister Esther survived. Mrs. Bob Hall survived, washed ashore at White Point. Mrs. Percy Reid survived and later found her husband and five-year-old son alive. Total casualties for the area were 357. The death toll in Corpus Christi was 284, but many believed that the toll was between 500 and 600 because so many unidentified bodies were buried in mass graves.

A close-up of the pile of debris cleaned up and dumped at the edge of the bay at Hall's Bayou. Spohn Sanitarium is in the distance.

Martial law was declared and National Guardsmen patrolled to prevent looting. Relief kitchens fed the homeless. North Beach was a sea of mud. The areas along the bayfront were covered with the splintered remains of buildings and bayfront piers. Rescue workers took notes on each body that was found. Maps showed the location of mass graves.

A month and a half after the storm, the Maxwell P. Dunne funeral home exhumed mass graves at Portland and White Point and floated the bodies across the bay on a barge for reburial at Rose Hill Cemetery. Later, the Red Cross erected a granite memorial in Rose Hill dedicated to the storm victims. The terrible 1919 hurricane was the greatest disaster in Corpus Christi's history, the storm of the century.

— July 24, 2013

HURRICANE — 2

The Weather Bureau warned on Friday, Sept. 8, 1961 that a dangerous storm named Hurricane Carla would hit the Texas coast, probably around Corpus Christi.

On Sunday, Corpus Christi residents started boarding up. The downtown was evacuated after reports warned that Carla's storm surge could top the seawall. North Beach and the islands were evacuated and 15,000 people sought shelter at the Courthouse and schools. The National Guard was called out even before the storm hit.

On Monday, Sept. 11, Carla, which had been aimed at Port Aransas, turned right and slammed into Port Lavaca. While there was damage at Corpus Christi, it was less than had been expected. Winds downed power lines, uprooted trees, and broke windows. Bridges were washed out on Ocean Drive and old island passes were reopened. The Padre Island Causeway was damaged.

It was a lucky near miss for Corpus Christi. Experts said if Carla had struck Port Aransas straight on the pass would have funneled the storm directly at Corpus Christi, and it would have swamped North Beach and the downtown, even with the seawall, like the deadly hurricane of 1919.

Six years later brought Hurricane Beulah. Corpus Christi was on the upper edge of the storm, which produced record rains and flooding after it stormed ashore near Brownsville on Sept. 20, 1967. One effect from Beulah was that commodes all over Corpus Christi backed up from increased pressure in the sewer system. Afterwards, people would say that something with a bad odor smelled like Beulah.

Sunday Aug. 2, 1970 was a sunny day in Corpus Christi. Many expected the approaching storm named Celia to hit Port Lavaca, like Carla, and hurricane watchers dismissed Celia as "more show than blow."

337

As Celia turned west, police in squad cars with loudspeakers patrolled North Beach, urging people to leave. As a yacht was lifted out of the water by a mobile crane at the marina, it began to spin wildly. The winds reached 112 mph and any chances of getting the other yachts out of the water were gone. Patients at Spohn Hospital were moved away from the east-facing windows.

By 1 p.m., wildly flapping red and black hurricane flags at the marina were ripped to shreds by gale-force winds. By 2 p.m., the eye of the storm compacted, from 40 miles wide to 10 miles wide. Like an ice skater who brings in her arms to spin faster, the storm gained speed and intensity.

By 3:30 p.m., Celia's winds reached 140 mph. The center of the storm was just south of Port Aransas. Ten minutes later, hurricane winds whipped inland with hard, driving, horizontal rain. Power went out. Celia's eye was over Corpus Christi Bay. At 4:30 p.m. in Corpus Christi, the force of hurricane winds uprooted trees, broke windows, tore off roofs, filled the air with flying debris. By 5:30, the winds reached 161 mph. Three hours later, it was over. The winds died down as darkness fell.

On Tuesday morning, 450,000 people in Corpus Christi and surrounding towns were without electricity. Dazed residents found neighborhoods in shambles, with uprooted trees, splintered fences, caved-in walls, crushed cars, downed telephone poles and roofless houses. In the next few days, with power out, people held barbecue parties to cook meat before it spoiled. Ice was in great demand.

Celia left 11 dead in Texas. Experts described it as very unusual. Corpus Christi received most of its damage from the left side of the storm, usually the weak side, and experts were shocked at how quickly the storm became "super-energized." Compared to Carla, Celia was a weak storm, but people would never forget the awful destructive power of a storm that was supposed to be more show than blow.

In August 1980, Hurricane Allen looked to be one of the worst storms that had ever threatened the Texas coast. This Category 5 storm, with 190 mph winds, was so large it covered the western Gulf of Mexico and the Weather Service posted a hurricane warning for the entire Texas coast. Nearly a million residents evacuated.

The storm pointed toward Brownsville, but experts predicted a right turn toward Corpus Christi. On Saturday, Aug. 9, Allen stalled and lost intensity. When it made landfall, it did turn right, but the

Hurricane Celia crammed shrimp boats against the north end of Conn Brown Harbor at Aransas Pass. Some boats were blown ashore and some were piled on top of others.

brunt of the storm hit remote King Ranch, the least populated area along the coast. Still, the storm surge at Corpus Christi was the highest, at nine feet, since the 1919 storm. North Beach was covered with water; piers along the bayfront were destroyed; the JFK Causeway and parts of Flour Bluff were under water.

As with Carla, Allen was a near miss for Corpus Christi. It was a powerful storm that weakened before it made landfall below the city. It was such a dangerous storm, and so many people left town before it hit, that it created a sense of complacency about these terrible storms that is still with us today.

People who lived in Corpus Christi in 1970 always remember Celia. They remember what it was like without power, the dark nights, no air-conditioning, the heat thick and still. But who remembers Bret? For Corpus Christi, Hurricane Bret, a category 3 storm, was another near-miss.

On Aug. 23, 1999, Bret was aimed at Corpus Christi, but it turned south and made landfall in Kenedy County. As the case with Allen,

A man surveys the wreckage of the Gateway Mobile Home Park on Lexington Boulevard after Hurricane Celia struck.

this was the best possible place for a hurricane to strike, at least it was for Corpus Christi. A lot of people left the city, clogging I-37 from Corpus Christi to San Antonio. Bret brought a lot of rain and, after it was over, the same complacency that prevailed after Allen.

We have had some near misses, with hurricanes in the 1930s and 1940s. We had Celia. But no great destructive storms have hit Corpus Christi since 1919, which was the single greatest disaster in Corpus Christi history. The official death toll was 284, but the toll may have been much higher. We are six years away from the 100th anniversary of that terrible storm. No one could say that we're overdue for a major hurricane, but there's no denying that we have been very lucky.

—July 31, 2013

THE BORDEN BROTHERS

We all know that Gail Borden Jr. is famous for inventing the process to condense milk, although in Texas the Borden name is older than canned milk. The Borden brothers were active participants and fighters in the Texas Revolution.

Thomas Henry Borden, second oldest of four brothers, migrated to Texas in 1822 and became surveyor for Stephen F. Austin's colony. He was followed by older brother Gail Borden Jr., Paschal Pavolo Borden, and younger brother John Pettit. Their father, Gail Borden Sr., brought the rest of the family and set up a blacksmith shop at San Felipe de Austin.

Gail Borden Jr. farmed on the Colorado River at Egypt, Texas, then moved to San Felipe to succeed his brother as surveyor. When Stephen F. Austin was imprisoned in Mexico, he managed Austin's affairs during his absence.

At San Felipe in 1835, Gail, Thomas and Joseph Baker started a newspaper, the Telegraph and Texas Register, which became the mouthpiece of the Texas Revolution. When San Felipe was evacuated during the Runaway Scrape in March 1836, Gail moved the paper to Harrisburg and as the issue for April 14 was being printed, the ink not dry, Gen. Antonio López de Santa Anna arrived. His soldiers dumped Borden's press and type trays in with the alligators in Buffalo Bayou.

Gail's brothers were busy fighting. John was with George Collinsworth's squad that captured Goliad in October 1835 and he was with Ira Westover's Texans who captured Fort Lipantitlán without a shot. Thomas was with Ben Milam in the siege of Bexar and with Jim Bowie in the Grass Fight. John and Paschal were in Moseley Baker's company at the battle of San Jacinto.

After the war, John Borden was appointed the first land commissioner of the Republic. Thomas helped lay out the city of Houston and entered the real estate business. Paschal opened a general store in Columbia and Gail Jr., who sold the Telegraph and Texas Register, was appointed customs collector at Galveston.

Like his blacksmith father, Gail Jr. showed a natural talent for inventing things. In Galveston, he invented a "locomotive bath house" for women to use to bathe in the Gulf of Mexico. He invented a process to boil meat until it was reduced to a thick paste, then mixed it with flour and baked it. He called it a meat biscuit.

Borden was trying to prepare a portable soup for friends going to California during the Gold Rush of 1849. He set up a large kettle and boiled 120 pounds of veal, reducing it to 10 pounds of extract, which was like melted glue. It was hot and humid in July and when he couldn't dry it out it occurred to him to bake it. "To my great satisfaction," Gail said in a letter, "the bread was found to contain all the primary principles of meat, and with a better flavor than simple veal soup."

Borden's patent meat biscuit won a gold medal at the Great Exhibition in London in 1851 and it won a medal at Henry Kinney's Lone Star Fair in Corpus Christi in 1852. But the prize-winning meat biscuit didn' sell because people didn't like the taste. After the meat biscuit, he developed, in 1853, a process for condensing milk in a vacuum and eventually opened factories around the country. His Eagle brand of condensed milk became known around the world. He died at Borden, Texas on Jan. 11, 1874.

We follow the Borden story to San Patricio County. Gail's youngest brother, John Pettit Borden, married Mary Susan Hatch, daughter of George Hatch, and moved to the Ingleside area in 1855. Borden bought land, started a ranch, and the couple had four daughters and one son.

John's son was Sidney Gail Borden. He enlisted in the Confederate Army at 19. After the war, he returned to San Patricio County and bought land and opened a store on what had been a sheep ranch owned by a man named Sharp.

This marked the beginning of the Sharpsburg, named after the sheep rancher, but it was Borden's town. As it grew, it gained a gristmill, blacksmith shop, cotton gin, school, post office and a population of 300. Robert Kinghorn, a blacksmith and carpenter, bought two 10-acre plots from Borden, and moved his family from Corpus Christi to Sharpsburg. Sharpsburg was north of Nuecestown on a slight rise near the Nueces River. Borden owned a ferry on the river near where I-37 crosses it today at Labonte Park. His business

Borden's Ferry in 1913 (top photo). The ferry crossing was located near where today's Highway 77 and I-37 cross the Nueces River. Below, Sidney Gail Borden's home at Sharpsburg in 1908.

partner in the store was D. C. Rachal, rancher at White Point. Borden planted grapes and sold wine labeled "Sharpsburg's Best" and "Rachal's Choice." The river was swift and navigable then. Borden and Rachal owned a flat-bottomed schooner named Nueces Valley which carried cotton and wool down the river and brought back commercial goods. Capt. Andrew Anderson recalled that he often sailed his vessel "Flour Bluff up the river to Sharpsburg.

Gail Borden Jr., John Pettit Borden, Judge Sidney Gail Borden

Once, when the river was in flood stage, he unloaded lumber from his ship at Borden's store. He said the river must have been about five miles wide.

After Borden was elected justice of the peace in 1872, he was called Judge Borden. In the Nuecestown Raid on Easter weekend 1875, Borden was one of several people held hostage. The bandits took his white horse and gold watch. After the captives were freed and the bandits rode away, Borden raised a posse at Sharpsburg and tracked the bandits to Laredo, where they crossed the river to safety. "Boys, I've brought you on a wild-goose chase," Borden said. "We'd better head for home."

Borden married Mary Sullivan, built a cotton gin at Sharpsburg, and subdivided land west of his ranch into farm tracts. He was an early promoter of converting ranchland into cotton acreage. Borden was elected county judge, county surveyor, and appointed postmaster at Sharpsburg. He had the first telephone line strung in San Patricio County, which connected Sharpsburg to Corpus Christi 20 miles away.

Sidney Gail Borden, nephew of Gail Borden Jr., died at his home in Sharpsburg on Jan. 31, 1908 and was buried in Rose Hill Cemetery in Corpus Christi. There is nothing there today to mark the site of the old Borden home or his once thriving river town of Sharpsburg.

— August 7, 2013

344

BETWEEN THE WARS — 1

On Sunday, Nov. 10, 1918, the Caller advised readers, "When peace comes, avoid crowds, but yell a little and insist that the bells ring and whistles blow. It would be too cow-like to chew a cud in silence when the world receives official notice."

On Nov. 11, the great war was over. More than 10 million men had been killed. In a single day, Britain lost 60,000 soldiers on the Somme. More than 1.2 million were killed at Verdun. In Corpus Christi, with news of Armistice Day, church bells were ringing and horns blowing as people took to the streets to celebrate, waving flags and cheering.

Anita Lovenskiold, a 16-year-old, wrote in her diary: "Oh, what a grand and glorious day! The war has ended. This morning the whistles blew, bells rang, and music began to play. We heard a lot of yelling. It was a parade and we sure did some running to catch up. I lost my money and goodness knows how many hairpins."

Days later, the flu pandemic was declared over and the city lifted the ban on public gatherings. Schools, theaters, and soda fountains were reopened. With the quarantine lifted, soldiers at the Camp Scurry Army base held a dance to celebrate the end of the war and the end of the epidemic.

A year later, on Sunday, Sept. 14, 1919, Corpus Christi was hit by the worst storm in the city's history. The downtown and North Beach were devastated; as many as 500 people died and the bodies of the victims washed up across Nueces Bay. As it entered the decade of the 1920s, Corpus Christi was trying to recover from the storm, efforts that led to building the port and eventually the seawall.

Nationally, Prohibition began on Jan. 16, 1920, but Corpus Christi had been dry since citizens voted for countywide prohibition in 1916. This began the era of bootleg liquor, backyard stills and tequila smuggled on pack mules from Mexico.

For the first time in history, women voted for president on Nov. 2, 1920. The Caller, which had opposed women's suffrage, noted: "We see that we should have read the signs of the times as well as appreciated the justice of the plea. But all is well that ends well."

The first traffic crossed the temporary Nueces Bay Causeway on Oct. 21, 1921. This wooden bridge replaced the first causeway, destroyed in the 1919 storm. Some merchants opposed building it, afraid it would take more business out of town than it would bring in.

A fire on Nov. 20, 1921 destroyed the downtown generating plant, leaving the city without electricity. To print the newspaper, the Caller hooked up a Fordson tractor to run the press, something learned after the 1919 storm. The city was without power for months.

President Warren Harding signed legislation on May 22, 1922 to construct the Port of Corpus Christi. A bond election to establish the navigation district passed 10 to 1 that October.

In 1922, the city built the Pleasure Pier off Peoples Street at a modest cost of $8,200. It became a favorite place for strolling and fishing, one of the first places visited by tourists who wanted to get out over the water. The Pier Café opened in 1926 in an old fisherman's shack at the foot of the Pleasure Pier. It was later moved into a new building on the south side of the pier entrance.

A sensational murder case dominated the news in October when reputed Klan leader Fred Roberts was shot to death. Sheriff Frank Robinson and three others were indicted for murder, but acquitted in a trial in Laredo. The former sheriff, fearing Klan retaliation, moved to Mexico.

Three years later, on July 5, 1925, a shootout at a house of sporting girls left four men dead. In the sequence of events, three men left Bessie Miller's on Sam Rankin Street: Paul McAllister, George Ryder, and Rufus McMurray. Two constables, C. M. Bisbee and R. R. Bledsoe, drove up and shots were fired. Four men were killed.

On Nov. 9, 1924, a train called the Blackland Special left Corpus Christi with farmers and businessmen wearing pearl-gray Stetsons on board. The train, with exhibit cars filled with farm products, promoted the blackland farming of South Texas.

Work began on a breakwater in 1924. A railroad trestle was built into the bay and granite rocks were hauled to the end of the line

Aerial photo in 1928 shows the Pleasure Pier jutting into the bay in front of the Nueces Hotel. On the bluff is the Nixon Building, erected in 1926, and next to it is the Plaza Hotel, which was still under construction.

where a barge-mounted crane dropped quarried boulders to the bay floor. As the breakwater took shape, the crew pulled up the trestle as they moved backwards. It was completed in 1926.

Seven years to the day after the great storm, on Sept. 14, 1926, the Port of Corpus Christi opened. Excursion trains brought 25,000 visitors to double the city's population. The city was draped in bunting for a parade from downtown to Cargo Dock One. Three U.S. destroyers arrived for port opening day.

During the boom that followed, Maston Nixon built the 12-story Nixon Building, which began the conversion of the bluff from cattle barons' mansions to the city's first tall buildings. The Plaza Hotel, then the Driscoll, followed the Nixon Building, as the artistic and beautiful were cleared away for the commercial and practical.

Gutzon Borglum, who became famous as the Mount Rushmore sculptor, was hired in 1928 to design a bayfront plan for Corpus Christi. His plan called for a seawall and a 32-foot-high statue of Christ inside the breakwater, but the city had no money and the plan was shelved.

The port in 1929 led the nation in cotton tonnage. During cotton-picking time, Leopard Street on Saturdays was crowded with cotton pickers and families. Corpus Christi at the end of the decade was a prosperous place.

William Ashley "Billy" Sunday, a former baseball pitcher turned evangelist, opened a five-week revival in Corpus Christi on March 3, 1929. The revival meetings were in a shed at the Port Compress. The city repaired the roads leading to the port area in anticipation of the thousands who would attend the evangelist's meetings. Most of the evening sessions drew 5,000 to 6,000 people.

Billy Sunday's sermons were covered in the Caller. A few of his quotes were: "Nightclubs are the vestibules of hell." "Generations unborn have the inherent right to be born right." "The Constitution was cradled in prayer." "In an endeavor to serve God and mammon, the church is cross-eyed." "We came from the Garden of Eden, not from a zoological garden."

On Oct. 29, 1929, the stock market crashed and $30 billion in paper value was lost, banks closed, jobs vanished, families were put on the road, farms were repossessed. This marked the beginning of the Great Depression.

— Aug. 14, 2013

BETWEEN THE WARS — *2*

In Corpus Christi in the 1930s, Sunday, Monday and Tuesday were called "Prosperity Days" meant to encourage positive thinking, said the newspaper, since the difference between hard times and good times was mostly psychological. "If we can just actually feel that we are on the way back to prosperity, by golly, we are."

In January 1930, a new bakery opened at Leopard and Palm. Fehr Baking made Fair-Made Bread. That summer a dance marathon on North Beach lasted 31 days, from July 24 until Aug. 25. One couple got married as they danced. The winning (and exhausted) couple received $675, a lot of money then.

In the 1930s, Corpus Christi firemen made $2 a day, but steak was 15 cents a pound and pork chops 10 cents a pound. An Erskine automobile at Winerich Motors cost $895. As the Depression deepened in 1931, Corpus Christi was trying to stay positive. Oil was discovered in the Saxet Field and the city's port, five years old, led the nation in cotton tonnage. But it was hard to stay positive as cotton prices fell from 18 cents to five cents a pound and farm workers on Chapman Ranch were let go. On King Ranch, 250 head of cattle were rounded up to furnish meat for hungry families in Kingsville.

During the "bank holiday" in March 1933, the Chamber of Commerce issued trade certificates for $1 each that were accepted by town merchants. Many were never redeemed; they were saved as souvenirs.

In the 1930s, the bascule bridge became a nuisance. When the port opened in 1926, the bascule was the top attraction and in the early days there was always a crowd gathered to watch the bridge go up and down. But the thrill didn't last. When the siren sounded, signaling the approach of a ship, motorists were in for a long wait, 20 minutes or more.

The nuisance for motorists was an outright danger for ships. The 97-foot opening was a tight squeeze for the large vessels visiting the port. Ships often brushed against the bridge's fenders. Part of the hull of "Old Ironsides" was scraped off when it smashed into the bascule in 1932. Navigating the bascule opening was called threading the needle.

As the New Deal took hold, the Works Progress Administration opened a sewing room at 613 Waco where women were paid up to $43 a month to sew clothes for the needy. Another WPA project in 1935 was to terrace the slope at Cole Park to prevent erosion.

Around the country, crude camps of the homeless and destitute sprouted on the outskirts of cities. Corpus Christi's migrant camp was on the north end of North Beach.

Construction of the seawall began in 1939. In the early stages, creosoted pilings were driven to provide a footing for the embankment. Reinforced concrete was poured in 40-foot lengths. The area behind the seawall, the levee, was built up with dredged fill from the bay bottom. The two T-heads and L-Head were part of the plan. Originally, there was supposed to be another L-head. In building the T-heads, wooden pilings were driven to outline the structure, then bay fill was pumped into the enclosures. When work was completed, the city had been extended two blocks and the bayfront elevated 14 feet above sea level, or 3.7 feet above the high water mark of the 1919 storm.

When the seawall improvement project began, John Govatos, owner of the Pier Cafe at the foot of the Pleasure Pier, moved up to the bluff to run the Nixon Café. His brother Jim took over the Pier Café. It was on Water Street, but the water was now a block away. The cafe did not thrive next to an expanse of churned-up mud.

When they filled in the waterfront, John Govatos said, it made a mess of the Pier Café. The water was gone, and the glamour was gone. With the extension of the bayfront, the Pleasure Pier was dismantled and both the Nueces Hotel and the Princess Louise were no longer at the water's edge and lost their standing as a seashore attraction.

As the seawall was taking shape, the Naval Air Station was being built, in a record seven months, beginning in June 1940. It represented an investment of $100 million, an investment that would pay during the war in the Pacific. While the seawall and NAS were under construction, the city was humming with activity,

A crew at work on the seawall in 1941. Photo by Doc McGregor.

hotels were packed and extra beds were put in lounges. The migrant camp on North Beach filled with workers and families who came hoping to get work building the Navy base.

Corpus Christi was one huge construction site. New sewer lines were being laid, ditches dug, streets paved or dug up for water and sewer lines. The downtown was a maze of detours. Dredge soil from the bay was piled in small mountains for use in raising the grade below South Bluff. As the bayfront was being transformed, the city's largest building, the 20-story Robert Driscoll Hotel, was rising on the bluff.

Corpus Christi's population in 1940 doubled from the last census 10 years earlier, to 57,301. Within a year, it had gained 30 percent, to 75,000. People grumbled about the disruption and the increase in prices that came with the growth. At Shoop's Grill, the price of a roast duck dinner shot up from 50 cents to 80 cents.

Sunday, Dec. 7, 1941 was a cool, placid day in Corpus Christi. Shortly after noon, people heard on radio that Japanese planes attacked U.S. bases at Pearl Harbor. At the Naval Air Station, leaves

An aerial shot by Doc McGregor in 1941 shows the white strip of reclaimed land between Water Street and the new seawall.

were cancelled. At the Caller-Times, printers in Sunday clothes began work on a special edition. In the midst of the chaos, reporters laughed when a man called wanting to know the time. That Monday at the Assembly & Repairs hangar at NAS, civilian workers stood in stunned silence to listen to Roosevelt's "a date which will live in of infamy" speech. After the president finished, people looked at each other, every face reflecting unasked questions, knowing their world was in for a change.

— Aug. 21, 2013

TRAINING GROUND

In June 1845, war with Mexico loomed as Texas prepared to join the U.S. Gen. Zachary Taylor was ordered to move the forces under his command from Fort Jesup in Louisiana to the contested region in Texas between the Nueces River and the Rio Grande. Corpus Christi, Taylor was told, would make a good staging place for the army.

The 3rd Infantry, commanded by Lt. Col. Ethan Allen Hitchcock, boarded a steamer at New Orleans on July 22, 1845. Three days later, the ship arrived at the Aransas Pass channel and the American flag was planted on St. Joseph's Island, the first to fly over Texas soil. "We have found good water," Hitchcock wrote in his diary, "and had fish and oysters for breakfast."

Taylor was undecided about where to concentrate the army, trying to choose between Corpus Christi and Live Oak Point. He visited Aransas City at Live Oak Point and dined at the home of James Power before he decided that Corpus Christi had certain advantages, including a natural theater of ground on the bluff where troops could drill. A disadvantage, he soon learned, were mudflats that made navigation across the bay difficult.

Moving the first companies across the bay was not easy. The lighter Undine drew four feet, but there were only three feet of water over the extensive mudflats across the bay. Taylor ordered two companies to embark on the Undine which promptly ran aground. Fishing boats were hired to ferry companies K and G, which landed on North Beach at sundown on Aug. 1, 1845. It was too rough to land their supplies so they ate hard ship's biscuits and slept on the sand.

Next morning they killed rattlesnakes by the hundreds and put up tents. Within days, army tents stretched across the slough toward Corpus Christi. When officers dined with Corpus Christi merchant Frederick Belden and his wife Mauricia (Arocha), they were given a dish made of corn meal, chopped meat, and cayenne pepper wrapped in corn husk and boiled. Capt. W. S. Henry said, "I know of nothing more palatable."

Hitchcock had embankments thrown up for defense and since no artillery had arrived he borrowed two old cannons from Henry Kinney which, one officer said, "were more dangerous to ourselves than to any enemy." Taylor called the encampment Fort Marcy, after Secretary of War William Marcy.

The troops spent their days with drills and target practice. "The Mexican Army being largely composed of cavalry," Lt. Abner Doubleday wrote, "our infantry were constantly drilled in forming square to resist cavalry." A sergeant wrote that they had been firing ball cartridges at targets "and in almost every instance, at a hundred paces, the targets fall shattered to the ground."

A well was dug in what would be called Artesian Park, but the water tasted bad so they hauled water from the Nueces River for drinking and cooking.

During a thunderstorm on Aug. 24, a lightning bolt hit a tent pole, killing a slave owned by Lt. Braxton Bragg. A baby born during the storm, Henry wrote, should have been named Thunder. From a distance, the thunder sounded like cannon and the Army dragoons, who had traveled overland from Louisiana and were at San Patricio, thought Taylor was being bombarded. They galloped toward Corpus Christi in relief, only to meet Taylor riding out to visit them.

Next day, the steamship "Alabama" arrived with the 7th Infantry. As troops were boarding a lighter, Lt. Ulysses S. Grant mistakenly fell into the bay. The men were laughing as he was pulled up like a wet parcel.

On Sept. 12, the steamboat Dayton exploded and the wounded and dead were brought to Corpus Christi. Hitchcock picked a burial site (today's Old Bayview Cemetery) where ten men were buried. Henry wrote, "May the God of Battles receive and cherish them."

Lt. Grant, who loved horses, bought four mustangs, which were cheap in South Texas. When they ran away, an officer joked, "I heard that Grant lost five or six dollars' worth of horses the other day." Horse races were popular diversions. Capt. Henry described one race between two mustang ponies. "One pony bolted and, not at all alarmed by the crowd, cleared two or three piles of rubbish, knocked one man down, threw his rider, stopped, turned, and snorted, as much as to say, 'Beat that if you can.' "

Gen. Zachary Taylor visited Live Oak Point before he decided to concentrate his army at Henry Kinney's village of Corpus Christi. From the Library of Congress.

On. Dec. 3, a norther struck and every tent was covered with ice. The temperature dropped to 23 degrees and cartloads of fish were gathered on the shore. One lieutenant, suffering from chills and fever, wrote home that, "Uncle Sam made a mighty poor bargain when he got Texas, even though he did get it for nothing."

Gen. Taylor celebrated New Year's Day 1846 by drinking eggnog with his officers. A play called "The Wife" opened at the Army Theater and the Union Theater featured performances of "The Ambassador's Ball." On Feb. 16, as Texas joined the Union, an Annexation Ball was held at the Union Theater. Music was provided by the army bands. Officers at the Annexation Ball included several future generals in the Civil War — Ulysses S. Grant, James Longstreet, George Meade, Braxton Bragg, John Magruder, among others.

As the army prepared to leave for the Rio Grande, Taylor sent patrols to look for a route of march. One traveled down Padre Island and another followed the old Matamoros Road. Because of a

Daniel P. Whiting's lithograph of the U. S. Army encamped along the Corpus Christi Bay shoreline on North Beach in October 1845.

shortage of forage for horses on the island, Taylor chose the inland route, which became known as Taylor's Trail.

"We are delighted at the prospects of the march," Henry wrote, "having become restless and anxious for a change. We anticipate no little fun, and all sorts of adventure, upon the route."

For seven months, Corpus Christi had been the training ground for the coming Mexican war. Separate units were melded into a real army whose fighting abilities would be tested at Palo Alto, Resaca de la Palma, and greater battles ahead in Mexico. The army began to depart on March 8, 1846, a day of blue skies and sunshine. Elements of the 3rd Infantry, the first to arrive, were the last to leave. As they marched away to the tune of "The Girl I Left Behind Me," Henry looked back. "The fields of white canvas were no longer visible and the campground looked like desolation itself. But the bright waters of the bay looked as sweet as ever."

—*Aug. 28, 2013*

GHOST TOWNS OF COAST - 1

New towns emerged on the coast after the Texas Revolution, beginning with Aransas City, Lamar, Corpus Christi, Copano, St. Mary's, Indianola, Saluria, and Aransas village on St. Joseph's. With the exception of Corpus Christi, these nascent towns flourished, declined and died.

Aransas City was established in 1836 on Live Oak Point on Live Oak Peninsula between Aransas and Copano bays. The sandy shores were empty wilderness. Karankawas who had lived there were gone, or were mostly gone, and Mexican rancheros in the region had departed after San Jacinto.

Most of this wilderness was owned by James Power and James Hewetson, the empresarios who contracted with Mexico to bring in Mexican and Irish colonists; Mexico wanted Catholics to settle in Texas as a buffer against North Americans. In payment for bringing in settlers, Power and Hewetson were granted 250,000 acres covering the shores of Copano and Aransas bays, Live Oak, Lookout and St. Charles peninsulas, Matagorda, St. Joseph's and Mustang islands.

After his wife Dolores died in child-birth, Power married his sister-in-law Tomasita Portilla. In 1836, he built a home and store at Live Oak Point near the old Spanish fort of Aranzazú, built to command the entrance to Copano Bay. Power planned a town called Aransas City near the south end of where Copano Bay Causeway is now.

The site was chosen to be a confluence of trade between the Chihuahua region of Mexico and New Orleans. Besides Aransas City, other coming coastal towns were connected to the Mexican trade. Power's store was a great emporium handling leaf tobacco, staple groceries, hardware, guns, calico, wines, whisky, and products destined for Chihuhua. Wool, hides and crude silver bars came in by ox-cart from Mexico. A wharf from Power's store stretched into the bay where ships docked. The Republic put up a customs house and appointed George W. Fulton customs collector.

President Sam Houston asked his friend Power to sign a peace treaty for the Republic with Lipan Chief Castro. The chief and his retinue, in full ceremonial dress, arrived in January 1838 and the treaty was signed. Power laid out his new town with 75 lots, one street named Washington and one named Market. In April 1838, he advertised the sale of town lots in the Houston Telegraph & Register. Two weeks later, the paper reported that the sale was postponed "due to rumors circulating relative to the incursion of the Mexicans."

They were not rumors. Mexico, still claiming Texas, sent a cavalry detachment to Aransas City, one of several incursions by Mexican forces after independence. Power's store was plundered and he was taken to Matamoros as prisoner. He was freed after five months.

Back home, Power learned that a town was being built on Lookout Point across the bay. He could see it from his porch. The new town was the work of James Byrne, a veteran of the Revolution whose life was spared in the massacre at Goliad. Byrne named the town "Lamar" after Mirabeau Lamar who succeeded Houston as president.

Seth Ballou, a former sailor, started a steam-powered ferry service between Lamar and Aransas City. A man named Willis Roberts wrote President Lamar that the air at Lookout Point was delightful, the water good, the sea-bathing luxurious. Fish, turtles and oysters were abundant. "My little Negroes can go out and get what they want."

Aransas City, incorporated in 1839, gained a mail route, Gideon Jaques opened a tavern, Benjamin F. Neal had a law office and new merchants were Henry Kinney and William Aubrey who, like Power, were engaged in the Mexican trade.

Byrne asked President Lamar to move the customs house from Aransas City to Lamar, pointing out that Aransas City had 12 buildings and 30 residents while Lamar had 20 houses and 60 residents. President Lamar was offered a bribe (a frame house and waterfront lot) to move the customs house. Politicians were no more honest then than now. Lamar ordered it moved.

Citizens at Aransas City met, with Henry Kinney presiding as chairman, and drafted a petition, which stated that the town of

A painting of Live Oak Point in 1842. James Power's first town, Aransas City on Live Oak Point, was in decline and within five years would be gone.

Lamar could not be reached by ships drawing seven feet of water, that Aransas City by contrast had an excellent harbor and seven feet of water within 100 yards of shore. But President Lamar could always resist pressures brought by allies of Sam Houston, his great enemy. The decision stood.

Henry Kinney left Aransas City in September 1839 to establish a trading post on Corpus Christi Bay, which was more convenient to the Mexican market. What became Corpus Christi was the westernmost port and settlement in Texas. Other residents of Aransas City moved to Corpus Christi, including Benjamin F. Neal, who would later become Corpus Christi's first mayor, and William Mann, who became Corpus Christi's wealthiest merchant.

William Bollaert, an Englishman who traveled through Texas in the 1840s, wrote in his journal for March 18, 1842: "10 a.m., came to anchor at Live Oak Point. This spot is the residence of Mr. James Power, an old empresario settler. He received us most hospitably. Had 'beefs' killed for us, supplied us with milk and fish. He was here with his family and had secreted in various parts of his house and behind doors an armament of loaded rifles and muskets, in case of a sudden attack."

In late July 1845, Gen. Zachary Taylor visited Power at Live Oak Point. Taylor's advance troops were on St. Joseph's Island and he

359

was trying to choose a site to concentrate his army: either Live Oak Peninsula below Aransas City or Corpus Christi. He decided on Corpus Christi.

As Aransas City declined, Lamar flourished. James Byrne paid to build a church, St. Joseph's Chapel, later called Stella Maris (Star of the Sea). Seth Ballou, the ferryman, and his slave Moses built the shellcrete church, which still stands. The gun-makers Samuel and James Colt bought a quarter interest in almost the whole of Lookout Peninsula and Goose Island, with the exception of Byrne's salt works near the Big Tree. In the 1870s, Lamar lost out to a new town built south of the old site of Aransas City called Rockport. By 1918, when the post office closed, old Lamar was a ghost town. Nothing remains of Aransas City. A forlorn granite slab beside Highway 35, near the south end of the causeway, marks the site of Power's house on Live Oak Point. It doesn't mention Aransas City.

— Sept. 4, 2013

GHOST TOWNS OF COAST - 2

Early coastal settlements of Aransas City, Lamar, Corpus Christi, Copano, St. Mary's, Indianola, Saluria, and Aransas village on St. Joseph's were connected in one way or another.

Irish empresario James Power founded Aransas City at Live Oak Point. He also founded the town of Copano and Saluria. Henry Kinney left Aransas City in 1839 to start his own town — Corpus Christi. Lamar and St. Mary's were competitors of Aransas City and Copano. Histories of these early towns are interwoven. with shared histories.

Aransas City was Power's town at Live Oak Point, near today's Fulton. It lost its custom house to Lamar, built on Lookout Point on Copano Bay. As Aransas City was dying, Power picked the old Copano landing place across Copano Bay to begin another town. This was five miles east of the present town of Bayside.

Copano already had a long history. With the deepest water in the western part of the Gulf, Copano was used as a port as far back as the 1700s. Supplies were landed there for Spanish garrisons at Bexar and La Bahia. A road connected Copano with the mission at Refugio. In the early 1830s, Copano was the place where Irish immigrants landed on their way to San Patricio and Refugio. At the beginning of the Revolution, Copano was considered vital by Texas and Mexico.

As Mexico prepared to put down the insurrection in Texas, a report by Juan Almonte pointed out that Copano "seems to be the deepest port in Texas. It has 15 to 18 feet of water at the bar and 10 or 12 throughout the bay. Ships can anchor within a very few yards of land. There are two roads from this port to Goliad." As Almonte's report makes clear, Copano was important, since an army from the Rio Grande moving into Texas would have to haul its supplies by mule trains from Mexico unless it controlled Copano.

In September 1835, Gen. Martin Perfecto de Cós landed 500 troops at Copano, the first hostile act of the Texas Revolution. James Power, from his vantage point at Live Oak Point, watched the unloading of the Mexican ship and sent a warning to Texans gathered at Refugio. For the Texans, Cós' landing was an act of war.

As the war unfolded, volunteers from the United States arrived at Copano, including the Mobile Greys, Kentucky Volunteers, Huntsville Volunteers, and the Invincibles. After the fall of the Alamo and the slaughter at Goliad, as Houston played hide-and-seek with Santa Anna, Copano was abandoned.

One of the unusual stories of the Revolution occurred at Copano. Gen. Thomas Rusk, secretary of war, sent Maj. Isaac Burton to scout the coast with 20 mounted Rangers. They followed the coastline around Mission Bay to reach Copano. Burton knew the Mexican army had been defeated at San Jacinto, that Santa Anna has been captured, but he didn't assume that the war was over.

Burton watched a suspicious ship arriving at Copano on June 2, 1836. He thought it might be bringing reinforcements for the Mexican army. Next morning at sunrise, Burton's Rangers signaled the ship to send a boat to shore. Five men from the ship came ashore and were captured. Burton put 16 Rangers on the boat and approached the ship, The Watchman." The captain of the ship surrendered without a shot fired. Using the Watchman as a decoy, Burton's men captured two other Mexican vessels loaded with supplies for the Mexican army. Burton's Rangers became known as the Horse Marines.

As Aransas City on Live Oak Point was dying in 1845 and 1846, James Power began promoting Copano. The townsite, near the old port, was surveyed and platted by 1847. Power began building a two-story shellcrete home on Power's Point, between the town and Mission Bay. A dozen houses were built on the bluff overlooking Copano Bay. Power's son-in-law, Walter Lambert, built a store and a pier and the Norton brothers built another store and pier. The Norton store served as a post office.

Before his plans could mature, Power died at his home on Live Oak Point on Aug. 15, 1852. He was buried in a vault on the grounds of his home; the body was later moved to Refugio. Power did not live to see his new house completed at Power's Point across the bay, but his widow Tomasita moved there.

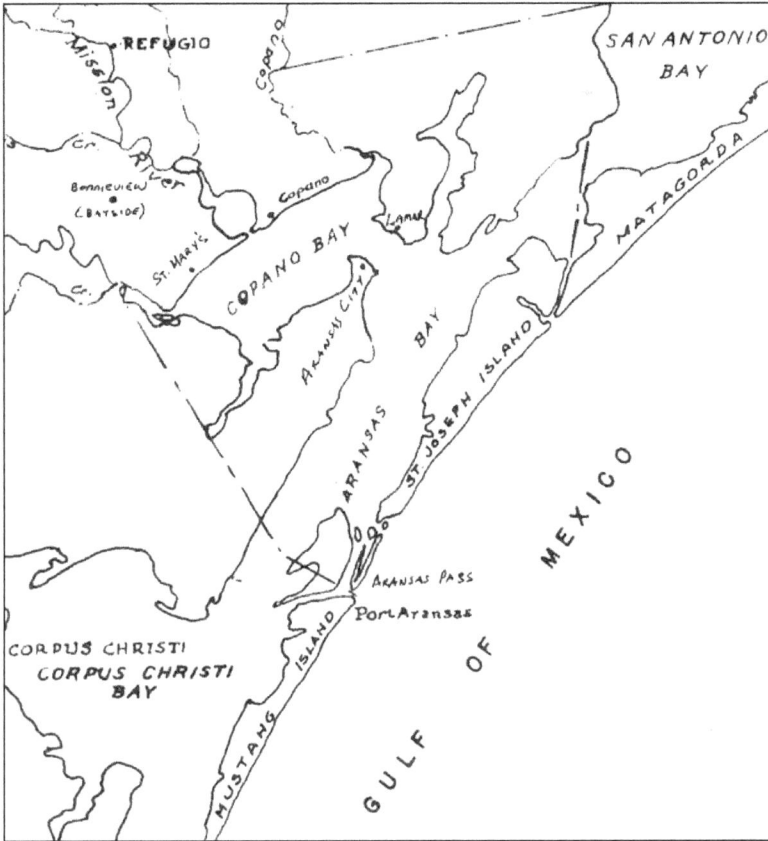

Map of Copano and St. Mary's fronting on Copano Bay. The village of Copano to the north and St. Mary's to the south. Map also shows the location of Aransas City at Live Oak Point and Lamar at Lookout Point.

Hobart Huson in "Refugio" quoted Judge W. L. Rea, who said he last visited Copano in 1870. "At that time, it was quite a settlement. There were about a dozen shell-concrete buildings. The old two-story shell-lime building in which Henry and Charles Norton had their store was standing, but not in use. A number of houses were vacant. The widow of the old Empresario lived in her two-story shell-lime house near the reef. At that time there was a thriving shipping business. Three-masted schooners came into port, and there was a prosperous business in shipping tallow and hides. These products were shipped from Copano to New Orleans. All the young men of Copano were engaged in loading boats. Vessels came within about 300 yards of the shore. The wharfs were not used. The hides were lightered from shore to the ships. Moses Simpson floated barrels of tallow on the water to the boats."

This was near the end for the town of Copano. Lack of freshwater was always a problem; Copano residents relied on captured rainwater stored in concrete (actually, shellcrete) cisterns. As Copano dwindled and the bay in front of the town silted up, closing off water-borne commerce, the residents moved to Refugio or to St. Mary's. By 1880, the post office was closed and the following year poor old Copano was merely listed as a place six miles northeast of St. Mary's, which had always been its main rival.

What is left of Copano is not easy to get to for anyone trying to reconcile the landscape with the written history. There is no road and the only way to get there is by boat. Vestiges of the old town are on the soft edge of a bank that is crumbling into Copano Bay. A study in 2005 warned that the remaining ruins of shellcrete houses and a cistern would fall into the bay because the shoreline is steadily eroding. Preservation Texas named Copano as one of Texas' most endangered historic places. The old town, once an important place in Texas history, is almost gone. Almost.

— Sept. 11, 2013

GHOST TOWNS OF COAST - 3

The history of St. Mary's on Copano Bay began with Joseph F. Smith, a lawyer who came to Texas from Arkansas and joined his uncle, Henry Smith, who served briefly as provisional governor of Texas during the Revolution.

Joseph F. Smith joined the punitive expedition to Mier in 1842 and was among those imprisoned at Perote Castle. Israel Canfield, a fellow prisoner, wrote in his diary that Smith "was one of the meanest men God ever put breath into." Probably not an objective observation, since John Henry Brown, who knew Smith, wrote in Indian Wars and Pioneers of Texas that he was "an eminently just man."

James Power, the empresario, would have agreed with Canfield. Smith, with an acquisitive eye, could ferret out weaknesses in land claims. He bought land certificates issued by the Republic, which were worthless unless land could be found that had not been filed on. Land that had not already been granted had to be surveyed, field notes filed with the land office, and patents issued. Smith reached the conclusion that some of Power's "premium" lands required final approval of the federal executive in Mexico, a step not taken by the empresario. The legal entanglements are beyond my scope, but essentially Smith thought the grants invalid.

Smith located his land certificates on Power's lands around Black Point on Copano Bay and requested patents. Power got a court injunction which resulted in a lawsuit. The case bounced around the courts until 1856, four years after Power's death, when the verdict was returned in Smith's favor.

With that judgment, Smith dusted off plans that had been shelved since 1839 for a town called St. Mary's of Aransas. The first site chosen was where Bayside is today, but the site was moved two miles up the coast where soundings revealed deeper water close to shore. The site was six miles southwest of Copano.

St. Mary's was laid off in seven tiers of 13 blocks fronting on the bay. Smith kept one block for his own use and built a three-story home on the site. St. Mary's became a thriving town, famous as a lumber port where longleaf pine from Florida was unloaded from three-masted schooners. The first wharf and warehouses were built by Thomas Taylor Williamson, one of Smith's associates. J. T. Cottingham and John Vineyard operated lumberyards. Dr. Rufus Nott built a drugstore and doctor's office. Early settlers included John Howland Wood, Cyrus Egery, and the Clark brothers. The town featured two hotels, the Neel House and the Ellis Hotel.

Like other coastal towns, it endured hard times during the Civil War. St. Mary's suffered because of the federal blockade that stifled commerce. In August 1861, Lt. John Kittredge took command of the USS Arthur in charge of the Union blockade in the Aransas Pass area and kept the coastal towns in an uproar.

In July of 1842, a time of panic on Corpus Christi and Aransas bays, Kittredge's shallow-draft warships entered Copano Bay and captured a blockade runner at Lamar. The ships anchored off Copano as residents hid in the brush, fearing the worst, but Kittredge's ships sailed on to St. Mary's and sent a landing party ashore.

At St. Mary's, wounded Confederate soldiers were hidden in the brush as Union sailors and marines searched the town. The late Keith Guthrie in Texas Forgotten Ports related a story told by Mrs. Clara Dugat: "Shortly after the Yankees landed, a horseman rode into town to warn people that the federal fleet was headed for St. Mary's. Not knowing it had already arrived, he dashed up to the home of Dr. Carpenter and shouted 'The Yankees are coming!' At that moment, a raiding party was searching the Carpenter home and it came out and took the horseman prisoner."

Union raiders returned to Copano Bay in February 1864. They burned wharves and warehouses at Lamar and St. Mary's. The raiders retreated when one of their lookouts warned that Confederates were hiding in ambush behind a fence. As it turned out, the Confederates were cattle grazing behind a fence at John Howland Wood's original home.

After the war, shipping facilities were repaired and the Morgan Line added St. Mary's as a port of call. The town's founder, Joseph Smith, joined die-hard Confederates in exile in the Tuxpan colony in Mexico, where he died. Four years after the war, the county seat

The ground floor of the old Neel House of St. Mary's in 1949. The top floor of the hotel was destroyed in the 1886 hurricane. From the Special Collections and Archives at Texas A&M University-Corpus Christi.

of Refugio was moved to St. Mary's, but one recalcitrant judge refused to move and the result was that Refugio remained the county seat.

The history of St. Mary's is linked to that of Corpus Christi. The man who defended Corpus Christi during Kittredge's bombardment in 1862, Alfred Marmaduke Hobby, came from St. Mary's. A well-traveled road connected Corpus Christi to St. Mary's busy port. In 1871, the first telegraph line to reach Corpus Christi came through St. Mary's from Indianola. John Vineyard, one of the founders of Ingleside, owned a lumberyard at St. Mary's. Capt. John Low, who rode with Jack Hays, was a carpenter-contractor in St. Mary's; he had been assessor-collector in Corpus Christi. Clara Driscoll, who "saved" the Alamo when they were going to tear it down to build a liquor warehouse, was born at St. Mary's.

St. Mary's went into decline after the storm of 1875 damaged wharves and warehouses. It was also facing stiff competition from Rockport on Aransas Bay, then the railroad from San Antonio bypassed St. Mary's. The storm of Aug. 20, 1886 delivered the final blow. Buildings that were not destroyed were taken down and moved away.

367

Clara Driscoll, ranching family heiress known as the woman who saved the Alamo, was born at St. Mary's.

Today, the town of Bayside seems older than it is, partly because it has grown to overlap what used to be the southwest end of St. Mary's. The old St. Mary's Cemetery, a mile from the bay, is there. John Howland Wood's second home, built in 1877, occupies the center of Bayside.

The town of St. Mary's had a brief life, from 1856 to 1886, but it was eventful. The early coastal towns of Aransas City, Lamar, Copano and St. Mary's — places where saltwater and ingenuity met — are ghosts today, ghosts of a time when the early history of South Texas was still being written.

— Sept. 18, 2013

GHOST TOWNS OF COAST - 4

The village of Aransas on St. Joseph's Island was home to sailors, ranchers, and lightermen who unloaded the large ships that couldn't come through the pass or cross the shallow inner bays.

The town was laid out in 1845 on the southwest end of the island, on the site of Jean Lafitte's old fort, across the channel from where the Lighthouse stands today. Legend says some of Lafitte's pirates settled at the new village and, the story goes, some old pirates of vague employment may have become "wreckers," that is, shining a false light from the sand dunes to cause a shipwreck providing an opportunity for plunder.

The village of Aransas was on the bay side of the island, across from the pass. On a map today, the site be a mile inland from the pass, across from the lighthouse, because the pass moved south at a steady rate before the jetties were built. When the lighthouse went up in 1856, it stood directly behind the mouth of the pass, shining its strong light to ships entering the pass. The lighthouse today is north of the pass. They called the settlement Aransas, which should not be confused with Aransas City on Live Oak Point.

Early settlers on the island included John Baker, William Roberts, Capt. L. Bludworth, Capt. Peter Johnson, James Mainlan and Capt. John Low. One prominent citizen at Aransas was James Babbitt Wells, who commanded the Texas Navy yards at Galveston during the Revolution. Wells moved to St. Joseph's, owned a ranch and a schooner and served as the official wreckmaster. The channel in front of the lighthouse was named for his wife, Lydia Ann, and Jim Wells County was named for his son, who became the political boss of Brownsville.

Many residents of Aransas made their living guiding ships through the pass or unloading goods from sea-going vessels to shallow-draft lighters, thus they were called lightermen. Robert Mercer, patriarch of a family of bar pilots who kept a log of events on the islands, lived at Aransas before he moved across the pass to found the Mercer settlement, which later became Port Aransas.

Another prominent citizen of Aransas was Capt. Peter Johnson, who owned schooners "Belleport" and "Fairy" and ran a stage line from Saluria on Matagorda Island to Aransas on St. Joseph's. Passengers could take one of Johnson's ships from Indianola to Saluria then take the stage down the island. At Vinson's Slough, where an old man named Vinson lived, a ferry took the stage across Cedar Bayou. Then it traveled down the beach to Aransas and from there passengers could board the "Fairy" to cross the bay to Corpus Christi.

During the Civil War, the Union blockade caused havoc with the maritime commerce on which Aransas depended. Raiding parties from blockading ships made the situation worse. On Feb. 25, 1862, the second year of the war, sailors and marines from the U.S. warship "Arthur" burned houses at Mercer's settlement on Mustang Island then crossed to St. Joseph's and burned homes and warehouses at Aransas. Island families moved to the mainland for the rest of the war.

A few bar pilots returned to St. Joseph's after the war, but it was never the same. There was an attempt to revive the village in the 1870s when Capt. Cheston Heath built a store and warehouse and renamed the place Aransas Wharf, but his operation was destroyed in the 1875 storm and residents of Aransas Wharf moved across the pass to what is now Port Aransas.

* * *

From the 1840s to the 1860s and the beginning of the Civil War, the village of Aransas was linked by stagecoach to Saluria on the northeastern corner of Matagorda Island. Saluria was an important town, with a lighthouse and thriving commercial port. Capt. Johnson's stage line ran from Saluria to Aransas on St. Joseph's, crossing Cedar Bayou at Vinson's Slough.

Like the village of Aransas, Saluria was projected in 1845, founded by James Power, the Irish empresario, and Alexander Somervell, who led the punitive raid into Mexico in 1842 that resulted in the battle of Mier and imprisonment of captured Texans at Perote Castle. But that's another story. Power deeded most of the town to Somervell and two other men.

View of the settlement of Saluria on Matagorda Island as seen from the bay, September 1860. From the Library of Congress.

Somervell was killed in 1854 after he left Lavaca on a boat for Saluria carrying a large amount of money. His body was found lashed to the mast and the money was gone.

The 1850 census showed 200 people on Matagorda Island, most of them residents of Saluria. In 1862, during the Union blockade, Saluria's residents fled to the mainland and Confederate soldiers at nearby Fort Esperanza were ordered to destroy bridges and ferries linking Saluria to Indianola. For reasons never explained, Saluria was burned by Confederate troops on the orders of Gen. John ("Prince John") Magruder.

The late Paul Freier, who wrote articles for the Port Lavaca Wave on the history of the region, wrote that no similar action was ordered by the Confederate command for Galveston or Houston. "Some believed that the Galveston-Houston interest urged Gen. Magruder to destroy the Matagorda Bay area which represented a commercial rival." The story was by no means proved, but it's the kind of story that is so bad it could be true.

After Union forces captured Fort Esperanza in late 1863, in the invasion of the coast by Gen. Nathaniel Banks' army, vacant homes and empty buildings in Saluria that had not been burned by the Confederates were torn down for firewood.

371

An undated photo of the Saluria Life Station at Pass Cavallo. Special Collections and Archives, Texas A&M University-Corpus Christi.

After the war, efforts to rebuild Saluria were dashed by the hurricane of 1875, the same storm that destroyed about 75 percent of Indianola, damaged Aransas Wharf, St. Mary's and Saluria. The Mercer diaries on Mustang Island described the storm on Mustang Island: "Wind blowing fearful . . . the tide up to the gate . . . the boats roar and snort at it in earnest . . . several chickens had the life blowed out of them . . . the wharf is gone, lock, stock and fluke . . . Joe Hall lowered the whisky bottle three inches at one drink, and Barnes took seven long swallows."

— Sept. 25, 2013

GHOST TOWNS OF THE COAST - 5

In the summer of 1840, a Comanche war party of as many as 500 braves burned houses, stole horses and captured hostages at Victoria and headed for Linnville on Lavaca Bay.

When it was founded in 1831 by John J. Linn, a merchant at Victoria, it was called Linn's Landing. During the Revolution, provisions and U.S. volunteers for the Texas army came through the port at Linnville.

When the Comanches attacked, residents escaped on boats in the bay. The Indians plundered warehouses filled with goods destined for San Antonio and the Mexican market of Chihuahua. They put on fancy top hats and tied colorful ribbons on their ponies. They took away captives and plunder as a large force of Texas volunteers assembled to chase them. When the Texans caught the Comanches at Plum Creek, it resulted in one of the worst defeats the Comanches ever suffered, with 85 braves killed in the battle.

After Linnville was burned, its residents moved to the south on a bluff overlooking the bay, which became Lavaca. In 1843, the town became a shipping point for cattle and grew when Charles Morgan made it a port of call for Morgan Line ships. The name was changed to Port Lavaca.

Twelve miles down the shore from Port Lavaca, Prince Karl of Solms-Braunfels, head of the German Immigration Society, picked a spot to land German families. In December 1844, the first shipload of German immigrants landed at Indian Point, which was later called Karlshafen (Karl's Harbor) for Prince Karl. Indian Point was on a mile-wide peninsula thrusting three miles into Matagorda Bay and separated from the mainland by Powderhorn Lake. A tent city grew up on the shore as German settlers arrived at Karlshafen, before they moved on to New Braunfels and Fredericksburg.

Meanwhile, Port Lavaca made a fateful decision to raise wharf fees and Charles Morgan moved his operations 12 miles to the south. He built a wharf on Powderhorn Lake, down the beach from Karlshafen, and established steamer service with New York, via Galveston and New Orleans. This became a center of commercial activity. The community sprouting up around it was known as Powderhorn, then Indianola.

The bustling port city of Indianola, with immigrants pouring in from Germany and elsewhere in Europe, had a cosmopolitan flavor. Wharves stretching into the bay were piled high with hides, pecans, oats, corn, cotton, gold bullion destined for the U.S. Mint at New Orleans. Longhorns were driven to the docks for shipment east. In 1856, the first contingent of camels for a U.S. Army experiment arrived at Indianola.

The cart road from Indianola to San Antonio was said to be the busiest freight route in Texas. In 1857, the cart war broke out between Hispanic and Anglo freighters. Gov. E. M. Pease called out the Rangers to put an end to violence on the cart road.

C.C. Cox, a rancher in the Lagarto area, wrote about Indianola in his diary in 1860. "Indianola at that day was a very important place, and did a large business, being the shipping point for all West Texas — including San Antonio — it was in fact the only sea-port west of Galveston."

Corpus Christi and Indianola shared a lot of history. Walter Merriman and John S. Givens were lawyers in Corpus Christi and Indianola. The great photographer Louis de Planque, who had been in Matamoros, had a photography studio on Main Street in Indianola before he moved to Corpus Christi. Morris Lichtenstein closed his department store in Indianola and moved to Corpus Christi.

During the Civil War, Indianola was occupied when Union forces captured Galveston in 1862 and again in 1863 after Gen. Nathaniel P. Banks' army captured Brownsville, Fort Semmes on Mustang Island and Fort Esperanza on Matagorda Island. Indianola was held briefly before Union forces were withdrawn near the end of the war.

After the war, Indianola, the Queen City of the West, passed Galveston as a port and became one of Texas' greatest cities before two catastrophic storms spelled the end of Indianola.

The storm on Sept. 16, 1875 was the beginning of the end. Indianola was all but destroyed and all Matagorda Bay suffered in one of the most destructive storms to ever hit Texas. The Signal Service, forerunner of the U.S. Weather Bureau, called it one of the

Main Street in Indianola (above) in 1873 two years before a hurricane destroyed much of the town. In the lower photo, one home stands in the middle of destruction after Indianola was hit by a second storm in 1886. Photos from Special Collections and Archives, Texas A&M University-Corpus Christi.

most perfect types of tropical storm since the tracking of hurricanes began.

Indianola was terribly vulnerable, being near sea level and surrounded by water. When the storm surge hit, the streets turned into rivers. Trains couldn't run with the tracks underwater. People were trapped in wooden buildings that collapsed in the storm surge. People clung to lumber and cotton bales. many human tragedies were enacted in the storm. A four-year-old girl, her hand caught in a rooftop, was found 15 hours later, alive, but crazed from the ordeal. Nearly 200 Indianolans were killed in the storm.

The town was wrecked. Twelve new bayous cut across the downtown streets of Indianola. Huck's Lumber Yard, the Casimir House hotel, the Indianola Bulletin, and three of every four buildings were destroyed.

But people of Indianola began to rebuild. Then, on Aug. 20, 1886, Indianola was hit by another powerful storm. This one was followed by a fire that consumed what the storm left standing. This last disaster left little to build on and the place was abandoned. Population figures reflect the story. The population of Indianola in 1870 was 2,221. In 1880, after the first storm, it was 1,739. In 1890, after the second storm, no one was living at Indianola. Today, it is a small fishing village with an old cemetery dating back to when it was the Queen City of the West.

The now-disappeared old coastal towns — Aransas City, Lamar, Copano, St. Mary's, Aransas on St. Joseph's, Saluria, Linnville, and Indianola — are linked to early Texas history and to each other. We see their successors thriving as modern cities. Today's Rockport/Fulton area succeeded James Power's Aransas City. Bayside succeeded St. Mary's and Port Aransas succeeded Aransas on St. Joseph's. Only Saluria and Copano have no modern descendants. Even though it is not in close proximity to Indianola, the successor of that great port city is Corpus Christi.

— Oct. 2, 2013

HENRY KINNEY - 1

The founder of Corpus Christi, Henry Lawrence Kinney, was born on June 3, 1814, the same day Napoleon was exiled to Elba. He was the third of six children born to Simon and Phoebe Kinney at Sheshequin near Towanda, Pa.

Kinney's father Simon studied law and owned a store in Towanda. He was admitted to the bar the year Henry was born. When Henry was six, his father was elected to the Pennsylvania Legislature and served two terms. He later ran for Congress but was not elected.

On the last day of 1832, Henry Kinney, 18, got into a fight with a man who accused him of seeing his wife. Kinney was fined $1 for assault and not long afterwards he left Pennsylvania for New Orleans. Accounts later said he visited the Irish colony at San Patricio but no records confirm that.

What is known is that in 1834 Kinney arrived in Illinois, 100 miles west of Chicago. He opened a general store, with Ulysses Spaulding, and bought a farm called White Hall. How he came up with the money is a mystery. Kinney's store was the first commercial building in what became Peru, Ill.

As Peru began to grow, Kinney built a hotel and bought a riverboat steamer operating between Peru and St. Louis. He named it "The H. L. Kinney." Kinney became a contractor for part of the Illinois and Michigan Canal. Henry Beebe in "History of Peru" wrote that Kinney's contract amounted to nearly a million dollars and he became the most influential man in western Illinois. Kinney was also considered one of the best horsemen around, famous for a marathon ride of 100 miles in 24 hours, from Peru to Chicago, without getting out of the saddle.

Kinney became an agent for Daniel Webster, the great statesman and senator from Massachusetts who was investing in land in Illinois. Kinney was authorized to purchase land for the senator.

Webster wanted to make money in Illinois and Kinney was good at telling people what they wanted to hear. In a letter to Webster on May 24, 1836, Kinney touted the possibility of profits of 100 percent a year to be gained from land speculation in Illinois. Webster bought a farm next to Kinney's White Hall.

Besides attending to his own enterprises, Kinney was overseeing Webster's farm Salisbury. Kinney became a friend of Fletcher Webster, the senator's son and, though he was in his 20s, Kinney was called "Colonel" based on his professed role in the Black Hawk War. No records support that; he did not reach Illinois until two years after the war. But no one questioned his use of the title; people took him for what he claimed to be. He was always called "the Colonel" by Daniel and Fletcher Webster.

Webster sent Fletcher to help Kinney turn Salisbury into a paying proposition. In 1837, Webster took the entire family to visit, the party including his second wife and his daughter Julia, who was 19. Kinney was in charge of the welcoming committee in Peru.

Sometimes history and myth get mixed together and we can't tell which is which. The story has been told that on this occasion Kinney fell in love with Julia Webster. The late Coleman McCampbell who wrote "Saga of a Frontier Seaport" thought the story a myth until he read an account by Nathaniel Brown, who was there. Brown wrote that on the eve of the departure of the Webster family a ball was held in their honor in Chicago. Kinney presented Webster with a team of matched horses and carriage and that evening proposed to Julia. She turned him down. It was surmised that her rejection caused a broken-hearted Kinney to leave Illinois. It may be true, or partly true, but Kinney's over-extended financial predicament hastened his departure.

Kinney was a major contractor in building the Illinois and Michigan Canal, an immense undertaking with the possibility of immense profits that fired Kinney's imagination. The canal would connect Chicago on Lake Michigan with the Illinois River and from there down the Mississippi to New Orleans. Kinney hired Irish immigrants to dig the canal. The first dirt was turned on July 4, 1836. A year later a financial panic spread to Illinois and, since the canal was being built on borrowed money, when the flow of money stopped the canal stopped. Kinney's days as a canal builder were over. Kinney had speculated on the success of the canal and with its completion in doubt, his debts crowded in. He was "caught in a

Henry Kinney in 1840. Photo was taken by Alberto Fahrenberg in Monterrey, Mexico. From the Special Collections and Archives, Texas A&M University-Corpus Christi.

vise of delinquent debtors and insistent creditors," according to Maurice Baxter in "One and Inseparable: Daniel Webster and the Union."

Kinney traveled to Washington in May 1838 to see Webster, who endorsed four notes of $10,000 each to Kinney (worth about $1.2 million in today's purchasing power). At the same time, Kinney sold his farm to Webster for an undisclosed amount. In another letter, Webster wrote, "I have made an arrangement with Col. Kinney respecting enlarging Salisbury. It is all agreed that White Hall (Kinney's farm) shall be added to Salisbury. When Kinney failed to repay the $40,000 loan, Webster was forced to make good.

Elmer Baldwin in the "History of La Salle County" wrote that "probably what hit Peru the hardest — and no place suffered more — was that the canal was being built on borrowed money and since there was no money to proceed, the work was stopped and the laborers thrown out of employment. Kinney must bear his share of the blame. He had taken contracts for a large amount of the work on the canal and was unable to meet his obligations. He left town, but many of the people who had come here at his instigation, and had either lived on his bounty or been employed in his enterprises, were ruined by his failure."

Kinney gave power of attorney to his father to manage whatever property he was leaving then departed from Illinois, leaving his Irish canal workers unpaid, according to Baldwin's account.

Kinney landed on the Texas coast. He and William Aubrey opened a trading post at Aransas City on Live Oak Point to engage in the Mexican trade. Kinney put up the capital, perhaps from that $40,000 loan he obtained with Daniel Webster's endorsement. Kinney quickly settled in and became right at home in Texas, where people didn't want to say where they came from or why. He was still calling himself "Colonel" and no one questioned the title's pedigree.

In June 1839, Kinney was elected chairman of a meeting at Aransas City to protest a decision to move the customs house from Aransas City to the new town of Lamar. That September Kinney moved his trading post to a site on Corpus Christi Bay that was more convenient to the Mexican trade. The site was known as a place where schooners carrying dubious cargoes could land.

— Oct. 9, 2013

HENRY KINNEY - 2

After Henry Kinney built a trading post on Corpus Christi Bay, Mexican traders arrived to sell wool, hides, and buy bolts of unbleached cloth, bales of leaf tobacco, and manufactured goods unavailable across the Rio Grande. The trading post consisted of a store and house surrounded by a stockade. Below the trading post, north of where the arroyo emptied into the bay, he had a landing place. His Rancho del Oso was eight miles from the settlement.

The trading post was called Kinney's Rancho. It was founded for trade with northern Mexico. There was no *sub rosa* purpose; Kinney was not establishing a presence in the contested territory of the Nueces Strip to justify the Texas claim to the region. While it would eventually serve that purpose, it was wholly accidental.

Kinney brought in merchandise from New Orleans and sent back wool, hides and Mexican products. Since this trade was illegal in Mexico, Kinney technically was a smuggler, though he was never considered as such in Texas. Other traders moved in, including Frederick Belden, Henry Gilpin, John Peter Kelsey, and William Mann. In May 1841, Philip Dimmitt, a hero of the Revolution, set up a trading post a few miles south of Corpus Christi. Soon afterwards, Mexican cavalry raided Dimmitt's store and seized Dimmitt. The Mexican soldiers camped near Kinney's place but left Kinney alone.

When Dimmitt was killed or committed suicide in Mexico, Kinney and William Aubrey were accused of instigating the raid to get rid of a competitor. It was no secret that Kinney had influence with military leaders in Mexico. Kinney and Aubrey were tried in Victoria and found not guilty, but suspicion that they were implicated in the Dimmitt affair never went away.

The lucrative Mexican trade was threatened by "cow-boys" who raided in the Nueces Strip. After caravans of Mexican traders were attacked, Kinney wrote President Mirabeau Lamar to warn that if the activities of the cow-boys were not curbed, all would be lost at Corpus Christi. In response, Texas created spy companies to patrol the Nueces Strip. One company was stationed at Corpus Christi with John Yerby in command. This group became as bad as the "cow-boys" they were supposed to put down. Kinney called them "robber Texians."

Yerby's band attacked a Mexican trade caravan on its way to Corpus Christi and killed eight men. The attack invited a reprisal raid from a force of Mexican soldiers and rancheros who tracked down and killed some of Yerby's band.

To protect his trading post, Kinney put some of the "robber Texians" on his payroll, including Mustang Gray. Kinney's other hired guns included J. R. Everitt, H. Clay Davis, and Henry Berry, who was elected the first sheriff of Nueces County.

Kinney later faced other troubles. The land his trading post and the settlement around it occupied was claimed by Mexican Army Capt. Enrique Villareal. He had been granted ten leagues of land, the Rincon del Oso, in 1831. Villareal arrived with 200 men to reaffirm his claim to 400 square miles of land on the shores of Corpus Christi Bay.

Kinney employed 40 hired gunmen, but when they saw the size of Villareal's force all but eight rode away to follow other pursuits. Kinney, however, went out to parley. He warned Villareal there were buried bombs about the place that could be detonated. At the same time, he said he recognized Villareal's claim and would offer him a fair price for the land. Kinney later bought one league of Villareal's 10 leagues for $1,000 in gold and $2,000 in trade goods. Five years later, Kinney bought the other nine leagues, paying the equivalent of about 15 cents an acre.

Kinney was clearly attuned to the political cross-currents around him and was adroit in working both sides of the border. He invited President Lamar to visit Corpus Christi and sent him a gift of brandy. He cultivated contacts in Texas and Mexico and could use one side or the other as needed. One day he would write Lamar or Sam Houston and next day write Mariano Arista, commander in chief of the Northern Army of Mexico. In the perpetually antagonistic relations between Texas and Mexico, Kinney was sometimes accused of spying for Texas or spying for Mexico.

After Texans were captured in the descent on Mier, Mexico in December 1842, some 200 captives were marched under heavy

Henry Kinney moved from Illinois to Texas and built a trading post on the bluff overlooking Corpus Christi Bay. Sketch of Kinney, circa 1851, is from the Hortense Warner Ward Papers at the Corpus Christi Central Library.

Guard to Mexico City while the wounded were left behind at Matamoros. Kinney visited the wounded in a hospital at Matamoros and gave one of the men, James Rice, $500 to buy necessities. Rice and seven men used the money to bribe their guards and escape. Kinney was arrested and charged with aiding their escape. After several months, he was released. During his prolonged stay in Matamoros, Kinney began an affair with Genoveva Perez, who bore him a daughter, Adelina.

Kinney was a famous horseman in Illinois and he gained the same reputation in Texas. In 1844, in a riding contest at San Antonio, first prize went to one of Jack Hays' Rangers, second prize went to Kinney, and third prize went to a Comanche chief. A man who knew Kinney said he was the most graceful of all the riders. "Everything he did seemed to be done without effort or without

383

Henry Kinney built a trading post at the edge of the bluff next to the arroyo where the Southwestern Bell Telephone building stands today on Upper Broadway.

any extra exertion on his part," wrote J. Williamson Moses. "He could throw a dollar (coin) before him and, with his horse in full stride, pick it up, leaning from his saddle. There was nothing which could be accomplished in the saddle which he could not do when mounted on his favorite horse, Old Charlie."

In May 1844 a Comanche war party attacked Corpus Christi. Kinney and 11 other men chased the Indians. Both sides dismounted and after firing at each other for some minutes, a Comanche chief rode to the front taunting the Texans. When they fired, the bullets bounced off the tough rawhide shield and before they could reload the Indians rushed Kinney's men. Nearly all the Indians were killed or wounded and three of the Corpus Christi men were killed and three wounded. Kinney appealed to Austin for help. On Dec. 14, 1844, he was authorized to raise a company of 40 Rangers to protect Corpus Christi.

— Oct. 16, 2013

HENRY KINNEY - 3

Henry Kinney's father Simon was elected to the Pennsylvania Legislature when Kinney was a boy. Kinney, following in his footsteps, was elected to the Senate of the 9th Congress of the Texas Republic in 1844. The following year, he helped ratify terms of the Republic's annexation to the United States and took part in writing a new state Constitution.

As annexation moved ahead, Kinney was quick to see the possibilities, which might mean war with Mexico and might require the presence of an American army. Kinney wrote Andrew Jackson Donelson, U.S. *chargé d'affairs* in Austin, that Corpus Christi would be a good place for Gen. Zachary Taylor to concentrate his army when he moved from Fort Jesup, La., to Texas. Kinney pointed out that Corpus Christi was ideally situated, being the same distance, 150 miles, to any potential trouble spot from Laredo to Matamoros. Donelson passed it on to Taylor, adding that "Corpus Christi is said to be as healthy as Pensacola."

Kinney's lobbying had its effect. After looking at Live Oak Point, Taylor chose Corpus Christi. When the first units of his army landed on July 31, 1845, Kinney was in Austin attending the annexation convention. In late August he returned to Corpus Christi with his two Lipan escorts whom he used for protection.

Kinney rented buildings to the Army, including Taylor's headquarters, and set up several businesses, including the Kinney House hotel. During the army's seven-month stay, from August 1845 until March 1846, half the soldiers of the U.S. Army were camped at Corpus Christi. During that time, Taylor turned to Kinney for advice and news on Mexico. Kinney was an expert at interpreting Mexican politics and Kinney's spy, Chipito Sandoval, furnished information on army movements in Mexico.

When Taylor's army departed, the settlement of Corpus Christi was reduced to a pale specter of its former self. The magnetism of war and adventure attracted most of the town's residents who left to "see the elephant." A Houston paper noted the downfall of Kinney's town: Since the removal of the U.S. Army from Corpus Christi, the population has dwindled from nearly 2,000 souls to a few hundred. The 200 grog shops that were the glory of the citizens, the faro banks and roulette tables, have disappeared. A few stores are about all that is left of the late flourishing town of Corpus Christi.'

Kinney's partner, William Aubrey, went to the border with a wagonload of whisky and Kinney left with the army. He was appointed to the staff of Gov. J. Pinckney Henderson in command of Texas troops attached to Taylor's army. Kinney served as a quartermaster. Chipito also joined Taylor's army, serving as a guide and spy; he would enter Mexican cities and return with information on troop strength and location.

As quartermaster, Kinney relied on his old trading partners in Mexico to purchase beef, horses, and pack mules for the army. At the battle of Monterrey in September 1846, Kinney served as an aide-de-camp and was cited for bravery in carrying dispatches through enemy fire. He later joined Gen. Winfield Scott's army at Veracruz and, according to some accounts, was able to buy mules and horses from Gen. López de Santa Anna's own agent.

On July 17, 1846, the American Flag newspaper in Matamoros printed a report from an unnamed correspondent, most likely Kinney, who was able to visit Corpus Christi during the war. "According to promise," the correspondent (Kinney) wrote, "I write you what information I have been able to gather since my return to Corpus Christi. I found the old inhabitants of the place, almost to a man, had departed for the Rio Grande. Corpus Christi is indeed deserted. But when they have 'seen the elephant' and find that his haunts afford no resting place so lovely and calmly beautiful as this delightful village, they will return."

And they did return when the U.S. and Mexico signed a treaty on Feb. 2, 1848 ending the Mexican War. And Kinney returned to take a renewed interest in the town he founded.

That August, Mexican War veterans calling themselves "buffalo hunters" camped on St. Joseph's Island. They planned to invade Mexico to establish a Republic of the Sierra Madre. They grew restive and came up with a scheme to rob Kinney, who was tipped off and sent word to Ranger Capt. J. S. Sutton at San Patricio. When the buffalo hunters arrived at Kinney's house on the bluff, they

Henry Lawrence Kinney, circa 1855, when he was 41 years old. Photo by Mathew B. Brady from the Library of Congress.

were met by Rangers and convinced to leave peacefully. Soon afterwards, the buffalo hunters returned to New Orleans.

The leader of the expedition, Capt. L. A. Besançon, wrote to the Democratic Telegraph and Texas Register in Houston apologizing to Kinney for "having brought down men for the purpose of engaging in what has been called the Sierra Madre expedition. Had I been aware of your (Kinney's) own opinion, and not relied upon Madame Rumor, I should have saved the expense of subsistence and transportation of a large body of men." Kinney, in his own letter to the Houston newspaper, disclaimed any connection with the affair. He pointed out that the United States was at peace with

Mexico and "it would certainly be a breach of neutrality to organize a force in our limits to invade any portion of her territory, and I certainly would not, with my consent, lend my name for such a purpose."

Corpus Christi was down to 300 people and Kinney set about trying to improve the town's fortunes, realizing, as he had in Illinois, that the promotion of a place could be useful for promoting his own interests. He tried to re-establish the trade link with Mexico and promoted Corpus Christi as a "jumping off place" for the California goldfields.

Kinney had other ideas. He started a slaughterhouse on North Beach where mustangs were killed for their hides. He was a partner in a beef packing house in Corpus Christi. He bought a steam dredge to dig a ship channel across the bay. He bought hundreds of wagons and mules, war surplus, and formed a partnership with William Mann and William Cazneau. Kinney invested $10,000 in the plan to open a trade route to Chihuahua.

After gold was discovered in California, Kinney placed newspaper ads claiming that the best route to the goldfields started at Corpus Christi. The town filled up with emigrants heading West, brought in by steamers and packet boats. The gold-seekers purchased wagons, mules and horses that Kinney had acquired as Army surplus.

Meanwhile, the "Great Chihuahua Train" began to take shape. Kinney and partners hoped to make a profit from the sale of goods in Chihuahua and they hoped to re-establish trade with northern Mexico. Great teams of oxen pulling a long train of wagons filled with trade goods departed in April 1849.

Kinney, Cazneau and Mann lost money on the trade trip and the traffic of gold-seekers through Corpus Christi came to a halt after word spread that the route across arid and harsh northern Mexico was very difficult and very dangerous.

— Oct. 23, 2013

HENRY KINNEY - 4

Henry Kinney, founder of Corpus Christi, adopted his illegitimate daughter Adelina in 1850. On June 13, 1850, he married a widow with older children, Mary Elizabeth Herbert, daughter of Judge James Webb. He met her while attending the Legislature in Austin.

Kinney was also having a scandalous affair with Matilda Ohler, wife of a Corpus Christi merchant. Maria von Blucher wrote her mother — "Mrs. Ohler is the public paramour of Col. Kinney. The most ignominious aspect of the affair is that Mr. Ohler, because of his pecuniary relations, tolerates the affair with the Colonel and even favors it."

Kinney maintained a second house in Brownsville where his mistress Genoveva lived with Adelina. Kinney would send presents to his daughter. A letter from a friend in Brownsville said — "Those articles all reached your little girl. She and her mother are well. The girl is at school and learning rapidly."

Some relatives followed Kinney to Texas. Though his father Simon, a respected lawyer, stayed in Illinois, two of Kinney's married sisters moved to Texas and so did his younger brother, Joseph Warren, and a cousin, Somers Kinney. The brother was killed on his way to Austin in 1851 when his pistol went off as he was putting it in his holster.

Kinney, whom many believed was one of the wealthiest men in Texas, was in debt. J. W. Wilbarger wrote that Kinney, seeming to think his purse would replenish itself, ran through his fortune in a few years after the Mexican War.

Trying to get out of debt, Kinney borrowed more money to hold a fair at Corpus Christi. He may have been inspired by the Great Exhibition in London. Kinney hoped to attract visitors to Corpus Christi who might buy land and settle in South Texas. He expected 20,000 visitors and borrowed $45,000 to cover expenses. As he had done in Illinois, Kinney financed his obsessions with other people's money. He sent "Legs" Lewis to New Orleans to buy engraved silver cups to be awarded as prizes.

As May 1, 1852, the day for the beginning of the fair, drew near, every movement around Corpus Christi seemed to have some connection with the fair. Kinney bought a steamboat to ferry visitors from ships anchoring off Aransas Pass.

J. Williamson Moses said Corpus Christi "grew as if by magic into a big city for the time at least. The town presented the novel and picturesque appearance of an immense camp and village in one. Tents, large and small, were pitched everywhere. Lots that had been vacant a day or two before were covered with canvas houses. There were soda-water fountains, ice-cream stands, confectioneries and restaurants everywhere. All over the place, wherever you looked, a gay and lively scene met the eye."

There were cockfights, riding contests, a bullfight, livestock auctions, horse races and circus acts. Tents with refreshments were located throughout the town and the streets were crowded with Indians, mustangers, soldiers, sheepherders, gunfighters. Richard King, who would soon begin his ranch, came up from Brownsville. Rip Ford attended and so did Sally Skull.

Kinney's friend, Gen. José M. Carbajal, head of the Federalist army at war in Mexico, spoke at the fair, setting forth his cause against the central government in Mexico City, but attracted little support.

Exhibits included Mexican blankets, saddles, bridles, spurs, farm products. Silver cups were awarded for the best flock of sheep, best herd of brood mares. Kinney won three prizes, for a stallion, Mexican bridle, and milk cow and his wife Mary took a prize for the cotton grown on their Oso Ranch. Each prize bore the inscription — "From H. L. Kinney and General Committee of the Lone Star Fair, Corpus Christi, May, 1852."

On the last day, Kinney was presented a silver urn and fruit basket for his hospitality. He spoke of chances taken when he moved his trading post from Live Oak Point to Corpus Christi but, he resolved, pointing toward the bay, "to live or die on the spot."

By Kinney's expectations, the fair was a failure and his creditors were crowding in again, with their hands out. Kinney was forced to give up his Mustang Island ranch and mortgage other holdings, including his Oso ranch. The $50,000 he spent to hold the fair was borrowed money and he was in deep financial difficulty.

Henry Kinney led a failed filibustering expedition to the Mosquito region of Nicaragua in 1855. Photo from the Texas State Library and Archives Commission.

When he was in debt in Illinois in 1837, Kinney turned to Daniel Webster to secure a loan of $40,000; in Texas in 1852, he turned to his friend and benefactor, John P. Schatzel, a wealthy trader from Matamoros who had retired to Corpus Christi. When Schatzel died, Kinney was forced to repay the estate the money he had borrowed.

He was in trouble at home, too. In a letter to her parents, Maria von Blucher wrote, "After three years of war with each other, the Kinneys have finally realized they will never be able to make peace, and Mrs. Kinney has gathered up all her goods and chattels and departed, not scuttling secretly away, but with the full consent of her husband."

Kinney, by nimble footwork, had always been able to get out of a tight spot. When in trouble, he took off for distant places, as he had when he left Pennsylvania for Illinois and Illinois for Texas. After the failure of the fair, Kinney's sources of credit were almost exhausted. While he owned a vast amount of land, there were no buyers. To raise money for his next venture, he mortgaged his property several times over.

Kinney appointed M. P. Norton guardian over his daughter Adelina, drew up a will leaving his estate to Adelina, and left Corpus Christi on Sept. 4, 1854. He was bound for the Mosquito region of Nicaragua, where he proposed to establish his own government.

Soon after Kinney's departure, Norton received a letter from Adelina in Brownsville — "I send you a letter to tell you that I am very poor because my mother don't send me some money to a long time. They tell me my mother is married. I am very mad with my mother because she don't send me a letter. If my mother is married you must give the money to me and my grandmother . . . I want you to send me some money to buy some dresses, and if you please tell me something of my father."

— Oct. 30, 2013

HENRY KINNEY - 5

Corpus Christi founder Henry Kinney planned to establish his own empire in Central America. His scheme was one of two filibustering expeditions in Nicaragua in 1855. The other was led by William Walker of Tennessee.

In New York, Kinney wrote M. P. Norton on Nov. 8, 1854: "The Central American Company met at my rooms last evening. Several of the great men of the nation attended and made speeches. All agree that I shall go down at the head of the New Government of Central America."

Kinney formed a partnership with Joseph Fabens, who claimed to own a large tract of land in Nicaragua, and the two planned to set up their own government with Kinney at the head. When Kinney's chartered steamship United States was ready to sail, Kinney and Fabens were indicted on charges of violating U.S. neutrality laws. They were arrested then released on bond. Kinney's steamship was blocked by U.S. Navy destroyers, but he chartered another ship, the Emma on which he made his escape. Among his followers on board was the grandson of Daniel Webster.

After the Emma wrecked on a reef, Kinney sailed on the Huntress for San Juan del Norte where he landed on July 18, 1855. He wrote Norton: "I am at last on Central American soil with 100 men and more. This is a beautiful place and is to be the principal of the world. I have a larger space to act in than I had at Corpus Christi and the result of my undertakings in Central America can hardly be imagined."

Kinney hoisted his own flag, started a newspaper, and busied himself appointing government officials. His government lasted 16 days. He was forced to resign because of the opposition of William

Walker, who had become a power in Nicaragua. Kinney's filibuster never had a chance to succeed. A visitor to San Juan del Norte reported that Kinney was broke, was drinking hard and looked like a man who had been in a fight, as he indeed had.

He landed at Galveston on June 21, 1858 and was presented with the news his divorce was final. Back in Corpus Christi, the city he founded welcomed home as a returning hero, despite the fact he owed many people in town. A reception and ball were held in his honor and soon after he was elected to the Texas Legislature.

Kinney resigned from the Legislature in March 1861 to protest secession. He wrote President Lincoln asking to be appointed to a diplomatic post in Mexico, but Lincoln did not respond. He then wrote to offer his services to Jefferson Davis. While he was not given an official appointment, he may have been employed to buy munitions for the South in Matamoros. A lot was going on in wartime Matamoros, the backdoor of the Confederacy. It was where Kinney met his end.

As history sometimes presents us with incompatible versions of the same event, we have conflicting accounts of Kinney's death. In one, he was shot to death in June 1861 during a gang fight. John B. "Red" Dunn relayed this version, which is repeated in the Texas Handbook. Charles G. Norton, grandson of Judge M. P. Norton, wrote that Kinney was shot down in the street during a difficulty.

A public notice printed in the Nueces Valley newspaper by B. F. Neal concerning Kinney's estate said he was killed in Matamoros on March 3, 1862 while fighting under Gen. Carbajal. Coleman McCampbell in "Texas Seaport" related: "It is 1865. Kinney is in Matamoros. He has become involved in a petty skirmish between two factions, the Crinolinos and Rohos. While attempting to pass through a breach in a wall, a bullet pierces his heart. He topples, dying instantly."

Still another account says Kinney was killed in the last days of February when he made an early morning visit to another man's wife. This version says he was shot at the front door of his former lover Genoveva, who had married while he was in Nicaragua, by her husband, Cesario Falcon. Supposedly, there were two companions with Kinney — Julius Henry and Martin Hinojosa — and Henry lifted Kinney up as he was dying. He was 47 years old. He was buried in Matamoros in an unmarked grave. No funeral, no flowers, no phony eulogies.

No official records have survived to show the date and circumstances of Kinney's death. That he was killed in 1865, as McCampbell asserts, can be discounted since his will was filed for probate in March 1862. Two statements from people at the time, which ring true, support the Genoveva story. James B. Wells, longtime political boss of Brownsville, said Kinney was not killed in the Crinolino-Rohos riot and Fred Starck, grandson of Petra Kenedy, said Kinney was paying a social call on a woman in Matamoros when he was shot. Kinney's friends may have concocted a cover story to protect his reputation. In any event, we may never know the true story of his death.

We do know that Kinney was a contradictory and enigmatic man, a man of enthusiasm who could fire up people around him, as he did in Illinois when he convinced the sage Daniel Webster to invest a fortune in land speculation, which plagued Webster to the end of his life. And in Texas, Kinney convinced prudent businessmen to invest in his Lone Star Fair. When that failed, he convinced New York financiers to underwrite his Nicaraguan disaster. He could trim his beliefs to fit the occasion, as when he offered to work for Abraham Lincoln and then Jefferson Davis. He resigned from the Legislature in protest over secession then became an agent for the Confederacy.

It was said that Kinney was not overly honest, that he had glaring faults and sterling qualities. He founded three towns, Peru, Ill., Nuecestown, and Corpus Christi. A county is named for him in far west Texas and his statue stands in the lobby of the Nueces County Courthouse. Was he a hero or rogue? More likely, he fell somewhere in between, fluctuating between the two poles depending on his own needs.

None of his schemes turned out as planned, but Henry Kinney was a most unusual man who lived in interesting times. We will not see his like again.

— Nov. 6, 2013

Henry Kinney in 1840 in Monterrey, Mexico. Sketch of Kinney from about 1850. Kinney in 1855, photographed by Mathew Brady. Kinney in the late 1850s.

Kinney in about 1861 photographed by Louis de Planque in Matamoros not long before his death in 1862.

LICHTENSTEIN'S LITTLE STORE

I went down to closed-off Chaparral and Lawrence and watched as a front-end loader knocked holes in the wall of the Lichtenstein building, raising a cloud of white dust. The sad relic of a building was barely recognizable compared to what it was when it opened in December 1941. I stopped to reflect about Lichtenstein's history and how it began so long ago.

It began with Morris Lichtenstein, who emigrated from Germany to the United States in 1852 when he was 17. He traveled to St. Louis, where he learned English, then he clerked at a hotel in Omaha. He left to prospect for gold and got lost in a snowstorm. Nearly frozen to death, he found shelter in an Indian village. In 1857, he came to Texas and went to work for Joseph and Alfred Moses in a store near Victoria.

When the Civil War began, Lichtenstein enlisted in the Confederate Army and was mustered in as a private in the Fourth Texas Cavalry, Sibley's Brigade.

Henry Sibley led an invasion of New Mexico as a springboard to capture Colorado and California for the Confederacy. In New Mexico, Sibley's brigade won the battle of Valverde and Sibley moved against Fort Union, but his advance guard was overcome by Colorado miners called Pikes Peakers. Sibley's brigade defeated the federals at Glorieta, but it was a Pyrrhic victory; the brigade lost its supplies, took a torturous route across the mountains, and in the retreat Sibley lost a third of his 2,500 men.

After the battle of Valverde, Lichtenstein was left behind to help the wounded. He was taken prisoner and sent to Camp Douglas outside Chicago. He was exchanged in 1863 and rejoined his old unit.

After the war, Lichtenstein sold pecans until he made enough money to open a drygoods store in Victoria. His brother Louis came down from Chicago to join him but the partnership soon ended. In

1868, after he bought Koehler's dry goods in Goliad, Lichtenstein married Selina Egg, sister of an army comrade. Morris and Selina had four children, three sons and a daughter. In 1870, Lichtenstein moved his store to Indianola. He relocated in Corpus Christi in 1874, a lucky move since Indianola was hit by the hurricane of 1875, the first of two storms that destroyed the city.

In Corpus Christi, Lichtenstein set up his business in a wood-frame building on Chaparral, the site later occupied by the Nueces Hotel. He sold ladies' and men's apparel and made regular trips to New York to buy the latest fashions. He stocked guns and ammunition and after the Nuecestown Raid in March 1875, Rangers led by Leander McNelly stopped at Lichtenstein's on their way to clean up the border. Lichtenstein supplied them with Sharps carbines and told them not to worry about paying him, that he would rather give the guns away than let bandits steal them.

In 1889 Lichtenstein moved into the Uehlinger Building, which later became the home of Montgomery Ward. Corpus Christi was booming in the 1890s, brought on by promoter Elihu Ropes. When his plans collapsed and the city returned to its pre-Ropes lethargy, Lichtenstein's continued to flourish.

In 1903, Morris formed a partnership with sons Julius and Albert and renamed the business Lichtenstein & Sons. A year later, Morris, after a toe was amputated, got blood poisoning and died. Julius and Albert took over the store.

In 1911, the store was moved from the Uehlinger Building into a new structure on Chaparral at Schatzel, the third location but the first built for the main purpose as a department store. The new building featured the city's first elevators and fire-protection sprinkler system.

After Julius died in 1923 and Albert in 1929, the business was operated by Simon and Sylvan Weil, related by marriage to the Lichtensteins (Carrie Weil, a sister of Simon and Sylvan, married Julius Lichtenstein). In 1932, Morris L. Lichtenstein, son of Albert and grandson of the founder, was working at the store as a buyer of men's clothing. He borrowed enough money to buy a controlling interest in the business from Simon and Sylvan Weil and other members of the Lichtenstein family who were still financially involved.

The purchase price was $50.000. One fourth, or $12,500, was paid in cash. A newspaper account said that Morris had to count his pennies to raise that amount. The deal was concluded on a Sunday and Morris went to the home of the store's advertising manager, Gordon Moore, and told him to plan for a big sale that would start on Monday morning. He had to bring in enough cash to meet the next payroll on Saturday.

After Julius died in 1923 and Albert in 1929, the business was operated by Simon and Sylvan Weil, related by marriage to the Lichtensteins (Carrie Weil, a sister of Simon and Sylvan, married Julius Lichtenstein). In 1932, Morris L. Lichtenstein, Albert's son, borrowed money to buy a controlling interest from Simon and Sylvan Weil and other Lichtensteins. He paid $50,000. The deal was made on Sunday and Morris began a sale on Monday to raise enough cash to make payroll.

Morris persuaded his brother Albert to come into the business. Albert sold his insurance agency and took over the financial end while Morris handled merchandising. Morris would circulate and greet shoppers while Albert stayed in his office. It was said Albert hated tobacco smoke; when people lit up in his office he would take out a bottle of Air Wick he kept in his desk.

The next move came in 1941, seven days before the attack on Pearl Harbor, when a new store opened on Chaparral, where the St. James Hotel once stood. It was not a beautiful building, with a curved front to suggest modernity, but no doubt functional. When the new store opened, Lichtenstein's was near the top of its commercial apogee, with sales of $5 million a year. At the ribbon-cutting ceremony, Morris L. said, "We like to feel that this store is more than a store, that it is a part of the lives and hopes of Corpus Christi."

In 1948, while Albert was in Colorado Springs, he thought of buying a small hotel to give him something do while on his annual vacation, then he thought of the Breakers Hotel on North Beach and, three weeks later, he bought the old hotel for $170,000. He soon found himself spending more time at the hotel than at the department store.

Albert was elected mayor in 1953. In the tunnel-bridge controversy, he backed digging a toll tunnel. When the City Council voted to build a high bridge, he resigned in protest, leaving his seat at the council table and taking a seat in the audience.

After Morris died in 1970 and Albert soon afterwards, a fourth generation of the family took over. It was a bad time. The downtown was dying and the store couldn't compete with the new malls. In 1972, two years shy of the store's 100th anniversary, Lichtenstein's was sold to Frost Bros. and then closed a few years later. The long run of success that began with the first Morris Lichtenstein came to an end. As I looked at the demolition site, it was sad to see the old building being knocked down.

—Nov. 13, 2013

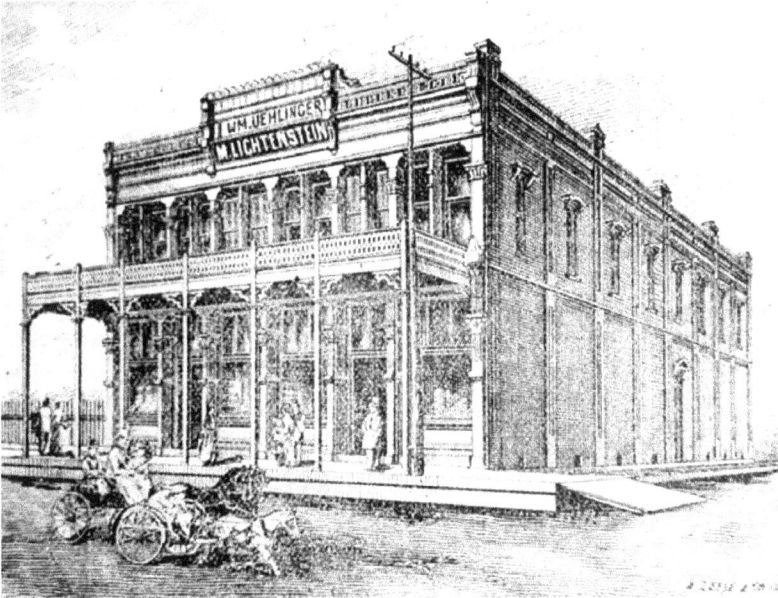

Lichtenstein set up his store in Corpus Christi in a wood-frame building on Chaparral, the site later occupied by a grocery store (top photo). In 1889 Lichtenstein's was moved into the Uehlinger Building at Chaparral and Peoples, which later became the site of Montgomery Ward.

In 1911, Lichtenstein's was moved from the Uehlinger Building into a new structure on Chaparral at Schatzel (top photo). The new building featured the city's first elevators and fire-protection sprinkler system. Lichtenstein's was moved into its fourth location (below) in 1941, seven days before the attack on Pearl Harbor. The new store was located on Chaparral where the old St. James Hotel once stood.

As Corpus Chisti grew southward, Lichtenstein's followed. This is an architectural rendering of their store in Parkdale Plaza.

MALTBY BROTHERS

One day in 1863 two brothers who had not seen each other for years met on a packet steamer on the Mississippi River below Vicksburg. One was a Union general and the other was a Confederate captain, a prisoner of war.

Dr. Norman Delaney takes this wartime reunion as his starting point for "The Maltby Brothers' Civil War." The book is about three brothers from Ohio divided in loyalty as gigantic forces clash in war. Two brothers had moved to Texas and were loyal to the Confederacy and a third rose high in the ranks of the Union Army.

The story of Henry and William Maltby runs parallel to the history of Corpus Christi from the 1850s through the 1870s. Henry came to Corpus Christi for Henry Kinney's Lone Star Fair in 1852. As Delaney tells us, he had become the proprietor of a circus which he brought to Kinney's fair. Performances at Maltby's Circus were staged under a canvas tent on the beach near Ohler's Wharf.

The circus moved on and by the end of 1852 Maltby was out of the circus business. In 1855 he returned to Corpus Christi, was elected mayor, and less than a year later resigned and traveled to Nicaragua, where Henry Kinney and William Walker were embroiled in their empire-making filibusters. Whether Henry Maltby was part of the filibustering efforts is unclear, but he soon returned to Corpus Christi and in October 1859 began to publish the Ranchero newspaper. His younger brother William joined him. The first issue of the Ranchero was printed on Oct. 22, 1859.

As the country moved toward war, the two Ohio brothers in Texas were more Southern than Southerners as they argued the cause of the South. A Ranchero editorial said: "Whatever position the South may decide on taking, we are with her to the fullest extent. We believe the right of secession is complete with every state, and should be exercised as a last resort whenever the equality of States is destroyed."

In February 1861, Henry Maltby and Dr. Philip Luckett were elected to represent Nueces County at the Texas Secession Convention in Austin. Maltby and Luckett were among 168 delegates who voted to secede; only eight voted no. A funny item in the Ranchero (written by William, who fancied poetry) read: "What will teach northern fanatics a lesson? Secession. What will make a man frisky? Whisky. What will build the graveyard fence? Pence. What is sweeter to us than honey? Money. What is needed by the Ranchero? Dinero."

William joined an artillery company formed for self-defense and in July 1861 married Mary Grace Swift. He was 23 and she was 14. Henry, the next year, married Hannah Franke.

In the first year of the war, publication of the Ranchero became erratic as the blockade made it difficult to get newsprint. "This is the first time we have missed an issue," Henry fumed. "We trust the (Devil) will lay malevolent hands on Old Abe and anchor him in the middle of the lake of fire and brimstone . . ."

After the bombardment of Corpus Christi in August 1862, Henry moved the paper to a ferry settlement on the Nueces River below San Patricio called Santa Margarita. William, meanwhile, was in charge of a Confederate artillery company at Fort Semmes on Mustang Island. When Fort Semmes was captured during the invasion of the Texas coast by forces under Gen. Nathaniel Banks in November 1863, William was taken prisoner and sent to New Orleans and then Vicksburg.

William met his brother Gen. Jasper A. Maltby on the river near Vicksburg. Jasper was a brigadier general in the Union Army, a fighting general, not a parade-ground soldier, who was wounded at Fort Donelson and in the siege of Vicksburg. In July 1864, William was exchanged and allowed to return to Texas.

After William's return from Vicksburg, Henry moved to the border to publish the Ranchero from Brownsville. When Brownsville was occupied, he moved across the river to Matamoros where he fulminated against occupation authorities and Reconstruction policies. William wrote that Henry "is not desirous of ever living on United States soil again," but Henry eventually moved back to Brownsville.

William returned to Corpus Christi and started his own newspaper, The Advertiser and signed his columns as "Bro. Bill." Three years after his wife Grace died in the yellow fever epidemic

Cover of Dr. Norman Delaney's "The Maltby Brothers' Civil War" published by Texas A&M University Press.

of 1867, he married Anna Marie Headen, daughter of a wealthy wool merchant.

William retired in 1873 but didn't stay retired long. Four years later, he teamed up with Eli Merriman to found the Corpus Christi Free Press, which became the genesis in 1883 of a new paper, the Corpus Christi Caller.

William Henderson Maltby, "Brother Bill," died in Corpus Christi on August 20, 1880 when he was 43. Henry Alonzo Maltby died in

Brownsville on May 18, 1906. His obituary said he was a man of staunch principles who remained true to his conception of what he thought was right. In a later assessment, Eli Merriman wrote that the Maltby brothers "were expert printers and newspaper men of the highest class — ready writers, brilliant and well-informed; Democrats always."

I take the liberty of quoting a passage from the book, which sums up the chronicle of the Maltby brothers: "Their lives provide a timeless story of how war can affect families and communities. All three men had deep convictions, Henry and William as devotees of the Lost Cause and Jasper of the Union he cherished . . . The Civil War was indeed a brothers' war, pitting friends and families against one another while strengthening the bonds of others."

Dr. Delaney, author of The Maltby Brothers' Civil War, taught history at Del Mar College for 40 years before his retirement. His book was published by Texas A&M University Press. The book includes 256 pages with 27 photographs with a sale price of $32.95. Some years ago I wrote two columns about Henry and William Maltby, but I did not undertake the kind of in-depth and painstaking research Delaney has assembled. This book — The Maltby Brothers' Civil War — is a valuable contribution to our knowledge of the Civil War and Reconstruction in South Texas, framed by the unique and colorful story of the Maltby family. It is also a very good read.

— Nov. 20, 2013

HARBOR ISLAND

Harbor Island, between Aransas Pass and Port Aransas, has a long and colorful and history. In 1720, France sent a ship to explore the Texas coast in search of a place to locate a colony. In his reconnaissance, Jean Béranger discovered the pass between Mustang and St. Joseph and landed on Harbor Island. He killed a rattlesnake coiled on oyster shells and watched Karankawas whip the water to attract fish, then shoot them with arrows. Béranger buried an engraved lead tablet by a live oak tree, which has never been found.

In 1857, long after Béranger, the U.S. government built a lighthouse on Harbor Island, a brick tower 67 feet above the tidal flats. The lighthouse stood at the mouth of the pass dividing Mustang and St. Joseph's; its light shone directly into the pass. Over the years, the pass drifted south as Gulf currents deposited sand on the south end of St. Joseph's and washed away the north end of Mustang. During the Civil War, Confederates tried to blow up the lighthouse but succeeded only in destroying the interior circular staircase. They buried the valuable French lens in a sand dune.

In 1907, Congress approved $123,000 in appropriations to dredge Turtle Cove, the mud-clogged channel between Harbor Island and Mustang Island, to a depth of eight feet. Two years later, Rep. John Garner convinced the House Committee on Rivers and Harbors to survey a 25-foot-deep channel through Turtle Cove, a vital first step if Corpus Christi was to obtain a deepwater port. The survey resulted in dredging Turtle Cove to 12 feet.

That year, Corpus Christi's hopes for a deepwater port were dashed when the U.S. Army Corps of Engineers decided the best place for a deepwater port was not at Corpus Christi but Harbor Island, which was 20 miles closer to the Gulf, would require less dredging and therefore would be cheaper.

When Turtle Cove was dredged to 25 feet, the spoils were dumped on Harbor Island, raising it by eight feet and providing a roadbed to build the Aransas Terminal Harbor Railroad, which was completed in 1912. Built on a six-mile-long causeway, it connected the port on Harbor Island with Southern Pacific in Aransas Pass.

The new port at Harbor Island opened to ocean-going vessels with the arrival of the ship Brinkburn on Sept. 7, 1912, which set off a celebration at Port Aransas, incorporated the year before, and the new town of Aransas Pass.

In 1918, during World War I, steel was in such short supply that shipbuilders decided to build oil tankers out of reinforced concrete. Several shipyards in the South, where it was warm enough to pour concrete year-round, began building concrete vessels. One was on Harbor Island.

Work began in June 1918 when the France & Canada Steamship Co. selected the site on Harbor Island with plans to build 10 concrete tankers, each 212 feet long and capable of carrying 15,000 barrels of oil. The plan was to use the tankers to carry Mexican oil from Tampico to terminals on Harbor Island.

Each day 600 workers were transported from Aransas Pass to Harbor Island on a special train operated by the Aransas Harbor Terminal Railroad. A Model-T truck with wheels adapted to fit rails had benches to sit on and it pulled a long trailer with seats. Workers called this train the Toonerville Trolley, after a popular comic strip titled "Toonerville Folks." Besides the Tooneverville trolley, the comic strip featured Little Woo-Woo Wortle, who had never been spanked, Aunt Eppie Hogg, the fattest lady in three counties, and Mickey McGuire, the tough Irish kid who was the town bully.

The 1919 storm destroyed the port facilities and oil storage tanks on Harbor Island and severely damaged the terminal railroad. The shipyard continued to build the concrete ships but under difficult conditions. With the Toonerville Trolley knocked out, workers were transported to the shipyard by boat.

Almost a year later, in July 1920, the first of two concrete ships built on the island, the Durham, was launched. It was named for Robert P. Durham, the engineer in charge. It was not a success. On its maiden voyage to Tampico, the ship wallowed, it was said, like a fat boy in a nightmare. The crew quit at Tampico and refused to make the return trip until the captain promised to have the "fat boy" towed back to Harbor Island.

The Durham, a cigar-shaped concrete oil tanker, on launching day July 24, 1920. The Durham was one of two concrete tankers built in Port Aransas between 1918 to 1920 by the France & Canada Steamship Company.

W.A. Scrivner, who was traffic manager of the Aransas Harbor Terminal Railroad, said once that the concrete tankers made two trips, "but they didn't navigate well, having to have a tugboat alongside at all times. One sank en route to Galveston and the other was tied up in the Sabine River above Port Arthur for a number of years." The shipyards were abandoned after the failure of the concrete tankers, which proved there are limits to human ingenuity.

After the railroad tracks from Aransas Pass to Harbor Island were repaired, the railroad began transporting automobiles on flat cars by using the old Model-T truck to pull a string of flat cars loaded with autos, many of them belonging to fishermen on their way to Port Aransas. At Harbor Island, the automobiles were driven onto the ferries to cross the ship channel. The terminal railroad carried thousands of fishermen and their automobiles to Port Aransas.

But other than transporting automobiles of fishermen, there was little need for a railroad to Harbor Island; the deepwater port for the region was now at Corpus Christi. In 1931, the railroad tracks were paved over and the six bridges planked over to create the Port Aransas Causeway, a toll causeway.

Nueces County purchased the old causeway in 1951 and the county operated the ferry boats plying between Harbor Island and

411

The Aransas Harbor Terminal Railroad used a Model-T with wheels adapted to fit the rails to pull flat cars loaded with automobiles. Photo from JoAnn Morgan.

Port Aransas until the state took over the ferry service in 1968. The Port Aransas Causeway was closed to traffic in April 1960 when the state finished building a new causeway from Aransas Pass to Harbor Island.

But Harbor Island was not the destination, just the place passed over on the way to Port Aransas. The glory years when the region's major port was being built on the island, when the Toonerville Trolley was making its daily run from Aransas Pass, were long gone.

— Nov. 27, 2013

MARTIN CULVER

William Sydney Porter, who worked on a South Texas ranch before he turned to fiction as O. Henry, called cattlemen grandees of grass, barons of beef and bone. Such a baron was Martin Smythe Culver, whose story covers a critical period of South Texas history after the Civil War.

Culver was born in Louisiana in 1838, the son of a steamboat captain on the Mississippi River. When his father was killed in a boiler explosion, his mother remarried and moved to San Antonio. Culver in his teens went to work for his uncle, J. T. "Tom" James, who owned a ranch in Live Oak County. James also ran cattle on Mustang Island and built the St. James Hotel in Corpus Christi.

At the end of the Civil War, Culver came out of the Confederate Army with plans to begin his own cattle operation. He had worked for his uncle long enough to know the business. He bought a small herd and hired Milton Dodson of Dinero to round them up. Culver then bought Rancho Perdido, the Lost Ranch.

It really had been a lost ranch for J. P. Harrison from Baltimore, by way of Corpus Christi, who bought the 600 acres that comprised the ranch in 1860, built a crude house, and planned to begin a ranch on the Penitas. The location was three miles southwest of Casa Blanca, 50 miles north of Corpus Christi. His ranching venture failed with the coming of the Civil War. In 1868, the 600 acres were sold to Culver. Land was cheap then, but he still got Rancho Perdido for a bargain at $1 an acre.

Martin Culver wasn't interested in land. He was at the other end of the spectrum from Richard King, who founded King Ranch. King wanted to own the ground he was standing on and all the land next to it while Culver wanted just enough land to serve as headquarters for his cattle that would graze on the open range.

After buying Rancho Perdido, Culver moved his cattle to Penitas Creek. He had married Kate Pugh of Gussettville and they moved into the crude ranch house built by J. P. Harrison in 1860.

South Texas after the war was overrun with unbranded cattle and Culver burned his brand on every longhorn he could find. His main brand was KL, which stood for his wife Kate and daughter Lizzie. Besides Milton Dodson, his foreman, Culver hired some 100 Mexican-American vaqueros to work the cattle. Though few of them knew English, they learned enough, and Culver and Dodson learned enough Spanish, to communicate. Their talk was a mixture of cow camp English and Spanish.

Culver began sending herds of 1,000 head up the trail to the new rail-head towns in Kansas. As trail-herding became more proficient, the herds increased to 3,000 or more. In a short time, within three or four years, Culver became a wealthy cattleman.

In 1868, Culver's half-sister, Mary Susanna Burris, rode down from San Antonio to visit and, a year later, she married Culver's foreman Milton Dodson. In 1870, Culver built a new ranch house for Rancho Perdido (in today's Jim Wells County) on Penitas Creek. Culver had lumber shipped from Florida and freighted overland by wagon. A former sailor designed the house and did all the carpentry. It included nine rooms, a wide front porch that extended along the front and one side and it was painted London purple with white trim. It was a show place.

In 1871, some 700,000 head of cattle went up the trail from Texas to Kansas, which flooded the market and beef prices fell to almost nothing. The value of a longhorn dropped to the value of the hide, tallow, horns and bones. Beef slaughter houses, also called packing houses or packeries, began operating on the coast. Culver built a packery at Nuecestown, which was in operation after 1871.

During that time, Culver took three vaqueros to the Dunn place outside Corpus Christi to buy horses. A vaquero got on a horse that spooked, trying to throw him, and the man's spurs got tangled in the stirrup, a dangerous situation. Culver quickly drew his pistol and shot the horse dead, saving the man's life.

Another story has been told of Culver. During the Nuecestown Raid in 1875, a wounded bandit was brought to Corpus Christi on an ox-cart. Looking for a place to hang the bandit, several men climbed to the roof of the Catholic Church and were fixing a rope to the steeple when Culver, who was Catholic, made them get down, and told them not to desecrate a house of worship. The bandit was taken on down Leopard Street and hanged from a gate.

Martin S. Culver ran cattle on the open range in the Nueces Valley. He later founded Trail City on the Kansas-Colorado line and presided over the end of the trail-driving era.

With the spread of barbed wire fencing the open range and free grazing were coming to an end. Culver could read the signs. He sold Rancho Perdido for $5,000. It was bought by his brother-in-law and foreman, Milton Dodson. Culver moved to Dodge City, where he became Trail Commissioner, responsible for inspecting herds up from Texas, making sure they carried the right brands and cutting herds that were to go north.

Martin Culver's ranch house at Rancho Perdido was built in 1871. The photo shows Culver's brother-in-law, Milton Dodson, who bought the house from Culver, sitting on the porch with other members of the Dodson family.

In 1885, the Kansas Legislature, afraid of the spread of Texas tick fever, passed a law preventing Texas cattle from entering Kansas. Culver traveled to Washington where he was able to secure a lease for a three-mile strip of territory along the Kansas-Colorado line. Herds from Texas could be taken up this new trail, skirting Kansas, and then on to Ogallala.

Culver moved his family to Coolidge, Kansas and then he established a new town across the state line in Colorado called Trail City. Saloon girls and gamblers in Dodge City and other Kansas cattle towns, out of work because of the quarantine of Texas cattle, moved to Trail City, which became known as the most sinful town in Colorado.

Trail City didn't last long. The coming of railroads ended cattle drives. Culver died about the same time, on Oct. 5, 1887, from appendicitis and he was buried in Coolidge, Kansas. Martin S. Culver was a successful free-range cattleman, a baron of beef and bone, who saw the beginning and the end, the prologue and epilogue, of the great trail drives out of South Texas.

— Dec. 4, 2013

EATING HORSE STEAKS

This is the season, between Thanksgiving and Christmas, when our thoughts turn to food so I thought about the kind of food people ate in early Texas. Compared to the almost infinite variety of foodstuffs we have to choose from on supermarket shelves, the contrast could not be greater.

Early settlers lived on corn and venison and relished wild game we would not look at today, much less eat. Staples that were shipped in — sugar, flour and coffee — were expensive and in short supply.

Noah Smithwick in "Evolution of a State" described coming to Texas on a schooner in 1827. At Green DeWitt's colony near Gonzales, he found that meals invariably consisted of venison sopped in honey. Later, on the Brazos, Smithwick said people feasted on corn that was in "roasting ear." When the corn turned hard, they made graters from tin-ware punched with holes and then, when cold weather came, hominy was boiled in iron kettles.

On a smuggling trip to the Rio Grande, Smithwick and his companions ran out of food. There was no game, but wild horses were abundant. The thought of eating horseflesh sickened him but "the other boys had been in Texas long enough to get rid of any fastidious notions. When provisions ran out, they killed a mustang. I said I would rather starve before I would eat it. On the third day of my fast, I went for a big horse steak which I could scarcely wait to cook. The boys said I was broke in."

A new arrival in Texas, J. C. Clopper, described the making of tortillas in San Antonio in his travel journal in 1828. "The way they (Tejanos) obtain their bread is worthy of notice. They raise only Indian corn — this is soaked in lime or lye till the rind of the grain is taken off. It is then ground on a concave stone about 12 inches wide and 20 in length . . . A handful of corn is laid on this and masticated with another stone resembling a roller but cut so as to fit the concavity. The operation is always performed by women, and in a kneeling posture. If they wish to treat their friends to very white bread, the whole family gathers round the pot of corn and, grain by grain, bite off the little black speck at the end of the germ. When the dough is ready, a small portion at a time is taken and patted in the hands till thin as a flannel cake. These cakes are baked on sheet iron and when eaten hot with butter or gravy are very palatable."

John Holland Jenkins, who grew up near Bastrop, described how settlers made do with limited materials. "It seems difficult to understand how corn could be grated into meal without machinery of some kind. Then we had no sieve, and no oven, but our old mortar and pestle was a first-rate grist mill, though tedious. Our sieve consisted of a wooden hoop, over which buckskin was stretched, and this was perforated with a red-hot wire. On our 'Johnny Cake' boards was baked as good a bread as was ever taken from oven or store. Our coffee was tied in a piece of buckskin and beaten on a rock with another rock."

Mary Austin Holley, a cousin of Stephen F. Austin, made several trips to Texas in the 1830s and socialized with rich planters. In May 1835, she described a dinner at Bolivar, in Brazoria County, which consisted of rabbit soup, a piece of "Yankee pickled pork," venison steaks, snap beans, "remarkably fine Irish potatoes" and lettuce fresh from the garden. On another occasion, she wrote of venison they ate at dinner: "Nothing could be finer. One need not complain of fare when tables are loaded with venison, oysters and beef of the finest quality. These meats are exceedingly tender. They live sumptuously here. Supper handsome — dressed cakes and sugar pyramids — other confectionary, with oranges brought from New Orleans."

J. Williamson Moses, who worked as a surveyor along the Llano and San Saba in 1848, once wrote: "The amount of meal or flour we could take on packhorses or mules was so small we did not pretend to keep up a supply of breadstuff. But as long as we had coffee and salt, we could do very well. There were times that for months we never ate a mouthful of bread and had no vegetables of any kind. We generally had a supply of bear, antelope and deer, not to mention wild turkey, goose and small game. We would eat our partially dried meat as bread, and the fresh, fat meat as meat. As to vegetables, we had none. A little sage and wild onions were a rare treat."

J. Williamson Moses, a surveyor, Texas Ranger and mustanger, said their diet in the field consisted of bear, antelope, deer, wild turkey, goose and small game.

The Mercer family of bar pilots on Mustang Island kept a daily ship's log. In an entry for Jan. 14, 1871, one of the Mercers noted: "This morning the wind N.E. Ned, Tom Lacey, Captain Clubb went up to the schooner Whisper. The captain of the schooner would not go out. Came home and went to planting potatoes. Planted about two-thirds of a barrel. Planted 12 rows of them. Roberts came from St. Joseph's (Island) and wanted to go to Rockport. Ned went with him. Brought back a keg of pigs' feet and two sacks of coffee. So ends the day."

J. Frank Dobie in "Vaquero of the Brush Country" described how to roast a wild turkey in its feathers. The cook would dig a pit, build a fire in it, heat the ground, then take out the coals. Having removed the entrails of the turkey and salted and peppered the bird, he would put it in the warm hole, cover it with hot earth and build a fire on top. About 20 hours later, the turkey could be lifted out by its feet. The skin and feathers would drop off by their own weight. The result was meat so tender, he wrote, it melted in the mouth.

Another dish I would not try at home comes from the "Slave Narratives." A former slave named Abram Sells described how possum was cooked. "We would parboil him then bake him plumb tender. Then we stacked sweet potatoes around him and poured the juice (from the cooking possum) over the whole thing. Now, there's something good enough for a king."

Uh, maybe. People were not as picky back then as we are today. They couldn't afford to be. They ate whatever they could catch or shoot, and were no doubt glad to get it. Today, spoiled as we are by HEB, we would have to be awfully hungry to eat roast possum with sweet potatoes or fricassee of wild turkey cooked in its own feathers. Both were described as delicious, and maybe they were, but I'll take their word for it.

— Dec. 11, 2013

420

CHRISTMAS IN WARTIME

When I looked at a photo of Chaparral Street in December 1945, I couldn't help but wonder what Christmas was like during the war years. Grim times, I thought, with so many away fighting in distant places. The whole country had to be in a turmoil of anxiety. But a search through newspaper microfilm reels told me that in the midst of war, Christmas shopping never slumped. And that was surprising. Even when the store shelves were almost bare, shoppers bought whatever was available.

To put the war years in perspective, in 1940 some 15,000 job-seekers flooded Corpus Christi looking for work at the naval air station being built. They did not see the city at its best. Streets were dug up for new water and sewer lines and with the seawall under construction the bayfront was a sea of mud.

In the first week of December 1941, Mrs. Edith Phillips, a teacher at Wynn Seale, was called for jury duty but sent home; women were not seated on juries then. Christmas lights were turned on downtown and that Friday Santa Claus landed in a Navy seaplane on the bay and toured the downtown in a car. Bob McCracken, the Lookout columnist in the Caller-Times, complained that modern-day Christmas featured too many Santas who moved too fast in planes and cars.

Two days later, on Sunday, people heard the news that Japan attacked U.S. bases at Pearl Harbor. That Monday at the Assembly & Repairs hangar at the Naval Air Station, sailors and civilians gathered to hear President Roosevelt's "a date which will live in infamy" speech. Three days later, Hitler declared war on the U.S. and young men began receiving life-changing letters that began with "Greetings."

Even with the nation at war, Christmas 1941 broke all previous sales records. The Caller-Times said no one could remember seeing such large crowds in Lichtenstein's and Perkins Brothers. People decided that it might be the last Christmas they would be able to celebrate for awhile, so they spent with abandon. Merchants didn't know whether to laugh or cry — glad because profits were up but sad because they didn't know if they would be able to restock their merchandise.

On Dec. 22, Grisham Ice Cream Company held its Christmas party at the Nueces Hotel. At the Naval Air Station, cedar trees next to the administration building were decorated with lights. Some 10,000 officers, enlisted men, cadets, and civil service workers were at the base, unable to travel for the holidays. Plans were made for "Pearl Harbor Dances" to benefit the Red Cross.

By 1942, the war brought new bureaucracies to ration sugar, meat, whisky, gasoline and tires. Housewives saved leftover cooking fats to increase the grease supply. A sign at a local grease collection point said — "Ladies, Put Your Fat Cans Down Here."

The Navy in 1942 established a super-secret radar training school on Ward Island. People in town had no idea what the secret was until after the war. Security measures were imposed and military guards stopped cars and searched for cameras. Some beaches were off-limits and people were not permitted to take a boat out in the bay or the Gulf without a photo ID.

The first blackout drill was Jan. 19, 1942. The next blackout, 10 days later, was the real thing, prompted by a U-boat sighting off Port Aransas. During 1942 and 1943, U-boats sank many ships in the Gulf, mostly tankers carrying oil and gasoline, the lifeblood of war.

By December 1942, it was expected that the war, a year old, would have a telling effect on Christmas celebrations and shopping. A letter to the editor said, "This Christmas season is different from any previous ones. Our lives have been built around the spirit of the war. This year the presents have been less and we save by lighting the tree only when the kids are around to see it."

But the war did not shrink Christmas sales, which were a repeat of the exuberant spending of the year before. Crow's Nest columnist Bob McCracken wrote of the holiday frenzy: "People had money to spend and decided to get while the getting was good. After all, there might not be any next year."

On Christmas Day, empty places around Christmas dinner tables were filled with servicemen from the Naval Air Station. With gas and tire rationing, traveling was difficult and people stayed home.

On Chaparral in December 1945, looking north, a time-exposure shot shows the Nueces Hotel on the right with the Palace Theater down the street. Christmas lights were strung for the first time since December 1941 when the war began.

On April 21, 1943, President Roosevelt and Mexico's President Avila Camacho visited the Naval Air Station. At the time of their visit, 20,000 civilians were employed at the station, many of them young women in civil defense jobs. The Naval Air Station played a major role in the war in the Pacific. Some 35,000 aviators trained for combat at NAS and its outlying fields.

At Christmas 1943, the newspaper reported that, "Goods and gifts available last year have long since been cleaned off the shelves, yet buying this year has broken all records, in wild, crazy, extravagant fashion." Abstemious they were not.

In 1944, two German POWs escaped from a prison camp at Mexia, 360 miles to the north, and fled to Corpus Christi, hoping to escape to Mexico. They were captured on North Beach. The Germans refused to answer any questions and arrogantly demanded that their captors call them sir.

On April 12, 1945, the nation mourned the news that President Roosevelt died. Students at George Evans Elementary gathered at the flagpole and sang the president's favorite songs, "Home on the Range" and "Abide With Me." Harry Truman became president, the Russians captured Berlin, Hitler committed suicide, and Germany surrendered. After atomic bombs destroyed Hiroshima and Nagasaki, Japan gave up on Aug. 15, 1945, bringing to an end the most destructive war in the history of the world.

In December 1945, for the first time since 1941, two downtown streets were decorated for Christmas. Lights and decorations were strung on Chaparral from Laguna to Starr and on Leopard Street from Broadway to Sam Rankin. Few stores, however, had Christmas lights for sale and only those who kept their pre-war strings could decorate their trees.

It was a sad Christmas for many families who had lost loved ones in the war. The Caller-Times noted that there were many missing faces among the old corner gangs — "the boys who used to gather at the drug stores and never took life seriously until their country was in danger. Many are gone and many will never be the same." But in December 1945, after four long years, the war was over and on Leopard and Chaparral the Christmas lights were back on.

— Dec. 25, 2013

NOTES ON SOURCES

CHAPTER 1
"Corpus Christi: A History," page 101 on Market Hall. Undated newspaper clip, "Bluff's Concrete Balustrade Was First Major Improvement." Articles on bluff tunnel, Feb. 23, 1977 and May 31, 1991. Bill Walraven column on civic improvements, Jan. 11, 1984. Caller-Times articles on the 1914 Courthouse: March 15, 1964 and March 23, 1989. M.G. column on Reef Road, Oct. 13, 1999. Times article on the causeway, Oct. 1, 1946. Corpus Christi Press, June 23, 1949 on causeway and Reef Road. Newspaper stories on the Nueces Hotel, Jan. 20, 1914, Sept. 22, 1929, Oct. 29, 1932, Dec. 26, 1958.

CHAPTER 2
Compiled from interviews conducted in the late 1930s and early 1940s by Marie Blucher with William Rankin, Anna Moore Schwien, Eli Merriman, E.H. Caldwell, John B. Dunn and Andy Anderson. Vertical files, Corpus Christi Central Library.

CHAPTER 3
Handbook of Texas on George C. Hatch. Nueces Valley, Sept. 5, 1872. Undated newspaper clip, "Civil War Chapter Uncovered" on Hatch's departure from Texas to British Honduras after the war. May 18, 1954 article on J. C. Hatch. Personal correspondence with descendents Richard J. Hatch and Norma Loveless. John B. Dunn, "Perilous Trails of Texas" and Eli Merriman's reminiscence. On Eunice Hatch's murder: Jim Davis, "Bloody Hatchet Murderer of Southern Texas" in January 1971 edition of Real West. Corpus Christi Caller, April 25, 1902; May 26, 1902; Corpus Christi Crony, April 26, 1902; May 3, 1902.

CHAPTER 4
On William Long Rogers, research papers of Frank Wagner; E. H. Caldwell's memoirs; Caller-Times, Dec. 7, 1941 and April 27, 1952; Bill Walraven columns, Sept. 15, 1978 and April 8, 1981. Fire in 1892, article by Anne Dodson, Nov. 20, 1955. Annual firemen's ball, "Saga of a Frontier Seaport," Coleman McCampbell. Caller-Times on replacing Market Hall, Sept. 22, 1929. On the fire bell, Eli Merriman's reminiscences. New water system, Dee Woods, July 13 and 14, 1939. A History of Corpus Christi's Municipal Water Supply, John S. McCampbell.

CHAPTER 5
"When I Was Young in Corpus Christi," recollections of W. S. Rankin, from interviews in 1939 and 1940, vertical files, Corpus Christi Central Library. Corpus Christi Times, April 17, 1942; Times, Sept. 26, 1947; Caller, Sept. 27, 1947. Undated clipping, "W. S. Rankin Recalls Excitement of Residents When Union Gunboats Bombarded City in 1862." Obituary, Times, April 12, 1948.

CHAPTER 6
J. L. Allhands "The Gringo Builders" and "Uriah Lott." "Who Built the Lines to the Lower Rio Grande Valley?" by L. J. Polk, Corpus Christi Times, May 1, 1936.

Caller-Times, April 27, 1952 and Jan. 18, 1959. Undated by E.T. Merriman, "Southwest Texas Owes Undying Debt of Gratitude to Uriah Lott..." Bill Walraven article, Jan. 18, 1959, and column, Nov. 23, 1977. Eleanor Mortensen article on Uriah Lott, Caller-Times, 1972. "The Excursion to Laredo," Caller-Times, July 29, 1925. "A Thumbnail History of the Texas Mexican Railway," undated. "Perfectly Exhausted With Pleasure," Bruce S. Cheeseman.

CHAPTER 7
War of the Rebellion, Official Records of the Union and Confederate Armies. Ernest Morgan, articles, Corpus Christi Caller-Times, Feb. 5, Feb. 19, March 5, March 12, 1961. William Adams, "The Bombardment of Corpus Christi," vertical files, Corpus Christi Central Library. Andrew Anderson, "Do You Know the Story of Corpus Christi?" biographical files, Corpus Christi Central Library. Eugenia Reynolds Briscoe, "City by the Sea". Norman C. Delaney, "The Vicksburg of Texas," Corpus Christi Times, Aug. 14, 15, 16, 1977. "Military Events in Texas During the Civil War, 1861-1865." Biographical Sketch of John W. Kittredge's career in the U.S. Navy, dated Jan. 25, 1939. The Ranchero, July 13, 20, 1861, Aug. 19, 1962.

CHAPTER 8
Biographical account of Perry Doddridge, Frank Wagner's research papers. "The King Ranch," by Tom Lea. Nueces Valley, July 3, 1858. "History of Nueces County." J. L. Allhands, "The Gringo Builders." Mary Sutherland, "The Story of Corpus Christi." Eugenia Reynolds Briscoe, "City by the Sea". Obituary, Corpus Christi Caller, June 13, 1902. Corpus Christi Crony, June 14, 1902.

Chapter 9
Carlos E. Castaneda, "The Mission Era: The Finding of Texas, 1519-1693," Volume 1. Castaneda translated the story of Agustin Padilla Davila in "Our Catholic Heritage in Texas." Report by the Texas Antiquities Committee, "Introduction to the Davila Account and Related Sources." Hodding Carter, "Doomed Road of Empire." Vernon Smylie, "The Early History of Padre Island." Dee Woods, "Blaze of Gold." Dee Woods, articles, June 15, 1939 and Sept. 21, 1939. Writers' Round Table, "Padre Island." Caller-Times article on Alex Meuly, July 2, 1969. Bill Walraven, column, May 12, 1981. Article on Lafitte, June 14, 1964.

Chapter 10
M.G. columns, Nov. 15 and Nov. 29, 2000. Bill Walraven column, Nov. 2, 1983. Handbook of Texas, individual entries on towns and cities. Caller-Times, Dec. 11, 1949, Jan. 18, 1959, Aug. 7, 1964, June 26, 1966, Feb. 26, 1969, Jan. 25, 1970, Jan. 27, 1976, Nov. 2, 1983, Aug. 3, 1992.

Chapter 11
Caller-Times, May 21, 1939. Caller-Times, June 15, 1941. Undated clipping from 1941, "City Stretches Its Facilities to Meet Population Gains." "Corpus Christi Is Suffering Growing Pains," Corpus Christi Times, Dec. 16, 1940. Caller-Times, "It's Bundles for Britain Day." Caller-Times, "NAS Dedication Was a Day to Remember," Jan. 18, 1959. Ernest Morgan, "A Quiet Week Became Chaotic in a

Flash," Caller, Dec. 7, 1961. Eleanor Mortensen, "It was a calm Sunday until . . .," Caller, Dec. 7, 1976. Caller-Times, "Instructions for Blackout Drill," Jan. 16, 1942. Caller-Times, "46,729 Sign Up For Ration Books," vertical files, Corpus Christi Central Library. Caller-Times, "6,000 Car and Motorcycle Owners Register for Gas," Nov. 20, 1942. April 21 and April 22, 1943, Caller-Times. Times, "Food Establishments in City Divided On Question of 'Meatless Tuesday'," Oct. 5, 1943. Jan. 28, 1982 Caller, Bill Walraven column. Article with no byline, Caller, Aug. 23, 1945, "Navy for First Time Describes 42-43 Nazi Sub Action in Gulf." Undated article, Caller-Times, "Sea War Came Close to Home in Summer of '42." M.G. column, Sept. 29, 1999.

Chapter 12
Caller-Times, Feb. 9, 1969, Grady Phelps, "The Hunt for Escaped POWs." "Corpus Christians Still Stunned by News of Sudden Death of President," Times, April 13, 1945; Times, "Flags at Half Mast as City Pays Its Respects to Memory of Roosevelt." "City in Mourning for Roosevelt," Caller, April 14, 1945. Juliet Knight Wenger, "News To Me." Caller-Times, Sept. 2, 1945, "When Johnnie Comes Marching Home . . ." From 'Beam,' March 15, 1946, on German POW camp. Caller-Times, Dec. 20, 1945.
Caller-Times, "City Faces Meat Famine as Only Local Packing Houses Are Shut Down," vertical files, Central Library. Mary Mahoney, "Loaves Disappear Here After Rush," Caller-Times, April 30, 1946. Centennial Journey, p. 62. Corpus Christi Times, "Boats Which Served In Coast Guard Returned To Owners," Feb. 1, 1946. Caller-Times, June 17, 18, 1946.

Chapter 13
Ernest Morgan, "1950s Found City Moving and Growing," Caller-Times, Jan. 1, 1960. Writers Roundtable, "Padre Island." Jim Greenwood, "First Visitor Shows at Five," Corpus Christi Times, June 17, 1950. Caller-Times, "Causeway to Padre Opened New Resort," Jan. 18, 1959. Corpus Christi Caller, "No Question At All About It, The United States Is At War," July 3, 1950. John W. Johnson, "Tears and Pride Mixed As Local Marines Leave," Caller-Times. Caller- Times, Jan. 30 through Feb. 1, 1951 editions.
Lynn Pentony, article, Times, Feb. 22, 1982. Bill Walraven, column, Caller, April 16, 1975. Centennial Journey, p. 92. Caller-Times, June 19, 20, 1954. Juliet K. Wenger, "News To Me." Caller-Times, Feb. 1, 1954, "KVDO Goes On Air Today." Charles Branning, "1953 remembered as a miserably dry year," Nov. 1988.

Chapter 14
Caller-Times' Harbor Bridge edition, Oct. 23, 1959. "Bridge vs. Tunnel Was Great Debate for Three Years," Oct. 23, 1959.
Bill Walraven, "El Rincon: A History of Corpus Christi Beach." Caller-Times, "City Losing Bayside Playground," Sept. 15, 1957.
Corpus Christi Caller, "Council Changes Name of Beach," Feb. 26, 1959. Corpus Christi Caller, "Old 'North Beach' Spans 125 Years of Varied History," Dec. 8, 1969. M.G. column on drive-ins, Jan. 12, 2000. Centennial History, "O&R closing spread gloom," p. 91.

Chapter 15
"The Mercer Logs: Pioneer Times on Mustang Island, Texas," compiled by John Guthrie Ford.

Chapter 16
Noakes Diary, 1865-1866, Corpus Christi Central Library.

Chapter 17 and 18
Hortense Warner Ward, "The First State Fair of Texas," Southwestern Historical Quarterly. Charles G. Norton, "Colonel Henry L. Kinney, Founder of Corpus Christi." Bruce Cheeseman, "Maria von Blucher's Corpus Christi," p. 71-72. Indianola Bulletin (on microfilm): March 11, 1852; March 18, March 25, April 8, April 15, April 22, April 29, April 30, May 6, May 13, May 20, 1852. Texas State Gazette, March 6, May 8, May 22, May 29, 1852.
Chapter 19 Corpus Christi Star, Oct. 17, Oct. 24, Dec. 16, 1848. Corpus Christi Star, April 21, 1849. Paul Horgan, "Great River," p. 492, 495, 496. The Lamar Papers, II, p. 457. The "History of Nueces County to 1850," master's thesis, Marvin Lee Deviney. Eugenia Reynolds Briscoe, "City by the Sea," p. 116, 126. Nueces County History, p. 58. W. R. Gore, "The Life of Henry Lawrence Kinney," master's thesis. Anna Marietta Kelsey, "Through the Years." E. H. Caldwell's memoirs, Eli Merriman's reminiscences. J. W. Williams, "Old Texas Trails." Brownson Malsch, "Indianola: The Mother of Western Texas," p. 27, 33-34, 44-47, 308-315. Hodding Carter, "Road of Empire."

Chapter 20
Certificate of Henry Addington Gilpin receiving the 30th Degree, Rite of Scotttish Freemasonry, August 1877. "The History of Kings County, Nova Scotia." Frank Wagner's research papers. Ruth Dodson, "Judge Gilpin and the Penitas Ranch," first printed in Texas Historical Association Quarterly and reprinted in "Recollections of Other Days," edited by Murphy Givens and Jim Moloney. "Reminiscences of C.C. Cox," Texas Historical Association Quarterly."

Chapter 21, 22, 23, 24
Z. N. Morrell, "Flowers and Fruits in the Wilderness." "Texas Ranger: Jack Hays in the Frontier Southwest," James Kimmins Greer. A. J. Sowell, "Life of Bigfoot Wallace." "Recollections of Early Texas: The Memoirs of John Holland Jenkins." Robert J. Casey, "The Texas Border." Paul Horgan, "Great River." Joseph D. McCutchan, "Mier Expedition Diary." Gen. Thomas J. Green, "Journal of the Texian Expedition Against Mier." "George Washington Trahern: Cowboy Soldier from Mier to Buena Vista," edited by Russell Buchanan, Southwestern Historical Quarterly. "Journal of Lewis Birdsall Harris," Southwestern Historical Quarterly. "Border Wars of Texas," James De Shields. Henderson Yoakum, "A Comprehensive History of Texas." Leonie Rummel Weyand, "Early History of Fayette County." L. V. Spellman, "Letters of the 'Dawson Men' From Perote Prison, Mexico, 1842-1843," Southwestern Historical Quarterly. Handbook of Texas.

Chapter 25
Corpus Christi Caller, April 2, 1952. Robstown Record, Diamond Anniversary edition, Nov. 18, 1982. "Role of 'Blacklanders' Is Described by Nixon," Caller, Oct. 13, 1954. Times, Aug. 19, 1965. "Local Blacklanders Made History In 1924," Robstown Record, Oct. 31, 1957. Corpus Christi Caller, Nov. 9 and 10, Nov. 13, Nov. 17, 18, 19, 23, 1924. Times, Jan. 24, 1983. Copy of audit report of Blacklanders' expenses, author's possession. Centennial Journey, p. 57. The Independent Petroleum Monthly, March 1961. Maston Nixon's obituary, Caller-Times, April 3, 1966.

Chapter 26
"Zachary Taylor in Corpus Christi," by the author, 2006. Corpus Christi Caller, Oct. 20, 1905. Caller, Jan. 10 and Jan. 31, 1908. Caller, Jan. 18, 1959. Times, Aug. 18, Sept. 14 and Oct. 12, 1965, April 21, 1966. "Building Corpus Christi," p. 46. Centennial History, p. 85. Sanborn maps, 1900 to 1909. City Directory, 1913. Andrew Anderson's memories, from "Recollections of Other Days." Corpus Christi Caller, March 5, 1941. Corpus Christi Caller, Oct. 3, 1983. Times, March 6, 1926.

Chapter 27
"Shanghai Pierce: A Fair Likeness," Chris Emmett. "The Trail Drivers of Texas," J. Marvin Hunter. Clara M. Love, "History of the Cattle Industry in the Southwest," Southwestern Historical Quarterly. "Reminiscences of C.C. Cox," Southwestern Historical Quarterly. "Cowboy Culture," David Dary. "The Cowboy," Philip Ashton Rollins. "The Day of the Cattleman," Ernest Staples Osgood. "Longhorns," J. Frank Dobie. "Cowboy Lore," Jules Verne Allen. "Texas After the Civil War," Carl H. Moneyhon. John Young and J. Frank Dobie, "A Vaquero of the Brush Country." Tom Lea, "The King Ranch." Sam P. Ridings, "The Chisholm Trail."

Chapter 28
February, March and April, 1915 editions of the Corpus Christi Caller and Daily Herald. Caller-Times, Oct. 26, 1956. Ernest Morgan, Caller-Times, March 11, 1962. Bill Walraven column, Jan. 14, 1986. Letter to the Editor, B.C. Baldwin, Oct. 12, 1957, Caller. Caller-Times, April 27, 1952. Maude T. Gilliland, "Horsebackers of the Brush Country." Centennial Journey, Jan. 23, 1983, p. 43. Louis Rawalt in "Recollections of Other Days."

Chapter 29
James Rowe, Corpus Christi Caller, Jan. 12, 1973. Caller, Feb. 26, 1954. Spencer Pearson, Jan. 11, 1973. Caller, May 23, 1957. Sid Richardson's obituary, Sept. 30, 1959, Times. "Texas Coastal Bend," Alpha Kennedy Wood. Corpus Christi Star, Sept. 19, 1848 and March 26, 1849. Brownson Malsch, "Indianola." Hobart Huson, "Texas Coastal Bend Trilogy."

Chapter 30
Caller, Jan. 18, 1959. Alpha Kennedy Wood. Corpus Christi Star, Sept. 19, 1848 and March 26, 1849. Brownson Malsch, "Indianola." Hobart Huson, "Texas Coastal Bend Trilogy." Bill Walraven column, May 28, 1985. Hobart Huson, "St.

Mary's of Aransas." Huson, "Iron Men." Huson, "Refugio." Frontier Times, March 1931, on Henry Smith. Caller-Times, May 17, 1984, article on Lamar. Handbook of Texas. Robert Lee Moore, "History of Refugio County," thesis. "Texas Irish Empresarios," William H. Oberste. Lamar Papers. Refugio County History. Houston Telegraph and Register, April 7 and April 18, 1838. "Empresario's Children," Bill and Marjorie Walraven. "William Bollaert's Texas," edited by W. Eugene Hollon and Ruth Butler. Keith Guthrie, "Texas Forgotten Ports." Memoirs of Mary A. Maverick. Spencer Pearson, "Little remains of once-thriving port," Aug. 8, 1988. Paul Freier in "The Wave," Feb. 20, 1974, April 17, April 24, 1974, and May 17, 1978. Lester Fitzhugh, "Saluria, Fort Esperanza, and Military Operations on the Texas Coast, 1861-1865," Southwestern Historical Quarterly. Corpus Christi Caller, "Towns Dotted Coast Islands in Old Days," May 8, 1959.

Chapter 31 and 32
A series of articles, Corpus Christi Caller-Times, Jan. 1, 1970, "City Was on the Go in Decade of 60s." Caller-Times, March 6, 1961; April 4, 1961; May 10, 1961; June 3 and June 21, 1961; Aug. 5, 1961; . Caller-Times, Dec. 31, 1961, "Hurricane Carla Was the Big News Maker." June 30, 1962. Sept. 28, 1962. Caller-Times, Dec. 30, 1962, "Annexation, Polio and Gas: Big News of '62." Flour Bluff annexation articles: Sept. 15, 1962; Jan. 14, 1964, Oct. 2, 1963, April 22, 1964. Laguna Madre slayings: April 12 and 15, 1965; Jan. 2, 1966. May 12, 1966. Aug. 9, 1969. NASA tracking station, "Wings of Gold: 50th Anniversary." Hurricane Beulah, Sept. 20, 1967, Caller-Times. Padre Island dedication, April 8, 1968.

Chapter 33
Noah Smithwick, "Evolution of a State." Correspondence with Bobby Lewis, Alvin, on Pappy O'Daniel. Hortense Warner Ward, "The First State Fair of Texas," Southwestern Historical Quarterly. David McComb, "Galveston." Handbook of Texas.

Chapter 34
Memoirs of Mary A. Maverick. Mary Austin Holley, "Texas Diary, 1835-38." The Memoirs of John Holland Jenkins. "Texas by Teran," edited by Jack Jackson, John Wheat.

Chapter 35
Bascom N. Timmons, "Garner of Texas." Caller-Times, Nov. 8, 1967, news article and editorial. Associated Press biographical account, Jan. 1, 1955. Caller-Times, Oct. 1936. Corpus Christi Caller, July 29, 1904. Coleman McCampbell, "Saga of a Frontier Seaport," p. 152-153. "King Ranch Papers," p. 191. U.S. News & World Report, Nov. 21, 1958. Corpus Christi Crony: May 17, 1902; June 14, June 28, July 19, July 26, Aug. 2, Sept. 13, Sept. 20, Sept. 27, Oct. 25, Nov. 8, Nov. 15, 1902; Jan. 31, 1903. Richard A. Laune, "Journal of South Texas" on port development. "Boss Rule," Evan Anders. "Seaport of the South," Carl Helmecke. Caller-Times, Jan. 1, 1950, April 27, 1953. Undated, Eli Merriman, "Fight for Turtle Cove Channel..."

Chapter 36 and 37

War of the Rebellion , Official Records of the Union and Confederate Armies: Operations in Texas and New Mexico, April and June 1861; operations of the Gulf Blockading Squadron in January and February, 1862; operations in Texas, New Mexico and Arizona, March 1862; operations of the West Gulf Blockading Squadron, November, December 1862; Confederate correspondence, November 1863; the Rio Grande Expedition, November, December 1863; reconnaissance of Matagorda Peninsula, January 1864; operations of the West Gulf Blockading Squadron, February 1865. Edwin B. Lufkin, "History of the 13th Maine Regiment." Henry Augustus Shorey, "The Story of the 15th Regiment." William Allen, Sue Hastings Taylor, "Aransas." Alpha Kennedy Wood, "Texas Coastal Bend." Lester N. Fitzhugh, "Saluria, Fort Esperanza, and Military Operations on the Texas Coast, 1861-1864," Southwestern Historical Quarterly. Handbook of Texas. Hobart Huson, "Refugio." Bill Walraven column in the Caller-Times, Dec. 20, 1975. Brownson Malsch, "Indianola." Dudley G. Wooten, "A Comprehensive History of Texas: Military Events and Operations in Texas and Along the Coasts and Border, 1861-1865." Ernest Morgan, "North Recaptures Coast Easily," Corpus Christi Caller-Times, May 28, 1961. Linda Wolff, "Indianola and Matagorda Island." Centennial History of Corpus Christi.

Chapter 38

Juliet K. Wenger, "News To Me." Caller-Times Centennial Issue, 1983. Editorial in the Caller on Bob McCracken's death, Oct. 31, 1958. Bill Walraven column, Aug. 31, 1984. Obituary, Caller, Oct. 30, 1858. McCracken column, Feb. 11, 1944 on German POW escapees. John Stallings' column, June 18, 1977. Caller-Times biographical form, Dec. 7, 1954. Times, Feb. 20, 1951, Dec. 2, 1957, Oct. 30, 1958. Caller, March 13, 1959.

Chapter 39

Vladimir Nabokov, "Speak, Memory." J. Frank Dobie, "Tales of Old-Time Texas." Handbook of Texas. Frontier Times, "The Headless Horseman." William Edward Syers, "Off the Beaten Trail." J. Frank Dobie, "The Mustangs." Grady Phelps, undated article in the Caller-Times, "Living on Ranch, O. Henry Caught Texas Flavor." Caller-Times, May 2, 1985. Webb Garrison, "A Treasury of Texas Tales." "Best Stories of O. Henry." Autobiographical Sketch by J. Frank Dobie, Dec. 29, 1958. Caller-Times, Oct. 27, 1963, "J. Frank Dobie: Texas Most Outspoken Maverick." Caller-Times, June 5, 1955. Undated newspaper article, "Dobie Captures True Color of Southwest." J. Frank Dobie in "Lagarto: A Collection of Memories," Hattie Mae Hinnant New, p. 62-67. Caller-Times, Jan. 18, 1959, "J. Frank Dobie Writes Of His Boyhood In Live Oak County." J. Frank Dobie, "Coronado's Children."

Chapter 40

Mary Austin Holley, "Texas Diary, 1835-38." "Roemer's Texas," Dr. Ferdinand von Roemer. "William Bollaert's Texas," edited by W. Eugene Hollon, Ruth Butler. "Emma Altgelt: Sketches of Life in Texas," by Henry Dielmann, Southwestern Historical Quarterly.

Chapter 41
Bill Walraven columns, Feb. 19, 1982, Oct. 20, 1983, Nov. 11, 1983, Caller-Times. Mat Nolan letter to Col. John S. Ford, transcribed by Frank Wagner. Corpus Christi Ranchero, several editions from August 1860. Eugenia Reynolds Briscoe, "City by the Sea." Centennial History, Caller-Times, 1983. Undated article, Ernest Morgan, "The Century-Old Mystery: Why Was Mat Nolan Killed." Frank Wagner, "The Shooting of Sheriff Mat Nolan," Wagner's research papers, Central Library. "Rip Ford's Texas," edited by Stephen B. Oates.

Chapter 42
"The Flight of the Grand Eagle: Charles G. Bryant, Maine Architect & Adventurer," James H. Mundy, Earle G. Shettleworth Jr. "Indian Wars and Pioneers of Texas," p. 109. The New York Herald, Feb. 11, 1850. "Texas Indian Papers, 1846-1859," p. 111-113. Walter Prescott Webb, "The Texas Rangers," p. 142. "Rip Ford's Texas," edited by Stephen B. Oates. Corpus Christi Gazette, Jan. 1, 1846. Eugenia Reynolds Briscoe, "City by the Sea."

Chapter 43
Mary Jo O'Rear, "Storm Over the Bay." Caller, Aug. 21, 1936, "Everybody Got Drunk and Happy" for All County Elections in "The Good Old Days". Corpus Christi Caller and Daily Herald, May 14, 23, 25, 26, 30, 1915; June 6 and 9, 1915; Sept. 1, 3, 4, 7, 18, 1915. "Boss Rule," Evan Anders. Frank Wagner's research papers. "Rip Ford's Texas," edited by Stephen B. Oates. John J. Linn, "Fifty Years in Texas." J. Williamson Moses, "Texas in Other Days," edited by the author. "Famous Speeches by Noted Indian Chiefs," edited by W. C. Vanderwerth, William R. Carmack.

Chapter 44, 45, 46
Keith Guthrie, "San Patricio County History," p. 177. Grady Phelps, "Old oyster reef provided passage across Nueces Bay," Caller-Times, May 26, 1974. The Taft Tribune, Feb. 18, 1969. Handbook of Texas. "Zachary Taylor in Corpus Christi," by the author, 2006. John Dunn, "Perilous Trails of Texas." Hortense Warner Ward, "Great Slaughter Made Coast A Boneyard," Caller-Times, Jan. 18, 1959. Caller-Times, Jan. 18, 1959. "El Rincon: A History of Corpus Christi Beach," Bill Walraven. "A Picture Postcard History," Anita Eisenhauer and Gigi Starnes. Caller-Times, Jan. 1, 1950. Caller, Dec. 8, 1969. Caller, several editions in 1895. Caller, July 14, 1905. Times, May 5, 1951. Caller-Times, Oct. 22, 1939. Times, Sept. 5, 1947. Caller-Times, Sept. 29, 1940. Caller, Feb. 26, 1959. Caller, Dec. 8, 1969. Caller-Times, July 13, 1990. Caller-Times Centennial Issue, 1983. "1919: The Storm," by Jim Moloney and the author. Corpus Christi Caller and Daily Herald, Dec. 10, 1915. "Engineering Record," March 18, 1916. Notes on Nueces Bay Causeway, Cathy Nix, Feb. 26, 1976. Caller, May 2, 1920, Jan. 23, 1921, Oct. 5, 1921, Oct. 8 and 9, 1921, Sept. 9 and 14, 1933, Sept. 21, 1933. Caller-Times, Harbor Bridge edition, Oct. 23, 1959. "Corpus Christi: A History," by the author and Jim Moloney. Bill Walraven column, Sept. 29, 1976. Caller-Times special section, "The Light of Other Days," July 18, 1999. "City won't be the same without Napoleon's Hat," M.G. column, Nov. 22, 2006.

Chapter 47
"The Kickapoo Holy Week Raid, 1878," Frank Wagner's research papers. E. H. Caldwell's memoirs, "The Last Indian Raid." "The Mexican and Indian Raid of '78" from a pamphlet published at Corpus Christi including affidavits of witnesses and officials, Texas Historical Quarterly. Handbook of Texas.

Chapter 48
"Saga of a Frontier Seaport," Coleman McCampbell. Obituary, Corpus Christi Caller, July 18, 1942. "Falfurrias," Dale Lasater. Trail Drivers of Texas. Corpus Christi Caller-Times, Oct. 27, 1935. Maude Gilliland, "Rincon." Jim Hogg County, 50th Anniversary brochure. John Young and J. Frank Dobie, "A Vaquero of the Brush County." Margaret Lynn Moser, "The Biography of a Particular Place," Vol. 2. "Cattle Kings of Texas," Dian Malouf. Anna Marietta Kelsey, "Through the Years." Caller, May 18, 1979. Caller, Sept. 9, 1939. Caller-Times, Nov. 13, 1938, Oct. 29, 1936, Jan. 26 and Nov. 13, 1938. Invitation to the formal opening of the Nueces Hotel, Jan. 18, 1913, Corpus Christi Central Library. Corpus Christi Caller and Daily Herald, Jan. 20, 1914. Undated clipping, "Nueces Hotel Showed Faith of Residents." Caller, Jan. 6, 1922. Theodore Fuller, "When the Century and I Were Young," p. 42-43. Times, Sept. 22, 1929. Caller, Oct. 29, 1932. Caller-Times, Oct. 23, 1932. Caller-Times, March 18, 1971. Corpus Christi Caller, Nov. 18 through 27, 1932, on Arthur Dowd slaying. Caller-Times, Nov. 24, 1935. Caller, Sept. 25, 1936. Caller-Times, Jan. 18, 1959. Caller, April 13, 1937 and Dec. 4, 1938. Caller, March 13, 1958. Dec. 26, 1958. Caller-Times, March 26, 1961. Times, Sept. 9, 1968. Caller-Times, May 30, 1971, Aug. 8, 1971. Letter from Bill Langham on building the Nueces Hotel, Sept. 27, 1974. Caller, June 16, 1988.

Chapter 49 and 50
"The Dragon Grill," Gigi Starnes, Nueces County Historical Commission, November 1989. Gary Cartwright, "Galveston." Marguerite Johnston, "Houston: The Unknown City." Spencer Pearson column, Caller-Times, June 22, 1985. Charles Branning, Dec. 31, 1987. Undated Caller-Times clip, "Shadowy Past Brought to Life." Tom Mulvany article, Aug. 6, 1947. Corpus Christi Press, Feb. 14 and 21 and March 28, 1946. Times, Sept. 28, 1945. Caller-Times, June 30, 1940. Caller, April 27, 1941. Caller-Times, Jan. 16, 1944.

CHAPTER 51
"Zachary Taylor in Corpus Christi," by the author, 2006. Galveston Weekly News, Jan. 10 and 31, 1854. Maria von Blücher's Corpus Christi. Letters From The South Texas Frontier, 1849-1879. Bruce Cheeseman. Nueces Valley newspaper, January 1854. Mary Sutherland, "The Story of Corpus Christi." Eugenia Reynolds Briscoe, "City by the Sea". "Corpus Christi: A History." Undated newspaper clip, "Bluff's Concrete Balustrade Was First Major Improvement." Articles on bluff tunnel, Feb. 23, 1977 and May 31, 1991. Caller-Times, Jan. 18, 1958. Bill Walraven column, Sept. 28, 1978. Caller-Times, Jan. 22, 1961. Caller, April 1920. Ruth Dodson, "The Noakes Raid," Frontier Times, July 1946. Leopold Morris, "The Mexican Raid of 1875 on Corpus Christi," Southwestern Historical Quarterly. Corpus Christi Weekly Gazette, March 27, 1875. Dee Woods, Aug. 26, 1939. Caller-Times Centennial Issue, 1983.

CHAPTER 52
Caller, May 13, 1952. Handbook of Texas. James Crutchfield, "Tragedy at Taos." Frontier Times, "Detail History of the Santa Fe Expedition." Paul Spellman, "Forgotten Texas Leader." Maria von Blücher's Corpus Christi. Letters From The South Texas Frontier, 1849-1879. Bruce Cheeseman. John Henry Brown, "Indian Wars and Pioneers of Texas." Nueces County News, July 14, 1939. The Ranchero, Matamoros, July 12, 1865. Caller-Times, Feb. 17, 1946.
Corpus Christi Democrat, Oct. 30, 1912. Caller-Times Feb. 1, 1941: Bill Barnard, "Death Takes Native Resident Who Grew Old Gracefully in Landmark Dwelling." Margaret Meuly's deposition seeking reimbursement for Civil War damage to a Meuly house, March 3, 1871, Central Library. Keith Guthrie, "Raw Frontier." "On This Bluff," Centennial History, 1867-1967, First Presbyterian Church.

CHAPTER 53
Bob McCracken column on Fred Gipson, reprinted in the Centennial Issue, 1983. Bill Walraven column, Oct. 28, 1980, Sept. 1, 1981, Nov. 15, 1978. Caller-Times, article, June 4, 1963 and March 9, 1964, July 4, 1963 and July 18, 1963, May 22, 1955, June 8, 1958. Undated clipping, Dean Chenoweth, "A Lot of Fred Gipson in His New Book 'The Home Place'." Caller-Times articles, May 24, 1959, March 12, 1956, Dec. 2, 1956. Bill Walraven article, Jan. 5, 1967. Times, June 2, 1956. Times, Dec. 19, 1980. Obituary, Caller, Aug. 15, 1973: 'Old Yeller' author, Gipson, died at Texas ranch home." Glen Lich, "Fred Gipson at Work." Goat Raiser, October 1969, Fred Gipson, "Easy Money, This Goat Money." Column in the Caller-Times, Aug. 9, 1939: "Of Pelicans and Horned Toads: Gipson Dwells on Nature Again, Until Hell-Bent Motorist Honks." Undated Caller-Times clipping, "Fred's First Day as a Waterfront Reporter …"

CHAPTER 54
E. H. Caldwell's memoirs. John Dunn, "Perilous Trails of Texas." Corpus Christi Caller, April 2, 1920: "When Mexican Raiders Swooped Down on Corpus," by John Dunn. Ruth Dodson, "The Noakes Raid," Frontier Times, July 1946. Leopold Morris, "The Mexican Raid of 1875 on Corpus Christi," Southwestern Historical Quarterly. Corpus Christi Weekly Gazette, March 27, 1875. Dee Woods, Aug. 26, 1939. Caller-Times Centennial Issue, 1983. Thomas John Noakes, "Raid by Mexicans in 1875," Frontier Times, reprinted from Corpus Christi Caller, Dec. 22, 1912. Caller-Times, May 23, 1988. Bill Walraven columns, Caller, Jan. 9, 1981. Caller, April 7, 1982, Feb. 26, 1988, . Undated clipping from Caller-Times: "Pioneer Woman Recalls Bandits' Raid on Corpus Christi in '70s." Times, March 28, 1950. Bill Walraven, article, Caller-Times, Jan. 18, 1959. Evansville Daily Journal, March 29, 1875. St. Louis Globe, March 30, 1875. Handbook of Texas. Times, Feb. 3, 1946. Dee Woods, Caller, June 29, 1939 and Aug. 26, 1939. Tom Lea, "The King Ranch." "History of Nueces County." George Durham and Clyde Wantland, "Taming the Nueces Strip." M.G. columns: Aug. 18 and 25, Sept. 1 and 8, 2004.

CHAPTER 55
"The Journey of Alvar Nuñez Cabeza De Vaca," translated by Fanny Bandelier. Harbert Davenport , Southwestern Historical Quarterly. John Upton Terrell, "Journey Into Darkness." Robert S. Weddle, "Spanish Sea." J. W. Williams, "Old

435

Texas Trails." Bill Walraven column, April 11, 1986. Lamar Papers. Keith Guthrie, "Raw Frontier." Frontier Times, "Lipantitlan." Hobart Huson, "Refugio." Joseph Milton Nance, Attack and Counter-attack: The Texas Frontier, 1842." George Coalson, "The Battle of Lipantitlan, July 7, 1842," The Journal of South Texas, Spring 1990. Lena H. Crofford, "Pioneers on the Nueces." W. G. Sutherland, undated clipping: "Sage of Bluntzer Tells History of Famous Nueces River..." Also by Sutherland: "Nueces River Has Played An Important Role In The Drama Of Early History." "Life of General Don Manuel de Mier y Teran," Southwestern Historical Quarterly. John J. Linn, "Fifty Years in Texas." Caller-Times, March 26, 1967. Dan Kilgore, Caller-Times, Jan. 18, 1959: "Texans Ousted Mexicans From Nueces County Fort." Caller-Times, Feb. 8, 1988. Walraven column, Aug. 5, 1986. Caller, Oct. 3, 1983. Article, July 29, 1982.

CHAPTER 56
Undated article, Corpus Christi Crony, "Pen Picture of Ward's Island." Corpus Christi Caller and Daily Herald, Nov. 8, 1914; May 23 and June 23, 1916; July 6, 13, 18, 19, 28; Aug. 3, 8, 12, Oct. 8, 1916. Caller-Times, March 12, 1923, March 27, 1942. Undated clipping: "U.S. Checks for $143,406 Ready for Owners of Ward Island Property." Caller-Times, Aug. 20, 1943. Caller, Aug. 15, 1945. Undated clipping, 1947: "Dubbed 'Radar Island,' Few Knew Its Meaning." Undated clipping: "Fame of Ward Island Dates From Ropes Boom in '90s." Caller-Times, May 18, 1945, July 1, 1954, Aug. 4, 1953, Feb. 14, 1972. Times, Nov. 25, 1947. Copies of affidavits on Ward Island property by: Charles Heck Jr.; Jewel Westerman; J. Patrick McGloin; and Jack Maddux.

CHAPTER 57
Caller-Times, Jan. 1, 1950, "A Sometimes Trolley." Caller-Times, June 13, 1965, Aug. 19, 1973, Centennial edition, April 27, 1952. Nov. 12, 1939. Caller, Aug. 19, 1973. Times, Jan. 15, 1970. Caller, Dec. 10, 1941. Caller-Times, Nov. 10, 1963. Caller, Aug. 19, 1973. Caller-Times, Golden Anniversary Edition. Times, April 1, 1943. Caller, July 4, 1949. Times, Sept. 18, 1967. Bill Walraven columns, March 30, March 31, 1982, and June 20, 1983. Margaret Ramage, streetcar timetable, Aug. 19, 1973. Notes from 1898 edition of the American Street Railway Journal, vertical files, Central Library. Garnet Menger, letter, June 29m 1953. Notes from the Corpus Christi Caller: March 29, May 17, June 7, June 14, June 28, July 26, Aug. 2, Aug. 9, Sept. 20, Oct. 4, Oct. 11, Nov. 8, 1890. Electric Railway Journal, Sept. 22, 1917, "Meeting the Menace of the Private Automobile at Corpus Christi." Copies of assorted streetcar maps. Notes on Peter Herdic's Transportation Museum, Williamsport, Pa. M.G. columns: Nov. 28 and Dec. 5, 2001.

CHAPTER 58
Caller, May 18, 1979. Caller, Sept. 9, 1939. Caller-Times, Nov. 13, 1938, Oct. 29, 1936, Jan. 26 and Nov. 13, 1938. Invitation to the formal opening of the Nueces Hotel, Jan. 18, 1913, Corpus Christi Central Library. Corpus Christi Caller and Daily Herald, Jan. 20, 1914. Undated clipping, "Nueces Hotel Showed Faith of Residents." Caller, Jan. 6, 1922. Theodore Fuller, "When the Century and I Were

Young," p. 42-43. Times, Sept. 22, 1929. Caller, Oct. 29, 1932. Caller-Times, Oct. 23, 1932. Caller-Times, March 18, 1971. Corpus Christi Caller, Nov. 18 through 27, 1932, on Arthur Dowd slaying. Caller-Times, Nov. 24, 1935. Caller, Sept. 25, 1936. Caller-Times, Jan. 18, 1959. Caller, April 13, 1937 and Dec. 4, 1938. Caller, March 13, 1958. Dec. 26, 1958. Caller-Times, March 26, 1961. Times, Sept. 9, 1968. Caller-Times, May 30, 1971, Aug. 8, 1971. Letter from Bill Langham on building the Nueces Hotel, Sept. 27, 1974. Caller, June 16, 1988. "1919: The Storm," by Jim Moloney and the author.

CHAPTER 59 and 60
Caller-Times, March 2, 1947. Undated clipping, 1940, "Something Is Finally Going To Be Done About Confusing Street Names in City." Caller-Times, Sept. 14, 1978. Times, Feb. 26, 1965. Caller, April 19, 1947. Times, Sept. 22, 1929. Caller-Times, May 11, 1978. Caller, Aug. 5, 1961. Caller-Times, Jan. 22, 1998. Times, Feb. 13, 1984. Caller, Aug. 4, 1981. Caller, March 11, 1941. Caller-Times, May 11, 1941. Caller-Times, Aug. 17, 1972. Caller-Times, Dec. 8, 1961. Caller, June 30, 1960. Times, Dec. 13, 1965. Times, Nov. 7, 1946. Caller, June 15, 1978. Times, Nov. 7, 1946. Times, June 23, 1969. Times, March 31, 1970. Caller, June 23, 1939. Caller-Times, Nov. 30, 1941. Caller-Times, Dec. 16, 1962. Undated clipping, "Corpus Christi's Delightful Street Names." Caller-Times, July 28, 1968. Caller, Jan. 29, 1988. Letter from Margaret Ramage, June 23, 1999. Bill Walraven columns, Feb. 1, 1978, March 6, 1978, Jan. 29, 1987.

CHAPTER 61, 62, 63, and 64
Caller-Times, April 8, 1956. Caller-Times, Feb. 5, 1939. Bill Walraven, June 18, 1981. Caller-Times, Jan. 23, 1942. Caller-Times, June 4, 1971. Vernon Smylie, "The Secrets of Padre Island" and "The Early History of Padre Island." Carlos E. Castaneda, "The Mission Era: The Finding of Texas, 1519-1693," Volume 1. Castaneda translated the story of Agustin Padilla Davila in "Our Catholic Heritage in Texas." Report by the Texas Antiquities Committee, "Introduction to the Davila Account and Related Sources." Hodding Carter, "Doomed Road of Empire." Dee Woods, "Blaze of Gold." Dee Woods, articles, June 15, 1939 and Sept. 21, 1939. Writers' Round Table, "Padre Island." Margaret Wead, Padre Island History, Sept. 1980. Dallas Morning News, June 19, 1972. Caller-Times, Jan. 18, 1959. Caller-Times, Sept. 26, 1954. Houston Chronicle, Feb. 22, 1938. Dee Woods, June 15, 1939, July 3, 1939, July 18, 1939, Sept. 21, 1939. Copy of Lt. Edmund Blake's report on the reconnaissance of Padre Island in 1846. Clipping from 1881 reprinted in the Caller in 1921: "Long Islands Fringing Gulf, Full of Romance." Times, Sept. 1, 1965. Caller-Times, June 17, 1950. Caller-Times, Sept. 26, 1954. John Stallings' column, June 17, 1978. Pauline Reese, "A History of Padre Island," a thesis, 1938. Times, July 2, 1978. Caller-Times, Oct. 29, 1967. Caller, June 21, 1965. Times, Aug. 22, 1973. Letter, Caller, March 4, 1963. Kerrville Daily Times, Aug. 25, 1963. Caller, Dec. 27, 1985. Map of restricted areas on Padre Island during World War II. Caller-Times' special edition on the opening of the Padre Island Causeway, June 17, 1950. Caller-Times, Feb. 11, June 10, and July 27, 1951. Caller-Times, Sept. 26, 1954. Kansas City Star, Nov. 7, 1954. Houston Post, March 28, 1954. Caller, Nov. 15, 1954. Caller-Times, Feb. 9 and Feb. 27, 1955, April 8, 1956, Oct. 31, 1956. Kansas City Star, Nov. 21, 1957. Caller-Times, Nov. 21, 1957. Times, Jan. 25 and June 8, 1960. Caller-Times, May 17, 1959. Dee

Woods, letter, Sept. 20, 1977. Dee Woods, article, Caller-Times, Jan. 18, 1959. Caller-Times, Jan. 18, 1961. Betty Callaway, "History of Padre Island." Bill Duncan, the Caller-Times, April 24, 1966, "The Long White Island." Assorted clips from 1965 to 1968 on land acquisition for the Padre Island National Seashore. Caller-Times, April 26, 1970, June 16, 1978, Oct. 19, 1978, Jan. 29, 1978, Jan. 1, 1979. Ernest G. Fischer, 10 articles on Patrick F. Dunn, Caller-Times, 1927. Houston Chronicle, March 25, 1977. Undated article by Bernard Brister, 1938: "Old Padre Island, Lonely and Legendary, To Be Converted Into Swank Watering Place." Undated clipping, Bill Walraven column. Caller-Times, Aug. 29, 1965. Robstown Record, June 17, 1965. Mathis News, June 2, 1966. Grace Dunn Vetters, article on Pat Dunn's ranch house, May 3, 1973.

CHAPTER 65
Anna Moore Schwien: "When Corpus Christi Was Young," memoirs based on interviews conducted in 1939 and 1940 by Marie von Blucher, reprinted in "Recollections of Other Days," by Jim Moloney and the author. Bill Walraven columns, Feb. 6, 1981, Aug. 13, 1985 and one undated: "Interviews with former slave sketch early history of city." Caller-Times, Sept. 15, 1968. Fayette Copeland, "Kendall of the Picayune." M.G. column on Forbes Britton, Aug. 22, 2007. "Daniel P. Whiting: A Soldier's Life," edited by the author.

CHAPTER 66
"Texas by Teran," edited by Jack Jackson, John Wheat.

CHAPTER 67
Correspondence with Judge Max Bennett who relayed the account of reporter James Rowe and King Ranch bourbon. Corpus Christi Crony, May 24, 1902. Caller-Times Centennial Issue, 1983, on the Fred Roberts slaying. Corpus Christi Caller-Times, Oct. 15, 1922; Caller, Oct. 16, 1922.

CHAPTER 68 and 69
Caller-Times, Jan. 18, 1959 on Garza Falcon. Caller-Times Golden Anniversary edition: "Title to Land Here Involved In Old Action." Caller-Times, Jan. 25, 1979. Caller, May 6, 1892. Caller, Dec. 1, 1893. Caller-Times, Sept. 25, 1988. Copy of extracts made by Eli Merriman on Levi Jones and J. Temple Doswell suit. Handbook of Texas on Levi Jones. Undated clipping: "Old Files Tell of Days When Land Titles Hereabouts Were Swept Away Under Aggravating Circumstances." Copy of deed records: "In the Matter of Ten Leagues of Land Called 'Rincon del Oso.' " Frank Wagner's research papers. Copies of original title of lands of Blas Maria Falcon, nine pages translated and certified by the General Land Office. Copies of court action, Nueces County, spring term, 1858. Paul Shuster Taylor, "An American-Mexican Frontier: Nueces County, Texas."

CHAPTER 70 and 71
"The Journey of Alvar Nuñez Cabeza De Vaca," translated by Fanny Bandelier. Fayette Copeland, "Kendall of the Picayune." Dee Woods, Caller, Aug. 4, 1939. Caller-Times, John C. Rayburn, "First Rainmaking – 1891," Jan. 18, 1959. Various editions, Corpus Christi Advertiser, 1870. Caller-Times, Jan. 18, 1959, "J. Frank Dobie Writes Of His Boyhood In Live Oak County." Bruce Cheeseman,

438

"Maria von Blucher's Corpus Christi." Corpus Christi Gazette, Dec. 1872 and January 1873. Tom Lea, "The King Ranch." Thomas Noakes' Diary, Corpus Christi Central Library. J. Frank Dobie, "The Longhorns." Roy Bedichek, "Karankaway Country." John Young and J. Frank Dobie, "A Vaquero of the Brush Country." William Syers, "Off the Beaten Trail." Caller-Times, undated clipping: "1954 City's 4th Driest." Caller-Times, July 2, 1953, Jan. 5, 1954, July 31, 1966, April 2, 1962. Caller-Times, King Ranch Edition, 1953: King Ranch Venture With Rainmakers Unsuccessful." Elmer Kelton, "The Times It Never Rained." Dick Frost, "The King Ranch Papers." Don Graham, "The Kings of Texas." Caller, June 22, 1939. Corpus Christi Crony, April 19 and Aug. 16, 1902, March 13, 1903. Undated clipping: "The Artesian Well Destined to Work a Revolution in Nueces County." King Ranch Edition, 1953: "Names of Water Wells Tell History of Ranch." Caller, March 13, 1903. E. H. Caldwell's memoirs. A. Ray Stephens, "The Taft Ranch." Dale Lasater, "Falfurrias." Diane Solether Smith, "The Armstrong Chronicle: A Ranching History."

CHAPTER 72
Bill Walraven column, Aug. 29, 1975. Corpus Christi Weekly Gazette, May 16, May 28, June 6, 1874. Caller-Times, May 3, 1931. J.B. (Red) John Dunn, "Perilous Trails of Texas." Jim Davis, Frontier Times, November 1970. Bill and Marjorie Walraven, "Empresario's Children."

CHAPTERS 73, 74
J.B. (Red) John Dunn, "Perilous Trails of Texas." Dunn: "Miscellaneous Recollections," vertical file, Corpus Christi Central Library. Bill Walraven column, Aug. 17, 1984. Obituary, Caller, Nov. 4, 1940. Copy of letter, Lilith Lorraine, May 26, 1936. Unpublished brochure on Dunn's Museum. Mrs. Frank DeGarmo, "Pathfinders of Texas."

CHAPTER 75
Holland McCombs, "Matamoros: Cotton Trading Capital of the World," Caller-Times, Jan. 18, 1959. Lt. Col. Arthur Lyons Fremantle, Diary. John Warren Hunter, "Heel-Fly Time in Texas." Eugenia Reynolds Briscoe, "City by the Sea." Robert W. Delaney: "Matamoros, Port for Texas during the Civil War," Southwestern Historical Quarterly. "Rip Ford's Texas," edited by Stephen B. Oates. Tom Lea, "The King Ranch." Judi Hopkins McMordie, "Los Algodones: the Cotton Times," UDC Magazine, December 1997. Ronnie Tyler, "Cotton on the Border, 1861-1865," Southwestern Historical Quarterly. Robert and William Adams, memoirs, vertical files, Central Library, also reprinted in "Recollections of Other Days," by Jim Moloney and the author. War of the Rebellion , Official Records of the Union and Confederate Armies: the Rio Grande Expedition.

CHAPTER 76
Bill Walraven, "Texans hated first Republican governor," Caller-Times, Nov. 9, 1978. Dave Allred, "Ex-Corpus Christi Law Student Was Stormy Governor," Caller-Times, April 15, 1956.
John Salman Ford, "Rip Ford's Texas," edited by Stephen B. Oates. Nueces Valley, April, 1858. Marie v. Blucher, "E. J. Davis House," vertical files, Corpus Christi Central Library. Ranchero, April 21, 1861. Edna May Tubbs, "E.J. Davis,

Only Republican To Ever Govern Texas Came From Corpus Christi," Caller, Aug. 27, 1939. Ernest Wallace, "Texas in Turmoil, the Saga of Texas: 1849-1875." Tom Lea, "King Ranch." E. T. Merriman, "Random Recollections of Nearly Ninety Years," Corpus Christi Central Library. "History of Nueces County." Anna Moore Schwien, "When Corpus Christi Was Young," reprinted in "Recollections of Other Days," by Jim Moloney and the author. T. R. Fehrenbach, "Lone Star." Garth Jones, "A Hated Texan: His Monument Towers Highest in State Cemetery," Caller-Times, Feb. 20, 1958. Eugenia Reynolds Briscoe, "City by the Sea." Frontier Times, August 1930: "The End of Carpet-Bag Rule in Texas." Bill Walraven, undated column. Hobart Huson, "Refugio." Southwestern Historical Quarterly, Vols. 77, 78. Handbook of Texas on Davis' State Police. Carl Moneyhon, "Texas After the Civil War." James Smallwood, Barry Crouch and Larry Peacock, "Murder and Mayhem: The War of Reconstruction in Texas." Barry Crouch, Donaly Brice, "The Governor's Hounds." M.G. columns: July 9, 16, 23, 2003.

CHAPTER 77
Lester Fitzhugh, "Saluria, Fort Esperanza, and Military Operations on the Texas Coast, 1861-1865," Southwestern Historical Quarterly. War of the Rebellion , Official Records of the Union and Confederate Armies: the Rio Grande Expedition, November, December 1863. Edwin B. Lufkin, "History of the 13th Maine Regiment." Henry Augustus Shorey, "The Story of the 15th Regiment." Letters by Maj. Thompson of the 20th Iowa, Corpus Christi Central Library. Eugenia Reynolds Briscoe, "City by the Sea." M.G. column, Nov. 6, 2002. Capt. C. Barney, "Recollections of Field Service with the 20th Iowa." Ernest Morgan, Caller-Times, May 28, 1961. Allen W. Jones: "Military Events in Texas During the Civil War, 1861-1865," Southwestern Historical Quarterly. A Comprehensive History of Texas: Military Events and Operations in Texas and Along the Coasts and Border, 1861-1865," compiled by Charles Evans. M.G. columns: Nov. 6, 13, 20, and 27, 2002.

CHAPTERS 78, 79
Report of the United States Commissioners to Texas, Joint Resolution of Congress approved May 7, 1872. Reports of the Committee of Investigation Sent in 1873 by the Mexican Government to the Frontier of Texas.

CHAPTERS 80, 81
Jim Moloney and the author: "1919: The Storm." Lucy Caldwell's letter, written on Sept. 21, 1919, related the events of the storm to her mother. Theodore Fuller recounted his and his sister's survival in "When the Century and I Were Young." Both were reprinted in "1919: The Storm." Caller, Nov. 19, 1922: "Big Monument to Unknown Dead Now in Cemetery." Caller-Times, Sept. 14, 1961 and Sept. 9, 1962. Warren Hogan: "Hurricane Carla: A Tribute to the News Media." Caller-Times, Aug. 4-9, 1970. Aug. 3, 1971. Caller-Times special edition: "Celia Remembered," Aug. 3, 1980. Michael Ellis, "The Hurricane Almanac," 1987. Caller-Times web site for stories on Hurricanes Allen and Bret.

CHAPTER 82
Dee Woods, column, Aug. 10, 1939. Caller, July 9, 1039. Keith Gutherie, "Texas Forgotten Ports" and "History of San Patricio County." Ernest Morgan, July 20, 1963. Handbook of Texas. Obituary, Sidney G. Borden, Caller, Feb. 7, 1908. Caller-Times, Sept. 17, 1982. Times, April 6, 1964. Travis Moorman, Caller-Times, Jan. 18, 1959: "Gail Borden's Brother, Nephew Active Here." Stephen Hardin, "Texian Iliad." Z. N. Morrell, "Flowers and Fruits in the Wilderness." Frontier Times, January 1936. Lota M. Spell, "Pioneer Printer." "Saga of a Frontier Seaport," Coleman McCampbell. E. H. Caldwell's memoirs. Noah Smithwick, "Evolution of a State." Capt. Andrew Anderson's memoirs, reprinted in "Recollections of Other Days" by Jim Moloney and the author. Joe Frantz, "Newspapers of the Republic of Texas," a thesis. Marilyn Sibley, "Lone Stars and State Gazettes: Texas Newspapers before the Civil War." Hortense Warner Ward, "The First State Fair of Texas," Southwestern Historical Quarterly.

CHAPTERS 83, 84
Article, Gigi Starnes, Nov. 7, 1985. Anita Lovenskiold diary, Corpus Christi Central Library. M.G. column, 2007, 2007. Caller, Aug. 27, 1918, Oct. 5 and 6, 1918, Oct. 18 and 18, Oct. 22, 25, 26, 27, 30, 1918; Nov. 9, 11, 1918. Jim Moloney and the author: "1919: The Storm." Caller, Aug. 19, 1920. Caller-Times, Oct. 29, 1936. Caller-Times, Sept. 9, 1951. Caller-Times, Sept. 15, 1926, Aug. 16, 1930, Aug. 20, 1930, Caller-Times, Oct. 30, 1931, Jan. 30, 1932, Feb. 21, 1932, Oct. 6, 1933, Dec. 6, 1933, Oct. 6, 1988. Caller-Times Centennial Issue, 1983. Marshall Anderson, June 2 and Oct. 6, 1988. Caller-Times, Jan. 23, 1983. M.G. columns: April 12, 2000; Feb. 4, 2001; Feb. 28, 2001; May 30, 2001; June 6, 2001; Nov. 28, 2001; Dec. 5, 2001; June 1-5, 2004; Dec. 5, 14, 25, 2005. Undated clippings, 1921: "Corpus Christi Light Plant Goes Up in Flames" and "Force of Electricians Begin Work to Arrange For Emergency Service." Caller on port opening day, Sept. 15, 1926. Caller on Billy Sunday, March 20, 1929. Times, Dec. 16, 1940.

CHAPTER 85
Pamphlet, "Zachary Taylor in Corpus Christi" by the author, 2006. K. Jack Bauer, "Zachary Taylor." Eugenia Reynolds Briscoe, "City by the Sea." Corpus Christi Gazette, 1846. Napoleon Jackson Tecumseh Dana, "Monterrey Is Ours." George K. Donnelly, letter, from Bill Walraven column, Oct. 10, 1985. Joseph Fry, "A Life of Zachary Taylor." Charles Masland, letters, Corpus Christi Central Library. Ethan Allen Hitchcock, "Fifty Years in Camp and Field." U.S. Grant, "Personal Memoirs." Holman Hamilton, "Zachary Taylor: Soldier of the Republic." N. S. Jarvis, "Army Surgeon's Notes on the Mexican War." John James Peck, "The Sign of the Eagle." Justin H. Smith, "The War with Mexico." M.G. columns: Nov. 25, Dec, 2, Dec. 9, 1998; Dec. 1, 8, 15, 22, 2004.

CHAPTERS 86, 87, 88, 89, 90
Caller-Times, Jan. 18, 1959. Frontier Times, March 1931 on Henry Smith. Bill Walraven column, May 28, 1985. Caller-Times, May 17, 1984. Times, Feb. 21, 1957. Handbook of Texas. Hobart Huson, "Refugio." Robert Lee Moore, "History of Refugio County," thesis. William H. Oberste, "Texas Irish Empresarios." Lamar Papers. Refugio County History. Houston Telegraph & Texas Register, April 7

and April 18, 1838. Alpha Kennedy Wood, "Texas Coastal Bend." Keith Guthrie, "Raw Frontier." Bill and Marjorie Walraven, "Empresario's Children." "William Bollaert's Texas," edited by W. Eugene Hollon and Ruth Butler. Keith Guthrie, "Texas Forgotten Ports." William Allen, Sue Hastings Taylor, "Aransas." Hobart Huson, "Texas Trilogy." T. Lindsay Baker, "More Ghost Towns of Texas." Caller-Times, Oct. 28, 1996. Hobart Huson, "Saint Mary's of Aransas," articles, 1937. Times, July 20, 1961. Caller-Times, March 8, 1961. Hobart Huson, "El Copano: The Ancient Port of Bexar and La Bahia." Caller-Times, May 31, 1957. Lester Fitzhugh, "Saluria, Fort Esperanza, and Military Operations on the Texas Coast, 1861-1865," Southwestern Historical Quarterly. Corpus Christi Caller, "Towns Dotted Coast Islands in Old Days," May 8, 1959. 1850 Census, Refugio County (St. Joseph's Island). Paul Freier in the Port Lavaca Wave, Feb. 20, 1974, April 17, April 24, 1974, and May 17, 1978. Corpus Christi Star, March 26 and Sept. 18, 1849. Brownson Malsch, "Indianola: The Mother of Western Texas." Linda Wolff, "Indianola and Matagorda Island."

CHAPTERS 91, 92, 93, 94, 95
Elmer Baldwin, "History of LaSalle County." "The Past and Present of LaSalle County, Illinois." "Peru Centennial, 1835-1935." Maurice Baxter, "One and Inseparable: Daniel Webster and the Union." Robert Vincent Remini: "Daniel Webster: The Man and His Time." Daniel Webster correspondence, Brandeis University, folders 86 through 89. Edwin David Sanborn, "The Private Correspondence of Daniel Webster." Clyde Duniway, "Daniel Webster and the West." Elijah Kennedy, "The Real Daniel Webster." Coleman McCampbell, Journal of the Illinois State Historical Society, Spring 1954. Coleman McCampbell, Frontier Times, "Romance Had Role in Founding of Corpus." McCampbell, Crystal Reflector, "Colonel Kinney's Romance With Daniel Webster's Daughter." Hobart Huson, "Refugio." Caller-Times, Jan. 18, 1959. Eugenia Reynolds Briscoe, "City by the Sea." Journals, Sixth Congress, Republic of Texas. Tom Lea, "King Ranch." Pamphlet, "Zachary Taylor in Corpus Christi" by the author, 2006. Homer Thrall, "History of Texas." Thomas J. Green, "The Perote Prisoners." Lamar Papers. Hortense Warner Ward, "Abduction and Death of Philip Dimitt." Letters written to President Lamar by Aubrey & Kinney, 1841. Joseph McCutchan, "Mier Expedition Diary." Senates of Republic: the Senate of the Ninth Congress, 1844-45. Encyclopedia of the Mexican-American War, entry on Kinney. Corpus Christi Star, Oct. 17, 1848. Hortense Warner Ward, "The First State Fair of Texas," Southwestern Historical Quarterly. Charles G. Norton, "Colonel Henry L. Kinney, Founder of Corpus Christi." Bruce Cheeseman, "Maria von Blucher's Corpus Christi," p. 71-72. Indianola Bulletin (on microfilm): March 11, 1852; March 18, March 25, April 8, April 15, April 22, April 29, April 30, May 6, May 13, May 20, 1852. Texas State Gazette, March 6, May 8, May 22, May 29, 1852. Bill Walraven column, May 8, 1985. Coleman McCampbell letter, Nov. 13, 1954. Earl Fornell, "Texans and Filibusters in the 1850s," Southwestern Historical Quarterly. Edward S. Wallace, "Destiny and Glory." Stanley Siegel, "A Political History of the Texas Republic, 1836-1845." John Hoyt Williams, "Sam Houston." Michael Collins, "Texas Devils." W. R. Gore, "The Life of Henry Lawrence Kinney," thesis. Charles G. Norton, "Colonel Henry L. Kinney," from Corpus Christi Times, May 16-31, 1938. Hortense Warner Ward, "Physical Courage, Moral Cowardice Found in Kinney," Caller-Times, Jan. 18, 1959.

Hortense Warner Ward, "Kinney's Trading Post." Ward's notes and research on Kinney, Corpus Christi Central Library. Bill Walraven columns, June 28, 1976; Nov. 23, 1978; Feb. 6, 1984; Aug. 20, 1985; May 21 and Dec. 2, 1986. Bruce Cheeseman, "Maria von Blucher's Corpus Christi." John (Red) Dunn, "Perilous Trails of Texas." Times, Jan. 5, 1960.

CHAPTER 96
Frank Wagner's research papers. Obituary of Morris Lichtenstein, Aug. 12, 1904. Undated clipping, 1933, "City's Oldest Retail Establishment." Obituary, Julius Lichtenstein, Feb. 20, 1923. Caller, June 23, 1939. Caller, April 25, 1940. Caller-Times, Feb. 22, 1942. Undated clipping, 1949, "Lichtenstein's, City's Oldest Firm, Marks 75th Anniversary." Times, Jan. 27, 1949. Caller-Times, 1954, Mayor Lichtenstein resigns. Caller, July 30, 1955. Times, Nov. 14, 1955 and April 3, 1957. Caller, Jan. 11, 1958. Times, Oct. 6, 1958. Caller, Oct. 25, 1962. Obituary, Albert Lichtenstein, Caller, Dec. 11, 1976. Obituary, Morris S. Lichtenstein, Caller-Times, May 19, 2007. Caller, April 18, 1972. Brownson Malsch, "Indianola: The Mother of Western Texas." M.G. column, Feb. 3, 1999. Mrs. Frank DeGarmo, "Pathfinders of Texas." Ralph Wooster, "Texas and Texans in the Civil War." Victor Rose, "History of Victoria County." Handbook of Texas. George Durham and Clyde Wantland, "Taming the Nueces Strip." "A Picture Postcard History," Anita Eisenhauer and Gigi Starnes. Caller, Jan. 21, 1883. Caller, Aug. 30, 1885. Caller-Times, Sept. 26, 1954, Nov. 26, 1933, July 14, 1966, Sept, 26, 1954.

CHAPTER 97
Norman C. Delaney, "The Maltby Brothers Civil War." Mrs. Frank DeGarmo, "Pathfinders of Texas." Caller, Feb. 22, 1963. Columns by the author: July 1. 1998; March 16, 17, 2005. Maltby family records, Corpus Christi Central Library. Bill Walraven column, Feb. 17, 1977, Oct. 7, 1981. Nueces County History. Hortense Warner Ward, "The First State Fair of Texas." Corpus Christi Ranchero, various editions from Oct. 22, 1859 to 1863, and Corpus Christi Advertiser.

CHAPTER 98
Keith Guthrie, "San Patricio County History." Undated clipping, James Rowe, "Lighthouse Beacon at Aransas Pass Has Warned Men at Sea For 84 Years." Undated article, Dee Woods, 1939 and Aug. 15, 1939. Caller-Times, Jan. 18, 1959. Caller, Nov. 26, 1959. Roy Miller, "The Legislative History of the Port of Corpus Christi," Central Library. Caller-Times, Sept. 9, 1951. Grady Phelps, undated clipping: "Old Port Aransas Causeway Once Adventure in Driving." Eli Merriman, "Opposition Plentiful in 60-Year Struggle for Deep Water." Caller, Sept. 9, 1951. Caller, March 1, 1907. Caller-Times, Jan. 1, 1950. "Seaport of the South," Carl Helmecke. Alpha Kennedy Wood, "Texas Coastal Bend." Linda Wolff, "Indianola and Matagorda Island." William Allen, Sue Hastings Taylor, "Aransas." Keith Guthrie, "Texas Forgotten Ports."

CHAPTER 99
Sister Mary Anne Roddy, "Rancho Perdido," thesis. Ruth Dodson's papers, Special Collections & Archives, Texas A&M University-Corpus Christi. Edward M. Price, "Martin Culver," from the Dodson papers. Hortense Warner Ward,

"Great Slaughter Made Coast a Boneyard." The Cattleman, Feb. 1948. Susan Armitrage, Elizabeth Jameson, "The Women's West." Undated clipping, Ernest Dewey, "Old Border Town Now Hardly A Memory," from the Dodson papers. Dee Woods, undated clipping, "Cattleman of Rip-Roaring 70s." John Young and J. Frank Dobie, "A Vaquero of the Brush Country." Hattie Mae Hinnant New, "Lagarto: A Collection of Memories." "History of Nueces County."

CHAPTER 100
Noah Smithwick, "Evolution of a State." "Recollections of Early Texas: The Memoirs of John Holland Jenkins." Mary Austin Holley, "Texas Diary, 1835-38." J. Williamson Moses, "Texas In Other Days," edited by the author. John Young and J. Frank Dobie, "A Vaquero of the Brush Country." "The Slave Narratives of Texas," edited by Ron Tyler and Lawrence Murphy.

CHAPTER 101
Corpus Christi Caller and Caller-Times, Dec. 5, 7, 20, 21, 22, 23, 24, 25, 1941; Jan. 19, 1942, Dec. 24, 1942; Dec. 24, 1943; Dec. 24, 1944; Times, Dec. 28, 1944. Caller, Dec. 20, Dec. 22, Dec. 25, 1945. Caller-Times, Feb. 9, 1969, Grady Phelps, "The Hunt for Escaped POWs." "Corpus Christians Still Stunned by News of Sudden Death of President," Times, April 13, 1945; Times, "Flags at Half Mast as City Pays Its Respects to Memory of Roosevelt." "City in Mourning for Roosevelt," Caller, April 14, 1945.

INDEX

445

447

448

449

455

457

461

462

Corpus Christi – A History

1919 The Storm

A Soldier's Life

Great Tales from the History of South Texas

Recollections of Other Days

Columns   2009 – 2011

Perilous Trails of Texas

www.nuecespress.com